THE CAMBRIDGE COMPANION TO BEDE

As the major writer and thinker of the Anglo-Saxon period, the Venerable Bede is a key figure in the study of the literature and thought of this time. This *Companion*, written by an international team of specialists, is a key introductory guide to Bede, his writings and his world. The first part of the volume focuses on Bede's cultural and intellectual milieu, covering his life, the secular-political contexts of his day, the foundations of the Latin learning he inherited and sought to perpetuate, the ecclesiastical and monastic setting of early Northumbria, and the foundation of his home institution, Wearmouth-Jarrow. The book then considers Bede's writing in detail, treating his educational, exegetical and historical works. Concluding with a detailed assessment of Bede's influence and reception from the time of his death up to the modern age, the *Companion* enables the reader to view Bede's writings within a wider cultural context.

SCOTT DEGREGORIO is Associate Professor of English Literature at the University of Michigan – Dearborn. He has published extensively on Bede as a biblical exegete and Church reformer. His books include, as editor, *Innovation and Tradition in the Writings of the Venerable Bede*, and, as translator, *Bede: On Ezra and Nehemiah*, which won the International Society of Anglo-Saxonists' prize for best edition/translation published in Anglo-Saxon studies, 2005–7.

A complete list of books in the series is at the back of this book.

THE CAMBRIDGE
COMPANION TO
BEDE

EDITED BY
SCOTT DEGREGORIO
University of Michigan – Dearborn

CAMBRIDGE
UNIVERSITY PRESS

CAMBRIDGE UNIVERSITY PRESS
Cambridge, New York, Melbourne, Madrid, Cape Town, Singapore,
São Paulo, Delhi, Dubai, Tokyo

Cambridge University Press
The Edinburgh Building, Cambridge CB2 8RU, UK

Published in the United States of America by Cambridge University Press, New York

www.cambridge.org
Information on this title: www.cambridge.org/9780521730730

© Cambridge University Press 2010

First published 2010

Printed in the United Kingdom at the University Press, Cambridge

A catalogue record for this publication is available from the British Library

Library of Congress Cataloguing in Publication data
The Cambridge companion to Bede / edited by Scott DeGregorio.
p.   cm. – (Cambridge companions to –)   ISBN 978-0-521-51495-8 (hardback)
1. Bede, the Venerable, Saint, 673–735.   I. DeGregorio, Scott.   II. Title.   III. Series.
PA8260.C27   2010
270.2′092–dc22
2010000702

ISBN 978-0-521-51495-8 Hardback
ISBN 978-0-521-73073-0 Paperback

CONTENTS

CONTENTS

MAPS

ILLUSTRATIONS

MICHELLE P. BROWN is Professor of Medieval Manuscript Studies and Course Tutor to the History of the Book MA at the School of Advanced Study, University of London. She was for many years the Curator of Medieval and Illuminated Manuscripts at the British Library, where she remains as a part-time project officer, and was until recently a Lay Canon and member of Chapter at St Paul's Cathedral, London. Her books include *The Lindisfarne Gospels: Society, Spirituality and the Scribe* and *Manuscripts from the Anglo-Saxon Age*.

JAMES CAMPBELL retired in 2002 as Fellow of Worcester College where he had taught medieval history since 1957 and as Professor of Medieval History in the University of Oxford. He works on Anglo-Saxon history and urban history. Writings of his on the former subject are collected in *Essays in Anglo-Saxon History* and *The Anglo-Saxon State*. He is a Fellow of the British Academy.

SCOTT DEGREGORIO is Associate Professor of English Literature at the University of Michigan – Dearborn. He has published extensively on Bede as a biblical exegete and Church reformer. His books include, as editor, *Innovation and Tradition in the Writings of the Venerable Bede*, and, as translator, *Bede: On Ezra and Nehemiah*, which won the International Society of Anglo-Saxonists' prize for best edition/ translation published in Anglo-Saxon studies, 2005–7.

SARAH FOOT is Regius Professor of Ecclesiastical History at Christ Church, Oxford. She has published widely on the Anglo-Saxon Church, including *Veiled Women: The Disappearance of Nuns from Anglo-Saxon England* and *Monastic Life in Anglo-Saxon England, c. 600–900*.

ALLEN J. FRANTZEN teaches in the English Department of Loyola University Chicago. He is the author, most recently, of *Bloody Good: Chivalry, Sacrifice, and the Great War*; co-editor, with John Hines, of *Cædmon's Hymn and Material Culture in the World of Bede*; and editor of the Anglo-Saxon penitentials (www. Anglo-Saxon.net).

ARTHUR G. HOLDER is Dean, Vice President for Academic Affairs and John Dillenberger Professor of Christian Spirituality at the Graduate Theological Union in Berkeley, California. He is the translator of *Bede: On the Tabernacle*, co-translator of *Bede: A Biblical Miscellany* and editor of *The Blackwell Companion to Christian Spirituality* and *Christian Spirituality: The Classics*.

CALVIN B. KENDALL is Professor of English Emeritus at the University of Minnesota, a member of the University of Minnesota Academy of Distinguished Teachers and an Associate of the International Center of Medieval Art. He has edited Bede's *De arte metrica* and *De schematibus et tropis* for the Corpus Christianorum, and has published two translations, *Bede's Art of Poetry and Rhetoric* and *Bede: On Genesis*. He is also the author of *The Metrical Grammar of Beowulf* and *The Allegory of the Church: Romanesque Portals and Their Verse Inscriptions*.

ROSALIND LOVE is a senior lecturer in the Department of Anglo-Saxon, Norse and Celtic at the University of Cambridge, with responsibility for Insular Latin. She has edited two volumes of Anglo-Latin hagiography in the series Oxford Medieval Texts, the second of which, on the saints of Ely, jointly won the International Society of Anglo-Saxonists' prize for best edition published in Anglo-Saxon studies, 2003–5. She has published a number of articles on Latin hagiography in England. Her work for the Fontes Anglo-Saxonici project (http://fontes.english.ox.ac.uk/) catalogued the sources for many Anglo-Latin texts, including two of Bede's commentaries.

LAWRENCE T. MARTIN is Professor Emeritus at the University of Wisconsin – Eau Claire, where he works on Ojibwe language revitalization. He has published articles on Bede and on medieval sermon literature, as well as an edition of *The Verona Homily Collection* in the Corpus Christianorum Scriptores Celtigenae series, a translation of Bede's *Commentary on the Acts of the Apostles* and, with Dom David Hurst, a translation of Bede's *Homilies on the Gospels*.

DAVID ROLLASON has taught history at Durham University since 1977. His most recent research has been on the history of early medieval Northumbria and on early medieval books of life, for one of the most interesting of which, the Durham *Liber Vitae*, he is the co-editor of the edition and linguistic and prosopographical commentary. He maintains his earlier research interest in early medieval hagiography and the cult of saints and is developing further his research interest in the histories and chronicles of northern England.

SHARON M. ROWLEY is Associate Professor of English at Christopher Newport University. She has published on Bede's *Ecclesiastical History* and the Old English version of it, as well as on Old English homilies and textual studies. She received a

Fellowship from the National Endowment for the Humanities to work on her forthcoming book on the Old English Bede.

CLARE STANCLIFFE is Honorary Reader in Ecclesiastical History in the Departments of History, and of Theology and Religion, Durham University, where she teaches an MA course on Christian Northumbria 600–800. Recent publications include her 2003 Jarrow Lecture, *Bede, Wilfrid, and the Irish*, and her 2005 Whithorn Lecture, *Bede and the Britons*. Her current research project is a book entitled *'Celt' and 'Roman': An Evolving Controversy and its Impact on Identity and Historiography from Columbanus to Bede*.

ALAN THACKER is a reader and executive editor of the Victoria County History at the Institute of Historical Research at the University of London. His research interests include intellectual and cultural life in early medieval western Europe, and especially the early medieval Church. He has published widely on hagiography, saints' cults and pastoral care in the early Middle Ages, and on Bede as historian, exegete and reformer.

FAITH WALLIS is a professor at McGill University in Montreal, where she holds a joint appointment in the Department of History and the Department of Social Studies of Medicine. She has published widely on Bede's scientific writings, authoring numerous articles as well as the English translation *Bede: The Reckoning of Time*.

JOSHUA A. WESTGARD is Adjunct Lecturer at The Catholic University of America in Washington, DC. He is author of several articles on medieval historical writing, and on the manuscripts and transmission of Bede's works. He is currently completing an edition and study of the set of annals known as the *Continuatio Bedae*, and is also preparing a monograph on the transmission and reception of the *Ecclesiastical History*.

IAN WOOD is Professor of Early Medieval History at the University of Leeds. He has published extensively on early medieval history, especially on the Burgundians, Franks and Anglo-Saxons and on the history of mission. Recently he was one of the co-authors of *Fragments of History: Rethinking the Ruthwell and Bewcastle Monuments*. He is currently working on a new edition of Bede's *Historia Abbatum* and the *Vita Ceolfridi*.

Bede's works are usually cited in modern scholarship by their abbreviated Latin titles. In this volume, the following English titles (most of them employed by their published English translation) are used for the Latin. Titles marked by asterisks designate works not yet available in English translation; for the sake of uniformity, English titles have been devised for these works too and are utilized throughout the volume. For complete bibliographical details on English translations and Latin editions, see the Bibliography.

Abbreviated Psalter of the Venerable Bede, trans. Browne = *Collectio Psalterii Bedae Venerabili adscripta*, ed. Browne

The Art of Poetry, trans. Kendall = *De arte metrica*, ed. Kendall

Commentary of Bede the Priest on the Canticle of Habakkuk, trans. Connolly = *Expositio Bedae presbyteri in Canticum Habacuc*, ed. Hurst

Commentary on the Acts of the Apostles, trans. Martin = *Expositio Actuum Apostolorum*, ed. Laistner

Commentary on the Apocalypse, trans. Marshall = *Expositio Apocalypseos*, ed. Gryson

**Commentary on the Gospel of Luke* = *In Lucae euangelium expositio*, ed. Hurst

**Commentary on the Gospel of Mark* = *In Marci euangelium expositio*, ed. Hurst

Commentary on the Seven Catholic Epistles, trans. Hurst = *In epistola VII catholicas*, ed. Hurst

Ecclesiastical History of the English People, trans. Colgrave and Mynors = *Historia ecclesiastica gentis Anglorum*, ed. Colgrave and Mynors

Excerpts from the Works of Saint Augustine on the Letters of the Blessed Apostle Paul, trans. Hurst = *Collectio Bedae presbyteri ex opusculis sancti Augustini in Epistulas Pauli Apostoli*. Still unprinted

The Figures of Rhetoric, trans. Kendall = *De schematibus et tropis*, ed. Kendall

History of the Abbots (published as *Lives of the Abbots of Wearmouth and Jarrow*), trans. Farmer = *Historia Abbatum*, ed. Plummer

Homilies on the Gospels, trans. Martin = *Homiliae euangelii*, ed. Hurst

Letter to Albinus, trans. Meyvaert = *Epistola ad Albinum*, ed. Plummer

Letter to Bishop Egbert, trans. McClure and Collins = *Epistola ad Ecgbertum Episcopum*, ed. Plummer

Letter to Plegwin, trans. Wallis = *Epistola ad Pleguinam*, ed. Jones

Letter to Wicthed, trans. Wallis = *Epistola ad VVichthedum*, ed. Jones

Life of Saint Cuthbert, trans. Colgrave = *Vita Sancti Cuthberti*, ed. Colgrave

*Life of Saint Felix = *Vita Sancti Felicis*, ed. Mackay

Martyrology, trans. F. Lifshitz = *Martyrologium*, ed. DuBois and Renaud

*Metrical Life of Saint Cuthbert = *Vita metrica Sancti Cuthberti*, ed. Jaager

On Eight Questions, trans. Holder = *De octo quaestionibus*, ed. Gorman

On Ezra and Nehemiah, trans. DeGregorio = *In Ezram et Neemiam*, ed. Hurst

*On First Samuel = *In primam partem Samuhelis*, ed. Hurst

On Genesis, trans. Kendall = *In principium Genesis*, ed. Jones

*On the Day of Judgement = *Versus de die judicii*, ed. Fraipont

On the Holy Places, trans. Foley = *De locis sanctis*, ed. Fraipont

*On the Nature of Things = *De natura rerum*, ed. Jones

*On Orthography = *De orthographia*, ed. Jones

*On the Proverbs of Solomon = *In prouerbia Salomonis*, ed. Hurst

On the Resting-Places of the Children of Israel, trans. Holder = *De mansionibus filiorum Israel*, ed. Migne

*On the Song of Songs = *In Cantica Canticorum*, ed. Hurst

On the Tabernacle, trans. Holder = *De tabernaculo*, ed. Hurst

On the Temple, trans. Connolly = *De templo*, ed. Hurst

*On Times = *De temporibus*, ed. Jones

On Tobias, trans. Foley = *In librum beati patris Tobiae*, ed. Hurst

On What Isaiah Says, trans. Holder = *De eo quod ait Isaias*, ed. Migne

Passion of Saint Anastasius = *Passio S. Anastasii*, ed. Franklin

The Reckoning of Time, trans. Wallis = *De temporum ratione*, ed. Jones

*Retraction on the Acts of the Apostles = *Retractatio in Actus Apostolorum*, ed. Laistner

Thirty Questions on the Book of Kings, trans. Foley = *In Regum librum XXX quaestiones*, ed. Hurst

The Cambridge Companion to Bede is only the second volume of the many yet published in this series that focuses on the Anglo-Saxon period. The status of Bede in the Anglo-Saxon literary and historical tradition is fully evident in *The Cambridge Companion to Old English Literature* (1991), but that collection focuses on the vernacular tradition, and while Bede's influence is present there, the magnitude of his work merits a volume devoted to it. Because he wrote in Latin, Bede remains a somewhat obscure figure in literature departments, invariably linked to the story of the first Old English Christian poet Cædmon told in Book 4 of Bede's best-known work, the *Ecclesiastical History of the English People*. Scholars have always recognized the *Ecclesiastical History*'s importance as a masterful specimen of historical prose narrative, without which Cædmon and much else about early Anglo-Saxon England would remain unknown. But Bede's achievements reach far beyond that work. He is, in fact, the most prolific author of early medieval England, a writer who excelled in all the main genres of his age, a major literary personality in an age riddled with anonymity, an authority whose views were sought by later writers, and, without question, one of the intellectual giants of the Middle Ages.

This book, designed to introduce his life and writings, seeks to highlight the distinctive achievements and strains of thought that together make Bede an imposing and rewarding figure. The contents of the volume fall into three parts. Part I covers Bede's life and the social, political, religious and intellectual contexts of his environment that are necessary for in-depth study of his writings. Part II turns to the writings themselves, with individual chapters on the scientific works, the educational treatises, the biblical commentaries, the Gospel homilies and the historical writings. Part III ranges chronologically from Bede's death in the early eighth century to the modern era in order to sketch the historical contexts in which his writings were received and his influence and reputation determined. A brief selection of recommended readings follows; this is supplemented, at the end of the volume, by a complete bibliographical listing of all the scholarly works cited in the individual chapters. The specialists who wrote the chapters have geared them towards an audience of students and non-specialists, directing their coverage to received paradigms of understanding rather than new points of view. The hope nevertheless remains that more advanced readers too might find in the pages that follow something to stimulate their thinking about Bede, early Anglo-Saxon England and early medieval literary culture in general.

Readers may be surprised to find no individual chapter or chapters devoted exclusively to the *Ecclesiastical History*, surely the work most likely to be encountered by the students whom this book is meant to serve. Scholarship has always privileged the *Ecclesiastical History*, and it is now time to see Bede's works in a more integrated and holistic way, recognizing in his collective output a carefully structured body of knowledge whose interconnections are deliberate and therefore essential for interpreters to grasp. Perceiving the intricacies of this larger design depends on a careful and sensitive reading of all its interrelated parts, and so on appreciating the various points of contact between the *Ecclesiastical History* and other Bedan compositions. Accordingly, in the chapter entitled 'Bede and History', readers will find a general discussion of the *Ecclesiastical History* that attempts at the same time to situate the work alongside his other historical writings, while the chapters devoted to his scientific, educational and exegetical writings also make an effort to underline notable intersections with the *Ecclesiastical History*.

Today, most of Bede's Latin writings can be read in modern English translations. This is a fairly recent development, and one that certainly bespeaks the need for a comprehensive companion to help guide the wider audience of readers now able to encounter the full range of his work for the first time. As more than one contributor will emphasize, it is striking not only how much Bede wrote but how much he wrote about, moving as he did through nearly all the realms of Christian Latin learning known in his day. But for too long, the only way into his vast literary corpus was via mastery of the original language in which it was composed, not to mention acquiring access to the costly editions in which the Latin texts are printed. The availability of competent, inexpensive English translations of Bede's writings is thus an important advance that should significantly augment his modern readership. This volume makes use of those translations, and a word of explanation is necessary on the procedure of reference and quotation followed. The reader is advised to begin with the list of Bede's writings on pp. xii–xiii. Provided here is an alphabetized listing of English and corresponding Latin titles with the last names of the translators and editors (complete citations are provided in the Bibliography, pp. 246–8). Where an English translation is available, its title has been used in the list and employed throughout the volume; this is the case for most titles. In the handful of instances where English translations have yet to appear, an English rendering of the work's Latin title has been devised for the list and for use throughout the book; for ease of identification, these titles are marked in the list by an asterisk. Where these untranslated works are cited in the book, the authors have supplied their own English translations where necessary.

Bede was himself a great lover of books, blessed as he was with access to perhaps the greatest library of his age. From the multiplicity of textual roles he would fulfil over the course of his literary career, he knew full well that book-making was a collective effort, predicated on the work of many. And so it is with this volume, whose contributors I wish to thank for their enthusiasm for the project and the learning they devoted to its realization. As editor I especially wish to thank Calvin Kendall, Arthur Holder, Larry Martin, Allen Frantzen, Sharon Rowley and Joshua Westgard for their careful reading of various sections of the manuscript and their helpful recommendations for improving it. My thanks are also due to the University of Michigan – Dearborn for sabbatical leave in the fall 2008 semester when work on the project was in fullest swing. Finally, Sarah Stanton, Rebecca Jones and the others at Cambridge University Press are hugely deserving of my gratitude for all their assistance and encouragement in bringing this book to publication.

CHRONOLOGICAL TABLE OF IMPORTANT DATES

449	The date ascribed by Bede (*EH* I. 15) to the arrival of the Angles and Saxons in Britain
c. 540	The British monk Gildas writes *On the Ruin of Britain*, a major source for Bede's *Ecclesiastical History*
597	Augustine of Canterbury and his companions arrive in Kent to convert the English (*EH* I. 25)
604	Death of Pope Gregory I
625	The date ascribed by Bede (*EH* II. 9) to Paulinus's mission to Northumbria
627	Edwin king of Northumbria accepts Christian faith; he and his people receive baptism from Paulinus on Easter Day (*EH* II. 12–14)
628	Benedict Biscop born
633	Edwin slain at Hatfield Chase on 12 October by Penda, pagan king of Mercia (*EH* II. 20)
635	King Oswald invites Irish monk Aidan to Northumbria to teach the Christian faith; grants him island of Lindisfarne as his episcopal see (*EH* III. 3)
653	Benedict Biscop makes first of his five trips to Rome
664	Synod of Whitby rules in favour of Roman method of Easter reckoning (*EH* III. 25) Benedict Biscop's second visit to Rome

665	Benedict Biscop travels from Rome to the monastery of St Honorat on the island of Lérins in southern Gaul, where he takes monastic vows
667	Benedict Biscop's third visit to Rome
669	Theodore of Tarsus and the African Hadrian arrive; Theodore takes up office of archbishop of Canterbury (*EH* IV. 1–2)
671	Benedict Biscop's fourth visit to Rome
c. 673	Bede born, probably somewhere near Wearmouth-Jarrow (*EH* V. 24: 'in the territory of this monastery')
674	King Ecgfrith grants land to Benedict Biscop to build monastery of St Peter at Wearmouth
679	Benedict Biscop's fifth visit to Rome
680	Bede, at age seven, becomes an oblate under Benedict Biscop's charge at Wearmouth
c. 681	Ecgfrith grants land to Biscop to build sister monastery of St Paul at Jarrow At Benedict Biscop's request, Ceolfrith moves from Wearmouth to Jarrow to serve as abbot

685	Dedication of the church at Jarrow on 23 April
	    King Ecgfrith slain at the Nechtansmere on 20 May
	    Aldfrith succeeds
	    Cuthbert induced to accept episcopal orders, becomes bishop of Lindisfarne
	    Benedict Biscop's sixth and final journey to Rome

687	Cuthbert dies on 20 March
690	Benedict Biscop dies on 12 January; Ceolfrith takes charge of Wearmouth, presiding over both houses
692	Bede, at age nineteen, ordained deacon (*EH* V. 24) Archbishop Theodore dies
702	Bede, at age thirty, ordained priest (*EH* V. 24)
703	Bede writes *On Times* and *Commentary on the Apocalypse*, his first works

705   Aldfrith dies
        Eadwulf usurps throne
        Osred, Aldfrith's son, restored to throne

709   Wilfrid dies

716   Abbot Ceolfrith unexpectedly resigns abbacy of Wearmouth-
        Jarrow and departs for Rome, taking with him the Codex
        Amiatinus. He dies en route at Langres on 25 September
        Osred dies
        Cenred succeeds

718   Cenred dies
        Osric succeeds

729   Osric dies
        Ceolwulf, to whom Bede dedicates *Ecclesiastical History*,
        succeeds

731   Bede completes *Ecclesiastical History*, though work on the text
        may have continued hereafter
        Ceolwulf is deposed but quickly restored

734   Bede writes to Bishop Egbert of York on 5 November about abuses
        in Northumbrian Church

735   Bede dies on 25 May
        Bishop Egbert receives pallium, becomes archbishop of York

793   Vikings sack Lindisfarne

794   Vikings sack Jarrow

c. 900 Earliest extant manuscript evidence for Old English translation of
        Bede's *Ecclesiastical History*

1563   *Editio princeps* of Bede's works printed in Basel

1899   Bede declared Doctor of the Church

MAPS

Map 1 Anglo-Saxon England

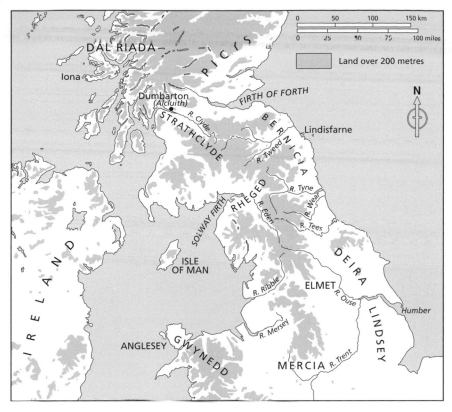

Map 2 The making of Northumbria: Bernicia, Deira and their neighbours in the early seventh century

Map 3 The Church in early Anglo-Saxon Northumbria

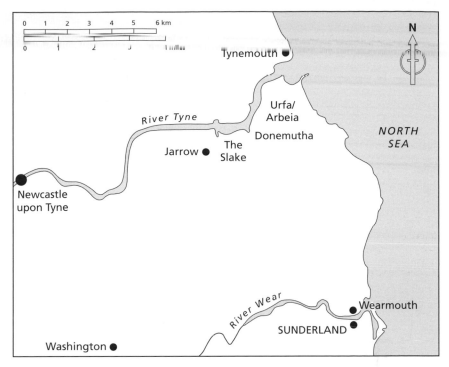

Map 4 Wearmouth and Jarrow, and the lower reaches of the Tyne and Wear

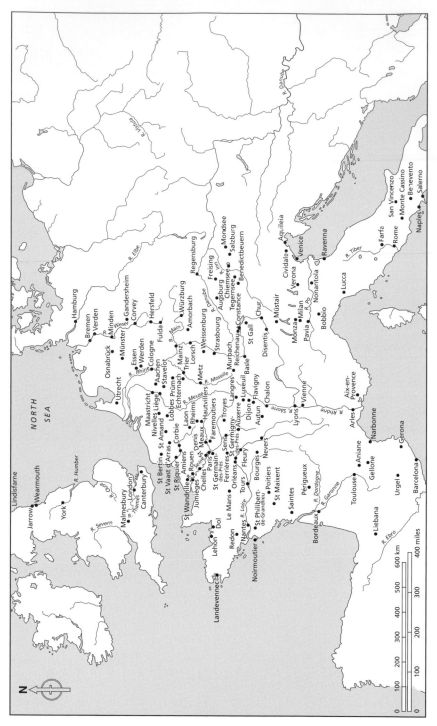

Map 5 Carolingian schools, scriptoria and literary centres

PART I

Bede's life and context

I

MICHELLE P. BROWN

Bede's life in context

Bede's biography and its sources

In AD 731, in the fifty-ninth year of his life, Bede concluded his *Ecclesiastical History of the English People* with an autobiographical note in which he stated that 'it has always been my delight to learn or to teach or to write' (V. 24, p. 567). The *Ecclesiastical History* gives us our primary route into the early Anglo-Saxon world, yet the sources for our knowledge of the famous scholar-monk's life are sparse: his brief autobiographical note, which includes a list of his own writings; an account of his death by one of his pupils, Cuthbert; his correspondence, notably the letters he wrote to Egbert and Plegwin; his prefaces to his prose *Life of Saint Cuthbert* and to Book IV of his *On First Samuel*. These can be contextualized somewhat by other written sources, such as the anonymous *Life of Ceolfrith* and passages in the *Anglo-Saxon Chronicle* which are based upon earlier annals, and by archaeological excavations and the remains of the material culture of the age. But for deeper insight into Bede's personality and philosophy of life we are reliant upon close reading and analysis of the nuances of his own works, in various areas of study, and upon examination of those things most familiar to him: his home, the twin monastery of Wearmouth-Jarrow, its buildings, fittings and artefacts and, most importantly, the books he so loved – those he consulted and those that he helped to produce in his roles as author, editor and scribe.

Bede's writings

The *Ecclesiastical History* is only one of the forty-four works in Bede's list (which is incomplete, omitting *On the Holy Places*, *On Eight Questions* and two letters, those to Albinus and to Egbert). Yet it is for the *Ecclesiastical History* that he is principally remembered, because of its pioneering methodology and because it remains the single most important source for the early Anglo-Saxon period. Through it, Bede sought to weave his people into the broader fabric of the Christian story of salvation, in sequel to Eusebius of

Caesarea's fourth-century *Ecclesiastical History* of the early Christian Church. Indeed, the very concept of 'Englishness' stems from Bede's attempts to construct a collective identity for the mêlée of peoples inhabiting the former Roman province of Britannia. However, the principal route to comprehending divine reality fully lay, for Bede and his peers, in the study of Christian Scripture and its interpretation by the Church Fathers. He therefore devoted the bulk of his research time, resulting in some twenty works, to biblical exegesis, and it is with these works of commentary, significantly, that his list of works begins. As later chapters in this volume will discuss, Bede's method in these exegetical writings involved excavating both the Old and New Testaments not only for literal meaning and archaeological detail but for multiple layers of allegorical interpretation through which the deeper spiritual meaning of Holy Writ might be discerned.

For understanding God's plan, nature also offered valuable insights; for as the Irish missionary Saint Columbanus (540–615) had proclaimed, nature is a second scripture in which God is perceived. So Bede's list includes works devoted to the operations of the natural world, of time and space. He wrote *On the Nature of Things*, building on the encyclopaedic approach to natural history of Pliny and Isidore of Seville (the work of Aristotle and the Alexandrian school having been lost to the West), and the volumes *On Times* and *The Reckoning of Time*. Chronological calculations had the potential to disrupt eternal harmony, especially when they related to Easter – the defining moment when God and humankind were reconciled. Bede's dating of the Incarnation to *annus mundi* ('the year of the world') 3952 – rather than the traditional date of 5199 established by Eusebius of Caesarea – led him perilously close to charges of heresy, as we know from his *Letter to Plegwin*, one of the precious few documents apart from his autobiographical note that sheds light on his life and personality. Bede's letter reveals his profound hurt, indignation and fury at being accused by 'lewd rustics' (*Letter to Plegwin*, p. 405), at the table of Bishop Wilfrid, of introducing dubious ideas of his own when conducting his chronological calculations, exposing him to suspicion of heresy on grounds of innovation. His friend Bishop Acca of Hexham had to encourage Bede to defend himself against similar criticism concerning his exegesis on the evangelists and their symbols.[1] As Bede was quick to point out in his reply to Acca, his critics' attacks stemmed from their own ignorance since, being less well-read than he, they were unaware of his implicit allusions to earlier authorities (*Commentary on the Gospel of Luke*, pp. 7–8). By way of practical response, he effectively introduced footnotes, inserting s-shaped marginal marks beside biblical quotations and alphabetic characters to denote authors cited. He took pains to credit his sources, stating in his autobiographical note that the

Ecclesiastical History was based on facts 'gleaned either from ancient documents or from tradition or from my own knowledge' (v. 24, p. 567), while his preface cites at length those who supplied data (pp. 5 7).

Bede also recounted the lives of saints so that they might serve as role models for society. He compiled an innovative martyrology, improved the translation of the Greek *Passion of Saint Anastasius*, reworked Paulinus's metrical *Life of Saint Felix* in prose and composed verse and prose lives of a new English saint in the making, Cuthbert, bishop of Lindisfarne (died 687). His objectivity as a historian may seem compromised, to modern readers, by his inclusion of miraculous events, but when writing hagiography it was unthinkable that miracles, the visible manifestation of sanctity, should be excluded as audiences expected them from their heroes. Yet, when writing about his personal heroes in the *History of the Abbots*, Bede eschewed such hagiographical devices because, in this instance, he was seeking to record their historical contribution, rather than to create cults for saintly founding fathers (see Chapter 12).

Bede devoted other works to language, the mechanics of which fascinated those who were becoming newly accustomed to communicating with the pen as well as the voice. Learning new languages also entails studying different patterns of thought and speech, and those encountered in Scripture inspired Bede to compose a treatise *The Figures of Rhetoric*, which he appended to his book on *The Art of Poetry*. A book of hymns 'in various metres and rhythms', a book of epigrams 'in heroic or elegiac verse', a treatise entitled *On Orthography* 'arranged according to the order of the alphabet' (v. 24, p. 571) and a collection of letters complete Bede's oeuvre.

Bede's life as a monk

The diversity of the writings included in Bede's list casts light on the nature of his educational background, steeped in the learning of the monastic schoolroom (on which see Chapter 7). In his autobiographical note, Bede tells us that he was born (672/3) on land belonging to Wearmouth-Jarrow (see Map 4). Wearmouth (Figure 1) was founded in 674 by the Northumbrian nobleman Benedict Biscop, who also founded Jarrow (Figure 2) in 681, and it is usually assumed that Bede's birthplace lay near the former in Sunderland. His family entrusted him to Abbots Biscop and Ceolfrith, successively, to be educated, and although we know nothing of his social background,[2] we may assume that he was of free birth and that his kin were Christians who aspired to learning and were wealthy enough to spare a son from other duties. Studying in the monastic schoolroom did not necessarily mean that pupils would embrace religious life, but one can imagine the boy Bede's omnivorous

1 The West Tower, St Peter's Church, Wearmouth (lower two stages and
the nave wall date from the 670s)

love of knowledge and his delight in the regularity of the monastic life
rendering him an eager novice. Bede spent the rest of his life at Wearmouth-
Jarrow, devoting himself 'entirely to the study of the Scriptures' (*EH* v. 24,
p. 567), observing the Benedictine-style communal rule of monastic life and
singing the Offices daily. He probably moved to Jarrow with Ceolfrith when a
community was established there in 681, although as the library was shared
between the two locations – some seven miles apart – it is likely that he
worked in both.

2 St Paul's Church, Jarrow. The current chancel consists substantially of the eastern of the two seventh-century churches and was used by the community, including Bede

It may seem harsh for a child to be separated from family and consigned to perpetual institutionalization in a monastery. Yet this is perhaps not so different from many university dons, progressing from boarding school, through university, to the regimen of college fellow, enjoying a communal life of teaching and research. Bede would likewise have been cushioned from many of the trials and tribulations of his day, with its virulent warfare and competition for limited resources hard-won from trade and the land. His personal regimen was not, however, typical of monks of his day. Monastic rules were devised by the leaders of individual communities, drawing to varying extents upon those of important founding figures such as Saints Pachomius, Basil, Cassian, Columbanus and Benedict of Nursia. These might place greater or lesser emphasis upon communal life or the more ascetic, eremitic traditions of the Eastern desert fathers. Most rules, however, advocated chastity, personal poverty and the performance of the Divine Office, which entailed reciting or chanting the psalms, prayers and biblical readings eight times throughout each day and night at the various canonical hours. Time was also set aside each day for personal prayer and meditative private reading of Scripture (*lectio divina*) and for manual labour, which might vary in accordance with the gifts of the individual. In Bede's case, an unusually large allocation of time would have been devoted to his research and teaching activities. He would have taught in the schoolroom, no doubt following the sort of curriculum established in the Canterbury school of Theodore and Hadrian – two learned figures from the Mediterranean world – in the late seventh century. This included the study of Latin, Greek, theology, exegesis, computistics, astronomy, medicine, poetry and Gregorian chant.[3] The rest of his study time would have been spent in the library, which we can imagine containing large book cupboards (*armaria*) of the sort depicted in the Codex Amiatinus, stocked with volumes from the early Christian Mediterranean, Byzantium, the Christian Orient, Frankia, Ireland and other parts of England (for which see Love's discussion in Chapter 3). He would also have laboured in the scriptorium, drafting his own works with a metal stylus on wax-covered tablets, copying his words or those of earlier authorities and of Scripture in a fine calligraphic hand onto prepared calfskin (vellum) with a goose-quill, using inks and pigments made from local mineral, plant and animal extracts, prepared in the scriptorium by the monks themselves and their novice assistants.

Bede would also have had to undertake other forms of arduous manual work, as a sign of his monastic humility, and would have relinquished personal property, and the joys, pains and distractions of relationships with wife and family. In exchange, he gained security, the fellowship of the monastic *familia* and the eternal communion of saints – and fame: known as 'the Venerable' from as early as the ninth century, he is the only English Doctor of the Catholic Church (since 1899). As later chapters in this volume discuss, by the 780s Bede's relics were considered miracle-working by Alcuin, were collected by York, Fulda and Glastonbury, and were claimed at Durham to have been stolen from Jarrow in the mid eleventh century by an acquisitive keeper of Saint Cuthbert's shrine, Alfred Westow, being placed alongside Cuthbert in his coffin in Durham Cathedral.[4] In 1370 Bede's relics were translated to the Galilee Chapel, where pilgrims were received and to which women visitors were restricted. There Bede lies, doorkeeper to this symbolic focus of Northumbria's identity, just as his *Ecclesiastical History* serves as portal to its origins.

Religious life was not always peaceful, however. The Jarrow community was decimated by plague in the late seventh century – one of the worst ever for pestilence and famine. From this event, however, possibly comes one further item of biographical information on Bede's life. According to the *Life of Ceolfrith*, at one point only Abbot Ceolfrith and 'one small boy' (long thought to be Bede) remained fit enough to sing the Office in the community's own church, the fabric of which survives as the present chancel of St Paul's Church, Jarrow – a place where Bede's presence feels very real indeed.[5] Ceolfrith would have learned chant from John, the pope's own archcantor, who spent time at Wearmouth-Jarrow in the 680s (*EH* IV. 18), for music was not written down until the ninth century and had to be taught *viva voce*. He would, in turn, have taught his brethren. Bede tells us, again in his autobiographical note, that at nineteen (692) he became deacon, responsible for reading the Gospel during the liturgy, and at thirty (702), the age at which Christ began his ministry, he was ordained priest. Most monks did not take priestly orders, but Bede was called to both vocations.

In addition to this episode from the *Life of Ceolfrith*, a later but equally momentous trauma in Bede's life is made known to us from the preface to the fourth book of his commentary *On First Samuel*. His work on this particular section of the Bible, and the fact that he interjects this highly personal preface as an aside within it, reveals that he harboured a telling personal affinity with Samuel, the prophet-priest, who anointed Saul and David and established the sacral role of kingship mediated through, and regulated by, the priesthood. Samuel was promised to the service of the Lord, by a mother desperate to conceive, and entrusted to the care of the high priest, Eli, in the temple of Shiloh. Bede evidently identified with this, casting his own father figure, Ceolfrith, in the role of Eli and himself as Samuel. Ceolfrith's sudden decision in 716 to vacate his abbacy and travel to Rome, to spend his last days among the tombs of the apostles, caused Bede such severe sorrow that his work on the commentary suffered. Here, in the preface to Book IV (p. 212), Bede shares his trauma and expresses his hopes for his community under Ceolfrith's successor, Hwætberht, nicknamed 'Eusebius'. In the fourth century, Eusebius of Caesarea had chronicled and legitimized the Emperor Constantine and the early Church, a service performed by Samuel for the early kings of the Israelites. By penning his own *Ecclesiastical History*, in emulation of Eusebius's earlier work, Bede fulfilled the prophetic role in respect of his own people, a task to which he evidently felt himself dedicated in the womb.

One final text conveys much important incidental insight into Bede's personality: his *Letter to Bishop Egbert*, written on 5 November 734, only months before his death in May 735. It may have been a sense of impending mortality that prompted him to unburden himself to the pastoral head of the Church in Northumbria, Egbert bishop of York, over his concerns for the spiritual and physical well-being of its people, and emboldened him to advance his own suggestions for their remedy. In urging Egbert to perform his pastoral role well, Bede dares to overstep the mark in outlining cases of episcopal abuse of power. An injustice that particularly incensed him was the extortion of payments from people in remote areas who scarcely ever saw a cleric, let alone a bishop (p. 347). Bede was not ambitious for advancement within Church and court life, ardently preferring the cloistered existence of the prophetic scholar, teacher and scribe. Nevertheless, he did not lack political astuteness. His letter suggests reforms (pp. 345, 349), laments the hypocrisy of those who founded pseudo-monasteries on their land for temporal benefits (pp. 351–2) and fears for the military strength of the kingdom should too many youths enter those bogus institutions (p. 350). The tone of this missive, like his letter to Plegwin and certain passages of the *Ecclesiastical History*, reveals that his personality was not entirely one of piety, prayer and scholarly objectivity. Bede, in characteristic human fashion, could harbour a measure of anger and resentment and had his prejudices, especially against those he considered enemies of Northumbria, and of orthodoxy: notably his own detractors, pagans and the ancient British Church.

Bede the 'Englishman' and the English vernacular

Bede had a well-developed sense of his own identity and of that which he was creating for his people, and of their place in the wider world and in posterity. To him may be attributed the very concept of 'Englishness', a collective nomenclature, derived from his own Anglian ancestry, for an amalgam of peoples of diverse Germanic and Celtic descent. He never travelled far from home, though he probably visited York, Hexham and Lindisfarne. Nonetheless, he dispatched research requests far afield, which were answered by Lastingham, East Anglia, Wessex, London, Barking and Canterbury. Nothhelm, a London priest and later archbishop, even undertook research on Bede's behalf in the papal archives. Abbot Albinus of Canterbury particularly supported Bede in writing the *Ecclesiastical History*, which was dedicated to King Ceolwulf of Northumbria, who in 737 subsequently abdicated and joined the Lindisfarne community. Bede evidently attracted influential friends, as well as jealous detractors, despite his relatively cloistered existence.

From his little cell Bede nonetheless used his imagination to envision the wider world and the heavenly kingdom. His *On the Holy Places*, reworking Abbot Adomnán of Iona's account of the Holy Places related to him by the Frankish pilgrim-bishop Arculf around 690, is one of the best early pilgrim guides, used by those who physically visited the Holy Land and those who, like Bede, journeyed there spiritually.[6] Closer to home, his vivid imagination was nurtured by oral tradition, vernacular poetry and song. Bede would have spoken Old English, in the Northumbrian dialect, resorting to Latin for his religious offices. He played an important role in the development of written English – a role that has been overshadowed by that of King Alfred and his circle in the aftermath of the Viking upheavals during the ninth century. In a letter recounting Bede's death – a genre calculated to promote his posthumous saintly status – one of his pupils, Cuthbert, describes his last days, spent in study and prayer, chanting psalms, antiphons and Old English verse: for he 'knew our poems well'. This account includes 'Bede's Death Song', perhaps of Bede's own composition:

> Facing that enforced journey, no man can be
> More prudent than he has good call to be,
> If he consider, before his going hence
> What for his spirit of good hap or of evil
> After his day of death shall be determined.[7]

This is the earliest recorded example of Old English poetry, along with 'Cædmon's Hymn', the preservation of which (in Latin translation) we also owe to Bede. As Bede told the story, Cædmon, a monk at Abbess Hild's Whitby, was so embarrassed at the prospect of taking his turn at singing at feasts that he hid with the beasts in the byre until God inspired him to sing:

> Now we must praise the Maker of the heavenly kingdom, the power of the Creator and his counsel, the deeds of the Father of glory and how He, since he is the eternal God, was the Author of all marvels and first created the heavens as a roof for the children of men and then, the almighty Guardian of the human race, created the earth.   (*EH* IV. 24, p. 417)

An Old English version of the poem, with dialectical variations, is preserved in the margins of several manuscripts of the *Ecclesiastical History* and in the 'Alfredian' translation of the latter into Old English (see Chapter 15).

The advantages of communicating orally in the vernacular, as well as being literate (i.e. Latinate) in Mediterranean fashion, were fully appreciated by Bede. His *Letter to Bishop Egbert* evinces deep concern that most of the thinly spread priesthood could not read Latin, leading him to translate the *Pater Noster* and Creed into Old English to help such 'illiterate' priests to conduct services and to teach their flocks (p. 346). Even during his final illness, Bede, free from the fears about vernacular Bibles that would later condemn Wycliffe and Tyndale, was translating into English John's Gospel, that the Good News (Old English *Godspell*) might better be shared with all.[8] For Bede, like fellow missionaries with the pen such as Ulfilas, Cyril and Methodius, recognized the necessity for vernacular translation.

Bede as evangelist-scribe, and contemporary manuscript culture

In response to a letter from Bishop Acca of Hexham Bede writes, in the preface to his *Commentary on the Gospel of Luke*: 'I have subjected myself to that burden of work in which, as in innumerable bonds of monastic servitude which I shall pass over, I was myself at once dictator, notary and scribe' (p. 7; my translation). This remark reveals that Bede regarded such work as holy labour, and that he differentiated between the functions of authors (who usually dictated rather than wrote themselves), secretary-copyists and scribal evangelists. The sixth-century monastic founder-publisher Cassiodorus wrote that the Spirit continues to work in those who translate, expand or humbly copy Scripture, as in the biblical authors.[9] Bede elaborates this theme in relation to Ezra the Scribe, who fulfilled the Law by rewriting its destroyed books, thereby opening his mouth to interpret Scripture and teach others (*On Ezra and Nehemiah*, pp. 108–11, 116). The act of writing is therefore presented as an essential, personal act for Bede as a scribe, a preacher and a teacher.[10]

Bede would have played a leading role in producing the three single-volume Bibles commissioned from the Wearmouth-Jarrow scriptorium by Ceolfrith, the greatest work of biblical scholarship and editing of the age. Two were to be retained for reference by Wearmouth and Jarrow; the third accompanied Ceolfrith on his final journey in 716 as a gift for the pope (*History of the Abbots*, ch. 15). It survives as the Codex Amiatinus (see Figure 3, and Chapter 3 for more discussion). Fragments of the others have resurfaced, some discovered by Canon Greenwell as binding fragments in a Newcastle antique shop (the Greenwell leaves). These formed part of one of the volumes retained by the communities, while other pieces (the Middleton leaves, see Figure 4, and Bankes leaf) may be from the other, donated by King Offa later in the century to Worcester, where it was already thought to have been made in Rome, so 'romanizing' were the Ceolfrith Bibles in style.[11] Indeed, Amiatinus, the dedication inscription of which was tampered with, was only recognized as having an English association in the 1880s (and not until the twentieth century was it acknowledged as actually English).[12]

Bede, the scribe, would probably have taken his turn in penning the Ceolfrith Bibles. We cannot firmly identify his hand, but it is probably one of the seven that wrote Amiatinus in a stately, romanizing uncial script, modelled upon that of Gregory the Great's Rome, with Roman rustic capitals being employed for rubrics and titles.[13] Another famous Wearmouth-Jarrow uncial manuscript is the little copy of Saint John's Gospel found inside Saint Cuthbert's coffin, thought to have been presented to his shrine in 698.[14] It is bound using 'Coptic sewing' and tooled in Eastern fashion, reflecting Eastern influences on the Insular world. An example of the continental uncial books that served as models survives in the Bodleian Library[15] – a sixth-century Greek and Latin copy of Acts from Sardinia which, judging from its close textual correspondences, may be the actual book Bede used for reference when working on his *Commentary on the Acts of the Apostles*. The Latin Creed in uncial (f. 226ᵛ) was probably added at Wearmouth-Jarrow – might this be an unidentified example of Bede's handwriting?

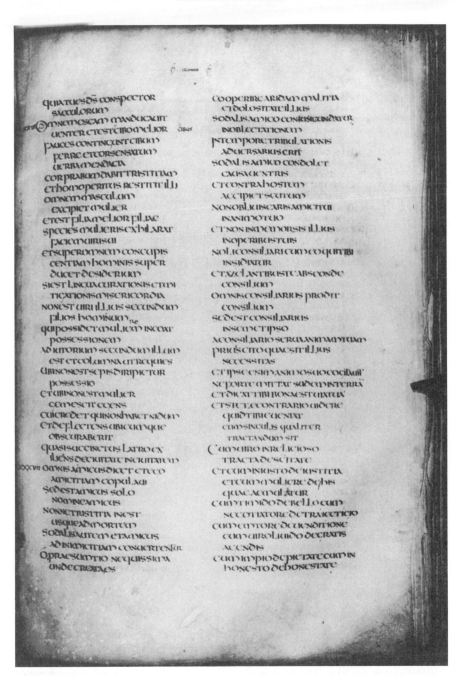

3 The Codex Amiatinus (Florence, Biblioteca Medicea-Laurenziana, Amiatino 1, f. 485ʳ),
Wearmouth-Jarrow, early eighth century (pre-716)

·ETLOCUTUSESTTIBI·
ETAIT ONICHEA;
UISURISES INDIE ILLA QUANDO INCRE
DIERIS CUBICULUM INTRACUBICULU
UT ABSCONDARIS,
ET AIT REX ISRAHEL;
TOLLITE ONICHEAM ETOANEAT APUT
AONON PRINCIPEON CIUITATIS·
ET APUT IOAS FILIUM AONOELECH·
ET DICITE EIS HAECDICIT REX;
ONITTITE UIRUON ISTUON INCARCEREM
ET SUSTENTATE EUON PANE TRIBULA
TIONIS ETAQUA ANGUSTIAE·
DONEC REUERTAR IN PACE;
DIXITQ; ONICHEAS;
SI REUERSUS FUERIS INPACE NONEST
LOCUTUS DNS INOE;
ET AIT AUDITE POPULI OONNES;
ASCENDIT ITAQ; REX ISRAHEL
ET IOSAPHAT REX IUDA INRAONOTH
GALAAD;
DIXITQ; REX ISRAHEL ADIOSAPHAT;
SUONE ARONAETINCREDERE PROELIU;
ET INDUERE UESTIBUSTUS;
PORRO REX ISRAHEL ONUTAUIT
HABITUON ET INGRESSUS EST BELLU;
REX AUTEON SIRIAE PRAECEPERAT
PRINCIPIB; CURRUUON TRIGINTA
DUOBUS DICENS·
NON PUGNABITIS CONTRAONINOREM
ET ONAIOREM QUEMPIAM;
NISI CONTRA REGEM ISRAHEL SOLUM;
CUON ERGO UIDISSENT PRINCIPES
CURRUUM IOSAPHAT·
SUSPICATI SUNT QUOD IPSE ESSET
REX ISRAHEL.
ET INPETU FACTO PUGNABANT
CONTRAEUON;
ET EXCLAONAUIT IOSAPHAT;
INTELLEXERUNTQ; PRINCIPES
CURRUUM QUOD NONESSET
REX ISRAHEL.
ET CESSAUERUNT ABEO;
UNUS AUTEON QUIDAM TETENDIT

ARCUON ININCERTUON SAGITTAON
DIRIGENS
ET CASU PERCUSSIT REGEM ISRAHEL,
INTER PULOONEON ETSTOONACHUON;
AT ILLE DIXIT AURIGE SUO,
UERTEON ONANUON TUAON ET EICEONE
DE EXERCITU·
QUIA GRAUITER UULNERATUS SUM;
COONONISUON EST ERGO PROELIUON
INDIE ILLA;
ET REX ISRAHEL STABAT INCURRU SUO
CONTRA SIROS ET ONORTUUS
EST UESPERI,
FLUEBAT AUTEON SANGUIS PLAGAE
INSINU CURRUS·
ET PRAECO PERSONUIT IN UNIUERSO
EXERCITU ANTEQUAON SOL
OCCUONBERET DICENS·
UNUSQUISQ; REUERTATUR INCIUITA
TEON ET INTERRAON SUAON;
ONORTUUS EST AUTEON REX
ET PERLATUS EST SAONARIAON;
SEPELIERUNTQ; REGEM INSAONARIA
ET LAUERUNT CURRUON INPISCINA
SAONARIAE,
ET LINXERUNT CANES SANGUINEON EIUS
ET HABENAS LAUERUNT IUXTA
UERBUON DNI QUOD LOCUTUS FUERAT·
RELIQUA UERO SERONONUON AHAB
ET UNIUERSA QUAE FECIT·
ET DOONUS EBURNEAE QUAON
AEDIFICAUIT·
CUNCTARUONQ; URBIUON QUAS EX
STRUXIT·
NONNE SCRIPTA SUNT HAEC INLIBRO
UERBORUON DIERUON REGUON ISRL·
DORONIUIT ERGO AHAB CUON PATRIBUS SUIS;
ET REGNAUIT OHOZIAS FILIUS
EIUS PRO EO
IOSAPHAT FILIUS ASA REGNARE
COEPERAT SUPER IUDAM ANNO
QUARTO AHAB REGIS ISRAHEL
TRIGINTA QUINQ; ANNORUM ERAT
CUON REGNARE COEPISSET·

4 A leaf from the Book of Kings, from one of the Ceolfrith Bibles, The Middleton Leaves (London, British Library, Add. MS 45025, f. 2ʳ), Wearmouth-Jarrow, early eighth century (pre-716). Bede probably served as one of the scribes of the Ceolfrith Bibles and his formal uncial hand would resemble this

5 The St Petersburg Bede, Wearmouth-Jarrow, mid eighth century (St Petersburg, National Library of Russia, Cod. Q.v.I.18), f. 26[v]

Bede would certainly have played his part in promoting the Wearmouth-Jarrow revival of the romanizing uncial style of book script. The eminent palaeographer E. A. Lowe once thought that he had detected Bede's hand in the colophon to one of the earliest extant copies of the *Ecclesiastical History*, the St Petersburg Bede (Figure 5), although this is now considered a copy.[16] The initials in this and in Cotton Tiberius A.xiv in the British Library[17] have coloured panelled infills recalling the stained glass of Wearmouth-Jarrow. These manuscripts, along with the Moore Bede,[18] represent the publishing response of Wearmouth-Jarrow and other Northumbrian scriptoria to demand, at home and abroad, for Bede's works following his death.[19] They are written in an elegant, highly legible minuscule script – a reformed version of the sort of lower case, cursive hand developed by earlier Irish and English scribes which was suitable for more mundane purposes than copying sacred text and which would have been written by Bede as his usual hand – and date to around the 740s–760s.[20] A further copy of the *Ecclesiastical History*

6 The Tiberius Bede, a copy of the *Ecclesiastical History* made at Canterbury, early ninth century
(London, British Library, Cotton MS Tiberius C.ii, f. 5ᵛ)

(BL, Cotton MS Tiberius C.ii; see Figure 6) was made in Kent in the early ninth century and has given its name to the 'Tiberius Group' of southern English manuscripts.²¹ Another Wearmouth-Jarrow copy of a Bedan text is Oxford, Bodleian, Bodl. 819, a late-eighth-century copy of his *On the Proverbs of Solomon*. It is unusual for so many early copies of early medieval

CODICIBVS SACRIS HOSTILI CLADE PERVSTIS
ESDRA DO FERVENS HOC REPARAVIT OPVS

7 Ezra the Scribe, Codex Amiatinus (Florence, Biblioteca Medicea-Laurenziana, Amiatino 1, f. v^r),
Wearmouth-Jarrow, early eighth century (pre-716)

texts to survive, but Bede's works, particularly the *Ecclesiastical History*, enjoyed tremendous popularity.

Ceolfrith, self-styled in his dedication page as 'abbot from the ends of the earth', intended the Amiatinus Bible to proclaim to Rome his people's contribution to the apostolic mission, worthy of the Church Fathers. A famous image of Ezra the Scribe (see Figure 7) features among Amiatinus's sacred *figurae* (schematic, symbolic images) on f. v^r. Given the interest in Ezra's role evidenced in Bede's writings,[22] it is likely to have been of great significance to him, and his own exegetical work sheds light on how this important image can be interpreted, giving insight into the mindset and motivation of Bede and his fellow makers of the Ceolfrith Bibles. The Ezra miniature has been interpreted as simultaneously representing Cassiodorus who likewise played a key role in preserving and disseminating Scripture in the post-Roman West, the nine volumes in the bookcase recalling his nine-volume edition of the Bible (*Novem Codices*), but bearing on their spines the names of various other editors of Scripture.[23] The image therefore symbolizes the ongoing process of transmission by scribes who, as Cassiodorus said, could preach with the hand and 'set tongues free with one's fingers', imitating the action of the Lord who wrote the Law with his all-powerful finger.[24] Bede furthermore described Ezra the Scribe as 'typus Christi', a 'type' (i.e. an Old Testament precursor) of Christ.[25] The Ezra miniature therefore depicts not only Ezra and Cassiodorus, but those who laboured on Amiatinus and other copies of Scripture, becoming the bearers of Logos. At one level, therefore, the image might be said to portray Bede, who reveals in his writings that he saw himself as the Northumbrian Ezra.[26] Once again, as in the case of Samuel the prophet and king-maker, Bede, the evangelist-scribe, imagines himself in the role of one of his biblical heroes.

Bede and the material culture of Wearmouth-Jarrow

Images, like words, therefore played an important role in Bede's life, just as they had for his ancestors who, for centuries, had signalled who they were and what they believed in by their art and artefacts. Freedom to explore relationships between word and image in the West – when iconoclasm was rife in the East – was established by Bede's hero Pope Gregory the Great, who wrote, 'What Scripture presents to readers, a picture presents to the gaze of the unlearned. For in it even the ignorant see what they ought to follow, in it the illiterate read.'[27] Benedict Biscop, founder of Wearmouth-Jarrow, embraced this approach when adorning his monasteries with treasures from his pilgrimages to Rome for, as Bede relates,

> he brought back many holy pictures of the saints to adorn the church of St Peter he had built: a painting of the Mother of God, the Blessed Mary ever-Virgin, and one of each of the twelve apostles which he fixed round the central arch on a wooden entablature reaching from wall to wall; pictures of incidents in the gospels with which he decorated the south wall, and scenes from St John's vision of the apocalypse for the north wall. Thus all who entered the church, even those who could not read, were able, whichever way they looked, to contemplate the dear face of Christ and His saints, even if only in a picture, to put themselves more firmly in mind of the Lord's Incarnation and, as they saw the decisive

moment of the Last Judgement before their very eyes be brought to examine their conscience with all due severity.   (*History of the Abbots*, ch. 6, pp. 192–3)

On his fifth journey to Rome, *c.* 685, Biscop returned with

a large supply of sacred books and no less a stock of sacred pictures than on previous journeys. He brought back paintings of the life of Our Lord for the chapel of the Holy Mother of God which he had built within the main monastery, setting them, as its crowning glory, all the way round the walls. His treasures included a set of pictures for the monastery and church of the blessed apostle Paul, consisting of scenes, very skilfully arranged, to show how the Old Testament foreshadowed the New. In one set, for instance, the picture of Isaac carrying the wood on which he was to be burnt as a sacrifice was placed immediately below that of Christ carrying the cross on which He was about to suffer. Similarly the Son of Man up on the cross was paired with the serpent raised up by Moses in the desert.   (*History of the Abbots*, ch. 9, p. 196)

The images adorning Biscop's churches therefore served as visual summaries of Scripture and of the relationship between the Old and New Testaments, illustrated by means of didactic typology – devices also employed by Bede in his writings.

Bede's work was made possible by access to the greatest library of its day which had been formed by Wearmouth-Jarrow's early abbots. Biscop had collected books from Italy (probably including Byzantine tomes), Gaul and southern England, where he served for a time as abbot of St Augustine's Abbey, Canterbury. On his fourth trip to Rome (671), 'he brought back a large number of books on all branches of sacred knowledge, some bought at a favourable price, others the gift of well wishers' (*History of the Abbots*, ch. 4, p. 190). Upon assuming the abbacy of both foundations in 689, Ceolfrith

doubled the number of books in the libraries of both monasteries with an ardour equal to that which Benedict had shown in founding them… For eight hides of land by the River Fresca he exchanged with King Aldfrid, who was very learned in the scriptures, the magnificently worked copy of the Cosmographers which Benedict had bought in Rome.   (*History of the Abbots*, ch. 15, p. 203)

This valuable riverside site would have supported at least eight families. By 716 Wearmouth-Jarrow owned 150 hides of land – worth nineteen such books in a library thought to have contained around 200 volumes. The library was the community's most valuable financial, spiritual and intellectual asset.

It was probably Bede who ensured that a copy of Wearmouth-Jarrow's prized sixth-century Neapolitan copy of Saint Jerome's Vulgate edition of the Gospels was sent to Holy Island to serve as an exemplar for the great cult-book of Saint Cuthbert's shrine, the Lindisfarne Gospels (see Figure 8).[28]

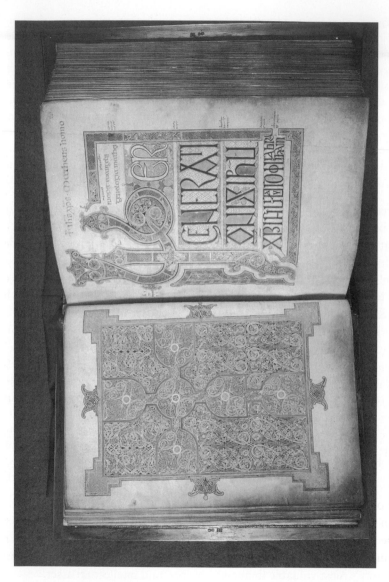

8 The opening of St Matthew's Gospel, The Lindisfarne Gospels (London, British Library, Cotton MS Nero D.iv, ff. 26ᵛ–27ʳ)

Amiatinus and Lindisfarne remain the best manuscript witnesses to Jerome's Vulgate edition, attesting to Northumbria's pivotal role as a preserver of the learning of late antiquity. The outstandingly beautiful, subtle illumination of the Lindisfarne Gospels skilfully and intellectually blends Celtic, Germanic, Roman and Eastern elements, reflecting their formative influences upon the English Church. The visual appearance of the Lindisfarne Gospels epitomizes the collaboration between Bishop Eadfrith and Bede and was designed to proclaim to those who viewed it, including innumerable pilgrims from across Britain and Ireland and from further afield, that their own people and culture had made a crucial contribution to this heady vision of eternal harmony for which Eadfrith and Bede laboured.[29]

The aesthetics of such a work, and their meaning, would not have escaped Bede, for the beauty of worship and ritual, and the sacred spaces in which they were performed, were very important to him.[30] As a boy, he would have observed the Frankish masons and glaziers imported by Biscop building Wearmouth and Jarrow, and seen them adorned with the prized images from Rome, and with the stained glass and sculptures in classical Roman and early Christian style (Figures 9 and 10), that remain there still. Classical balusters and the scrolling tendrils of the True Vine, inhabited by humans and other creatures, co-existed with the interlacing forms of Germanic animal art within splendid churches and monastic buildings, built *more romanorum* of dressed stone in an otherwise timber and mud world. Passages in Bede's *The Reckoning of Time* afford us glimpses of his mind meandering in meditation while in church, leading him to contemplate optical illusions of light and shadow and their scientific and spiritual interpretation. His commentaries *On the Temple* and *On the Tabernacle* (and their plans in the Codex Amiatinus)[31] also reveal his fascinations with the symbolic proportions, fittings and implements of sacred architecture.

The material culture of Bede's home therefore combines with archaeological, artistic and written sources to help us to reconstruct a resplendent image of his life and his well-illumined age. Among these sources shines the beacon of Bede's writings. We may not know the intimate details of his life, but the profile that we can construct of him from his own writings, from a few contemporary written sources and the vestiges of the places and things he knew, presents us with a remarkable mind living in remarkable times. Although Bede's external life was comparatively uneventful, this calm enabled a dynamic inner life, from which he watched events unfold and meditated upon their deeper significance. A routine of dedicated and gruelling cerebral work, punctuated by regular physical labour and by the

9 Stained-glass window depicting an evangelist, St Paul's Church, Jarrow, 680s
(Bede's World Museum, Jarrow)

uplifting and sustaining experience of worship, discipline and deep, deep prayer – this was the regime that allowed Bede to produce so much important and integrated writing, to give shape to the aspirations of an emerging nation and, most importantly of all, to gain a revelatory glimpse of a greater, eternal reality.

10 Inhabited vine-scroll, St Paul's Church, Jarrow, 680s

NOTES

1. Acca's letter to Bede appears as part of the preface to Bede's *Commentary on the Gospel of Luke*, pp. 5–6; on Bede's defence of his interpretation, see Stansbury 1999a: 72.
2. On the possibility that Bede was of high birth, see Campbell's comments in his chapter in this volume, p. 25.
3. Bischoff and Lapidge 1994; Lapidge 1995. See also Bodden 1988.
4. Kendall 1984.
5. *Life of Ceolfrith*, ch. 14, in Farmer 2004: 218.
6. O'Loughlin 2007.
7. *Cuthbert's Letter on the Death of Bede*, in Colgrave and Mynors 1969: 583.
8. *Ibid.*
9. Cassiodorus, *Institutions of Divine and Secular Learning*, trans. J. Halporn and M. Vessey, Translated Texts for Historians 42 (Liverpool University Press, 2004), ch. 30, pp. 163–4.
10. O'Reilly 2001: 24–30; DeGregorio 2004: 16–18.
11. For the Codex Amiatinus, see Alexander 1978: no. 7. For the surviving remnants of the Ceolfrith Bibles and the Worcester and Offa connections, see Webster and Backhouse 1991: 122–3, and M. P. Brown 1996: 166. On Ceolfrith's commission, see Wood 1995.
12. de Rossi 1888: 1–22. For summary, see Bruce-Mitford 1967 and Nordhagen 1977.
13. Lowe 1960.
14. T. J. Brown 1969.

15. Lowe 1934–72: vol. II, p. 251.
16. *Ibid.*, vol. XI, p. 1,621; also Lowe 1958.
17. *Ibid.*, Suppl. 1,703.
18. *Ibid.*, vol. II, p. 139.
19. Parkes 1982.
20. There is debate among scholars as to the palaeographical dating: for orientation, see Parkes, 1982; M. P. Brown 2003b; and Dumville 2007.
21. For an introduction to the manuscript culture of the Insular age, see M. P. Brown 2008.
22. See DeGregorio 2004, 2005 and 2006c.
23. Henderson 1993: 85.
24. Cassiodorus, *Institutions*, ch. 30, p. 163.
25. O'Reilly 2001.
26. DeGregorio 2004: 17–18 and 2006d: xxxv as well as his chapter in the present volume, pp. 137–9.
27. Gregory the Great, Letter XI. 10, to the iconoclast Bishop Serenus of Marseilles.
28. M. P. Brown 2003a.
29. M. P. Brown 2000 and 2003a.
30. Parsons 1987; also Henderson 1980; and Meyvaert 1979.
31. Farr 1999.

2

JAMES CAMPBELL

Secular and political contexts

Bede's rank

The present chapter is not concerned with Bede's intellectual achievement, but, rather, with the political, social and economic circumstances of his life. Much of what we know of these circumstances comes from his own historical work. Bede's prose is lucid, and his style engaging. Such qualities have helped to secure a warm home for his *Ecclesiastical History of the English People* in the hearts of readers in every generation since his own. Early England and its Church are generally seen through Bede's eyes. Necessarily so: he is the chief source. But the simplicity and apparent candour of his style may deceive. In his historical work Bede deployed outstanding abilities to support strong convictions and homiletic intentions. With him, as with others like him, it is nearly as important to attend to what he does not say as to what he does.

For example, mark that in the moving, almost elegiac, autobiographical passage in his *Ecclesiastical History* (v. 24) he fails to tell us who his father was. It is a fair guess (though unprovable) that his father was an aristocrat. Bede moved in the highest company. He sent a draft of his *Ecclesiastical History* to King Ceolwulf for comment. He was on visiting terms with Ceolwulf's cousin, Egbert, bishop (soon archbishop) of York; and it was to Egbert that he wrote the letter of detailed reformist rebuke which gives his harsh judgement on the Northumbrian Church. These relationships suggest that he was near to a circle of men in power. The suggestion is reinforced by the late eighth-century genealogical king-list for the kingdom of Lindsey.[1] It has a man called Biscop succeeding his father Beda at some time in the eighth century. It cannot intend to indicate that among the kings of Lindsey were our Bede and our Benedict Biscop, instrumental in the foundation of Wearmouth-Jarrow. But this document hints seriously that these were names current in a very grand family, one to which Bede and Benedict Biscop both belonged.

Benedict Biscop was certainly of noble race, very rich and often summoned to the presence of the king because of his wisdom and the ripeness of his judgement.[2] Two other great abbots in Bede's community were also of high birth. Ceolfrith's father had held high and noble office under a king; and Eosterwine was a cousin of Biscop's and had been in the personal service of King Ecgfrith.[3] Bede's possibly noble birth and the certain high status of some of his fellow monks need by no means have determined his views. He was too puritanical for that. But his account even of the conversion may derive from a stance among the ruling few. It is remarkable, is it not, that he pays so little attention to the conversion of the population at large?

The history of Northumbria

For approximately the first twelve years of Bede's life Northumbria was ruled by King Ecgfrith (670–85), the successful heir to a successful line. In the sixth century, the area which became the kingdom of Northumbria came to consist of two separate kingdoms, Deira in the south and Bernicia in the north besides areas remaining under British rule (see Map 2). When Anglian rulers established themselves there, it is uncertain how far they took over existing systems of rule or how far their accession to power was accompanied by folk migration,[4] or how far British invasions, persisting until at least 633, complicated the scene. The chain of events which led to the creation of a united Northumbria seems to have been begun by Æthelfrith (d. 616). Initially king of Bernicia, he gained authority over Deira. His successor as ruler of both kingdoms was Edwin (616–33), a member of the rival Deiran house. Edwin's successors as rulers of Northumbria were Æthelfrith's sons Oswald (634–42) and Oswiu (ruler of Bernicia from 642, of both kingdoms from c. 655). Ecgfrith was Oswiu's son and, until his defeat and death in 685, he was extending his power far northwards over Britons, Picts and Irish in the areas later called Scotland. Wearmouth and Jarrow may be seen as monuments to his power.

English polities and their relationships

The political history of Northumbria in the generations before Bede's birth shows developments and raises problems common to the Anglo-Saxon lands. Firstly, there is the union of smaller into larger units of authority. Early England held many small kingdoms. In Bede's time the principal kingdoms were East Anglia, Essex, Kent, Mercia, Northumbria, Sussex and Wessex (see Map 1). Northumbria was not the only one of these to have composite origins. The rising power of Mercia came to include the kingdoms of Lindsey and that of the Hwicce (in the west Midlands). It could well have absorbed other polities of which we know nothing.

It is not possible to fully understand the nature of the positions held by men in authority in early England. We read of kings, sub-kings (*reguli, subreguli*) and others of high authority (*principes, duces*); and of areas of authority or description categorized as *gentes, nationes, populus provinciae, regiones* and *tribus*.[5] The likely meanings of some of these terms overlap and their variety is indicative of a complicated scene with elements of flux. In some kingdoms, sub-kings who were members of the ruling house might have authority over part of the realm. A ruler of a once independent kingdom might become a subordinated sub-king. Complicated and stressed systems of succession could lead, at least in late seventh-century Wessex, to a period in which power was divided among sub-kings (see p. 29 below). Indeed in Wessex it may have been normal to have a number of sub-kings each in charge of a *scir* (possibly one of the shires still surviving today). These men would correspond to those termed *ealdormen* in the late seventh-century laws of King Ine. A key consideration in analysing such matters is that of the ambiguous relationship between subordination and delegation.

Consideration of relations between kingdoms centres on a famous passage in which Bede lists seven rulers who held superiority (*imperium*) within the Anglo-Saxon lands (*EH* II. 5). The first, surprisingly, is Aelle, king of Sussex, in the late fifth century. There follow Ceawlin of Wessex (560–91), Æthelberht of Kent (560?–616), Rædwald, king of East Anglia during the first generation of the seventh century, and the three kings of Northumbria who reigned from 616 to 670, Edwin, Oswald and Oswiu. Bede need not have intended to indicate continuous tenure of *imperium* throughout the period. He says that the first four overlords had authority over all the lands south of the Humber, the last three over all the English lands other than Kent. The holder of such overlordships is likely to have been termed *bretwealda*, probably meaning 'wide ruler'. Not all seven rulers need have exercised the same power. And others, not included in the list, could have enjoyed a comparable position, for example Bede's contemporary Æthelbald, king of Mercia (716–57), who he says exercised authority everywhere south of the Humber (v. 23). It is often asserted that the position held by the seven cannot be seen as resembling an office, but that, on the contrary, the term *bretwealda* was honorific, almost poetic, giving an important general impression, and no more. One may have doubts about the cutting power of so clear a distinction. There is a tendency among scholars to see the politics and governmental arrangements of this period as essentially confused and rough, to become more organized, refined and defined later. There was indeed much of violence and instability. But the men in power came from long-experienced societies and were capable of feeling the force of long-established conventions. Consider the astonishing account which Bede gives of the governmental arrangements of the continental Saxons in his day (v. 10). They had no single ruler; but were divided under the authority of men whom he calls 'satraps'. The Saxons, he tells us, united only in war when the 'satraps' drew lots to determine who should be in power for the duration. This sophisticated arrangement leads one to reflect on the possible sophistications of 'bretwealdaship', not to be brushed aside because we can, at best, catch no more than quick glimpses of them.

Bede saw 'Angles' as descriptive of all the Germanic inhabitants of Britain. This appears not only in the Latin title of the *Ecclesiastical History* but also in his statement that *lingua Anglorum* was one of the five languages of the island (*EH* I. 1). It is not easy to reconcile such emphases on unity or common culture with Bede's account of Angles, Saxons and Jutes as separate invaders, something reflected in the names of kingdoms. Nevertheless, eighth-century usage (including some of Bede's) indicates that the terms 'Angle' and 'Saxon' were seen as virtually synonymous; and this is indicated in such continental usages as *Angli Saxones*.[6] One of the elements which must have made for a kind of unity at a high level was the intermarriage of royal houses. All the royal marriages which Bede records are between people of royal or princely blood from different kingdoms. Queens took households and followers with them when they married and this must have strengthened the degree of connection between kingdoms. So similarly must the strong importance of exile which contributed to the emphasized diversity of the retinue of great men (see p. 33 below).

Royal successions

A major source of instability in Anglo-Saxon governments was the absence of a secure system of royal inheritance. It seems that sometimes any man who could colourably claim to belong to the royal family in an extended sense could have a claim to the throne. No doubt father could help son to succession, or brother brother. Cohesion in consent among the powerful could produce orderly outcomes. But there must have been strong and recurrent elements of faction and of feud.

Northumbrian history in Bede's time exemplifies this. Ecgfrith, after his death in battle (685), was succeeded by his half-Irish half-brother Aldfrith. This can hardly have been an easy succession; for there must have been dangerous, even murderous, enmity behind Aldfrith's having spent much of his life in exile in Ireland. Aldfrith died in 705 leaving a son aged eight, Osred. At this juncture one Eadwulf, whose origin is unknown, made an unsuccessful bid for the throne. Then, very remarkably, Osred was made king (the only child to hold such a position in early

England) and he held the throne until he was murdered in 716. Bede in his *Metrical Life of Saint Cuthbert* adverted favourably to Osred's youth, calling him a 'new Josiah' (p. 100). Other contemporary views were less rosy. Saint Boniface, with other bishops, said that he engaged in the adulterous violation of nuns and the destruction of monasteries.[7] His oppressive conduct towards the nobility was said to have been such that the *dux* Eanmund was driven to a monastic life.[8] Osred's unpopularity may have favoured the succession in 716 of a member of a distant branch of the royal family, Ceonred. But he only lasted for two years and on his death in 718 was succeeded by Osric who may have been a son of Aldfrith and ruled until his death in 729. He was succeeded by Ceolwulf, a brother of his predecessor Ceonred, and the king to whom Bede dedicated the *Ecclesiastical History*. Ceolwulf had an extraordinary career. Briefly deposed and tonsured but restored in 731, he resigned his throne in 737 and retired to the monastery of Lindisfarne where he lived for another twenty-three years or more.

Detailed knowledge of the complex and fraught politics of Northumbria, as of those of other kingdoms, is scanty. There must have been connections with hardly less complex ecclesiastical politics, not least with the stormy career of Wilfrid, but it is hardly possible to clarify these.[9] We depend on guesswork in trying to understand interconnected struggles for power in Church and state and can do no more than catch distant echoes. The point is well illustrated by Professor Wood, who in emphasizing the non-reclusive elements in Bede's environments suggests, reasonably, the considerable likelihood of Abbot Ceolfrith's unexpected retirement having been connected with King Osred's murder in 716. But, as Wood points out, we have to admit alternative, and opposite, explanations for this hypothetical connection. Maybe Ceolfrith was close to Osred and thought it as well to leave when the king fell. But maybe he left before Osred's death and because he found his regime intolerable. Of course neither motive may have applied, but maybe one of them did.[10]

Bede's accounts of other political events may sometimes have been determined by his selective judgement. In one slightly arresting example, Bede says that the death of Cenwealh, king of Wessex, in 672 was followed by a period of rule of *subreguli*, but the *Anglo-Saxon Chronicle*, which, though not a contemporary source, may rest on one, says that Cenwealh was succeeded for a year or so by his widow, Queen Seaxburh.[11] Merovingian parallels suggest that feminine rule of this kind was possible. This case is the only one known in early Anglo-Saxon history. One may wonder whether Bede had not heard of it, or did not believe in it, or omitted it because he disapproved of it.

The internal organization of kingdoms

By contrast with the often confused tale of royal successions, the laws of seventh-century Anglo-Saxon kings give an impression of ordered power. This is particularly true of those of Wihtred of Kent and Ine of Wessex, both from about the end of the seventh century. They contrast with the earlier Kentish laws in the importance they attach to physical penalties (penalties of death or flogging are not mentioned in the earlier laws) and also in presenting vigorous efforts to enforce Church requirements on, for example, baptism and Sabbath observance.[12]

It is tempting to regard such legislation as essentially aspirational, intended to display kings as legislators rather than to be very seriously enforceable.[13] The idea is attractive but there is solid evidence of organized royal power such that one should take the detailed provisions of the laws seriously. This evidence is that of the great dykes. The greatest is Offa's Dyke, over one hundred miles long, very probably belonging to the late eighth century. Such lesser, but very considerable earthworks as the East Wansdyke, the Devil's Dyke and the Fleam Dyke, probably belong to much the same period or a somewhat earlier one. Such works are great demonstrations of ordered power and of a public service providing for defence. Another public service, bridge-building, appears, like military service, as compulsory in eighth-century charters. It may be with surprise that one reads Bede's account of the good peace which King Edwin maintained and of his providing bronze vessels at drinking places along the public roads (*EH* II. 16). But we must bear in mind large possibilities for order as well as disorder in Anglo-Saxon polities, order which may have been linked to a sense of public responsibility.

Problems and possibilities in relation to the organization of kingdoms and between kingdoms come to a focus in the consideration of hidage assessments. Such consideration is important not least because it suggests quite elaborate organization both within kingdoms and in relations between kingdoms. Bede describes seven areas or islands in terms of the number of 'lands of one family' (sometimes just 'families'). Thus he says that the land of the north Mercians is of seven thousand families, that of the south Mercians of five thousand (*EH* III. 24). On other occasions he uses the same unit to describe grants of estates (e.g. IV. 3). His land of one 'family' is the assessment unit which in Anglo-Saxon was termed a 'hide' (*hiwisc*) and it appears in Latin equivalents in land grants surviving from the late seventh century on. The 'Tribal Hidage', colourably, regarded as a 'tribute list' of the seventh or the eighth century, lists hidages for varying areas including most of the Anglo-Saxon lands. The modern 'tribal' title of this document has encouraged interpretation in terms of antecedent 'tribal' settlement, underestimating the extent to which administrative units may have been listed in 'people' form. It is seriously arguable that the pattern of assessment has some direct connection with that of Domesday Book (1086).[14] The 'Hidage' is part of the evidence for Anglo-Saxon government having deployed detailed assessment on the widest scale, a scale consonant with that of the great earthworks of the period.

Land tenure

Themes related to land tenure are important for the understanding of Bede's circumstances and concerns. One of these plays a large part in his *Letter to Bishop Egbert*. Bede there complains about the prevalence of 'false monasteries'. Noblemen were setting up such institutions, he complains, in order to gain the benefit of a certain kind of land tenure such as to give them valued exceptions (pp. 349–53). The passages concerned have been much discussed. There is a consensus that the term concerned was that of what came to be known as 'bookland', i.e. tenure by written grant, which had been introduced by the Church. The privileges it bestowed must have involved departure from existing rules. There is incomplete consensus on what these rules may have been. It appears that kings granted land to followers on precarious tenure, for life only, or not for so long. A grant by charter would have substituted permanence for precariousness. Also, if, as is likely, some noble land was held by family tenure such that, on the death of a holder, lands held by him were redistributed according to known rules, then bookland would have been preferable by granting freedom of disposition. In addition, such tenure could have involved freedom from major services to a king, but it is disputed how far this was so. Major questions lurk unanswered here. Among them are these: How far may pagan religious institutions have had established endowments? How did kings come to claim the right to make grants by charter? Did such rights sometimes extend to sub-kings, as they seem to have done in early Wessex? Did overlords claim some right of supervision or participation in such grants?

The 'bookland' problem relates to the land of noblemen and of churches. But how did *their* tenants hold their land? What was the nature of peasant tenure in general? No definite and complete answer is possible. One broadly attractive hypothesis appears most convincingly in recent years in the work of Dr Faith and derives from observation of patterns of land tenure in the great Domesday survey of 1086 and in later sources, which seem to derive from earlier circumstances.[15] The key is a distinction often found in these sources between two categories of land tenure, one associated with 'inland', and the other with 'outland' or alternatively 'warland'. 'Inland' was land closely associated with a lord's centres of authority, cultivated to meet his household needs, the cultivators being people of much subordinated status. 'Warland', 'outland', appears as distinct, involving obligations to rulers or lords much lighter than those imposed on 'inland' tenants. These obligations involved public services for such purposes as war and bridge-building, seem to have been owed primarily to a ruler, and to have been part of a system of organization centred on the 'inland' centres termed on royal lands 'royal vills'. When Bede says (somewhat inscrutably) that when kings gave Benedict Biscop a place for building a monastery it was 'not taken away from some lesser persons, but granted from their own personal property' (*Homilies on the Gospels*, I. 13, p. 129), he may well mean that the land concerned was 'inland' rather than 'warland'.[16]

It is unlikely that peasants with substantial holdings represented the 'rank and file' of society in Bede's England. If the theoretical free peasants of the scheme just outlined correspond to the *ceorls*, the lowest class of freemen represented in the early laws of Kent and of Wessex, then it should be noted that these appear to have been allocated, respectively, wergelds of a hundred and two hundred gold tremises (or their equivalent) and would seem to represent (in later terms) a gentry or yeomanry. Below these rather grand freemen there could have been people who were half free, unlanded or slaves: a proletariat. We do not know how many such people there were. But possibly major monasteries such as Wearmouth-Jarrow were islands of wealth with a sea of poor people all around. This possibility is illustrated by an incident in an account of an important early ninth-century Northumbrian monastery which mentions poor people trying to keep warm in the ashes thrown out from the monastery's fires.[17]

War and exile

Prominent among the principal interests and commitments of rulers and noblemen was war. Important about war in Bede's England was that it could be a very long-distance affair. For example, the conquering king of Mercia, Penda (?632–55), is found ravaging as far north as Bamburgh (*EH* III. 16). The final, and fatal, battle (642) fought by Oswald, king of Northumbria, probably took place near distant Oswestry. He had established his power in 632 by defeating, somewhere near Hadrian's Wall, a British ruler whose base was in north Wales. Such evidence for far-flung warfare gives edge to what the *Anglo-Saxon Chronicle* (late ninth century as we have it) claims about Ceolwulf, king of Wessex (597–?611): 'He ever fought and made war, either against the English, or the Britons, or the Picts, or the Scots.'[18] That an Anglo-Saxon term for a main road was *herepaeth*, 'army road', gives another hint about long-distance warfare.

Specifically illuminating is Bede's account of a battle in 679 in which the Northumbrians defeated the Mercians (*EH* IV. 22). A Northumbrian noble-man called Imma was captured. When asked who he was, he said he was a peasant, there to carry food for the army. His captor, who was a *comes* (an important nobleman), did not believe this, but recognized him as noble by his appearance, bearing and speech; and he offered to spare his life provided that he confessed his identity. Imma did so. The captor did spare Imma and sold him to a Frisian in London when a difficulty arose. It proved impossible to keep him shackled. The Frisian therefore allowed him to ransom himself.

This is a very revealing series of events. Imma's captor said that he really should have killed him because all his own brothers and relations had been killed in the battle. This illustrates how, for the ruling class, war was war to the death. That is why kings not infrequently fell in battle and why the fate of so great a king as Oswald of Northumbria (634–42) was marked by his triumphant enemies' displaying his head and hands stuck on stakes (*EH* III. 12). The extermination of a rival dynasty was a normal goal in the game of power. After Cædwalla of Wessex conquered the Isle of Wight he put the king's brothers to death when he caught them (IV. 16; Bede rejoices in their having been converted and baptized between their capture and their killing). Bede's account of the fate of the family of King Edwin after his fall in 616 is instructive (II. 20). One of Edwin's sons fell in the same conflict as his father. Another fled to the king of the Mercians who later had him murdered. Edwin's daughter, Eanfled, fled to Kent with a young brother and a nephew. She sent them both to Gaul to the care of their relative, King Dagobert. Bede tells us why: *metu Eadbaldi et Osualdi regum*, 'for fear of kings Eadbald and Oswald'. What Bede (and Eanfled) probably had in mind was that Oswald (already a Christian and in due course a saint) would have killed these children (*pueri*) if Eadbald, king of Kent, might have been induced to hand them over. The handing over would presumably have been for appropriate recompense. When Edwin himself had been an exile at the court of Rædwald of East Anglia, his enemy Æthelfrith offered mounting rewards (accompanied by threats) to have him handed over or killed and Edwin escaped such a fate only by means verging on the miraculous (II. 12).

Wars and feuds to the death led inevitably to exile as a common, almost normal, episode in the lives of the high-born. For example, we first hear of Cædwalla (king of Wessex *c.* 685–8) as an exile of noble descent in the 'desert places' of the Chilterns and the Weald.[19] Exiles would have made an important component of the military followers of kings and royal adven-turers of whom we are told that their followings included very noble men 'from almost every kingdom' (*EH* III. 14, p. 257; this said of Oswine, king of Deira 644–51) or 'from various peoples and all directions' (said of Guthlac, future saint).[20] Exiles were not, of course, the only element in such retinues. We are told of the hero of the poem *Beowulf* (for which Professor Lapidge[21] has produced better evidence than had been found before for believing its origins lie in around the time of Bede) that it was observed that he and his companions must have come to Hrothgar's court, not as exiles, but out of daring and ambition (see lines 337–9). The same would have been true of the nobles who, Bede says, were in his day adventuring overseas.

Trade and economic conditions

A fundamentally important passage in Bede's story of Imma is that which speaks of his being sold to a Frisian merchant in London. Here is a point where war and commerce meet. Undoubtedly English slaves were exported to the continent. The famous story of Gregory the Great's encounter with such slaves on sale in a Roman market is an instance (*EH* II. 1). Instances like these are not such as to permit quantification. But if, as the Imma story suggests, it was normal for non-noble prisoners to be enslaved, then the connections between war and commerce could have been close and would provide some of the explanation for the way in which the kingdoms that could expand their frontiers at the expense of the Britons (Northumbria, Mercia and Wessex) prospered to dominance.[22]

Bede elsewhere says of London that it was an *emporium* for many people coming by land and sea. By *emporium* he means place of trade, and the term has passed into historians' usage to indicate major trading sites of between the seventh century and the ninth. There was an important such site at London, immediately to the west of the Roman city, and archaeology has revealed others of comparable importance just to the east of medieval Southampton, at Ipswich and at York.[23] There must be other such sites still undiscovered. Sea communication and sea power were essential to Bede's Northumbria. This is demonstrated by Edwin's having authority over Anglesey and Man, and Ecgfrith's invasion of Ireland. Not for nothing did Bede's monastery, like a number of others, lie beside a port which came to be known as the Port of Ecgfrith, the *Portus Ecgfridi* (see Chapter 6). The *loci* of no fewer than twenty-six of Bede's historical or hagiographical accounts lie on or near the North Sea coast of England.[24]

The mention in the Imma story of a Frisian is also important. English commercial and linguistic relations with Frisia were close in the late seventh and early eighth century and had what was in effect a common currency in the coin which numismatists call *sceattas*. This currency was astonishingly abundant. The evidence of individual finds suggests that there was more coin in circulation in England between *c.* 710 and *c.* 740 than there was at any other period before 1066.[25]

Hard and hostile elements in Bede's English economic environment were famine and plague. He mentions famine in Sussex so terrible that starving men in groups of forty or fifty would link hands and plunge to their deaths in the sea (*EH* IV. 13). In the 660s England was struck by an epidemic which may well have been of bubonic plague and if so could have been as damaging as the Black Death.[26] The *Life of Ceolfrith* says of a later attack of plague at Jarrow that the community was so stricken that only Ceolfrith himself and one boy – the *puerculus* could have been Bede himself – were left to maintain something of the liturgical round.[27]

The position of the Britons

Major problems relate to the position of the Britons in lands under Anglo-Saxon domination. No doubt there were major differences between one area and another. Thus the laws of Ine suggest a considerable British population in Wessex, some of whom enjoyed fairly high status. This may be related to the rapid overrunning of most of the southwestern peninsula by West Saxon kings during the later seventh century; and it is noteworthy that some of the earlier kings of Wessex had Celtic names. The position could have been different in other areas where an earlier Anglo-Saxon occupation may have had more of the character of folk migration, and where, by Bede's day, the capacity of dominant groups to outbreed their subjects could have had time to alter the racial balance.

Bede's account of the deeds of King Æthelfrith suggests the possibility of there having been rather more 'ethnic cleansing' and rather less British survival than is sometimes suggested. No ruler, Bede says, subdued more lands to the English people, making them available for settlement or tributary having 'exterminated or conquered' their inhabitants (*EH* I. 34, p. 117). A famous story by Bede (sometimes somewhat misunderstood) illustrates not only his opposition to the religious position of Britons (in his own day he saw them as 'inveterate and stumbling') but also his willingness to consider, without disapproval, massacre of many of them (V. 22). The story is that of Augustine's second meeting with representatives of the British churches (II. 2), most of whom came from the monastery of Bangor Iscoed and who had been advised by a hermit to pay attention to Augustine only if he rose to greet them. He did not do so. Bertram Colgrave has commented that his attitude 'does not seem very tactful'.[28] As Bede saw the incident it had nothing to do with tact. Augustine sat because he was sitting in judgement to give a terrible warning: if the Britons did not preach the way of life to the English 'they would suffer the vengeance of death at their hands'. So it proved. At the battle of Chester (?616) Æthelfrith was said to have killed twelve hundred of the monks of Bangor. Thus, Bede shows us (without a word of regret for the slaughter of the monks), was Augustine's prophetic judgement fulfilled. It is worth noticing that Britons need not have been the only victims of 'ethnic cleansing'. Bede says of the conquest of the Isle of Wight by Cædwalla of Wessex that he sought to exterminate all the inhabitants and replace them with men from his own kingdom (IV. 16).

Anglo-Saxon relations with the continent and Ireland

It is not easy to establish, and it may be too easy to underestimate, the scale and nature of early Anglo-Saxon involvements with other parts of Europe than those from which they came. The information we have on such relationships is episodic and normally can be interpreted only in terms of possibility. An obvious case is this. Saxons played a considerable part in the invasion of Italy by the Lombards from 568. How far may papal interest in England and Anglo-Saxon connection with Italy have been linked to this movement? A marriage with a Merovingian princess played a crucial part in the initiation of the Augustine mission. It is important to observe that Bede's account of the flight of her grandson and great-grandson to Gaul reflects a consciousness and continuance of dynastic relationship otherwise not known to us. Bede and Stephanus do something to indicate other dynastic connections with Gaul. Bede tells us that Sigeberht, apparently the first Christian king of East Anglia, had been converted while an exile in Gaul (*EH* II. 15). Stephanus relates that Bishop Wilfrid was partly responsible for organizing the return of Dagobert II (king of Austrasia 676–9) from long exile in Ireland.[29]

It is a question how far people from other parts of Europe were coming into England in the seventh century or later. It is slightly curious that, although the date of the initiation of Germanic settlement in Britain is considerably discussed by modern scholars, that of its cessation is not. Guthlac predicted, correctly, that his successor at Crowland would be someone not yet converted and the language of his biographer Felix makes it plain that this man, Cissa, had not yet come to Britain.[30] By contrast, the first Angles or Saxons we know to have become Christians were outside England: before *c.* 560 near Nantes, by 597 at Iona.[31] Of special importance in relation to the history of the conversion is the English involvement with Ireland. The key importance of the exile of the sons of Æthelfrith among the Irish is brought out by Bede as determinative in the conversion of a large part of England (*EH* III. 1–3). It is interesting that he tells us that both Oswald and Oswine were fluent in Irish. When Bede entered the monastery of Wearmouth-Jarrow it was part of the empire of King Ecgfrith, whose authority extended over the Irish settlements in modern Scotland. Indeed Ecgfrith was later believed to have been buried at

Iona. His half-brother Aldfrith was half-Irish, spent the early part of his life in exile in Ireland and was literate in Irish to the extent that we have poems attributed to him. (When he became king of Northumbria (685–705) he was the first English or part-English layman known to have been literate.) The evidence of the Irish annals, which is in important ways superior to anything comparable from England, indicates that there may have been considerable secular interchange between Ireland and England impelled by the pressures of war and exile. Thus Anglo-Saxons are found fighting in Ireland and Irish aristocrats in Britain.[32]

Conviviality

Bede sometimes indicates, though he hardly approved of, the role of conviviality, public conviviality, in Anglo-Saxon life. Thus, in describing a miracle associated with Oswald, he tells how a travelling Briton came to a village where he was kindly invited to a feast, so long and hospitable that it concluded with the building in which it took place being burned down (*EH* III. 10). At a different level, there is the famous story of Cædmon, a servant in the abbey of Whitby, who was inspired to compose religious poetry in English (IV. 24). Bede shows that, even in such humble circles at a feast, the harp passed from hand to hand and each man was supposed in turn to declaim a poem.

Such entertainment was characteristic of the higher orders also. The monks of Lindisfarne spent days at Christmas rejoicing, feasting and telling tales (Bede, *Life of Saint Cuthbert*, ch. 27). Another hint of such aspects of monastic life comes in the *Penitential* associated with Archbishop Theodore: a penance is prescribed for drinking to the point of vomiting, but this is remitted if it is for gladness at Christmas or Easter or any festival of a saint, and if the penitent in question has imbibed no more than is commanded by his seniors. The significance of the life of the hall with its poetry, music and drink is reinforced by *Beowulf*. This poem takes one into the religious and aristocratic life of the time. The poem's underlying values remain less religious than some of the frames of reference it adopts, relating to a body of warriors not in all respects unlike monks, a group of men, united under one leader in a common loyalty, eating and sleeping together. Bede's values and judgements may have differed not only from the secular ones of his time, but also from those of many clerics, including bishops, such as those he denounced in his *Letter to Bishop Egbert* of whom he says that their entourages were given to laughter, jokes, tales, feasting and drunkenness, and that they daily fed their stomachs with feasts more than the soul on the heavenly sacrifice (pp. 344–5).

Conclusion

The history of Christianity in the Anglo-Saxon lands has to be seen in the context of secular forces and circumstances of which our knowledge often is no more than fragmentary. Obvious examples are the ways in which marriage and exile created a web of connection across which the currents of Christianity moved. From another angle, one can imagine something of the organized power which built great dykes when Bede tells us of people being baptized in the River Glen for thirty-six days by Paulinus (*EH* II. 15). Not entirely volunteers, maybe? Or again, one can see how kings and nobles whose wars were wars to the death could have valued a religion with an emphasis (even if it was not a consistent one) on an association between faith and victory. Or then, consider the obvious great wealth of such monasteries as Wearmouth-Jarrow, with its fine buildings, its capacity to produce magnificent manuscripts, its possession of treasures, intellectual and other, bought in Italy. This reflects the generosity of royal and noble benefactors enriched by boom times. It may be disquieting to some to reflect on how far the affluence of such great men may have derived from a slave trade fuelled by conquest.

Another commercial connection is more certain. It can hardly have been a coincidence that the first English missionary efforts overseas were in Frisia, linked to England not only by language but by trade and a virtually common coinage. If political circumstances and organization inevitably affected the success of Christianity, so too did Christianity affect the exercise and nature of political power. 'The social and legal revolution involved in the conversion was extraordinary – probably too massive for us ever to fully comprehend.'[33] The contrasts between such laws as we have from the earlier seventh century and those from near its end probably have important connections with religious change. The problems and possibilities associated with bookland indicate how the introduction of Christianity affected the organization of power. A comparable development is seen most powerfully in the career of Wilfrid: the Church had produced a new kind of potentate, an ecclesiastical one, with a status and influence transcending the boundaries of a single kingdom.

The limpid prose of Bede's *Ecclesiastical History* does reveal ecclesiastical and secular connections and interactions. But in using his great work as a major source for the nature of the world in which he lived, we have always to remember that he was largely concerned to preach to and to judge that world and he was prone to omit that of which he disapproved. Not the least of such omissions is that of any serious account either of the partly vanishing world of paganism, or of its continuing influence. And it was one which our other sources fail to make good.

NOTES

1. Dumville 1976: 31, 33, 37.
2. *Life of Ceolfrith*, ch. 12, in Farmer 2004: 217.
3. *Ibid.*, ch. 34, p. 226, ch. 12, p. 217.
4. Rollason 2003: ch. 3.
5. Campbell 1986: 85–98; Thacker 1981; Murray 2007.
6. Brooks 1999; Levison 1946: 92.
7. *The Letters of Saint Boniface*, trans. E. Emerton (New York: Columbia University Press, 2000), p. 107 (no. 57).
8. *Æthelwulf: De Abbatibus*, ed. A. Campbell (Oxford: Clarendon Press, 1967), pp. 4–17.
9. To Goffart 1988: 235–328 contrast Higham 2006: 58–68.
10. Wood 2008b: 24–5.
11. *Two of the Saxon Chronicles Parallel*, ed. C. Plummer and J. Earle, 2 vols. (Oxford: Clarendon Press, 1892–9), vol. i, pp. 34–5, s.a. 672.
12. Campbell 2007.
13. Wormald 1999: 1–44.
14. Corbett 1900 and 1913: 550–1.
15. Faith 1997.
16. Wood 1995: 11.
17. *Æthelwulf: De Abbatibus*, pp. 38–9.
18. *The Anglo-Saxon Chronicle: A Revised Translation*, trans. D. Whitelock (London: Eyre and Spottiswode, 1965), p. 14, s.a. 597.
19. *The Life of Bishop Wilfrid by Eddius Stephanus*, ed. and trans. B. Colgrave (Cambridge University Press, 1985), ch. 42, p. 85.
20. *Felix's Life of Saint Guthlac*, ed. and trans. B. Colgrave (Cambridge University Press, 1985), pp. 80–1.
21. Lapidge 2000.
22. Maddicott 2000.
23. Russo 1998.
24. Naylor 2007 provides the relevant references.
25. Stevens 1985: 15.
26. Maddicott 1997.
27. *Life of Ceolfrith*, ch. 14, in Farmer 2004: 218.
28. Colgrave and Mynors 1969: 140, n. 1.
29. *Life of Bishop Wilfrid*, ch. 28, p. 55.
30. *Felix's Life of Saint Guthlac*, pp. 146–9.
31. Campbell 1986: 70.
32. Moisl 1983.
33. Wood 2008b: 13.

3

ROSALIND LOVE

The world of Latin learning

Arguably the two most famous products of the monastery of Wearmouth-Jarrow are the massive Bible known as the Codex Amiatinus and Bede himself. The one we still have as a tangible monument to the cultural aspirations of that community, while the other remains more elusive, but present to us as the mind behind the many thousands of words that make up his prodigious output of Latin writings. Amiatinus is powerfully symbolic of the world of Latin learning to which Bede was both heir and prolific contributor, and it reminds us of two things: the Scriptures lay at the heart of that world, and secondly, most of what Bede knew about it he had gleaned from a long, fruitful immersion in books. To understand why Bede wrote what he did, and how he fits into the bigger picture of Latin learning in Anglo-Saxon England and indeed in Western Christendom, it is instructive to begin with some comparisons between the man and the book, which will then lead us to an exploration of his library.

The Bible: the heart of all learning

As noted in Chapter 1, the Codex Amiatinus was made during Bede's lifetime in the scriptorium at Wearmouth or Jarrow, along with two other similarly large Bibles of which only scraps survive (Figures 3 and 4). It is extraordinary in many ways, not least for containing the whole Bible under one cover (a so-called 'pandect'), unremarkable now, yet exceedingly rare in the early Middle Ages, when part-Bibles were the norm, and a massive undertaking, in terms of the vellum and the man-hours required. The plan in Abbot Ceolfrith's mind, so Bede stated in his *History of the Abbots* (ch. 15), was to have one Bible each for Wearmouth and Jarrow; the third he hoped to take as a gift to the pope in Rome. Obviously the pope had plenty of Bibles already, but that was not the point of this gesture, which intended to make a statement about England's secure status as an outpost of Christianity, and of Western literate culture. To send a fine Bible to Rome meant sending a sample of high-quality craftsmanship and scholarship to the city where the apostles Peter and Paul founded the Christian Church and still lay buried, and where Latin had held sway as the language of civilization for a thousand years. Bede's fellow countrymen, one suspects, regarded him with similar pride: just ten years after his death, he was described as 'that keenest investigator of the Scriptures ... who, we have learned, shone forth among you of late as a lantern of the Church, by his scriptural scholarship'.[1]

Other features of the Codex Amiatinus take us further. We know from an examination of its script and artwork, alongside Bede's own comments (*History of the Abbots*, ch. 15), that it had an important model, a large Bible now lost. Benedict Biscop and Ceolfrith had expended much effort to supply the two monasteries with the books needed not only for the central activity of daily Christian worship – that is, Bibles and liturgical books – but also for study and teaching. The boys brought to join these communities would at the very least need to be taught Latin in order to read the Bible or say their prayers. Among the books which Ceolfrith bought in Rome was a large Bible, in what Bede describes as the 'old translation'. By that he meant the 'Vetus Latina' ('Old Latin') Bible, the first, often fumbling, attempts, from the end of the second century onwards, at rendering the Greek of the New Testament and the Greek translation of the Old Testament (the Septuagint) into a language which would make the Scriptures accessible to the increasing numbers of converts. The translation was 'old' because it had been superseded by a more correct and uniform translation, the Vulgate made by Jerome in the late fourth century, at the behest of Pope Damasus.

Why did it matter which version of the Bible one used? It mattered greatly: a faulty translation of the text at the heart of one's faith could lead to mistaken belief, even heresy. Words were important, but a complex matter, given that Western Christendom was dealing with Latin Scriptures translated from a mixture of Greek, Greek translated from Hebrew, and Hebrew itself. Hence, much of Bede's own biblical scholarship, as he built on what he had inherited from the Christian writers of the first three centuries of the Church, was concerned with minute scrutiny of the wording of the Scriptures. This was the starting point for biblical exegesis, with the words themselves, radiating out to a variety of perspectives: identifying plants or animals, places, people and their historical setting, but then delving deeper into symbolism and prophetic foreshadowing and drawing out lessons for this present life. The ways of interpreting the Scriptures which Bede inherited (see Chapters 9 and 10) represent a rich fusion of distinct intellectual traditions: a Semitic focus on the 'letter', that is, on the text's literal level, and its historical content (termed 'Antiochene' exegesis, since it was developed in fourth-century Antioch in

Syria), which gained strength as a reaction to a Hellenistic concern with going *beyond* the letter to allegorical readings, however fanciful they might seem (so-called 'Alexandrian' exegesis, named from the third- and fourth-century Greek schools at Alexandria).

To return to the Codex Amiatinus: in producing their three Bibles, the monks at Wearmouth-Jarrow replaced their model's actual text with something more up to date, while simultaneously imitating the physical aspects of the large book which Ceolfrith had bought – drawing inspiration from the fact that it contained the whole Bible, from its illustrations, its script, its layout. Scholars have seen the script and artwork of Amiatinus as deliberately and carefully imitative of what were perceived to be 'Roman' features of the model, and the whole project speaks eloquently of Rome's powerful attraction, an important force in the evolution of Latin learning in the Middle Ages.

Although Bede and his fellow monks did not realize it, at least not to begin with, the massive Bible which they were imitating had its own story.[2] In the 550s, Cassiodorus Senator (d. 570), an Italian aristocrat, weary of a political life divided between Rome, Ravenna and then Constantinople, in the service of Theoderic and his successors, kings of the Goths, retired to his family estates in southern Italy and to the monastic community he had set up, known as Vivarium, at Squillace (Calabria). Cassiodorus is an interesting representative of the world of Latin learning which Bede inherited. Like many of the Fathers whose works Bede studied so attentively, he belonged to an era when men of a certain social status still received an intellectual formation based on the Roman education system, even though he was one of the last few to do so. They had read and could quote from classical Latin literature, though, as we shall see, some then felt called to reject it. Cassiodorus had a relatively enlightened view of what the cultural activities of his sixth-century community should be: he wished to preserve the high values of the ancient world, of literature and book-production, in more dangerous and less civilized times, and in the service of Christian literature. We know about these ideas from his *Institutes of Divine and Secular Learning*, a practical handbook on the Christian intellectual life, in which he prescribed what should be studied and which books Vivarium ought to have. He unfolded his plan for a set of part-Bibles, handy for study, and also a volume containing the whole Bible, which Cassiodorus called his Bigger Codex ('Codex Grandior'). In his *Institutes* and elsewhere he provided specific information about the appearance of this Codex, enabling modern scholars (and Bede) to match the description with what we know about the model for the Codex Amiatinus. In other words, Ceolfrith had brought Cassiodorus's 'Codex Grandior' home to Northumbria.[3]

Bede's library

Just as the Codex Amiatinus is founded on the model of an ancient Italian book containing an old version of the Latin Bible produced by a man who still valued classical literature, so likewise Bede, as we know him in his large body of writings, built on an inherited model of learned culture, accessible to him principally in the books which he found around him. It is a *Latin* culture because, thanks to the sheer brute force of the expanding Roman empire, the Christian Scriptures, which began their spread westwards under that empire, were therefore translated into Latin. At the time this was for reasons of accessibility, even though, once Christianity reached non-Latin-speaking peoples, that accessibility was reversed, so that the Bible became the preserve of the educated until the first vernacular translations. Nevertheless, in the West, Latin continued to be the language of culture and scholarship. The majority of the learned literature which Bede read and imitated consisted of the writings of the Latin Fathers, principally Augustine, Ambrose, Jerome; from a more recent generation Cassiodorus, Isidore and Gregory; and at a remove, where these had been translated into Latin, the writings of the Greek Fathers, such as Eusebius, Basil, Origen and John Chrysostom. The literature which they produced was dominated by commentaries on the Bible and other aids to its study such as rudimentary onomastic dictionaries, theological treatises, sermons and letters, rules for monastic communities, but also accounts of the Church's early history, stories of the saints, Latin hymns for use in worship and other kinds of poetry too, even versifications of the Scriptures. Many of these works were among the volumes which came to Wearmouth-Jarrow. It is a sad fact that they have almost all vanished, so that the only way we can reconstruct Bede's 'library' is to identify quotations in his own writings.[4]

Before considering in more detail what Bede would have learnt from those books, we might attempt to conjure up a mental image of the library, or rather libraries, of Wearmouth and Jarrow. Scholars have suggested that we should be thinking in terms of some 200 volumes, containing roughly 250 distinct works, on the grounds that one codex might contain a compilation of works – selected writings of Augustine, say, or a collection of saints' lives – but conversely some very long works might run to more than one volume, depending on format and the size of script.[5] At the time it must have seemed an impressive collection, brought to Northumbria by Benedict Biscop and Ceolfrith from Gaul and Italy where they may also have had access to some Greek books too, and very likely from Ireland in the hands of missionaries or other travellers; by the latter means books from Spain and North Africa could also have reached Bede, if not via Gaul. Devastatingly, we have just one fragment that can with any certainty be said to have survived from the imported books Bede had, a strip of vellum containing verses from 1 Maccabees, now kept in the Durham Cathedral Library (MS B.IV.6), and deriving from a book written in sixth-century Italy. Such a small remnant is nevertheless eloquent, its script and small format indicative of the type of books brought for use at Wearmouth-Jarrow.[6] They were certainly not all on the massive scale of Cassiodorus's 'Codex Grandior'.

The wealth of reading available to Bede in the Wearmouth-Jarrow library introduced him to many strands of thought, some still relevant, others rather outmoded. It would be impossible to summarize the discourses of the entire patristic period here, but to understand Bede we need to catch some flavour of what he found in those books, surveying its themes rather than scanning the titles in his reading list.[7] The central importance of understanding Scripture means that the largest proportion of his library consisted of an impressive array of earlier commentaries by the Fathers. Next came works of theology: the early Church was concerned to establish key tenets of the Christian faith which were not only *correctly* in line with Scripture, and so orthodox, but also acceptable and common to the *whole* Church, that is, catholic. From these matters Christian writers could move towards what Augustine called faith seeking understanding, that is, the quest to make reasoned sense of their faith, on its own terms and in the light of other intellectual traditions such as Platonism, and to make it coherent, so as to be able to defend and communicate it. This meant working out areas of unclarity, issues on which the Bible was silent and those which arose out of contemporary society, for example about public and private morality – because patristic theology is firmly pastoral, that is, focused on instructing the Christian people. It also meant dealing with attacks on orthodox belief from within, threatening the Church's unity, namely the various heresies which arose over the years. Christological controversies, that is, disagreements over the nature of Christ and his Incarnation, were chief among those threats, from heretical positions such as Arianism, Gnosticism, Adoptionism, Nestorianism and Monophysitism. Also to be argued out was the concept of the Trinity – three persons in one God, holy and undivided. Then further points of division were to come over humanity's relationship to that Trinity: the soul and its immortality, the extent of man's sinful nature, the complex truth of divine grace (that is, the free gift of salvation from sin's effects), and all the social consequences of those doctrines, relating to how Christians should live their lives, whether as virginal celibates and ascetics or active in the world. Here a movement that was to provoke continuing controversy, and one that Bede felt moved to write against, was Pelagianism, which had its origins with a British scholar, Pelagius, and had apparently found support in his homeland in the fifth century.[8] Less directly theological yet still weighty matters included the Church's organization and discipline, regulation of the monastic life, and the increasingly powerful cult of the saints. Many difficult and controversial matters had been settled by Bede's day, so that he could turn to this or that commentary or treatise for an authoritative exposition. But he did, of course, have his own particular contexts to address: a people recently brought to Christianity, their own customs and innate flaws, and continuing threats to orthodoxy from within the Church itself, to name but a few.

Some of the genres of Christian literature mentioned above followed on from those of classical Latin – historiography and biography, letters and, of course, poetry. Writers like Augustine and Jerome were still very much in touch with the Roman world, and from the earliest times some Christian thinkers felt that, with all its connections to pagan polytheism, classical literature should be rejected. Gregory the Great is often cited as a prominent example of an outspoken rejection which actually has a long heritage: 'the praises of Jove and the praises of Jesus Christ cannot proceed from the same lips',[9] though the truth of his attitude is doubtless more nuanced than that exaggerated polarization. There were difficulties with this rejection, not least because the very act of learning Latin was still dependent upon the study of such literature in ways which we shall consider shortly. Moreover, men of sophistication saw continuing value in great works like Vergil's *Aeneid*, remnants of a people whose aspiration had been to 'rule over the nations, to impose the ways of peace, to spare the underdog and pull down the proud' (*Aeneid* VI. 851–3). Jerome, for example, famously felt within himself a great struggle between being a disciple of Christ and a disciple of Cicero, that is, between his deep love of the Scriptures and his appreciation of the great Roman orator's brilliant speeches. A glance at a work such as *The City of God* shows how frequently Augustine chose to quote a line of Vergil here, verses of Horace there. Thus the earlier classical world is inescapably present, perhaps somewhat elusive but persistent, within the Christian Latin literature which Bede inherited.

To a limited extent, Bede also had direct access to examples of classical Latin learning. The realm in which he was perhaps brought closest to it was the classroom (see Chapter 7). The secular Roman education system, which itself seems to have survived on into the early sixth century in a few places, had various stages, taking the pupil from the basics of Latin grammar to rote learning of specimens of literature, and thence, presumably for the cleverest, to study of poetic composition, oratory, dialectic and philosophy. Originally, while the Roman world was still fully conversant with Greek, study of arithmetic, geometry, astronomy and music also followed – once Greek culture disappeared in the West in the late fifth century, the avenues to these branches of scientific knowledge, and to philosophy, were temporarily closed off. To varying degrees in different places, the Christian Church took on the bare outlines of this system for schools based at churches and in monasteries: essential grammar, memorization of key texts, progressing to study of Scripture, the task for which everything else – including the basics of rhetoric and poetry, as well as some limited science – was preparatory.[10]

The rules of Latin grammar had to be written down at an early stage, not least once non-Latin-speakers became part of the Roman empire. Early grammar books and handbooks on versification nevertheless took for granted that the user already knew some Latin. Such books would nevertheless have been the means by which Bede learnt Latin (on his teachers, see Chapter 7). These third- and fourth-century technical handbooks were supplemented by those produced later, and all of them proceeded by presenting examples of Latin from earlier literature. Thus, in Bede's explanation of the difference between the formation of the genitive of the word for storm, *turbo* ('turbinis'), and the way to form it for the personal name *Turbo* ('Turbonis'), the latter is exemplified by a line of Horace's verse (*On Orthography*, p. 55; quoting Charisius's *Art of Grammar*). By this means, a reader at any period and in any place is instantly transported to the Roman world and its literature, and Bede was no exception. When he came to write his own manuals – *The Art of Poetry*, *The Figures of Rhetoric* and *On Orthography* – he drew extensively on these earlier textbooks (see Chapter 7), of which he seems to have had a reasonable collection.

Furthermore, there is unambiguous evidence that Bede did also have in his library copies of a few classical texts: certainly Vergil's *Aeneid*, his *Georgics* and *Bucolics* and perhaps an anthology of other verse; and from an entirely different branch of scholarship, also parts of the thirty-seven-book *Natural History* by Pliny the Younger. Bede's own poetry shows the strong influence of classical models, though not exclusively; he was deeply familiar, too, with the versifiers of the Scriptures, Arator and Juvencus, with the Christian epic of Caelius Sedulius, with the poems and hymns of Prudentius, Paulinus of Nola, Prosper of Aquitaine, and Venantius Fortunatus. These must have been the poets to whom Bede felt he should turn first, yet it is striking how often he let a stray line of Vergil creep into his prose. We may attribute this to a poet's appreciation of fine verse, known by heart; but it is nowhere near being the love affair with the classical world that we see in the writers at the court of Charlemagne in the late eighth century.

The sixth century: a period of transition

From this swift sketch of the distant landscape in Bede's intellectual background, we should move nearer the foreground by focusing on a few of the prominent figures of the century preceding his birth: still in some sense far off, yet either deeply influential upon him or typical of the changed world of which he was a part. The period experienced a sea change in intellectual life, as the old-style Roman schools at last dwindled away, Christian schools grew in number, and monasticism began to gain strength. Cassiodorus, the eldest of this group, we have already begun to consider. Scholars disagree over whether Bede had a copy of his *Institutes*, mostly doubting that he did, though its content, effectively a monastic curriculum and reading list, would have interested him greatly.[11] He definitely had Cassiodorus's *Exposition of the Psalms*, quoted it often, and was surely struck by Cassiodorus's preference for allegorical or mystical interpretations of a text which lay at the heart of monastic spirituality, by virtue of the fact that, in the Daily Office, a community such as Bede's would have recited the whole Psalter at least once a week.

Another of Bede's intellectual forebears, for whom he developed a profound reverence, was Gregory the Great (d. 604), the pope who initiated the mission to Kent in 597. The book collection at Wearmouth-Jarrow included the majority of his writings: indeed, one of the few surviving manuscripts from its scriptorium is a fragment of Gregory's *Morals on Job*.[12] Gregory's writings are strongly pastoral in emphasis, dominated by sets of homilies and talks, for a variety of audiences, both clerical and lay, and at every turn his influence can be discerned in Bede's own work. Strikingly, at much the same time Gregory's writings were also being studied attentively at Whitby, where an unknown author (or just possibly, authoress, since it was a double house, headed for a time by Abbess Hild) produced a *Life of Gregory* sometime between 680 and 710.[13] For lack of substantial information about the pope's life and miraculous doings, those writings served as that text's principal source.

Also to have a resounding impact was Isidore of Seville, whose extraordinarily influential *Etymologies* began to circulate in about 636, the year of his death. Isidore was of an aristocratic Hispano-Roman family, and a beneficiary of an education founded on ancient principles, in a country which had been thoroughly Romanized, but then less disturbed than some areas, at least from the point of view of culture, by barbarian invasion. He was prolific in his literary output, writing on theology, the natural world and history. Isidore has generally been characterized as no original thinker but rather as a gifted compiler of earlier knowledge, whether patristic theology or secular learning, in which, like Cassiodorus, he saw intrinsic value. Bede had copies of his most important works, which would have purveyed to him a great wealth of information. His oeuvre and approach have been likened to the Spaniard's, though the comparison does no justice to Bede's creativity. We may note with interest that he named Isidore just three times in his writings, on each occasion only to contradict him, and it has been suggested that, although initially very dependent on Isidore's works, Bede felt increasingly out of sympathy with his ideas.[14]

There are a couple of representatives of Latin learning in Gaul whose work warrants mention as background and comparison for Bede's own, namely Venantius Fortunatus (d. 601) and his friend Gregory of Tours (d. 594). Fortunatus, an Italian, had the benefit of an old-style education at Ravenna, though he spent most of his career in Gaul. He wrote a number of hagiographical works, at least one of which was known to Bede, on Saint Martin of Tours, but he is best-known for his poetry (hymns and secular verses), which was extremely influential as a glimpse of Rome's great poetic tradition, and left its mark upon Bede's own verse. Gregory, descended from a Gallo-Roman family in the Auvergne, was very conscious of his lack of literary polish; his Latin does indeed occasionally break grammatical rules, and this may show the distinction between the education available to Fortunatus and his own, though he was not necessarily representative of his fellow countrymen. Gregory's *History of the Franks*, recording contemporary events in a 'national' history, ends with a list of his own writings which some have suggested was the model for Bede's own biography and bibliography at the end of the *Ecclesiastical History* (v. 24).[15]

Insular Latin learning

When Bede joined the newly founded community at Jarrow, less than a hundred years had passed since the bringing of Christianity to the south of England, first to Kent in 597, by Augustine and his fellow missionaries. As well as enjoying an outpost of this Roman mission, led by Paulinus who baptized King Edwin of Northumbria in 627, the north of England had its own distinct encounter with Christianity and Latin culture through the Gaelic missionaries who came from Iona at King Oswald's request, headed by Aidan who arrived in 635 and established Lindisfarne as the base for his preaching.

These were obviously not Britain's first encounters with Latin – that came much earlier with the arrival of the Roman legions, and the administrative and cultural institutions which followed in their wake, eventually also bringing with them Christianity. We know only a little about the extent to which the native inhabitants engaged with Latin – the vulgar Latin spoken by soldiers and tradesmen, but also the Latin of official business and education. One might suppose that the infrastructure fell away quickly once the Romans left in 410 as the empire crumbled. Despite that, we have scattered evidence that Latin continued to be learnt and used in Britain.[16] The lives and the writings of men such as Patrick in the fifth century, and then Gildas in the sixth, suggest a small measure of continuity for Latin learning between the Roman occupation and the period of the Anglo-Saxons' conversion. Bede knew Gildas's venomous *On the Ruin of Britain*, and absorbed its anti-British invective: this was what he knew of earlier Latin in his homeland. Of Patrick he seems to have known little if anything at all, but he was well aware of the learned tradition which grew up in the saint's Irish mission field. He observed in his *Ecclesiastical History* that a generation of Anglo-Saxons had flocked to Ireland:

> There were at this time in Ireland many English both noble and common who left their native land during the episcopate of Bishops Finan and Colman [mid seventh century]. They retired thither either to pursue biblical studies or to lead a life of stricter discipline ... The Irish received all these students generously, gave them daily sustenance, books for study and free instruction.
>
> (III. 27, p. 313; translation modified)

It used to be thought that Ireland was never touched by Roman expansion, but recent archaeological evidence has begun to modify this view, which also ignores the reality of contact through trade.[17] Whatever the case may be, when it came to the adoption of Christianity's learned Latin culture, the Irish were quicker-witted pupils than the Anglo-Saxons. For the earliest surviving Insular Latin literature comes from Ireland or from the hands of Irishmen active elsewhere, from the late sixth century and throughout the seventh. The importance of Ireland for Bede is dealt with in Chapter 5, but it is worth noting here that what survives of the earliest Hiberno-Latin literature covers many of the same areas as Bede's own work: grammatical studies, biblical exegesis, lives of the saints, and also poetry in the form of hymns.

In England, Bede was immediately preceded on the Latin literary stage by Aldhelm (d. 709/10), so-called 'first English man of letters'.[18] We know from his correspondence that Aldhelm, a monk of Malmesbury (Wiltshire), had studied at the school established in Canterbury by Archbishop Theodore and his colleague Hadrian – a school whose wondrous character and prodigious pupils Bede described enthusiastically in his *Ecclesiastical History* (IV. 2). Theodore and Hadrian arrived in 669 and 670, bringing contact with the learned world both of Rome, from which they had come most immediately, and also of the Christian Greek world.[19] The surviving evidence for their activities at Canterbury – especially lists of glosses to staple texts, and biblical commentaries transmitted in the form of what may have been classroom notes – suggests an emphasis on Bible study and reading in the kind of patristic literature I have already described as forming the core of Bede's own 'library'.[20] In a letter to his diocesan bishop, Leuthere, Aldhelm outlined the Canterbury curriculum, adding some other subjects: *computus* and arithmetic, Latin verse, astronomy and law.[21] Sadly, apart from some lines of rhythmical verse, and the biblical commentaries just mentioned, little survives to represent directly the Latin learning of Theodore and Hadrian, though it assuredly lives on in their most prolific pupil, Aldhelm.

Aldhelm's writings, though fewer than Bede's and more restricted in range, are nevertheless remarkable. In some respects they are different from his, too, and represent what one might call a less 'consistent' performance. Aldhelm wrote a long handbook on Latin poetic composition, as derivative of earlier handbooks as Bede's own *Art of Poetry* was, but also thoroughly eccentric. Strikingly, the work is addressed to a king, Aldfrith of Northumbria (685–705), himself a deeply learned man, remembered by the Irish as *sapiens* ('a scholar'). Aldhelm introduces the subject, bafflingly, by an extended discussion of the number seven, and later illustrates the composition of Latin hexameters by incorporating one hundred poems of his own, namely his *Enigmata* or riddle poems. Although ostensibly an experiment in hexameters, the *Enigmata* are also an essay in natural history, allegory, cosmology and Isidorean-influenced etymology. A small collection of Aldhelm's letters also survives, on a variety of topics, including one that stands four-square in the patristic tradition of admonition, and handles topics entirely familiar to Bede, namely the irregular customs with regard to tonsure, Easter observance and other matters, on the part of the clergy 'on the other side of the River Severn's strait' (Letter IV to Geraint, king of Dumnonia [Devon and Cornwall]).[22]

Aldhelm's most substantial work is his treatise on virginity, in prose later matched by a poem covering some (but not all) of the same content. Aldhelm wrote in part to offer a paradigm of holy living to his monastic contemporaries. He sought to accommodate the particular issues of his context by allowing the widowed or divorced to have a share of holiness alongside virgins, redefining virginity as a spiritual, rather than solely physical, attribute.[23] Since the work is dedicated to a group of women, either an abbess and her community (assumed to be Barking in Essex, a 'double' house, containing men and women), or to a group of abbesses, striking are Aldhelm's expectations of his audience, for whom he pulls no punches in the challenging Latin addressed to them. One suspects that wrestling with his syntax was somehow part of the intended spiritual workout, and that Aldhelm saw study as one path to purity. The first part of the prose version discusses virginity's high status relative to that of marriage and the widowed (or divorced) state, then, swaying towards hagiography, Aldhelm provides a series of narratives describing the lives of exemplary virgins, concluding with a warning to his monastic audience about the dangers of caring too much about clothes.

The poetic version retreads the catalogue of virgins, abridging the introductory section, and adding new material at the end, on the virtues and vices. The whole twinned work, a fusion of regulatory text, theology and hagiography, is firmly if idiosyncratically founded on the patristic tradition of exhortatory discussions of virginity, and like Bede's own writings, seeks to synthesize and redirect that tradition towards his contemporary situation.

If Aldhelm's choice of subject matter seems comparable to Bede's, then his choice of style could not be more different. Whether under the influence of trends in Irish Latin or, perhaps more likely, styles he had encountered from the continent, Aldhelm wrote prose that is self-consciously long-winded (in his *De uirginitate* he referred to his own 'verbose garrulity and garrulous verbosity'), delighting to say the same thing repeatedly in different ways and seldom straightforwardly.[24] Bede, who was aware of the most important of Aldhelm's writings, described him as 'sermone nitidus' ('sparkling in discourse', *EH* v. 18, p. 515, translation modified), though he evidently had no interest in emulating that sparkle. If sparkle means ostentation, it is a tendency observable in some kinds of earlier Latin, and certainly one that was to be a hallmark of Latin written in England later on. Aldhelm's ostentation is twofold: vocabulary and syntax, linked so as to present seemingly opaque prose, even if that was not necessarily the intention. The quest for unusual vocabulary was driven by the desire for variation and repetition, which also added ever more layers of subclauses to the syntactical structure of sentences that can then run for a whole paragraph.

By contrast, Bede's aspirations lay elsewhere: his stated concerns were to educate and expound, and thus clarity would be essential; indeed, his style has often been praised for its simple elegance and restraint. The models for his prose lay in the materials to which he had immediate access, not so much the Latin Bible (which was in a relatively unsophisticated style of Latin, well suited to narrative in particular) as the writings of the Fathers.[25] It is unwise to settle for too monochrome a picture, though, given the wide spectrum of Bede's writings, and recent analyses suggest that he used a variety of textures, was indeed in this regard a 'chameleon', and was capable of considerable syntactical complexity or density of expression – particularly in his homilies, but also in some commentaries.[26] Abstruse vocabulary, however, was not to his taste, and although he learnt to read Greek, he never paraded Graecisms as Aldhelm did, or as some Hiberno-Latin authors chose to. He seems simply to have been immune to ostentation: truly the humble servant of Christ he portrayed himself as. Aldhelm also prided himself on being the first of his race to write in (and about) Latin verse, and crafted for himself a distinctive, if somewhat heavily monotonous, style. Bede's verse and his teaching on composition seem to be a reaction to it, and on the whole he emerges as the better and more sure-footed poet.[27]

The only other Anglo-Latin literature to precede, or run contemporary with, Bede is in the genre of hagiography. I have already mentioned the anonymous Whitby *Life of Gregory*; there also survives a *Life of Saint Guthlac* the hermit (composed between about 720 and 749), by an otherwise unknown Felix, writing somewhere in Mercia, and clearly influenced by Aldhelm's love of unusual vocabulary, if not his tangled word order.[28] There is no evidence that Bede could have known either of those texts. More significant is the pair of Northern hagiographies which reflect an ecclesio-political struggle, namely the anonymous *Life of Saint Cuthbert*, composed on Lindisfarne soon after Cuthbert's death in 687,[29] and Stephen of Ripon's *Life of Bishop Wilfrid* (composed between 710 and 720), which borrows extensively from the other life in ways clearly intended to make a point.[30] To some degree all of these lives, as well as those written in seventh-century Ireland, bear the strong impress of antique models – of Athanasius's *Life of Saint Antony* and Sulpicius Severus's *Life of Saint Martin of Tours* – which also, though less blatantly, inform Bede's hagiography. Throughout the history of Insular Latin, saints' lives feature prominently as an inherited branch of literature with the practical purpose of establishing legitimacy for native saints and their communities.

Among these Insular Latin authors, Bede stands out head and shoulders. He had much in common with them in his intellectual interests, even if not necessarily in his aesthetics. But in his monumental contribution to biblical scholarship, he seems much more distinctly like a bridge between the world of learning he encountered in the books at Wearmouth-Jarrow and the medieval world, truly deserving of the place often assigned to him 'among the Fathers' (see Chapter 9). He, above all others, acted as a conduit for that inherited learning, and it is striking that apart from the earlier Irish commentators, and Alcuin of York who wrote later in the eighth century, there are no other surviving exegetical texts from the British Isles from the early Middle Ages. There is also a very real sense of the baton having passed to England at this period: it has recently been noted that, after Gregory the Great, Italy itself could boast no Latin writer of note until the later eighth century.[31]

Let us conclude by returning to the Codex Amiatinus and to the illustration that served as its frontispiece, depicting a seated man engaged in the business of writing (see Figure 7). Intended to show Ezra rewriting the Jewish Law, it is thought to have been modelled on a picture in the 'Codex Grandior' of Cassiodorus copying out his Bibles, and reminds us compellingly of the physical labour of scholarship, to which Bede was no stranger. Scholars have tried in vain to identify his handwriting in the earliest manuscript of the *Ecclesiastical History*, but Bede himself gave a fleeting insight into a typical working day: in the preface to his *Commentary on the Gospel of Luke*, he observed that he had had to be at once author and scribe and copyist ('ipse mihi dictator simul notarius et librarius', p. 7). It is a striking image of a lifetime's dedication to scholarship.

NOTES

1. Boniface, Letter 76, in *The Letters of Saint Boniface*, trans. E. Emerton (New York: Columbia University Press, 2000), p. 112 (no. 59).
2. Meyvaert 1996: 827–31, revisited in Meyvaert 2005: 1,100–1.
3. Bruce-Mitford 1967: 196–7.
4. Lapidge 2006; Love (forthcoming).
5. Lapidge 2006: 37, 59–60. His figures exclude Bibles and liturgical books.
6. Marsden 1995: 43–5, 83–5.
7. Lapidge 2006:193–228 provides a very full list.
8. On Bede's attack on Pelagianism in his commentary on the Song of Songs, see Holder 1999.
9. Markus 1997: 36–9.
10. Lapidge 1986: 6–8.
11. Dionisotti 1982: 129; Meyvaert 2005: 1,100–1.
12. Parkes 1982: 4.
13. *The Earliest Life of Gregory the Great*, ed. and trans. B. Colgrave (Cambridge University Press, 1985).
14. Wallis 1999: lxxxi; McCready 1995a and 1995b.
15. Levison 1935: 132.
16. Orchard 2003: 194.
17. *Ibid.*, 192–3; Charles-Edwards 2000: 172–6.
18. Lapidge and Herren 1979: 1; for a recent important account, see Lapidge 2008.
19. Lapidge 1995: 141–68.
20. Bischoff and Lapidge 1994.
21. Lapidge and Herren 1979: 152–3.
22. *Ibid.*, 155–60.
23. *Ibid.*, 53–7.
24. *Ibid.*, 76.
25. Shanzer 2007.
26. Sharpe 2005.
27. N. Wright 2005.
28. *Felix's Life of Saint Guthlac*, ed. and trans. B. Colgrave (Cambridge University Press, 1985).
29. *Two Lives of Saint Cuthbert*, ed. and trans. B. Colgrave (Cambridge University Press, 1985).
30. *The Life of Bishop Wilfrid by Eddius Stephanus*, ed. and trans. B. Colgrave (Cambridge University Press, 1985); there is also a translation in Farmer 2004: 105–84. On the political dimension, see Kirby 1983 and 1995, and Thacker 1989.
31. Sharpe 2005: 339.

4

SARAH FOOT

Church and monastery in Bede's Northumbria

By his own account, Bede inhabited a world of limited horizons. In the oft-quoted autobiographical statement with which he concluded his *Ecclesiastical History of the English People*, he claimed to have lived all his life from the age of seven in the monastery of St Peter and St Paul which is at Wearmouth and Jarrow (v. 24). He thus viewed the Church in Northumbria not just through the lens of a monastery located on the eastern coast of the northern Northumbrian kingdom of Bernicia, but from a distinctive perspective within an exceptional religious community, one that arguably did not typify other monasteries of his day. When previously surveying the state of the whole English Church at the time of writing the *Ecclesiastical History* (*c.* 731), Bede had explained the wider institutional framework in which his own monastery lay: 'At the present time there are four bishops in the kingdom of Northumbria, over which Ceolwulf rules: Wilfrid in the church of York, Æthelwold at Lindisfarne, Acca at Hexham, Pehthelm in the place called Whithorn ...' (v. 23, p. 559). Of those bishops, Bede was, not surprisingly, closest to his own diocesan, Acca, the dedicatee of several of his commentaries with whom he maintained a regular correspondence. Yet it is clear from the preface to the *Ecclesiastical History* that Bede had connections elsewhere within the English ecclesiastical hierarchy, in other Anglo-Saxon monasteries and beyond.

Even if he did, indeed, never travel far from home during his long career, it would be an error to envisage that, beyond these intellectual contacts, Bede saw the world only from an isolated cloister, remote from outside physical, social or indeed ecclesiastical landscapes. Connections between Jarrow and the ruling royal house in Northumbria were close and the monastery's location on the mouth of the River Tyne placed it not only in proximity to other monastic houses, but overlooking one of the best and most active harbours in Northumbria.[1] To understand Bede's world, its wider institutional and social context thus needs some elaboration. The specific environment of the 'one monastery in two different places' (*History of the Abbots*, ch. 15, p. 202) where Bede lived we shall touch on below. This chapter's main focus, however, will be the ecclesiastical geography of Northumbria in Bede's day, dioceses and diocesan organization, and the range and diversity of monastic houses in the region. Shedding some light on the place of the Church within Northumbrian lay society in the late seventh and early eighth centuries, we may hope to illuminate something of the social and cultural context within which Bede wrote and so to explain some of his attitudes and presuppositions.

The ecclesiastical geography of Bede's Northumbria

Whatever residual traces of Christianity had persisted among the British population of Northern Britain after the withdrawal of Roman troops in the early fifth century and subsequent breakdown of episcopal authority, these had little direct impact on the character of the Church established among the newly converted Anglo-Saxons in Northumbria. Three central factors determined the territorial shape and organization of the Northumbrian Church in which Bede lived, worked and wrote: the process of conversion (first by Roman missionaries from Kent, then by Irish monks from Iona); the direct association between missionary activity (and the creation of monasteries) and the ruling Northumbrian royal houses of Deira and Bernicia; and the reorganization of English dioceses under Archbishop Theodore in the 670s. As Clare Stancliffe has shown (see Chapter 5), Bede's account of the extent of British involvement in Northumbrian Christian culture in the seventh and early eighth centuries requires some modification, but that question will not be reconsidered here.

Instead we should begin where Bede would have wished, with the Roman mission to Northumbria. Although its immediate effects were apparently relatively short-lived, Paulinus's mission to the court of King Edwin of Northumbria in the 620s retained a place in ecclesiastical memory for having laid the foundations of the Christian life among the Northumbrian people. Paulinus, a member of the first mission to Kent in 597, was consecrated as bishop in July 625 in order to minister to the Christian Kentish princess, Æthelburh, when she went to Northumbria on her marriage to the then-pagan Edwin. Once the king had accepted the faith, and persuaded his leading men to follow him in that choice, a large number of the common people were baptized with him at Easter in 627 in the hastily erected wooden church of St Peter at York (*EH* II. 14). The creation of an episcopal seat at York would prove the longest-lasting legacy of Paulinus's mission. Although the missionaries had some success in preaching and baptized large numbers into the faith, they struggled to build chapels or baptisteries in the earliest days of the Church in the north, despite working in near royal dwellings and using former Roman settlements, where possible. At least one of those that they did build (at the royal dwelling at Campodonum) was later burnt down (II. 14). The extent to which the success of the first mission had depended on royal support became clear after Edwin's death in 633, when his united kingdom of Northumbria broke into its constituent parts – Bernicia in the north and Deira to the south – and the kings who succeeded him in each part of his realm apostatized. For Paulinus and his protégée Æthelburh, the return of paganism meant that there was no safety except in flight and they returned to Kent (II. 20).

Yet more than the mere memory of the Roman missionaries survived Paulinus's tactical retreat. At least one of his companions, James the Deacon, remained at York and continued to teach and baptize, dwelling near Catterick where, as the number of believers grew, he taught the Roman method of singing (*EH* II. 20). Continuing devotion to the Church of Rome in Northumbria provides one index independent of Bede of the persistence of a view that Roman endeavour had brought the Northumbrians to the faith. The anonymous Whitby author of the earliest Life of Gregory the Great remembered him as 'our apostle' who would present the souls of the English to the Lord at the Day of Judgement; this text and Alcuin's (admittedly partisan) history of the bishops and saints of York both present the conversion of the Northumbrians as the work of Paulinus and his companions.[2] Direct Roman influence may be visible in the evolution of ecclesiastical structures in the north, especially through the establishment of churches and monasteries at or near former Roman settlements, but that whatever remained of the first missionary impulse had sadly diminished by the 660s seems clear. When Wilfrid finally assumed his position as bishop of Northumbria in 669 and came to the church of York, he found its stone buildings in a ruinous condition, with a leaking roof, unglazed windows and the whole structure filthy inside and out from rain water and birds' nests and droppings.[3] Other, lesser churches can only have suffered even worse damage. That York should, nonetheless, still at that time have been thought the most appropriate site for a bishopric charged with the care of the whole of Northumbria despite its location towards the south of the kingdom is interesting. York's historic claims and associations with Rome (and thus with the victorious party at the synod of Whitby in 664) may thus have taken precedence over more pragmatic considerations, at least until Archbishop Theodore sought to divide the unwieldy diocese.

In the intervening years since the Roman missionaries' ignominious withdrawal and the presumed collapse of most of the ecclesiastical structures they had instituted, the evangelization of Northumbria had continued, or perhaps more accurately, had begun again, led by monks from a quite different tradition. When he took possession of his kingdom of Bernicia in 634, King

Oswald looked to the Irish monks from Columba's island monastery of Iona among whom he had been converted and baptized while in exile for a bishop to teach the faith to his people. Aidan, the community's choice, accepted from Oswald the island of Lindisfarne as a site for his episcopal see. Until the synod of Whitby in 664, Lindisfarne served as the sole diocesan seat for the whole of the Northumbrian kingdom and Bede presented Aidan and his successors – Finan, Colmán and Tuda – as ideal exemplars of episcopal authority, combining asceticism and solitude with preaching and ministry. The austerity and frugality of the lifestyle of their community was most starkly evident on their departure for Ireland after the victory of the Roman party in 664, when the site proved to have few buildings other than the church, only those necessary to sustain the communal life (*EH* III. 26). Herein lay a fundamental distinction between the 'Roman' and 'Irish' modes of evangelization, which had a marked impact on the development of the Church in Northumbria. For while the Roman-trained missionaries had preferred to work out of royal centres and showed some preference for reusing existing stone structures, Irish methods relied less on fixed institutions and more on travel, sometimes quite distant travel, among the scattered rural population. Those ideals continued into the next generation through men trained in this mould such as Chad (bishop of Lichfield), John of Beverley and Cuthbert (bishop of Lindisfarne). Their renunciation of property and material wealth reflected their spiritual virtues without diminishing their episcopal authority. Their commitment to carry the word out from their monastic bases to a wider population attracted Bede's admiration, but also provided a stark contrast with what Bede perceived as the weaknesses in the Church of his own day. Then, as he said in his *Letter to Bishop Egbert* in 734, 'the places in the diocese under your authority are so far apart that it would take you more than the whole year on your own to go through them all and preach the word of God in every hamlet and field' (p. 345).

The need to provide more regularized institutional structures for episcopal oversight of Northumbria and the organization of pastoral care for all localities, not just those close to the existing bishopric and to royal centres, was not a novel problem but had preoccupied Archbishop Theodore in Bede's youth. One of the archbishop's first acts on his appointment and arrival in Britain in 669 had been to remove the uncanonically consecrated Chad from the Northumbrian diocese and restore Wilfrid to his episcopal seat in York. (Although he had been appointed to this post in 664 after Whitby, Wilfrid failed to take up his seat immediately, remaining absent for a long time in Gaul while he sought episcopal consecration from a canonically ordained bishop.) Bolstered by the resolutions of the first national synod of English bishops held at Hertford in September 672 or 673 and its agreement that 'more bishops should be created as the number of the faithful increases' (*EH* IV. 5, p. 353), Theodore subsequently sought to break up Wilfrid's monster diocese into smaller, more manageable units. With royal support, he removed Wilfrid from York in 677 and divided the see into three: Bosa became bishop of Deira with his seat at York; Eata took the bishopric of Bernicia, which he governed from either Lindisfarne or Hexham; and Lindsey acquired its own bishopric, held by Eadhæd (IV. 12). Theodore's eventual reconciliation in 686 with Wilfrid – who had turned to the papacy for support in regaining his see – restored the controversial prelate to York, but without unpicking Theodore's scheme for diocesan reorganization. Lindsey now lay in Mercian hands and had its own bishop; there were two sees in Bernicia – Lindisfarne and Hexham – to which Cuthbert and Eata were appointed; and the extreme north of Wilfrid's diocese fell into the care of a bishopric for the Picts at Abercorn. Unattractive as these new arrangements seemed to Wilfrid, royal support for the underlying principles of diocesan reorganization meant that they remained essentially in place. By 692 Wilfrid had abandoned his efforts to regain his former position in the north and retreated to Mercia, leaving the see of York to the man who had previously usurped him, Bosa (d. 706).[4]

This, then, was the shape of the episcopal structure in which Bede lived and worked. The once unitary Northumbrian diocese, with borders presumably equivalent to those of the united kingdoms of Bernicia and Deira, had become, following Theodore's reorganization, four bishoprics. York had responsibility for the area between the Humber to the south and the Tees to the north; Hexham covered the region between the Tees and the River Alne, extending westwards into Cumbria, although the westernmost part of Northumbria round the Solway Firth came under the aegis of the see of Whithorn (also known as Candida Casa: *EH* III. 4), established by 731. In the north of the kingdom, Lindisfarne was the bishop's seat; the see of Abercorn had proved fairly short-lived, for there was no bishop there after Trumwine had to flee in 685 (IV. 26). Northumbria's ecclesiastical geography owed, however, at least as much to the profusion of monastic houses established within its bounds as it did to diocesan structures.

Monasteries in Northumbria

Bede's own writings represent our best source for the nature of monasticism in early Northumbria, yet they also present the historian with some difficulties; for Bede reveals a great deal about a relatively small number of communities, leaving us to wonder just how representative a picture he has drawn. In his *Life of Saint Cuthbert*, he tells us parenthetically a good deal about the nature of the communities at Melrose, Ripon and Lindisfarne to which the saint at various times belonged, and offers some insight into other houses with which Cuthbert's ministry brought him into contact, such as the congregation at Tynemouth (ch. 3), or the dependency of Whitby where he dedicated a new church (ch. 34). Many monasteries found mention in the *Ecclesiastical History*, but Bede gave detailed descriptions of the way of life in only a few, namely those institutions from which he had obtained hagiographical material. Among Northumbrian communities the double house at Whitby stands out from the rest in his narrative, yet the level of detail which he provided in his account of the *History of the Abbots* about the nature of the daily round in his own house is unparalleled.

In many ways Wearmouth-Jarrow did not typify the seventh-century English minster. Its library alone distinguished it from other Northumbrian houses, creating an intellectual environment matched in the north perhaps only by the cathedral in York. Equally unusual was the apparent willingness of its abbots to engage directly in the more arduous aspects of the daily round, as exemplified in the case of Abbot Eosterwine's enthusiasm for winnowing and threshing, milking the cows and ewes, and labouring in the bake-house, garden and kitchen (*History of the Abbots*, ch. 8). We might further wonder how closely the liturgical round in these monasteries found echo in other Northumbrian minsters, for Bede's account supplied much more incidental detail about the precise content of the office (for example in chs. 14 and 17) than did other texts from this period.

The system for regulating the way of life within the two communities, however, appears more similar to arrangements adopted elsewhere. Although Bede expressed a commitment to uniformity of monastic observance and clearly himself knew the Rule of Saint Benedict well enough to quote from it frequently in his writings, neither that nor any other single rule regulated all aspects of his own monastery's actions. Bede mentioned Benedict and his Rule expressly by name only in his commentary *On Ezra and Nehemiah* (pp. 171–2), yet he referred to the Rule also in his account of Abbot Benedict Biscop's deathbed recommendations for the running of the houses after his death, where he did so to commend the detailed guidance it offers for the election of a new abbot (*History of the Abbots*, ch. 11).[5] Rather than pre-scribe any single rule, Benedict Biscop appears to have drawn up a composite set of guidelines to direct the running of his two houses, drawing on those he had encountered elsewhere (including the seventeen Gaulish monasteries he had visited: *History of the Abbots*, ch. 11). His regulatory advice may have been preserved orally rather than in a written rule. Ceolfrith brought to Wearmouth-Jarrow his further experience of the different lifestyle of the monasteries of Gilling and Ripon and thus a particular view of the proper conduct of the regular life, one which did not entirely endear him to some of the nobles among his fellow monks when first he was prior at Wearmouth.[6]

It seems that the monastic life in which Bede was trained and educated at Wearmouth and Jarrow, while outwardly similar to that of other minsters of his own time, represented a spiritually and intellectually more intense version than that experienced by religious in other communities. If his personal knowledge of communal monasticism did not reflect closely that of monks (and nuns) in other religious houses in Northumbria, we can scarcely be surprised if this coloured Bede's perception of the inadequacies of some monastic behaviour in his own day. Further, we might wonder whether Bede imposed his own ideas about the ideal monastic house onto those institutions which came to play a wider role in his history of the formation of the English as a nation chosen in the sight of God.[7]

Other texts can supplement Bede's account of early Northumbrian monasticism, for example the poem by Æthelwulf, *On the Abbots*, which describes the heads of a monastic cell of Lindisfarne, probably Crayke in North Yorkshire,[8] Alcuin's poem on the bishops and saints of York, or Stephen's *Life of Bishop Wilfrid*, which casts light on the bishop's favourite foundations at Ripon and Hexham as well as his monastic empire which spread south of the Humber. Our picture of Northumbrian monasticism remains, however, a fundamentally limited one, restricted to a small number of institutions well represented in surviving sources, and geographically oriented towards the eastern seaboard.[9] Of Cumbrian monasteries in the days of Bede we know from written sources only about the house at Dacre in the northern lakes, over which an Abbot Swithberht ruled (*EH* IV. 32), and Carlisle, a double house visited on one occasion by the anchorite Hereberht, who lived in a cell on an island in Derwent Water (*Life of Saint Cuthbert*, chs. 27–8). There was a monastery at Heversham on the mouth of the River Derwent in the ninth century but not necessarily in Bede's day, for the monks of the community of Saint Cuthbert stayed there when contemplating taking the relics of their precious saint to Ireland before turning back inland to stay at Crayke.[10] One might imagine that the standing crosses at Ruthwell, Hoddom and Bewcastle witness to the presence of religious communities of some sort in their immediate neighbourhood, since most Anglian sculpture is assumed to arise in monastic contexts, but as Wood has argued, not all of these need necessarily have been congregations of professed monks rather than ecclesiastics of other sorts.[11]

Bede had his own clear ideas about what constituted the regular life and views about institutions that failed to maintain it, such as Barrow where, he reported, only the vestiges of regular living survived in his day (*EH* IV. 3). Manifestly, he reported the serious irregularities observed by the visiting

Adamnan in the double house at Coldingham and the ultimate fate of the community (after fire destroyed their house) in order to stress the distance between that abbey's slide from grace and the inevitability of divine judgement (IV. 25).[12] Yet did that community, at least in some respects, resemble the norm among Northumbrian houses more closely than did the centre of spiritual and intellectual excellence where Bede found his home? Commenting on the list of behaviour undesirable among monks and nuns made at the Council of *Clofesho* in 747, Catherine Cubitt has remarked how much this sounded like Bede's description of Coldingham. That this council saw the need to ban poets, harpists, musicians and clowns, fine garments, feasting and drunkenness might suggest that these activities and pastimes occurred in contemporary monastic cloisters.[13] While accepting that its library inevitably marked Wearmouth and Jarrow out from the average monastery, putting it on a par with the best educational establishments in Britain (and indeed in western Europe),[14] we may still feel that other characteristics of Benedict Biscop's foundations set them spiritually as well as intellectually apart from the average nobleman's religious house. The difficulty is to know where to locate that hypothetical average institution on the spectrum between extremes represented by Bede's Jarrow (or Cuthbert's Lindisfarne) on one hand and Coldingham or the false monasteries set up for tax-saving purposes excoriated in Bede's *Letter to Bishop Egbert* on the other. Three issues may serve in the restricted space available to argue the wider point: the place of monasteries within the landscape of Northumbria; the ideal of poverty and the reality of monastic wealth; and prayer and contemplation.

One impression given by some of the prescriptive literature and the more idealized descriptions of monastic houses that we might challenge is that religious communities dwelt in isolated solitude. Although the desire to withdraw from the world and its distractions and preoccupations was an ideal central to all expressions of monasticism, in practice few if any religious communities contrived to obtain for themselves complete separation from lay society.[15] In part this reflected the geography of their locations. Many Northumbrian monasteries found themselves within close proximity of each other (see Map 3). Wearmouth and Jarrow lay not only a mere seven miles apart, but within easy reach of Gateshead (*EH* III. 21), South Shields (IV. 23; and *Life of Saint Cuthbert*, ch. 35) and Tynemouth (V. 6). Whitby and its dependency at Hackness (IV. 23), the community at Lastingham (III. 23) and the congregation presumed to have worshipped at Kirkdale similarly clustered in a tight area of North Yorkshire. Another group of communities, at least one probably episcopal rather than monastic, lay in the area north and east of Leeds, including Ilkley, Otley and Collingham (where surviving stone sculpture probably points to congregations of some sort), Addingham (also with surviving sculpture and mentioned as a property of the archbishops of York by Simeon of Durham)[16] plus the better-attested houses of Tadcaster (IV. 23) and perhaps Barwick in Elmet (if rightly identified with the monastery in Elmet where Abbot Thrythwulf lived: II. 14). Wilfrid's house at Ripon was not far away from any of these, and held estates in the same area of Yorkshire.[17] Other communities deliberately located their monasteries close to centres of royal administration, not just episcopal seats such as York and Lindisfarne (which was not far from the royal burh at Bamburgh), but Coldingham for example also lay near to a royal site. Economic necessity and pragmatic common sense made such juxtapositions inevitable. Even Bishop Aidan, whose personal desire for solitude Bede reported (III. 16), had a church and a cell at the royal burh at Bamburgh which he used as a base from which to go out and evangelize the countryside. However, the fact that, when he was close to death, his companions had to erect a tent there to shelter him from the elements during his last illness suggests that this could only in the loosest possible terms have been described as a dwelling place (III. 17).

Poverty lay at the heart of the monastic ideal, yet in order for monasteries to survive economically, they had necessarily to acquire sufficient lands and material wealth to liberate their members from the mundane grind of subsistence agriculture in order to devote themselves to prayer. They needed, further, to hold those possessions in perpetual right, free from secular interference. Some Northumbrian houses, such as Bede's own community in two places, Wearmouth and Jarrow, rested on substantial land grants; as discussed more fully in Chapter 6, King Ecgfrith originally gave Benedict Biscop seventy hides to found St Peter's at Wearmouth before later adding the forty hides which constituted the basis for the endowment of Jarrow (*History of the Abbots*, chs. 4 and 7). Wilfrid read aloud at the dedication of the new church in Ripon a list of the estates that kings had given to the monastery by means of charter, including not just land supposedly taken from the British Church, but also estates elsewhere in North Yorkshire.[18] His monastery at Hexham Wilfrid built on an estate given him by Queen Æthelthryth (wife of the Northumbrian king, Ecgfrith, later briefly a nun at Coldingham and then abbess of Ely); Stephen's account of the lavishness of the decoration of the church Wilfrid built there and Bishop Acca's subsequent ornamentation of the place with gold, silver and precious stones suggests again a substantial endowment.[19] Yet the willingness not just of kings and queens but of the Northumbrian aristocracy to donate land away from family ties for perpetual prayer, while a major spur to the spread of monastic institutions, could create its own problems.

Bede had his own severe reservations about the motives driving some men and women in his own day to acquire land in the name of religion and set up new communities which retained too much of a secular way of life while affecting monastic principles. In the hyperbolic and rhetorical letter he wrote to Egbert complaining about such institutions, Bede urged that 'the irreligious and wicked deeds and documents of earlier rulers' should be torn up, and the lands to which they related either be reformed so properly useful to God, or given to lay use (*Letter to Bishop Egbert*, p. 350). We might see that advice being implemented when, in 757 or 758, Abbot Forthred went to Rome to appeal to the pope for help in regaining possession of Stonegrave, Coxwold and *Donemutha*, a group of houses in North Yorkshire, which Forthred had been given by an abbess but which Eadbert, king of Northumbria, had appropriated to give to his brother. Alternatively, other less edifying motives might have lain behind this seizure. Writing to King Eadbert to instruct him to return the lands to Forthred, Pope Paul I recommended that 'when this wrongful and vicious seizure has been rescinded, permission may never again be granted to any layman or any person whatsoever to invade the possessions of religious places; but rather, that the things which are concerned with the purpose of the religious life may by your zeal be more abundantly increased'.[20] Various eighth-century English Church councils attempted to legislate against secular control of monastic property, seemingly with only variable success. This may in part explain the enthusiasm shown by many abbots, including Benedict Biscop and Wilfrid, for acquiring papal privileges to free their foundations from any outside interference.[21]

Similar scepticism might colour our reading of claims to personal poverty, despite the remarks Bede made about the absolute rejection of individual wealth by the monks of Lindisfarne (*EH* III. 26) and the prohibition on private possessions on which Hild insisted at her first monastery at Hartlepool and then at Whitby (IV. 23). Wilfrid stands apart (not for the first time) in his almost flamboyant distribution on his deathbed of the riches he had accumulated during his career. Among these, his gift of gold, silver and precious stones to the monasteries of Ripon and Hexham made so that they, too, might be able to buy the friendship of kings and bishops appears far removed from what we might – perhaps erroneously – imagine to have been conventional clerical mores.[22] Although more ostentatious than his peers, Wilfrid was not alone in retaining some wealth after taking monastic vows. Clearly the Coldingham women had sufficient wealth either severally or collectively to fund their ostentatious lifestyle (*EH* IV. 25), and one of the questions in Bishop Egbert's *Dialogues* dealt with how to handle disputes over personal property retained by monks and nuns after they had left the world.[23] Saint Cuthbert lived in notable austerity, yet his companions buried him with a seventh-century Northumbrian pectoral cross made of gold, inlaid with garnets and suspended on a silken and gold cord; this escaped the Henrician despoliation of Durham to be found with the saint's skeleton in 1827. Even Bede himself owned some small treasures in a box that he shared among his friends when he was dying, some pepper, napkins and a bit of incense.[24]

The quest for spiritual perfection was the ultimate goal of the monastic life, sought, not without difficulty, through corporate worship (and shared sacrament), private prayer and contemplation. While Bede defined his lifelong observance of regular discipline in terms of his daily singing of the Divine Office in church (*EH* v. 24), many texts stressed the intercessory role of monasteries. Bishops and abbots meeting at the Council of Clofesho in 747 decreed that 'churchmen and monastics should in their canonical hours entreat the divine clemency not only for themselves, but for kings, ealdormen and for the safety of all Christian people'.[25] Many donors endowed monasteries in return for prayer, for themselves or others. Dedicating his baby daughter Ælfflæd to perpetual virginity, King Oswiu gave twelve small estates to create new monasteries which, freed from earthly obligations, might be used for prayer without ceasing (*EH* III. 24). Brought up at Hild's Whitby, in adulthood Ælfflæd helped to ensure that her monastery played a significant role in the maintenance of the cult of the Northumbrian royal family. Her mother, Eanflæd, Oswiu's queen (and abbess of Whitby after Hild), founded Gilling, North Yorkshire, in expiation for her husband's murder of Oswine, the last king of Deira, in 651, to offer prayers for the souls of both kings (*EH* III. 14, 24). When he became bishop of York Bosa, formerly a monk at Whitby, encouraged his new community in constant praise of God, as Alcuin described:

> This father of the church endowed its fabric
> and made its clergy live a life apart from the common people,
> decreeing that they should serve the one God at every hour:
> that the mystical lyre should sound in unbroken strain,
> that human voices, forever singing heavenly praises
> to the Lord, should beat upon the heights of Heaven.[26]

Similarly, Eanmund, founder of the monastery described in Æthelwulf's *On the Abbots*, took seriously the advice of his mentor Egbert to send thanks towards the stars to God; the members of his community often spent all night in prayer without ceasing, one kneeling on the floor of the church, another outside in the cold night air.[27]

Contemporary writers preferred to emphasize individual examples of prayer and devotion over the regular recitation of the Daily Office, the central corporate act of monastic worship. Hagiographical convention portrayed the saints as continuously engaged in praise of God, ceaselessly chanting psalms and praying alone. Cuthbert recited psalms even before he entered the religious life and, once professed, sometimes chose to spend the night up to his neck in the sea in prayer rather than sleeping with his brethren (*Life of Saint Cuthbert*, chs. 5 and 10); Wilfrid continued to sing psalms perpetually even when in prison.[28] While Bede was dying, he spent all of his time when he was not teaching his pupils in reciting the Psalter, singing antiphons and repeating prayers, although he was too weak to attend the office with his brethren.[29] This concentration on individual acts of spiritual prowess may partly reflect the focus of especially hagiographical texts on the extraordinary deeds of the saintly, in comparison with which participation in the Office, which dictated the rhythm of the monastic day, seemed rather less noteworthy. The saints whom Bede most extolled in his writings, such as Cuthbert or Aidan, he depicted as exemplary figures to whose pastoral, ascetic and spiritual ideals all should aspire; in promoting their sanctity of course he dwelt on their private spirituality. It also seems clear, however, that many monasteries could frequently prove distinctly unquiet spaces, and only those with the internal spiritual strength and mental resources to cut themselves off from their peers would find the silence in which to seek God. In one of his homilies, Bede urged his brothers not to lose any opportunity presented to them to retreat to the oratory of the monastery, where they could thank God for his gifts or ask him for grace in private and quietness (*Homilies on the Gospels*, 1. 23). Aspiration and reality diverged here, as elsewhere.

Conclusion

Looking back in maturity, Bede seemed to believe that a golden age of English Christianity had passed; the English, he thought, had attained particular intellectual and spiritual heights during his own youth, in the time of Archbishop Theodore of Canterbury (669–90), to which age he looked back regretfully:

> Never had there been such happy times since the English first came to Britain; ... the desires of all men were set on the joys of the heavenly kingdom of which they had only lately heard; while all who wished for instruction in sacred studies had teachers ready to hand. (*EH* IV. 2, p. 335)

That era had defined the shape and structure of the ecclesiastical environment in which Bede had worked, creating a social and religious context which goes some way towards explaining his writings in various genres which later chapters in this volume explore. Reflecting on his career, Bede saw his role within his own monastery as primarily the study of Scripture, and (within the context of the discipline of the rule and the singing of the Office) said he had all his life delighted to learn, or to teach, or to write. We remember him most as a historian, but he listed first and placed the most importance on his works of biblical exegesis, on which his medieval reputation largely rested (*EH* v. 24). Life within the monasteries of Wearmouth and Jarrow did not, as we saw, cut Bede off entirely from the world around him. But if that life served as the index against which he measured other monastic houses, it may not have occasioned him to observe much health among the monastic or episcopal churches of his own day.

The success with which the early English Church integrated itself into Germanic familial structures was one of its most substantial achievements. Discussing the conversion of the Anglo-Saxon aristocracy, Patrick Wormald located the Church's triumph in its effective 'assimilation by a warrior nobility, which had no intention of abandoning its culture, or seriously changing its ways of life, but which was willing to throw its traditions, customs, tastes and loyalties into the articulation of the new faith'.[30] The enthusiasm of that same nobility for the institutions of monasticism, its readiness both to join such congregations and – much more significantly – to endow them with landed wealth from among its own possessions, made monasteries fundamentally aristocratic institutions. Much of the essential character of the noble lifestyle thus continued within the cloister. Bishops' households reflected similarly secular attributes, if we believe the admonitory letter that Bede wrote to his own diocesan in 734; bishops themselves sought to retain responsibility for large dioceses in order to maximize the dues exacted from the laity, while surrounding themselves at home with men given to laughter, joking, telling tales, feasting and drinking. He wrote to Egbert urging him to obtain the co-operation of King Ceolwulf to 'put the Church of our people into a better condition than it has been up to now' (*Letter to Bishop Egbert*, p. 348). All this was far removed from the world Bede knew at Jarrow and from the ideals espoused by those monks closest to his own heart, like Aidan and Cuthbert.

Yet the social context in which the majority of Anglo-Saxon monks and nuns, bishops, priests and other clergy practised their religious vocations probably lay closer to the picture Bede excoriated in that letter than it did to the rarefied atmosphere of Ceolfrith's Jarrow or Cuthbert's Lindisfarne. Most early English monasteries occupied a liminal space between the society of the secular aristocracy from which the majority of their professed members were drawn and the ecclesiastical society of the Christian Church. While part of particular noble and royal networks, they were bound by reciprocal bonds of hospitality and obligation. Yet as members also of the wider family of the

Church they could, if necessary, divorce themselves from their own kin (and from the local king) to appeal to a higher ecclesiastical authority of bishop, archbishop or even pope. Bede saw himself in a world apart, monks having a stature superior to that of the rest of fallen humanity (*On the Temple*, p. 26). We may understand him better if we perceive him and the Church of his day not apart from, but deeply enmeshed within, the secular society that lay outside his cloister's walls.

NOTES

1. Morris 2004: 6–7; Wood 2006: 72–3.
2. *The Earliest Life of Gregory the Great*, ed. and trans. B. Colgrave (Cambridge University Press, 1985), ch. 6 (Gregory as apostle to the English), pp. 82–3; chs. 14–19 (Paulinus's mission), pp. 96–107; Alcuin, *The Bishops, Kings and Saints of York*, ed. and trans. P. Godman (Oxford: Clarendon Press, 1982), lines 291–301, pp. 28–9.
3. *The Life of Bishop Wilfrid by Eddius Stephanus*, ed. and trans. B. Colgrave (Cambridge University Press, 1985), ch. 16, p. 35.
4. Cubitt 1989.
5. Van der Walt 1986; DeGregorio 2008.
6. *Life of Ceolfrith*, ch. 8, in Farmer 2004: 216.
7. Foot 2006; Wormald 1992.
8. *Æthelwulf: De abbatibus*, ed. and trans. A. Campbell (Oxford: Clarendon Press, 1967). For the identification with Crayke, see Lapidge 1996: 394.
9. Morris 1983: 35–8 (Table 3).
10. *Historia de Sancto Cuthberto: A History of Saint Cuthbert and a Record of his Patrimony*, ed. T. Johnson South (Cambridge: D. S. Brewer, 2002), pp. 58–9.
11. Wood 1987.
12. *Ibid.*, 25.
13. *Council of Clofesho*, ch. 20, in A. W. Haddan and W. Stubbs (eds.), *Councils and Ecclesiastical Documents Relating to Great Britain and Ireland*, 3 vols. (Oxford: Clarendon Press, 1869–78), vol. III, p. 369. Cubitt 1995: 121; Foot 2006: 187.
14. Lapidge 2006: 191–228.
15. Foot 2006: ch. 7.
16. Simeon of Durham, *Letter on the Archbishops of York*, ch. 3, in *Symeonis monachi opera omnia*, ed. T. Arnold, 2 vols., Rolls Series 75 (London: Longman, 1882–5), vol. I, p. 225. Wood 1987: 20–1.
17. *Life of Bishop Wilfrid*, ch. 17, pp. 34–7. Ripon itself was not far from Crayke (to whose history Æthelwulf's poem *De abbatibus* attests) and another cluster of houses belonging to an Abbot Forthred at Stonegrave, Coxwold and Donamuthe: see Whitelock 1979: 830–1 (no. 184); and for the possible location of the third of those places, Parker 1985.
18. *Life of Bishop Wilfrid*, ch. 17, pp. 36–7.
19. *Ibid.*, ch. 22, pp. 44–7.
20. Whitelock 1979: 830–1 (no. 184).
21. Cubitt 1992; Foot 2006: 130–4.
22. *Life of Bishop Wilfrid*, ch. 63, pp. 136–7.

23. *Dialogues of Egbert*, response 10, in Haddan and Stubbs (eds.), *Councils*, vol. III, pp. 407–8; see Foot 2006: 165.

24. See *Cuthbert's Letter on the Death of Bede*, in Colgrave and Mynors 1969: 585.

25. *Council of Clofesho*, AD 747, ch. 30, in Haddan and Stubbs (eds.), *Councils*, vol. III, p. 369.

26. Alcuin, *The Bishops, Kings and Saints of York*, lines 857–62, pp. 70–3.

27. *Æthelwulf: De abbatibus*, chs. 6–7, pp. 16–19.

28. *Life of Bishop Wilfrid*, chs. 36 and 38, pp. 74–5, 76–7.

29. *Cuthbert's Letter on the Death of Bede*, in Colgrave and Mynors 1969: 583.

30. Wormald 1978: 57.

5

CLARE STANCLIFFE

British and Irish contexts

Near the beginning of his *Ecclesiastical History of the English People*, Bede notes the use of five languages in Britain: English, British, Irish, Pictish and Latin (I. I). Latin was the language of the Church. For the rest, Bede's wording skilfully circumvents the problem that political frontiers did not necessarily march with linguistic frontiers. Broadly speaking, Bede presented Britain as inhabited by four major peoples: north of the Forth, on the east side of what is now Scotland, were the Picts. To their west were the Irish of the kingdom of Dál Riada, relatively recent colonists from Ireland. (We may note here that Bede's term for the Irish, *Scotti*, does not distinguish between those living in Ireland and those in western Scotland.) South of the Forth–Clyde isthmus was the land of the Britons, the original inhabitants of Britain. But after the Romans had withdrawn their soldiers, the Britons had invited in the 'English or Saxons' from across the North Sea to help defend their land (I. I 5). Settled in the east of Britain, these had soon seized control of land from the Britons. This trend continued, so that in the period covered by Bede's history the area under British control contracted towards the west, ultimately leaving them with just rump kingdoms: Dumnonia in the southwest, shrinking westwards to become Cornwall; Gwynedd, Powys and other kingdoms in what came to be Wales; and Strathclyde in what is now southwest Scotland.

There was, then, a British context for Bede's Northumbria, itself a shotgun marriage between the two neighbouring kingdoms of Deira (between Humber and Tees) and Bernicia (between Tees and Forth: see Map 2). The seventh century saw far-flung military overlordships, which brought the British kingdoms of northern Wales and Northumbria into direct conflict with each other. A succession of Northumbrian kings, Æthelfrith, Edwin and Oswald, took the offensive and fought at Chester against Powys, on Anglesey against Gwynedd, and in Meigen (around Welshpool) and at Maserfelth, probably to be identified as Oswestry. British kings fought back, prosecuting the war as far as Northumbria, often in alliance with the English Mercian leader, Penda. Bede focuses particularly on the exploits of the Gwynedd king, Cadwallon, who was the leader of the alliance responsible for slaying Edwin, the first Christian king of Northumbria. Bede highlights his ravaging of Deira and Bernicia 'like a savage tyrant, tearing them to pieces with fearful bloodshed' (*EH* III. 1, p. 213). By labelling Cadwallon 'the king of the Britons' (*ibid.*), Bede implies an ethnic dimension to this warfare; but it is more likely that these are simply wars for political dominance, with Britons and English collaborating against a common Northumbrian threat.

Alongside the continuing British kingdoms in what is now Wales, we may note that, right through Bede's lifetime and beyond, Strathclyde remained independent, and militarily formidable (see Map 2). Its chief royal seat was at Dumbarton on the north bank of the Clyde, but its territory lay largely south of the Clyde, where it marched with the northwest boundary of Northumbria. At the same time as these independent British kingdoms continued in the west, there will have been many British speakers brought under English rule during the reign of King Æthelfrith and his seventh-century successors as the English expanded westwards across the Pennines and along either side of the Solway Firth. Yet Bede says nothing of the Northumbrian conquest of British kingdoms like Elmet (in the Pennines) and Rheged (near the Solway Firth), and very, very little about those British speakers who were absorbed into Northumbria. They are effectively written out of his history. Thus, although we can discern that there was a British context for Bede's Northumbria, a major problem is that our evidence for it is slender, selective and biased.

The Picts were a neighbouring people with whom the Northumbrians had political relations, and some ecclesiastical ones too (see Map 2). However, attempts to expand Northumbrian domination north of the Forth ended in military disaster in 685, and so the relationship stabilized as essentially one between neighbours: it did not impinge in a major way upon Bede and his world, insofar as we can judge from the scant evidence.

It was different with the Irish of Dál Riada in western Scotland (see Map 2). After 616 when Æthelfrith, the Bernician king who had forcibly annexed Deira, had been killed in battle by the Deiran prince, Edwin, Æthelfrith's sons had to flee for their lives to somewhere beyond the reach of Edwin's vengeance. As a result Oswald and Oswiu had sought refuge in Dál Riada, and there been baptized in the monastery of Iona. This had been founded in the previous century by an Irish monk, Saint Columba, and headed a federation of monasteries that reached from Durrow in the Irish midlands up to Derry, and thence across the Irish Sea to the Hebrides where Iona and other dependencies were situated, and beyond, eastwards, into Pictland. So when Oswald won the kingdoms of Bernicia and Deira at the battle of Heavenfield in 634, it was natural for him to turn to Iona for missionaries to convert his people, still largely pagan despite some missionary work under Edwin. In this way, a close religious and cultural relationship developed between the English and the Irish, to such an extent that mid-seventh-century Northumbria has been termed 'a cultural province of Ireland'.[1] In 664 the synod of Whitby ended Northumbria's bishops being appointed from Iona, but links with Ireland remained close, and those with Iona were renewed or reinforced during the reign of King Aldfrith (c. 685–705), who himself had spent considerable time studying on Iona.

This explains why there are important British and Irish contexts for Bede and his world, but exploring their true significance poses a challenge. For instance, Bede's *Ecclesiastical History* presents the Irish as the major evangelists of Northumbria, particularly its northern component, Bernicia. Other sources, however, present a very different version of the Northumbrian Christian past.[2] A *Life of Gregory* written at the Deiran monastery of Whitby puts the emphasis on the Roman mission to the Deiran king, Edwin.[3] This is compatible with Bede's account of Edwin's conversion, and on its own might rank simply as a Deiran slant on the conversion process. Yet another source, Stephen of Ripon's *Life of Bishop Wilfrid*, goes much further. There, Wilfrid portrays the achievements of the Irish as 'weeds' that he had succeeded in 'rooting out' during his episcopate, when Roman links were restored after the unfortunate Irish interlude.[4] There were, then, contrasting views about how the Irish mission to Northumbria should be interpreted, and a recent work has emphasized that even Bede does not give a consistent view in all his works: his *Chronicle* that comprises chapter 66 of *The Reckoning of Time* highlights the conversion of Edwin, and omits all mention of the Irish mission.[5] This alerts us to the highly controversial nature of the Irish involvement in the Northumbrian Church, and the likelihood that all our sources – Bede, as well as Stephen – are writing from a particular angle. We therefore need to discover how Bede has slanted his narrative, and what the reality was.

Bede's presentation of the Britons and Irish

Bede's *Ecclesiastical History* is constructed in five books, and the main focus is the conversion and then establishment of the Church among the English, divided though they were into separate kingdoms. This in turn is set within a broader context of the island of Britain, with its four major peoples; and the work as a whole is given coherence by the way in which Bede interweaves the role of the different peoples with the dynamic of his history of mission. The main thrust of his story is that the Britons were Christian but sinful, and so were punished by God, being led to their fateful decision to invite the English to Britain. Further, a major sin of the Britons was their failure to preach the Gospel to the English, here presented as God's own chosen people

(I. 14 and 22). When Gregory the Great's Roman missionaries arrived and invited the Britons to drop their deviant practices, chiefly their dating of Easter, and to join them in the task of converting the English, the Britons refused; and they therefore deserved divine punishment in the form of military defeat and the slaughter of many of their monks. Thereafter the Britons are presented as *perfidi*, 'faithless ones', in some sense beyond the pale (II. 2).[6] The English, however, were converted in part by missionaries from Rome: these evangelized Kent and achieved at least temporary success elsewhere in the southeast, while the marriage of King Edwin of Deira to a Kentish princess brought the Roman missionary Paulinus to Edwin's court, where he eventually succeeded in converting the king. On Edwin's death in battle, however, Deira and Bernicia reverted to paganism, and so a new beginning was needed.

This was provided by Bishop Aidan and the Irish sent from Iona in response to Oswald's request; and Bede leaves us in no doubt that, although Aidan was incorrect in his Easter practice, he was nonetheless an exemplary missionary. Book III of the *Ecclesiastical History* is dominated by the Irish mission. Oswald gave Aidan the tidal island of Lindisfarne to establish a monastery, close to – but cut off from – his own royal stronghold of Bamburgh, but a far cry from Paulinus's see in the former Roman city of York. Bede paints an idyllic picture of King Oswald acting as Aidan's interpreter to his nobles when Aidan preached. Many Irish came to Britain, preaching and baptizing: 'Churches were built in various places and the people flocked together with joy to hear the Word; land and property of other kinds were given by royal bounty to establish monasteries, and English children, as well as their elders, were instructed by Irish teachers in advanced studies and in the observance of the discipline of a Rule' (III. 3, p. 221). Thus Oswald's people became Christian, and 'Oswald gained from the one God ... greater earthly realms ... among the speakers of four different languages, British, Pictish, Irish, and English' (III. 6, p. 231). Thanks to Northumbrian political influence, Irish and Irish-trained missionaries worked elsewhere within England: among the Middle Angles, a Mercian sub-kingdom, and among the East Saxons, and later in Mercia itself. Although Bede does not hide the fact that Aidan and the Columban Irish (i.e. those who acknowledged the abbot of Iona's ecclesiastical authority) calculated the date of Easter incorrectly, that does not prevent him from eulogizing Aidan as a saint, and highlighting the respect in which he was held even by bishops trained on the continent (III. 4–5, 15–17, 25). Their faulty Easter practice was excused as due to ignorance because they lived 'so far away at the ends of the earth' (III. 4, p. 225). This apart, their praxis was exemplary, as their loving willingness to share their Christian faith with the English showed.

After Aidan's death, however, and particularly after the return to Northumbria of Wilfrid, a Northumbrian instructed in the correct Roman observance on the continent, the dispute over Easter became highly charged. There are hints that the validity of baptisms performed by the Irish was being questioned. In addition, a political dimension emerged, with King Oswiu (Oswald's brother and successor) remaining loyal to the Columban tradition, while Oswiu's son Alhfrith, sub-king of Deira, was won over to the Roman point of view by Wilfrid. It became essential for Oswiu to assert his authority, and he summoned the parties to a synod held at Whitby in 664. There he decided in favour of Roman Easter practice; this was the only one to be observed in his kingdom in future. Colmán, the Irish bishop of Lindisfarne, who was unable to abandon the tradition of his mother-house, left, together with all the Irish and thirty of the English monks of Lindisfarne. Initially, however, there was some continuity. Colmán's immediate successor was Tuda, consecrated bishop in the south of Ireland, which had accepted Roman Easter practice long since. After his premature death from plague, a complex situation emerged, with Wilfrid being promoted by Alhfrith, while Oswiu chose Chad, a disciple of Aidan, who was consecrated by a West Saxon bishop together with two British bishops, thanks to the depletion of bishops through plague. However, once the papally appointed Archbishop Theodore arrived in England in 669, he deposed Chad and installed Wilfrid at Paulinus's former see of York.

Yet the Irish do not disappear from the pages of the *Ecclesiastical History*. Indeed, Bede goes out of his way to stress continuity, presenting Eata, a disciple of Aidan, as becoming bishop of Lindisfarne not long after Colmán's departure (III. 26), although it was in fact fourteen years later, and meanwhile expatiating on the numbers of English who chose to go to Ireland for religious reasons.[7] A Northumbrian raid on mainland Ireland in 684 was roundly condemned by Bede, who viewed the Northumbrian defeat in Pictland the next year as 'the avenging hand of God' for this attack on the Irish, 'a harmless race that had always been most friendly to the English' (IV. 26, pp. 429, 427). This defeat, in which the Northumbrian king was killed, appears to have ended Northumbrian political domination over the Picts, Dál Riada and Strathclyde. Yet contacts continued at the religious and cultural level, and Bede particularly highlighted those with a bearing on the Easter question: first, the personal conversion to the Roman Easter of Adomnán, abbot of Iona, during a visit which he paid to Bede's own monastery c. 688, when he had helpful conversations with Abbot Ceolfrith (V. 15); secondly, the conversion to the Roman Easter of King Nechtan of the Picts (c. 712), who sought information and stonemasons from Ceolfrith (V. 21). Finally, Bede celebrated the success of a Northumbrian,

Egbert, in converting the monastery of Iona to the Roman Easter and tonsure in 716. Bede interpreted this in terms of God's compassion for the Irish, recompensing them for their generous evangelization of the English. He then went on to highlight the contrast with the Britons, 'who would not proclaim to the English the knowledge of the Christian faith which they had', so, fittingly, they 'still persist in their errors and stumble in their ways' (v. 22, p. 555; cf. III. 4). This celebration of Egbert's conversion of Iona marks the culmination of Bede's *Ecclesiastical History*, coming virtually at its end. In the following, penultimate, chapter Bede celebrates the fact that the Picts and Dalriadan Irish are not hostile to the English, and again contrasts the Britons, 'who oppose the English through their intestine hatred, and the whole state of the catholic church by their incorrect Easter and evil customs' (v. 23, p. 561). Thus the contrast between the charitable and friendly Irish and the surly, hostile Britons runs right through the *Ecclesiastical History* from beginning to end.

Looking now to see how Bede presents the relationship between the Irish and the Roman missions, we may say that the Roman mission is portrayed positively, with a particularly warm appreciation of Pope Gregory; yet its limitations in Northumbria are not glossed over. Edwin's six years as a Christian saw mass baptisms in both Bernicia and Deira, but the building of only a tiny number of churches, at York and at a royal estate named Campodunum, both in Deira. No church, nor even cross, was erected in all Bernicia in those years (II. 14; III. 2). These tender Christian beginnings were snuffed out by the British king Cadwallon, whom Bede paints as a 'barbarian in heart', who slaughtered the English without mercy (II. 20, p. 203). Thus, far from contributing anything positive, the Britons actually destroyed what Paulinus had founded. Bede, however, strove to present an image of Christian continuity in Northumbria, ending Book II with the depiction of Paulinus's deacon James continuing to teach and baptize after Paulinus and the others had fled. Much the same happens later after the synod of Whitby and departure of the Irish, when Eata becomes the figure of continuity. Thus Bede evinces a concern to portray the Northumbrian Church as founded by Paulinus and continuing right through Cadwallon's devastation, the revival under Oswald and Aidan, the synod of Whitby and its aftermath, and culminating in the days of Eata and Cuthbert. All, whether Roman or Irish or English, and whatever their Easter allegiance, were part of the same Church.

Probing the reality behind Bede's portrayal

Despite Bede's reputation for accuracy, there are reasons for thinking that his portrayal is misleading in some respects. First, his depiction of the Britons and Irish as moral opposites, judged by whether or not they were missionary-minded towards the English, bears all the marks of a construct. Given his knowledge, Bede could have presented instances of virtuous Britons, and even a British mission to a neighbouring people, the Picts; yet he chose not to do so.[8] The strong contrast drawn between the two peoples is highly misleading: the Irish had been converted largely by the Britons, and relations between the two in the religious sphere remained close for much of the seventh century. Indeed, it is plausible to think of Aidan working in harmony with British Christians during his Northumbrian mission, and it is most revealing to discover an instance of British and English collaboration in consecrating Chad as bishop, even after the synod of Whitby.

A second way in which Bede's presentation misleads is, arguably, in glossing over the revolutionary changes that occurred *c.* 669 under Wilfrid of York and Theodore, archbishop of Canterbury.[9] Stephen's *Life of Bishop Wilfrid* differs from Bede in accusing the Columban Irish and British Easter practice condemned at Whitby of being heretical, not just mistaken. Further, he does not portray the synod of Whitby as ending the Easter dispute in Northumbria; rather, King Oswiu was still listening to Quartodeciman heretics when he decided to promote Chad to be bishop. True conformity with Rome came only *c.* 669 when Archbishop Theodore removed Chad and installed Wilfrid as bishop of York. The most plausible interpretation of our conflicting sources is that Stephen is here more truthful than Bede. Admittedly his presentation of Columban Irish and British Easter practice as 'Quartodeciman' is not literally true. Strictly speaking, Quartodecimans ('Fourteeners') were those who kept Easter on the fourteenth day of the lunar month Nisan regardless of the day of the week, so celebrating Christian Easter at the same time as the Jewish Passover, whereas Celtic Easter practice was always to celebrate Easter on a Sunday. However, if 14 Nisan fell actually on a Sunday, they accepted that as the correct date for Easter, whereas continental practice in those circumstances postponed Easter till the following Sunday (21 Nisan). This provided a pretext for dubbing Celtic Easter practice Quartodeciman – a usage found in Pope Honorius's letter to the Irish written in the 620s (*The Reckoning of Time*, ch. 66, p. 228). Its application to Celtic Easter practice during Theodore's episcopate can be corroborated by strictly contemporary sources, Theodore's *Judgments* and Aldhelm's letter to Geraint of Dumnonia.

The upshot of this is that the Northumbrian Church in the late seventh century was deeply divided. On the one hand, Wilfrid and his followers maintained that the traditional British and Columban Irish Easter practice was heretical, and that catholic Christians should not have anything to do with its adherents. We glimpse this mindset in Theodore's *Judgments*, which impose stringent penances even on Catholics who prayed alongside such 'heretics', or allowed them to celebrate the Eucharist.[10] On the other hand, there were Eata's Lindisfarne and Hild's Whitby, which themselves accepted Roman Easter practice at the synod of Whitby, but refused to disown all that the Irish had brought to the Northumbrian Church, and to regard Columban monks like Aidan as heretics. These formed a 'middle party' between the intransigent Wilfridians on the one hand, and Iona on the other, and the figure of Cuthbert provided a rallying point for them: an iconic holy man, whose uncorrupted body was translated on Lindisfarne in 698 to become the focus for a cult.

All this forms the complex Northumbrian scene into which Bede was born and with which he was still interacting when he wrote the *Ecclesiastical History* nearly sixty years later. The Romeward affiliation of Wearmouth-Jarrow is well-known, with the frequent continental journeys of Benedict Biscop, while Ceolfrith, Bede's abbot for much of his life, was a product of Wilfrid's monastery of Ripon. Yet there are reasons for thinking that Ceolfrith's conversations with Adomnán of Iona in the 680s were a two-way process.[11] Around the turn of the seventh to eighth centuries we witness the development of friendly relations between Wearmouth-Jarrow and Lindisfarne, with the loaning and gift of manuscripts, and with Bede's decision to write a *Metrical Life of Saint Cuthbert* followed some years later by his prose *Life of Saint Cuthbert*. Bede's *Ecclesiastical History* is also a product of this appreciation of Christian strands from many traditions. Its slant is quite different from that of Stephen's *Life of Saint Wilfrid*. It hushes up the Quartodeciman accusation, and instead adopts the line that fitted with Lindisfarne's post-664 stance: the Columban Easter practice was incorrect, but it was not a matter of heresy; in any case, the Irish should be excused on the grounds of their outgoing charity and willingness to convert the English. Thus Bede felt able to affirm all that was good about the Irish mission to Northumbria, in contrast to his own contemporary Church: their selfless evangelism, their readiness to walk miles and preach to the poor, their disregard of worldly gain (III. 4–5, 26).

This passing over shortcomings within the Church in silence and focusing rather on what was praiseworthy is a consistent trait of Bede's *Ecclesiastical History*; and while arguably it tallies with his own principles, we can also interpret it as an attempt to foster peace in a Northumbrian Church that was still threatened by factionalism. There is, however, one exception: Bede has no qualms about highlighting the sinfulness of the Britons, their unfriendly rejection of Augustine's demands, and their general hostility to the English. An edginess creeps into his voice when he is talking of Cadwallon's devastation of Northumbria or the Britons' continuing hostility towards the English. This may well be because Bede was worried that Northumbria was vulnerable to British attack, thanks partly to the formidable kingdom of Strathclyde to its northwest, and partly to its inclusion of large numbers of only partially assimilated Britons.[12] He makes a great deal of the meetings between Augustine and the British bishops c. 603.[13] After their refusal to conform he labels them *perfidi* and treats them almost as schismatics (*EH* II. 2). Yet British Easter practice was the same as that of the Columban Irish, so prior to 669 it did not necessarily debar them from contributing to the conversion of the English, and this has been plausibly argued for at least parts of the west Midlands.[14] It may be that their participation in the consecration of Chad c. 664 was but the tip of an iceberg. On the other hand, since Theodore and Wilfrid later regarded both Britons and Columban Irish as Quartodeciman heretics, we can understand why, if there were traditions of a British contribution to English Christianity, they were later suppressed. We therefore need to set aside Bede's dismissive comments, and re-examine the question.

The British contribution

That there was some British contribution to Christian Northumbria is clear: to look no further, those British areas with their churches that were taken over by the English when the latter were officially Christian must have passed from British Christian to English Christian hands. Whether this led to disruption and expropriation at one end of the scale, or to a seamless transfer of authority at the other, will have varied according to circumstance. For instance, British churches in the Lothians taken over under Oswald and Aidan probably fared better than those in the Pennines taken over under Ecgfrith and Wilfrid.[15] The clearest example of a major British church being taken over by the English as a going concern is Whithorn, on the north of the Solway Firth. Here, the British saint, Ninian, continued to be revered, and the church's episcopal status was soon revived, although major rebuilding works on a different orientation took place (*EH* III. 4 and V. 23).

Whether there was any active British involvement in the conversion of Northumbria is more problematic. Since there were close relations between British and Irish Christians at this period, it is likely that Aidan was able to establish good relations with British churchmen, and there may well have been some collaboration; but there is no direct evidence of it. The only surviving evidence we have is an entry in *The Welsh Annals*, together with a notice in the early ninth-century *History of the Britons*, to the effect that Edwin was baptized by a Briton, Rhun son of Urien.[16] The silence both of the contemporary papal correspondence and of Bede and the Whitby *Life of Gregory* means that this evidence is often dismissed out of hand. Yet early northern British annal entries were incorporated into the later *Welsh Annals*, and another claim in the *History of the Britons*, that Oswiu had a British wife, Rieinmelth, from the same Rheged dynasty as Rhun, is independently substantiated. It may well be the case that British churchmen collaborated with Paulinus's mission to Edwin, and that the baptism was a joint affair; and that British participation was subsequently written out of the English retellings of the story.

We reach surer ground with the question of an intellectual British contribution to Bede, for he makes no secret of his reliance upon a British work, Gildas's *On the Ruin of Britain*, which he could have obtained from Canterbury or Iona. He used Gildas to tell the story of post-Roman Britain: how the Britons had committed every sin in the book, and how this had brought on them retribution from God, leading to their calling in the Anglo-Saxons (*EH* I. esp. 14 and 22). It is important to realize that Bede does not simply take information from Gildas; the debt goes much deeper. Bede follows Gildas in aligning his own people with God's chosen people of the Bible, and in the idea that plague and military defeat are punishment for sin. What is more, he was able to take over Gildas's presentation of the sinfulness of the Britons unchanged; but whereas Gildas highlighted their sins in order to prompt a change of heart, Bede presented it as historical fact, and also used it to justify the Anglo-Saxons' brutal conquests.

The Irish contribution

Whatever role the Britons and Paulinus's mission may have played, those primarily responsible for the conversion of Northumbria were the Irish. Their thirty years up to the synod of Whitby allowed time for Christianity to put down roots to an extent denied the Roman mission. After the anti-Quartodeciman Wilfrid became effective bishop in 669, direct links with Iona were officially severed for a time; but those with the southern half of mainland Ireland, which had already adopted the Roman Easter, continued unabated, while Colmán and his former Lindisfarne monks founded new monasteries in Connacht, including 'Mayo of the Saxons', which long maintained its links with Northumbria.[17] On the accession of the Iona-educated Aldfrith *c.* 685, links with Iona were restored, and its abbot, Adomnán, visited Northumbria and Bede's own monastery (*EH* v. 15 and 21). This extended period of close interrelationship between Northumbria and the Irish continued well into the eighth century, and is exemplified by the development of a common style of writing and illuminating manuscripts, hence the convenient terminology of 'Insular' script and 'Hiberno-Saxon' art.

A firm foundation for the conversion of the whole of Northumbria, and not just an elite around the king, was laid by the work of Aidan. Whereas

Paulinus appears to have remained attached to the court of Edwin and his queen, Aidan, for all his close relationship with Oswald, was careful to maintain his distance. He used the network of royal vills; but he did not travel as part of the royal household,[18] preferring to walk so that he could talk to those he met (*EH* III. 5 and 14). Further, Aidan established his own monastic base on Lindisfarne, right from the start. The establishment of this monastery was crucial since it provided a training ground for Anglo-Saxon recruits, instructing them in the religious life, but also educating them in the Psalms and thence in Latin, in reading and writing, in the study of the Bible, and so initiating them into the whole world of Christian learning. This would fit Eata, Chad and others to become the Christian leaders of the future. In addition to Lindisfarne, Aidan was responsible for persuading the Deiran princess Hild to abandon her plan of joining her sister in a Frankish monastery, and instead to return to Northumbria where she soon became abbess of Hartlepool, and later of the double (i.e. female and male) monastery of Whitby. There, Hild insisted on high standards of biblical study as well as the religious life (*EH* IV. 23). Monasteries required endowments of land, and in 655 King Oswiu, in thanksgiving for victory over the Mercians, gave landed estates for the foundation of twelve monasteries, six in Bernicia and six in Deira. These could provide a network of pastoral care – another key function of monasteries at this period.

Besides establishing monasteries, the Irish mission may also have been better placed than Paulinus's to get alongside the Anglo-Saxons because they came from a not dissimilar society. The key role played by monasteries was itself an adaptation to providing the Church with bases in a society that was not organized around towns. There was also the crucial question of how to transmit a religion that had originally spread within the Roman empire, with its Scriptures and liturgy in Latin or Greek, to a 'barbarian' society that knew neither, and whose culture was orally based. The Irish had already pioneered the teaching of Latin as a foreign language. They adapted the Latin grammars of late antiquity to the needs of non-native speakers, and by 700 had produced five of their own.[19] They also pioneered the use of the vernacular, both prose and verse, for devotional and teaching purposes. Whether this influenced the relatively rapid use of Old English for similar purposes at Hild's Whitby, and by Bede himself, we cannot know; but it seems likely.

Thanks to their role as evangelists and teachers, the Irish contribution to Northumbrian Christianity was everywhere. Of course, it was one Gospel that was preached, whether by Aidan or Paulinus. There are, however, distinctive aspects of Irish Christianity that left their mark: the use of private confession and repeatable penance; various ascetic practices and devotions; a high regard for the hermit's life as facilitating contemplation of God – an attitude that translated into the establishment of hermitages on little islands; and, alongside this, ways of integrating pastoral care with periods of withdrawal for prayer, with Aidan preceding Cuthbert in using Farne for this purpose (*EH* III. 16).[20] In all this, there are just two points to draw out. First, the Irish transmitted to the Anglo-Saxons the ascetic concept of *peregrinatio* as exile or 'pilgrimage'. They regarded God's heavenly kingdom as the place where the Christian truly belonged, and therefore stressed the importance of not being totally absorbed by the society in which they lived. Rather, they voluntarily left their own kingdom for another, or, ideally, went overseas. The primary motivation was as an ascetic form of renunciation, but one of its consequences was a great deal of travel by churchmen. This led to missionary work where they found themselves; it also promoted contacts between Ireland, Britain, Gaul and Italy. The greatest Irish 'pilgrim', Columbanus, had founded monasteries in both Frankia and Italy, and thereafter the pilgrim currents had flowed in all directions: from the continent to Ireland and Britain, between the two islands, and from Ireland and Britain to the continent, with the specific Anglo-Saxon twist that many of them chose to go to Rome, a notable example being Bede's abbot, Ceolfrith. Thus a second point is that we should not think in terms of presenting Irish churchmen as in some sense opposed to or in conflict with continental churchmen. Apart from specific periods and areas of conflict over Easter, it was a time that saw much collaboration; and the continental missionaries who came to England independently of Augustine's mission often, perhaps always, turn out to have had links to Columbanian monasticism on the continent.[21]

In addition to ascetic renunciation and missionary work, a third reason for travel was the desire for learning; and here, seventh-century Ireland had considerable drawing power, thanks to the lively interest with which its scholars engaged with the Bible and Christian scholarship. Visiting students included the Frank Agilbert, one of the 'Roman' representatives at the synod of Whitby (*EH* III. 7). Above all, Ireland was the major destination for Anglo-Saxons. Bede talks of 'many' going to Ireland around the mid seventh century: 'some of these devoted themselves faithfully to the monastic life, while others preferred to travel round to the cells of various teachers and apply themselves to study. The Irish welcomed them all gladly ... and provided them with books to read and with instruction, without asking for any payment' (*EH* III. 27, p. 313). Bede's general picture is confirmed by Aldhelm, and we can name eighteen such individuals.[22] Unfortunately the survival of early Irish manuscripts is pitiful, above all in Ireland itself; and this, together with the tendency of the Irish to write anonymously, or use the name of famous authors like Augustine, makes it hard to identify compositions as being definitely the work of Irish scholars. In 1954, however, Bernhard Bischoff argued the case for Irish composition of an impressive number of biblical commentaries.[23] Since then, scholars have continued to refine and deepen our understanding of seventh-century Irish scholarship.

We may accept, then, that Irish scholarship was flourishing; and we may readily believe that a monastery like Lindisfarne probably derived much of its scholarship and many of its manuscripts from the Irish. Yet how significant was this for Bede? His own monastery was highly unusual in the number of manuscripts imported from the continent. It is therefore easy to assume that most of the library which made Bede's scholarship possible derived from the continent, and that the Irish contributed little beyond the odd rarity, such as the commentary of Philippus on Job. That, however, would be mistaken. In the first place, it has been established that in the field of computistics, at least, Bede's knowledge even of the Dionysian Easter materials, together with many other tracts, letters and excerpts, derived from a computistical collection put together in Ireland, not the continent. The same may well go for Bede's knowledge of Isidore. Secondly, we should not think solely in terms of the provision of books divorced from the context in which those books were used. The crucial thing to remember is that the Irish were the primary teachers of Christian Northumbria; and, as such, they introduced not simply texts, but *texts within a context of Christian teaching and learning.*

Let us begin with this last point. We know little about Bede's teachers, but one at least is named: Trumberht, who had been taught by Chad in his monastery. That takes us straight back to the Irish, since not only was Chad a monk in the tradition of Aidan (*EH* III. 28); he had also spent time in Ireland with Egbert as a young man, leading the religious life. The association with Egbert allows us to identify Chad's monastery in Ireland as Rath Melsigi, in southeast Ireland.[24] This is highly significant, as Rath Melsigi lies in the valley of the Barrow, just thirty-five miles east of a known network of monastic scholars that looked back to Manchian of Min Droichet (d. 652) as their master. This included the Irishman who called himself Augustine, and as such in 655 wrote a lively, original work *On the Miracles of Holy Scripture*, possibly known to Bede. This, in turn, influenced the Irish author of the *Book of the Order of Creatures*, that was definitely known to Bede. The circle also included other exegetes: Laidcenn of Clonfertmulloe, who compiled an abbreviated version of Gregory the Great's commentary on Job, and the anonymous Irish author of the earliest extant Latin commentary on the Catholic Epistles. This, in turn, was used by a second (probably Irish) commentator on the same epistles who wrote under the name of Hilary, and whose work was used – and sometimes criticized – by Bede.[25] In addition,

Ó Cróinín has argued convincingly that it was in this same area, and very probably in association with this same group of scholars, that the Irish computistical collection which Bede used was compiled in 658.[26]

Bede's dependence on this anthology illustrates the significance of Irish scholarship lying behind Bede's works. As well as being a collection of texts, the anthology contained an Irish *computus*; Bede 'borrowed freely both its structure and its content' when he came to compose his own books on time.[27] In his *On the Nature of Things*, Bede made considerable use of the cosmographical work already mentioned, *Book of the Order of Creatures*. This contributed to Bede's understanding of tides, where the Irish preceded him in making use of direct observation.[28] In addition we should note that several of these works used the grammatical works of an idiosyncratic author, probably Irish, who wrote under the name of Virgilius Maro the Grammarian. Bede used his *Epitomies* in his *On Orthography* and perhaps in *The Reckoning of Time*.[29] However, we must not assume that all the Irish works that Bede knew came from this area of southeast Ireland. The most extensive endorsement of any Irish work was Bede's decision to make an abridged version of Adomnán of Iona's *On the Holy Places*, as well as including lengthy excerpts in his *Ecclesiastical History* (v. 15–17).

What the Irish had to offer was thus something of far greater significance than the provision of certain manuscripts. We have identified scholarly circles in Ireland which were active in teaching and discussing texts, and which produced works of Christian cosmography, exegesis, *computus* and grammar. We have also located potential links between the monastic schools of southern Ireland, where many of these were written, and Northumbria, via the monastery of Rath Melsigi and the many Northumbrian *peregrini* to Ireland. Thirdly, we should note that Irish scholars were able to build upon the continental texts and traditions they received to create new works that were suited to their own needs: mastering Latin, interpreting the Scriptures and acquiring extensive computistical skills. The Irish thus pioneered a new curriculum for the new monastic schools. Most significant of all, the Irish transmitted their conviction that plumbing the depths of Scripture and of God's creation was an ongoing task, and that it was something to which contemporary Insular scholars could and should contribute, not just by teaching, but also by writing. Bede, with his excellent library and his outstanding intellectual gifts, was able to build upon this inheritance, and surpass it.

NOTES

1. T. J. Brown 1993: 150.
2. See further Goffart 1988: 256–96 and Bullough 1981.

3. *The Earliest Life of Gregory the Great*, ed. B. Colgrave (Cambridge University Press, 1985), chs. 12–19, pp. 94–104; cf. Bullough 1981: 342.
4. *The Life of Bishop Wilfrid by Eddius Stephanus*, ed. B. Colgrave (Cambridge University Press, 1985), ch. 47, pp. 94–5.
5. Higham 2006: 115–27. However, I reject Higham's view that Bede's *Chronicle* rather than the text of his *Ecclesiastical History* approximates to Bede's own views. See rather Thacker 1996: 50–1.
6. Thacker 2008: 134–44.
7. Thacker 1996: 46–8.
8. Stancliffe 2007.
9. Stancliffe 2003; Charles-Edwards 2000: chs. 7–10.
10. *The Penitential of Theodore*, I. v, in McNeill and Gamer 1990: 188–9.
11. For what follows, see Charles-Edwards 2000: 341–2.
12. Stancliffe 2007.
13. Stancliffe 1999.
14. Bassett 1992; Sims-Williams 1990: 54–86.
15. Stancliffe 1995: 76–80.
16. *The Welsh Annals* under 626; *History of the Britons*, ch. 63, both in *Nennius: British History and Welsh Annals*, ed. and trans. J. Morris (London: Phillimore, 1980), pp. 46, 86, and 38, 79.
17. Hughes 1971; Orschel 2001.
18. Charles-Edwards 2000: 314–15.
19. Holtz 1981.
20. Stancliffe 1989.
21. Campbell 1986: 55–9.
22. Aldhelm, letter 5, in Lapidge and Herren 1979: 160–3. Ó Cróinín 1984: 22, n. 2; Charles-Edwards 2000: 8, n. 2.
23. Bischoff 1954.
24. Cf. *EH* III. 27 and IV. 3. For the significance and identification of Rath Melsigi, see Ó Cróinín 1984.
25. Grosjean 1955; McNally 1973: xii–xv.
26. Ó Cróinín 1983. Cf. Wallis 1999: lxxii–lxxviii.
27. Jones 1943: 110.
28. Picard 2004: 142–4; Stevens 1985: 12–13; Smyth 1996.
29. Picard 2005: 56–7; Bracken 2006.

6

IAN WOOD

The foundation of Bede's
Wearmouth-Jarrow

Wearmouth-Jarrow is famously a single monastery in two places. This is what both Bede's *History of the Abbots* (chs. 7, 15, 18) and the anonymous *Life of Ceolfrith* (chs. 11, 16, 19, 25) tell us on numerous occasions.[1] However, the fact that the point is repeated in both these texts suggests either that it was not common knowledge, or that it was not universally accepted. It is not difficult to see that in certain respects the description of the two houses as forming a single monastery is misleading, hiding a rather more complex reality. St Peter's, Wearmouth, was after all founded in 674 and St Paul's, Jarrow, around seven years later in 681/2. Moreover, the fact that the two houses were founded some years apart meant that their standing in canon law was initially distinct. Thus, when Benedict Biscop secured a privilege from Pope Agatho in 678/80, it only covered the foundation at Wearmouth, since the sister-house was not yet in existence (*HA*, ch. 6; *LC*, ch. 16). Ceolfrith, therefore, had to secure a separate privilege for Jarrow, which he did from Pope Sergius in 701 (*HA*, chs. 16, 18; *LC*, ch. 20). There was, therefore, a period when the part of the monastery based at Wearmouth held a papal privilege, while Jarrow did not.

One might assume that the distinction between the two houses evaporated after Ceolfrith had secured a privilege for Jarrow. Yet even Bede and the author of the *Life of Ceolfrith* seem to have been confused as to whether they were talking about one house or two. In chapter 20 of the *Life of Ceolfrith* the author speaks of 'monasteries' (*monasteria*) in the plural; in the following chapter he uses the singular; in chapter 33 he uses both singular and plural – and one could argue that the singular refers to Wearmouth alone. One finds a similar failure to talk consistently of the monastery of SS Peter and Paul of Wearmouth-Jarrow in later correspondence: Alcuin, for instance, addressed one letter to Wearmouth-Jarrow, another to Jarrow alone, and a third to the monks of St Peter's, in other words Wearmouth.[2]

We might simply be dealing here with a question of shorthand: to address one was to address both. Certainly Hwætberht was elected abbot by the community of both Wearmouth and Jarrow (*HA*, ch. 18; *LC*, ch. 29), so that the title of abbot of St Peter's, which he adopted when addressing Pope Gregory, must be taken as referring to both centres. Yet in the preceding days Ceolfrith had treated the monks of Wearmouth and Jarrow rather differently. He broke the news of his departure to the community at Wearmouth alone, and told the monks there to preserve unity with their brothers at St Paul's (*LC*, chs. 23, 25). No wonder Bede, who appears to have been based at Jarrow at the time,[3] was so upset when he heard of Ceolfrith's imminent departure – he would not even have been among the first of those to be told. And the monks of the latter house actually seem to have played a secondary role in the election of Hwætberht, for only some of them were present at Wearmouth when the new abbot was chosen (*HA*, ch. 18; *LC*, ch. 29). Thus, even after Ceolfrith had secured a privilege from Pope Sergius, which presumably granted the same status to Jarrow as was already held by Wearmouth, the two communities seem to have been treated in slightly different ways. To talk of Wearmouth-Jarrow simply as a single community is to ignore the differences, however slight, between them.

In origin, however, those differences might not have been so slight. My purpose in this chapter is to look at the foundations of each of the houses separately, to show that they differed in significant respects, and indeed that they each faced different problems. I shall also look at the question of the relationship between the two houses, to suggest that Jarrow was not originally conceived as part of Wearmouth,[4] and that the amalgamation of the two was not as simple and straightforward as we have been led to believe. This, perhaps, may explain the failure to talk consistently of a single monastery, even after the death of Benedict Biscop.

The foundation of Wearmouth

Wearmouth, we are told by Bede, was founded by Biscop at Ecgfrith's command, on land granted to him by the king for that purpose (*HA*, chs. 4, 1; *LC*, ch. 5). The immediate context of the foundation would appear to be Biscop's return to Northumbria after his fourth visit to Rome. He had not intended to establish a community in his native country: according to Bede he planned to go to Wessex, but abandoned that idea because of the death of his erstwhile patron, the West Saxon King Cenwalh (*HA*, ch. 4). It is possible that Ecgfrith reckoned that there was a good deal of prestige to be gained in persuading Biscop to remain in Northumbria, especially as he brought with him a significant collection of religious treasure, gathered over the course of various continental visits.

There would appear to have been a gap of a year between the king's initial grant and the construction of the church at Wearmouth (*HA*, ch. 5; *LC*, ch. 7). It is unclear how much one should read into this: although, as we shall see, the foundation of the monastery seems to have been the cause of dispute, this may not have been a feature at the moment of its inception. What is certain is that Biscop spent that time gathering together the senior personnel for his new foundation: Ceolfrith, for instance, was transferred from Ripon, a move which doubtless involved some negotiation with Wilfrid (*LC*, chs. 4, 5) – though relations between Biscop and Wilfrid are likely to have been easier than they were later.[5] Equally important was the decision to build the church (although not, it seems, the conventual buildings) in stone. Securing masons from Gaul may also help account for the time lapse (*HA*, ch. 5; *LC*, ch. 7). There would be an even longer interval between the foundation of Jarrow and the completion of its stone church (*LC*, chs. 11–12).

The gap in time between Ecgfrith's grant and the establishment of Wearmouth is only one, and perhaps the slightest, of the oddities surrounding our knowledge of the origins of the monastery. Certainly more obvious is the conflict between the account of the size of the original land grant given by Bede and that given by the author of the *Life of Ceolfrith*. Bede talks of a grant of seventy hides (*HA*, ch. 4), while the anonymous author talks of fifty, a number that, he says, was later increased with further grants coming from the king and from unnamed nobles (*LC*, ch. 7). How one deals with this discrepancy depends in part on how one regards the relationship of the two texts. The norm is to date the *Life of Ceolfrith* to the decade following Ceolfrith's departure in 716, and to place Bede's *History of the Abbots* in the late 720s.[6] The result of this is that Bede's figures look to be a sharp correction of those in the *Life of Ceolfrith*. This ordering of the texts depends on the argument that when in 725 Bede compiled his *Chronica Maiora*, which forms chapter 66 of *The Reckoning of Time*, he used the *Life of Ceolfrith* rather than his own *History of the Abbots*, which, it has been argued, cannot have been written by that date.[7] It is difficult, however, to see why one should come to such a conclusion: the phrase in the *Chronica Maiora* which is supposedly drawn from the *Life of Ceolfrith* is more likely to have been taken from the *History of the Abbots*.[8] Once this argument has been rejected, Bede's account may most logically be dated to the period between news of Ceolfrith's death reaching Wearmouth-Jarrow, the most recent event contained in the *History of the Abbots*, and the arrival of Pope Gregory's letter of commiseration, of which Bede seems to have been unaware at the time of writing. It is almost unthinkable that he would have ignored so prestigious a source, which is, however, partially transcribed by the anonymous author (*LC*, ch. 39). The *History of the Abbots* should, therefore, be dated to late 716 or early 717, while the *Life of Ceolfrith* should be placed at some point later than the spring of 717, allowing time for the pope's letter to be delivered to Hwætberht and the community of Wearmouth-Jarrow, following the reopening of lines of communication between Rome and Northumbria after the end of winter. This ordering of the texts goes some way to removing any problems raised by the divergent statements concerning the original endowment of Wearmouth: the anonymous author was simply being more precise than Bede.

There does, however, remain a problem: the initial land grant for Wearmouth was clearly the cause of subsequent conflict, so much so, in fact, that Bede felt he had to address the matter in his homily on Benedict Biscop. There Bede states that the monastery was founded on royal land and not on property 'taken away from some lesser persons' (*Homilies on the Gospels* I. 13, p. 129). This is an extraordinary statement, and the fact that it was made in a homily written to commemorate the death of the founder makes it all the more striking. Why did Bede feel that he had to state to the members of his own community, and in the context of the liturgy, that Wearmouth was not founded on land taken from others? One can only conclude that there were some who did not believe that to be the case, and that the disbelievers included members of the first audience of Bede's homily, in other words monks of Wearmouth-Jarrow. Clearly there were some who did not accept that the lands on which Wearmouth was founded had come directly from the pool of land we know to have been held by the king, but believed it to be rather from property that had already been granted out to others.

Unfortunately we know nothing about who else claimed the land. It is just possible that the estate of Wearmouth had once been the site of a monastery governed by Hild, who is known to have lived the monastic life for a short period on a small estate on the north bank of the Wear (*EH* IV. 23). More important, those challenging the rights of Wearmouth seem to have been relatives of Biscop. The question of Biscop's family is one that clearly concerned Bede and the anonymous author. There is reference to a shadowy brother who seems to have been concerned to acquire Wearmouth (*HA*, ch. 11; *LC*, ch. 16) – one might guess that he wished to treat it as a monastery which belonged to his family. The threats posed by the family seem to have been noted in Agatho's privilege for the monastery, which in the paraphrase given in the *Life of Ceolfrith* (ch. 16) specifically banned succession to the abbacy solely on the grounds of blood relationship. The dangers posed by relatives are evoked on a number of occasions in the *History of the Abbots* (chs. 13–14, also 11), not least in the advice delivered by the dying Biscop to his community. The same theme appears at the equivalent point of the *Life of Ceolfrith* (ch. 16). That Bede also seems to associate the threats posed by family members with internal division may provide further evidence, alongside that of the homily on Biscop, to suggest that there were partisans of Biscop's brother within the community (*HA*, ch. 13).

Wearmouth was, therefore, a house seen by some as being founded on royal land, conveyed specifically to Biscop for the purpose, and by others as being a family monastery to which Biscop's brother, and presumably his descendants, had a claim. There were, it would seem, those who regarded Wearmouth as being no different from the family monasteries derided by Bede in his *Letter to Bishop Egbert*. One of Bede's principal concerns in the *History of the Abbots* would, therefore, seem to have been to address this very issue, and to make it clear that Wearmouth should not be so categorized.

We should, however, note the strength of the opposition's case. Although Biscop was intent on ensuring that no brother of his should take over the monastery, his first co-abbot, Eosterwine, was a relative (*HA*, ch. 8). So too was Ceolfrith, first abbot of Jarrow, and Biscop's ultimate successor at Wearmouth (*HA*, ch. 13). Indeed, it is worth remembering Ceolfrith's position as a relative of Biscop when one notes his initial transfer from Ripon to Wearmouth, and his subsequent progression through the monastery's offices (*LC*, chs. 5, 6, 8, 10, 12; cf. *HA*, ch. 7). His early position is described in notably vague and suggestive terms by the anonymous author: he is *adiutor et cooperator*, that is, a 'helper and fellow-worker' (*LC*, ch. 5, p. 215).[9] To Eosterwine and Ceolfrith one might perhaps add Bede himself as possibly being a further relative of Biscop: that is, if the curious text known as the Lindsey Genealogy has any relevance, for that list includes the names Biscop Beding and Beda Bubbing, that is, Biscop son of Beda, and Beda son of Bubba, which might suggest that Bede and Biscop were related.[10] If that were the case, it may be significant that Bede is said in the Old English translation of the *Ecclesiastical History* to have been born in Sunderland: that is, on the south side of the Wear, directly opposite Wearmouth.[11] Interestingly, the estate seems to have been purchased subsequently by Biscop, and conveyed to his monastery. All this might be construed as indicating that, for nearly half a century after its foundation, Wearmouth was dominated by the family of Biscop. Of course, Bede argued that Eosterwine and Ceolfrith gained their positions through virtue and not family connection, thus conforming to the privilege of Agatho (*LC*, ch. 16). But it is not difficult to see how some could have read the evidence differently: that a faction surrounding Biscop's brother thought that he, and they, had been badly done by; and that Bede felt the need to address them and their concerns, both in the *History of the Abbots* and also in his homily for the anniversary of Biscop's death.

Wearmouth, then, was founded by Biscop, albeit on land given by the king and on the king's orders. The grant of property, however – or perhaps the other estates subsequently conveyed – was such that members of Biscop's family rightly or wrongly thought they had a claim to the land or that they should have had some role in the running of the monastery. This was something that Biscop and his successors denied, and it is their position that is represented by Bede and the anonymous author. The arguments they put forward, however, supply us with our only evidence for the opposition's case.

The foundation of Jarrow

While some of these issues must also have affected Jarrow, other matters come to the fore when we consider what can be established of its foundation and early history.[12] Again our evidence derives almost entirely from Bede's *History of the Abbots* and from the *Life of Ceolfrith*. According to Bede, Ecgfrith was so delighted by Biscop's work at Wearmouth that he gave him a further forty hides for the construction of a new monastery at Jarrow. A year later Biscop built a monastery dedicated to Saint Paul, on the advice and command of the king, and sent Ceolfrith as abbot, together with seventeen monks (*HA*, ch. 7). The new foundation was to be joined to Wearmouth as the head is to the body: in short, the two houses were to be fully integrated. As we have already seen, this does not seem to be borne out by the facts.

Just as the account of the foundation of Wearmouth given by the anonymous author seems to depart in certain interesting ways from that provided by Bede, so too does that of the foundation of Jarrow. This time the two authors agree on the size of the grant, but in other respects the anonymous seems to modify Bede's picture or at least to provide further detail. Thus, he gives some important information on the first year of the community: having taken over the site, Ceolfrith and his followers had first to erect all the buildings necessary for the monastery (*LC*, ch. 11). These did not include the church, the construction of which was only begun after three years (*LC*, ch. 12). More intriguing is the disagreement of the two authors over the number of monks transferred from Wearmouth. According to Bede seventeen were involved; according to the anonymous there were twenty-two brothers, ten tonsured and twelve untonsured (*HA*, ch. 7; *LC*, ch. 11). This may, in fact, be the simple result of a scribal error. The seventeen in Bede's text may be a confusion of xvii for xxii in Roman numerals. Yet the *Life of Ceolfrith* provides some details which suggest that the original community at Jarrow was not simply made up of a group sent from Wearmouth. Strangely, the anonymous author asserts that not all the monks assigned to the new foundation could sing in the same style (*LC*, ch. 11). Given the emphasis laid on Biscop's success in bringing John the archcantor to Wearmouth to teach the monks how to sing in the Roman style, both by Bede and by the anonymous (*HA*, ch. 6; *LC*, ch. 10), this seems an extraordinary admission, and is surely best seen as an indication that the original community at Jarrow was not simply made up of monks from Wearmouth. One possible place of origin for some of the other inmates is a monastery two miles away at South Shields, which we learn from Bede's *Life of Saint Cuthbert* (see ch. 3) was transformed into a nunnery, probably at about this time. The monks presumably had to be accommodated elsewhere.

There are, however, additional indications that Jarrow was something other than an annexe to Wearmouth. Unlike the older house it was founded, as the *Life of Ceolfrith* asserts very precisely, by Ecgfrith 'for the redemption of his soul' (*LC*, ch. 11, p. 216). The vogue for donations *pro anima* was only just beginning at this time,[13] and it seems that Ecgfrith was very deliberately following a growing trend. His involvement in the foundation of Jarrow is further emphasized by the fact that he took care to mark out the place on which the altar of the monastery should stand (*LC*, ch. 12). It seems significant that the dedication stone of the church, which still survives, names Ceolfrith as abbot, and highlights the fact that the dedication took place in the fourth year of Ecgfrith's reign.[14] Equally notably, there is no mention of Biscop.

What is one to make of Biscop's role in the foundation of Jarrow? Both Bede and the anonymous author mention him as being the recipient of the estate on which the monastery was founded, and the *Life of Ceolfrith*, in its death notice for Biscop, claims that he took care of Jarrow through Ceolfrith (ch. 18). Interestingly, the language the author uses to describe his position at St Paul's differs from that used to describe his rule at St Peter's: in the later case he 'ruled' (*regebat*) and in the former he 'exercised care through Ceolfrith' (*per Ceolfridum curam impendebat*; my translation). It is clear that Ceolfrith and some monks were transferred from Wearmouth to the new centre, which must imply that the new foundation had Biscop's approval – although the presence of Ceolfrith, despite the fact that he was related to Biscop, does not of itself prove that the two men were working together: he had, after all, already returned from Wearmouth to Ripon on one occasion, because he was not happy at Biscop's foundation (*LC*, ch. 8). In addition, Biscop's involvement in the new monastery can be seen in the fact that he brought icons back from Rome to adorn its walls (*LC*, ch. 9). At the same time, the journey to Rome should raise suspicions about the extent to which he was really in charge of the new foundation, for it meant that he was in Italy at precisely the time that the church of Jarrow was dedicated.[15] This tends to support the impression given by the dedication inscription: that the main figures in the foundation of Jarrow were Ceolfrith and Ecgfrith. As for Biscop's purchase of icons, these may have been made at the king's request: certainly he would have needed royal approval to leave Northumbria and to travel to Rome.

There is one further indication that Jarrow, in its earliest years, was not so closely tied to Wearmouth that it could rely on support from the older house. Only a short while after the foundation of the new monastery, the house was badly hit by plague to the extent that, according to the anonymous author, all who could read, preach or say the antiphons and responses, died, with the exception of the abbot and one young boy. Unable to cope, Ceolfrith initially decided to perform a much reduced liturgy; but he found this so upsetting that he quickly reinstated the full course of worship (*LC*, ch. 14).[16] This story has been much commented on, because scholars have argued as to whether or not the young boy, who we are told was still alive at the time of writing and had spoken and written much in praise of Ceolfrith, was Bede himself – which is indeed likely. What has not been noted is the simple point that, had Jarrow been no more than an annexe of Wearmouth, Ceolfrith could have solved his liturgical problem by sending to the mother-house for assistance.

What we, therefore, seem to see is that Jarrow was not simply a daughter-house of Wearmouth, despite the rhetoric of unity which suffuses the *History of the Abbots* and the *Life of Ceolfrith*. Although Jarrow drew its abbot and some of its first inmates from the older foundation, and although Biscop clearly contributed in certain respects to the new house, not least in providing it with a set of icons for its church, it should initially be seen as Ecgfrith's foundation, established primarily for the redemption of his soul. While Ecgfrith provided the land for Wearmouth and commanded its foundation, at Jarrow in addition he specifically acted for his own salvation.

Ecgfrith and Jarrow

We can, I think, come a little closer to understanding Ecgfrith's interest in Jarrow, when we study its setting on the River Tyne more carefully. Jarrow overlooks what was once one of the finest harbours in the north of England, a set of mudflats, known as the Slake, now sadly concreted over to provide a car park for the Nissan car plant (see Map 4).[17] This great stretch of tidal water, protected from the open sea by the headland of South Shields, provided an ideal place to beach ships in the days when quays and jetties were not required. The area would seem to have given its name to Jarrow, since the name 'Gyrwe' refers to fen or marsh land,[18] but the harbour itself was known in the Middle Ages as the *Portus Ecgfridi*: the Harbour of Ecgfrith,[19] which suggests that it was a site with which the king had been closely associated. The proximity of the harbour, of course, should be taken into account when considering Bede's foreign contacts and his interest in the phenomenon of the tide.

One further name draws attention to the interest of the king in the region of the lower Tyne: *Ecgferthes mynster*, a nunnery which would seem to have been called *Donemutha* (Old English: 'mouth of the Don'), and was probably situated at South Shields, on the very headland which protected Jarrow Slake from the open sea (see Map 4).[20] It may well have been this house which was changed from being a monastery into a nunnery, thereby providing Jarrow with some of its earliest inmates.[21] Ecgfrith would seem, then, to have been particularly interested in the lower Tyne: his name was associated with the Slake and *Donemutha*, the *Portus Ecgfridi* and *Ecgferthes mynster*, and Jarrow was founded for the redemption of his soul.

There is at least one other site which is not associated with Ecgfrith in any source, but where he may well have stayed, and which certainly has importance for our understanding of Jarrow, and of Bede's work, especially of the *Ecclesiastical History*. It would seem that the Roman fort at Arbeia, on the top of the headland at South Shields, was still used in the Middle Saxon period (see Map 4). The evidence for this comes partly from archaeology,[22] and partly from information supplied to the antiquarian John Leland in the early years of the sixteenth century, when the monks of Tynemouth, a monastery on the north side of the Tyne, claimed that the Northumbrian king Oswine had been born in the nearby site of Urfa, which would seem to have been a corrupt form of the Roman name Arbeia.[23] If, as seems likely, Arbeia/Urfa was the site of a royal palace in the seventh century, this further highlights the extent to which the origins of Jarrow need to be understood in the context of Ecgfrith's policy in the lower Tyne. It also suggests that, when dedicating the *Ecclesiastical History* to Ceolwulf, Bede was addressing a man who may often have been resident within sight of St Paul's monastery.

It is worth speculating on the precise implications of all this for the dedication of the church of St Paul at Jarrow. The dedication stone records that this took place on 25 April 685. It is likely, given that the monastery was founded for the redemption of his soul and, also, given his interest in the placing of the altar, that Ecgfrith was present. Just under a month later, on 20 or 21 May,[24] he was dead, killed at the battle of Nechtanesmere, which is now thought to have taken place in the region of Lorne, in the western part of the Pictish kingdom.[25] He would seem to have travelled west, via Carlisle, where he probably took leave of his wife, who waited there for news of his expedition (*Life of Saint Cuthbert*, ch. 27). It was at Carlisle that she was told of the disaster at Nechtanesmere, and urged to flee for safety, to the *urbs regia*, which is usually identified as Bamburgh, but may at this time have been Arbeia/Urfa. The dedication of Jarrow, then, may have marked the last great public act of Ecgfrith.

In its very first years, then, Jarrow's profile was distinct from that of Wearmouth. However much it drew from the style of monasticism established by Biscop at the older house, it was more firmly a royal house, and needs to be understood in the context of Ecgfrith's interests in the lower Tyne. Its position next to the Slake may also explain one of the more puzzling aspects of the endowment initially of Jarrow, but subsequently of the combined monastery. From what we learn of the endowment of the house, both from Bede and also from the anonymous author, neither Wearmouth nor Jarrow was spectacularly rich in the extent of their estates. They do not, for instance, seem to have possessed as much land as Wilfrid's foundations.[26] It is, therefore, not easy to see where they found the resources to play the great role that has plausibly been assigned to them in the production of manuscripts in the years after Bede's death.[27] One solution is to suppose that, along with the estates granted to Jarrow by Ecgfrith, there were also some rights relating to the harbour that lay at the very gates of the monastery.

One monastery in two places

Given the differences between the two houses, how and why did they come together in such a way as to seem plausibly to reflect the rhetoric of unity that is such a feature of the *History of the Abbots* and the *Life of Ceolfrith*? There was, of course, a good deal to build on: Ceolfrith had been closely associated with Biscop; a significant number of the original monks at Jarrow would seem to have been drawn from Wearmouth (*HA*, ch. 7; *LC*, ch. 11); and Ceolfrith would seem to have been concerned to ensure that the new house followed the rule devised by Biscop, and that it performed the same liturgy (*LC*, chs. 11, 14). As we have already seen, Biscop acquired icons for Jarrow during the visit he made to Rome immediately after the foundation of the monastery (*HA*, ch. 9). And it is clear that Ceolfrith retained a close interest in Wearmouth even during the first years of Jarrow's existence. When Eosterwine died during Biscop's absence, Ceolfrith was involved in the election of Sigfrith as his successor (*HA*, ch. 10; *LC*, ch. 13). The choice may not have been to Biscop's taste: William of Malmesbury, who may have had access to evidence now lost, implies that he was not entirely happy at not being consulted.[28] Since Sigfrith was apparently the first of the abbots or leading figures of Wearmouth not to be related to Biscop, one might wonder whether he would have preferred the election of someone more closely associated with himself, despite his avowed desire to ignore family connections – a suggestion that might imply that the strongest opposition to the influence of relatives should be attributed to Ceolfrith and Bede rather than to Biscop himself.

A number of factors may well explain the tightening of links between the two houses from the summer of 685 onwards. The first of these is the death of Ecgfrith and the succession of his half-brother Aldfrith. Since Jarrow would seem to have been founded especially for the salvation of the soul of the former, we may assume that with his death it lost its main patron. Equally important, Ecgfrith seems not to have been on good terms with his successor. During his reign Aldfrith was in exile on Iona, and there may have been some apprehension about his return.[29] Aldfrith is unlikely to have been concerned to promote a house founded by Ecgfrith for his own salvation. At the same time there were a number of leading figures in Northumbria, including Cuthbert, who had been strongly critical of Ecgfrith's policies in his last years (*EH* IV. 26). Thus, there may not have been much of a faction inclined to celebrate the memory of the dead king. It would not, therefore, be at all surprising if Jarrow lost some of its prestige and independence in the context of Aldfrith's takeover of power.

Meanwhile Biscop had returned from Rome, only to find that Ecgfrith had been killed (*HA*, ch. 9). Biscop's return must have facilitated the tightening of ties between the two houses. Moreover, on his return he presented Jarrow with the icons he had purchased for St Peter's (*HA*, ch. 9). It could easily have been at this juncture that Wearmouth and Jarrow were essentially combined into a single monastery. On the other hand, it may be that the real point of amalgamation came with or just before Biscop's death. According to Bede, Ceolfrith acted as co-abbot at Wearmouth in the last year of Biscop's life (*HA*, ch. 14). On the latter's death he took the running of the monastery entirely into his own hands, thus exercising the same office there that he already exercised at Jarrow (*HA*, ch. 9; for a description of Biscop's intention, cf. *LC*, ch. 16).

Yet, as we have seen, even after Ceolfrith took over the rule of both houses, the two seem to have been treated slightly differently – as is apparent above all in Ceolfrith's apparent intention not to convey his decision to retire personally to the community of Jarrow; and this is echoed in the fact that the monks of Wearmouth would appear to have been better represented at the election of Hwætberht as his successor (*LC*, chs. 23, 25, 29; Bede is less forthcoming, *HA*, ch. 18). It would seem that, even at this stage, Wearmouth was treated as the senior house. Whether Jarrow ever came to be treated as a complete equal is unclear: if it was, one might wonder whether that simply reflected the prestige of Bede, who may have been based there: he seems to have been rather more closely associated with the house on the Tyne than with that on the Wear.

Conclusion

Although Wearmouth and Jarrow seem to have been amalgamated to form a single house, it is unlikely that they were so conceived at the time of the foundation of St Paul's. The picture of their unity from the moment that Jarrow was established seems rather to be a construct, and it seems to have been one that was contested. It appears that, in their opening years, different issues affected each of the houses, and that these issues actually played a part in making the image of a joint-house necessary. For Jarrow, the major issue seems to have been its association with Ecgfrith, which became something of a liability after his death. For Wearmouth, the claims made by Biscop's family seem to have been more important. And they would still seem to have been important in 716 when Ceolfrith ensured that his successor was elected without his family dominating the election. That this was still a live issue is clear from the emphasis placed on it by both Bede and the anonymous author, both of whom were writing only shortly after his departure. If Bede was, indeed, a relative of Biscop, who better could have attacked the threat of family influence or advocated a free election? We see Wearmouth-Jarrow above all through the eyes of one party addressing a particular issue, that of abbatial succession, at a precise moment – a major break in a family's control of a monastery. We need to be aware that we are looking at a history of monastic foundation through the eyes of two men who essentially represented a single side of an argument, and to note that what they offered was a construct that was contested at the time.

NOTES

1. In subsequent parenthetical references, these texts will be referred to as *HA* and *LC* respectively. Quotations are from the English translations in Farmer 2004.
2. Alcuin, Letters 19, 286 and 284, in E. Dümmler (ed.), *Epistolae Karolini aevi*, vol. 2, Monumenta Germaniae Historica 4 (Berlin: Weidmann, 1895), pp. 53, 444, 442.
3. This is an inference from Bede's famous statement in *On First Samuel*, p. 212.
4. For detailed accounts of the early years of Jarrow alone, see Wood 1995, 2006, and 2008.
5. *The Life of Bishop Wilfrid by Eddius Stephanus*, ed. and trans. B. Colgrave (Cambridge University Press, 1985), chs. 15–22, pp. 32–47, presents the period between 669 and 678 as a time when Wilfrid was well regarded by the king and court in Northumbria. After his fall from grace in 679 he may have found himself in direct conflict with Biscop, who may have presented Ecgfrith's case against him at the papal court: cf. *Life of Bishop Wilfrid*, chs. 29–34, pp. 57–71, with the accounts of Biscop at Rome in the same year in *History of the Abbots*, ch. 6 and in the *Life of Ceolfrith*, ch. 9.
6. Goffart 1988: 277, n. 195; Coates 1999: 72, n. 18.
7. Goffart 1988: 257, n. 112.
8. The idea derives from a footnote in Mommsen's edition of the *Chronica Maiora*, but the more recent edition, by C. W. Jones in CCSL 123B (Turnhout: Brepols, 1977), p. 534 n., more plausibly gives the *History of the Abbots* as the source.
9. Cf. Bede's *adiutor strenuissimus*, translated by Farmer as 'the greatest help' – *History of the Abbots*, ch. 7, p. 193.
10. Campbell 2004, as well as Campbell's remarks in this volume, Chapter 2, pp. 25–6.

11. Plummer 1896: vol. I, p. ix, n. 2.
12. See Wood 2006 and 2008a.
13. Fichtenau 1957: 141–4.
14. Wood 2008a: 3.
15. *Ibid.*, 12.
16. *Ibid.*, 14.
17. *Ibid.*, 6.
18. Cramp *et al.* 2005–6: 8–9.
19. Symeon of Durham, *Libellus de exordio atque procursu istius hoc est Dunhelmensis ecclesie*, ed. D. Rollason, Oxford Medieval Texts (Oxford: Clarendon Press, 2000), II. 5, pp. 89–91. See also Wood 2008a: 18.
20. *Anglo-Saxon Chronicle*, s.a. 794, in *English Historical Documents c. 500–1042*, ed. and trans. D. Whitelock (London: Eyre and Spottiswoode, 1955), pp. 167–8. See also Wood 2008a: 18–22. For a different reading, with a full list of the relevant sources, see Parker 1985.
21. Wood 2008a: 22.
22. *Ibid.*, 23
23. *Ibid.*, 23–4 and 2008b: 20.
24. Wood 2008a: 6.
25. Woolf 2006.
26. G. R. J. Jones 1995: 22–38.
27. Parkes 1982.
28. William of Malmesbury, *Gesta pontificum Anglorum*, ed. and trans. M. Winterbottom, 2 vols. (Oxford: Clarendon Press, 2007), vol. I, pp. 496–7.
29. See, for example, the *Anonymous Life of Saint Cuthbert*, III. 6, in *Two Lives of Saint Cuthbert*, ed. B. Colgrave (Cambridge University Press, 1985), p. 105; cf. Bede, *Life of Saint Cuthbert*, ch. 24, and *Ecclesiastical History* IV. 26.

PART II

Bede's writings

7

CALVIN B. KENDALL

Bede and education

Education in Britain and the West

The Venerable Bede occupies a pivotal place and moment in the history of Western education.[1] By the seventh century public schools no longer existed in Europe; only scattered remnants of the liberal aristocratic educational system of the Roman empire remained in northern Italy and Spain, none at all in Gaul and Britain. Bede's lifetime coincides with the revival of education and the beginnings of a new medieval Christian culture in the West.[2] Bede's monastery of Wearmouth-Jarrow is the nodal point and Bede the intellectual force that link the civilization of the ancient world with the Carolingian renaissance, which fuelled in its turn the renaissances of the twelfth and the fifteenth and sixteenth centuries.

In Britain, the old educational system had disappeared without leaving a trace. Missionaries from the continent and from Ireland, beginning with the Gregorian mission under Augustine in 597, carried out their work of conversion most effectively through the establishment of monasteries. Monks had to be trained for their vocation; monastic schools followed inevitably. Irish models of scholarship and monastic education exerted their influence throughout the seventh century. There was no formal division of the curriculum into subjects along the lines of the seven liberal arts of late classical antiquity. Pupils learned what they needed to know by a kind of apprenticeship system. Young boys were put under the tutelage of an older monk – a master with his disciples, possibly in groups of ten on the model of the *decania* described in the Benedictine Rule (ch. 21), although the Rule does not concern itself specifically with education. One learned in part by imitating and doing. Details elude us. If a room were set aside for instruction, the scene may have resembled a 'blab' school of the American frontier. Rote memorization, effected by repeating aloud the text to be studied, was the primary method of instruction, followed by dictation onto wax tablets. Oblates and novices needed only to acquire enough Latin to be able to perform the Divine Office.

99

With the arrival at Canterbury of Archbishop Theodore in 669 and Abbot Hadrian *c.* 670, we are on more solid ground. Theodore reorganized the episcopal school and gave Hadrian the monastery of St Peter and St Paul of Canterbury, where Benedict Biscop, the future abbot of Wearmouth-Jarrow, ruled for two years until Hadrian was ready to take up his duties. Bede informs us that Theodore and Hadrian 'were extremely learned in sacred and secular literature', and that they 'gave their hearers instruction not only in the books of Holy Scripture but also in the art of metre, astronomy, and ecclesiastical computation' (*EH* IV. 2, p. 333). Their students learned musical chant and Greek as well as Latin. Hadrian's pupil Aldhelm adds that he studied Roman law.

Education at Wearmouth-Jarrow

In evaluating Bede's achievement, it is important to underscore the symbiotic relationship between Bede and his abbots, Benedict Biscop and Ceolfrith. His achievement depends absolutely on their extraordinary and, one wants to add, improbable efforts to create a centre for learning in Northumbria. He is impossible to imagine without them, just as they would be an obscure footnote in history without his achievement. Bede stands on the shoulders of two giants. Benedict Biscop imported much of the programme of studies at Canterbury to Northumbria when he established the monastery of St Peter at Wearmouth in 674. Bede was probably born less than a year before this establishment, and he entered the monastery at the age of seven. A year or so later, in 681, Benedict chose a small number of monks, with Ceolfrith as their abbot, to build the sister monastery of St Paul at Jarrow. Whether the young Bede was in this initial group is unclear, but he certainly came under Ceolfrith's tutelage as a boy. In Bede's own words,

> When I was seven years of age I was, by the care of my kinsmen, put into the charge of the reverend Abbot Benedict and then of Ceolfrith, to be educated. From then on I have spent all my life in this monastery, applying myself entirely to the study of the Scriptures; and, amid the observance of the discipline of the Rule and the daily task of singing in the church, it has always been my delight to learn or to teach or to write. (*EH* V. 24, p. 567)

Despite the fact that the monastery of Wearmouth-Jarrow was no older than Bede himself, there must have been scholarship of a high order there already in Bede's youth. Latin, which was not the native tongue of any inhabitant of Britain, was the language of instruction. No doubt Bede was a precociously advanced student and, as he implies in his *Letter to Bishop Egbert* (ch. 5), he certainly supplied deficiencies in his formal instruction from his own extensive reading. But fluent mastery of Latin requires contact with highly educated Latin speakers. Bede's Latin is classically correct, displaying none of the mannerisms of the flamboyant style favoured by Insular authors like Aldhelm nor any of the grammatical solecisms of continental authors like Gregory of Tours (see Chapter 3).

In addition to mastering the language, Bede was trained in Latin versification to the point where he could compose quantitatively correct classical metres and in mathematics and astronomy to the extent that he was able to work out the most difficult problems of the *computus* (roughly, the science of determining by astronomical calculation the date of Easter). It must be emphasized that both of these attainments are more remarkable than may at first appear. To compose quantitative verse in an age when speakers of Latin were no longer able to distinguish the difference between a long and a short vowel aurally, and when no dictionaries existed to preserve the historical vowel lengths of classical antiquity, necessitated committing to memory a prodigious amount of classical verse. And to carry out complex calculations that require long division or the use of fractions is several orders of magnitude more difficult and laborious when working with Roman than it is with Arabic numerals. Bede surely owed his accomplishment both to a superb memory and to an elite cadre of teachers.

Who were Bede's teachers and where were they trained? These questions are inextricably linked with the history of the twin monastery and the personnel whom Benedict Biscop brought with him to assist in the double foundation. Benedict himself would have had the opportunity of learning or improving his knowledge of Latin on his first trip to Rome in 653 at the age of about twenty-five, and of polishing it further in the course of his subsequent trips, especially his second trip *c.* 664, when, after several months in Rome, he left to spend two years in the monastery of St Honoratus at Lérins (*History of the Abbots*, chs. 1–2). On his return from Lérins to Rome, the pope appointed Benedict to be Theodore and Hadrian's guide on their journey to Britain and interpreter of their teachings when they got there (*History of the Abbots*, ch. 3). The appointment presumes his bilingual fluency.

But Bede's opportunities to be tutored by Benedict would have been limited. Benedict was in Rome during a good part of 679, at approximately the time when Bede entered Wearmouth as an oblate. Shortly after Benedict's appointment of Ceolfrith as abbot of the new foundation of Jarrow (681) and of Eosterwine as abbot of Wearmouth (682), he again set out for Rome, not to return until after Eosterwine's death in 686 (*History of the Abbots*, chs. 8–10). It was precisely on account of his frequent absences that he named these men to be abbots under him. After suffering for three years from a creeping paralysis, Benedict died in 690 when Bede was seventeen or eighteen (*History of the Abbots*, chs. 11 and 14).

It is widely assumed that Bede's principal teacher was Ceolfrith. Ceolfrith received his training in several monasteries around England, among them Wilfrid's monastery of Ripon, where he seems to have been Wilfrid's protégé.[3] He accompanied Benedict Biscop on his trip to Rome in 678–9 (*EH* IV. 18; *History of the Abbots*, ch. 7). After having been abbot of Jarrow since 681, Ceolfrith was appointed abbot of both monasteries in 690, when Bede was about sixteen, and he remained in that post until 716 when he resigned his office and departed for Rome. The two monasteries were only about seven miles apart and there must have been much intercourse between them. Nevertheless the physical separation can only have increased the constraints upon Ceolfrith's time as he exercised his duties as abbot. In his later years he is reported to have chanted the entire Psalter twice each day.[4] Even if he did so in an abbreviated format this would have constituted a substantial temporal drain on a day already filled with administrative obligations and the routine of the Divine Office. Bede inserted a letter from Ceolfrith to Nechtan, the king of the Picts, into the *Ecclesiastical History* (V. 21), which letter Bertram Colgrave describes as being 'one of the clearest accounts of the Easter controversy to be found anywhere in writers ancient or modern'.[5] There is some doubt whether the letter is the work of Ceolfrith or of Bede. But, even if Bede drafted the letter, he surely would not have presented it as he did in the *Ecclesiastical History* if he and the monastic community did not regard Ceolfrith as an authority on the Easter question and the *computus*. It is therefore possible that Ceolfrith instructed Bede in the *computus* and perhaps in the mathematics on which it depends. One cannot help but wonder whether he would have had time to teach Bede much else.

In addition to Benedict Biscop and Ceolfrith, we know of several other highly educated men who might have engaged intellectually with Bede during his formative years. At the instance of Pope Agatho, Benedict and Ceolfrith brought John, the archcantor of Rome, with them back to Wearmouth after their trip to Rome in 678–9 to teach the monks the Roman mode of chanting. John remained at the monastery for a year or so, training its cantors in singing and reading, and instructing singers from other monasteries all over Britain who came to hear him (*EH* IV. 18). Though the precise length of John's stay at Wearmouth is unknown, it certainly overlapped with Bede's initial time as a novice there. John may have been a formidable influence at a very impressionable moment in Bede's early years.

Eosterwine and Sigfrith were successive abbots of Wearmouth under Benedict Biscop. Bede lauds Eosterwine (abbot 682–6) for his piety and humility, but says nothing about his scholarship. He describes Sigfrith (abbot 686–9) as being 'well-grounded in scriptural knowledge' (*History of the Abbots*, ch. 10, p. 197), although he was hampered by his infirmities.

How much opportunity the young Bede, seven miles away at Jarrow, would have had to be instructed by either of them is unclear. Bede informs us that 'one of those who taught me the Scriptures' was the monk Trumberht (*EH* IV. 3, p. 343). Trumberht had been educated at the monastery of Lastingham under the direction of Bishop Chad. Chad, who is described as being 'learned in the scriptures' (III. 28, p. 317), was a disciple of the Irish monk Aidan. The Celtic connection is significant (see Chapter 5, pp. 78–82); Wearmouth-Jarrow was at the confluence of streams of influence from the principal intellectual centres of western Europe – Ireland, Frankish Gaul, Rome, Spain and Canterbury. Bede himself had a high regard for the calibre of Irish schools (e.g. III. 27). Another of his teachers could have been Witmer, a man whom he describes as being 'well-versed in every branch of secular learning as well as in the scriptures' (*History of the Abbots*, ch. 15, p. 203). Witmer entered the monastery of Wearmouth as an older man in Ceolfrith's time. He was wealthy enough to make an important donation of land to the monastery and one wonders where he might have received his education (at Canterbury?). But again, Bede being at Jarrow, his opportunities to learn from him may have been circumscribed.

Bede's contemporary, Hwætberht, like Bede, entered the monastery at an early age. When he was elected abbot in 716, he had been a priest for twelve years. Hwætberht's master was Abbot Sigfrith of Wearmouth. There he had been taught 'the arts of writing, chanting, reading and teaching' (*History of the Abbots*, ch. 18, p. 206). This programme is instructive both for what it includes and for what it omits. Reading, writing and chanting were fundamental to the monastic curriculum. There is no mention of the *computus*, but Bede adds 'teaching'. Bede's passionate commitment to teaching is beyond question. This statement, whether it refers to the subjects to be taught or the methods to be employed in teaching them, is precious evidence that other teachers at Wearmouth-Jarrow thought about what they were doing and made a conscious effort to pass those reflections on to the next generation.

There must be teachers and scholars whose names we do not know – some missing persons in Bede's educational background with more time to tutor the young Bede than Ceolfrith and others just mentioned. The most conservative (hence classical) speakers of Latin in the seventh century would have been found in Spain. It is possible that one or more of Bede's teachers were Spanish or had Spanish connections, perhaps through Ireland. This would be consistent with, and might help explain, the fact that manuscripts of Isidore of Seville's works were second in number only to those of Gregory the Great's in Anglo-Saxon England in Bede's time.[6] Bede drew extensively on Isidore's works, especially his *Etymologies* and *On the Nature of Things*, and on his deathbed, according to his pupil Cuthbert, he was compiling a series of extracts from, or corrections to, the latter work, possibly in English translation.[7]

On his later trips to Rome Benedict Biscop went to great lengths to collect manuscripts for the monastic library, and Ceolfrith followed his example. When Ceolfrith set out for Rome for the last time his travelling party consisted of some eighty men, which suggests ample capacity to carry books (*History of the Abbots*, ch. 21).[8] Thanks to their efforts, in Bede's maturity the library of Wearmouth-Jarrow may have been the most extensive in western Europe (see Chapter 3). Laistner listed seventy-eight authors as being with a greater or lesser degree of probability among Bede's sources.[9] Most of them would have been in the Wearmouth-Jarrow library, though Bede may have borrowed some from elsewhere. The library was well supplied with patristic authors such as Ambrose, Augustine, Basil, Cassian, Gregory and Jerome. One of the treasures which Benedict Biscop brought back from Rome was the Codex Grandior of Cassiodorus, an Old Latin version of the Bible, which became the model for three enormous pandects (complete texts) of the Vulgate Bible produced in the monastery's scriptorium – one for Wearmouth, one for Jarrow, and the third, the surviving Codex Amiatinus, which Ceolfrith planned to present to the pope (see Figures 3, 4 and 7). The library possessed other editions both of the Vulgate and of the Old Latin Bible, as well as some parts of the Bible in Greek. Historians in the collection included Eusebius (in Latin translation), Gildas, Gregory of Tours, Josephus (in Latin translation), Orosius and Prosper. Late Latin poets and grammarians were well represented. But of the standard authors of classical antiquity there is hardly a trace. Parts of Pliny's *Natural History* and the works of Vergil were probably the only classical texts to which Bede had full access.[10]

Bede as educator

We think of Bede as the 'schoolmaster' of his monastery. In the first years of the fledgeling establishment, Abbot Benedict Biscop may have taken upon himself the responsibility of training his monks, but by the time of his death Wearmouth and Jarrow numbered some 300 monks, and under Ceolfrith their numbers doubled again. At this size, no single abbot or teacher could have handled all the educational needs of both monasteries. The choirmaster held a recognized position in the monastery. It is unlikely that there was a parallel 'schoolmaster', formally speaking. There was no term for such a position in common use at the time, and Bede may never have thought of himself as an educator *per se*. Was Bede only one senior monk among many who passed on what they knew to their pupils, or was he recognized as pre-eminent in this domain? Did he and the others implement a generally agreed-upon programme of studies, or was he at some point and in some way in charge of the curriculum of Jarrow? How was instruction organized? Was a room or rooms designated for the purpose of instruction? Questions like these can only be approached indirectly and with circumspection.

Bede's ordination as deacon in *c.* 691 perhaps coincides with the time he began instructing younger monks; a pressing need for qualified teachers coupled with his obvious abilities might explain his being made deacon at the uncanonical age of nineteen. Much of his time and energy in the decade before his ordination as priest and in the years immediately following apparently went into composing textbooks suited to the practical needs of monastic education at Jarrow – elementary Latin (*On Orthography*), Latin verse composition and scriptural studies (*The Art of Poetry* and *The Figures of Rhetoric*), and the *computus* (*On Times* and *On the Nature of Things*). With these basic needs taken care of, he could turn his attention in his later years to preaching, scriptural exegesis and ecclesiastical history. Carrying these conjectures a bit further, the fact that his ordination as priest at the age of thirty in 702 was immediately followed by the 'publication' of *On Times* and probably one or more of his other textbooks might suggest that, on being made a priest, he was recognized in some sense as a schoolmaster with responsibility for the curriculum. It is noteworthy that he composed only one more textbook after those mentioned above – *The Reckoning of Time* (725), which is a massive expansion of the earlier *On Times*.

Schooling at Wearmouth-Jarrow was probably organized around a broad division between elementary and advanced instruction. Bede loved the innocence of children, praised their readiness to learn, and regarded them as capable of wisdom, which hints that he may have enjoyed teaching the very young as well as more advanced students.[11] The Psalter was the elementary reader of the monastic school. Novices began by learning to write the letters of the alphabet and then syllables and words on wax tablets in order to sound out the (Latin) words of the Psalter, which they were required to commit to memory – a task which could take anywhere from six months to three years. They were aided by instruction in penmanship, spelling, grammar, word order, etc. Bede's *On Orthography* is a kind of handbook for the purpose, a collection of common spelling mistakes, ambiguities, peculiarities, irregularities and other items of interest in Latin, arranged alphabetically (by first letter only), e.g.:

> *Altum* [= high, deep] signifies both up and down. ...
> *Gracilis* [= thin] in the superlative is *gracillimus*, not *gracilissimus*. ...
> *Petra* [= rock] is both a Greek and a Latin noun, signifying the same thing in each language. Hence the name of the apostle *Peter* carries in each language the same significance of unconquerable faith, derived from *Petra*. ...

Tabes [= corruption] is only used in the singular; *tendiculae* [= snares] and *tenebrae* [= darkness], only in the plural   (*On Orthography*, pp. 12, 26, 39, 55)

At the same time the choirmaster would instruct the novices in the melodies of the chant, which had to be committed to memory since no system of musical notation had yet been invented. Possibly this elementary level of education included some simple finger calculation.

It was an innovation in Anglo-Saxon England that abbey schools admitted secular students. Wilfrid tutored sons of nobles, so that they might either enter the Church or return to the king as warriors.[12] Higher education was reserved for the elite – the sons of the nobility and youngsters who showed special aptitude. Fundamental to the advanced curriculum was instruction in all aspects of the Latin language, with the ultimate goal of proficiency in biblical exegesis.

In the classical world, the school texts for advanced study of Latin verse were heavily based on Vergil's poetry. The grammatical textbooks that Bede inherited from the late Roman empire took more of their illustrations from Vergil than from any other poet. Vergil was probably still the school author of Wearmouth-Jarrow when Bede was a schoolboy, as had been the case at Canterbury under Theodore and Hadrian. Bede seems to have been the one who determined to displace Vergil from this role. In *The Art of Poetry*, he usually, though not always, replaces quotations from Vergil and other classical poets in the late Latin grammarians with examples drawn from Christian Latin poets like Arator, Fortunatus, Paulinus, Prudentius and Sedulius.

The chief reason for studying the poets was to learn the rules of Latin verse composition and the proof that one had done so was one's ability to compose quantitatively correct poetry. The first eight chapters of *The Art of Poetry* offer instruction in the prosodic potential of the letters of the alphabet and rules for determining the metrical length (long or short) of initial, medial and final syllables. Chapters 9 through 23 constitute a treatise on Latin quantitative poetry. Bede focuses primarily on heroic and elegiac verse (dactylic hexameters and pentameters), with some attention to the lyric metres. In chapter 11, discussing stylistic graces, he asserts that

> the best and most beautiful arrangement of a dactylic hexameter verse is when the next to the last word agrees with the first word and the final word agrees with a word in the middle ... However, this should not be done constantly, but only after intervals of several lines. For if you always arrange your feet and your verses in the same way, even if it is the best way, your composition is at once cheapened.   (ch. 11, p. 103)

Generations of would-be poets remembered his praise and forgot his admonition. The medieval passion for leonine (internal) rhyme that reached its height in the twelfth century can be traced in part to this passage. Among the concluding chapters is one (ch. 24) analysing the distinction between quantitative and rhythmical (accentual-syllabic) verse – the first clear recognition of the revolution in poetic form that separates both the popular Latin and the vernacular poetry of the Middle Ages (and the modern world) from the poetry of classical antiquity. Throughout the work we hear the voice of Bede the teacher: 'But I urge the student who has not yet reached this point to examine in the meantime even more attentively ...' (ch. 4, p. 63).

An explanation for the survival of the study of poetry as well as for the persistence of interest in the figures of rhetoric in the vocational environment of the monastic school, which was hostile to all forms of secular art and learning, must be sought. Bede himself more than once dismisses these arts as distractions from the word of God. But he does so strictly in the context of secular learning. The eloquence that may be frivolous in pagan literature is part of God's word in the Bible. Early Christian apologists sought to justify their new religion by arguing that the Hebrew Bible of Moses anticipated all the learning and wisdom of the classical world, including the metres of the poets and the eloquence of the rhetors. Saint Jerome was Bede's authority for the belief that the Psalms were written in lyric metres and that much of the Book of Job was composed in hexameters. Knowledge of these metres was therefore essential for full understanding of the sacred texts.

Acquaintance with the 'schemes' and 'tropes' of rhetoric was equally essential in order not to be misled about the literal and figurative meanings of the Bible. *The Figures of Rhetoric* is a textbook of Christian rhetoric for the guidance of fledgeling exegetes. Bede takes his definitions of the rhetorical figures from the late Latin grammarians, but more rigorously than he did in *The Art of Poetry* he replaces illustrative quotations from classical authors like Cicero with examples from the Vulgate Bible. *The Figures of Rhetoric* is based on the principle that deviance is both a formal aesthetic property of language and an analytic tool for uncovering hidden meaning. The textbook is arranged in two parts. The first part is a catalogue of seventeen schemes. Schemes include such artificial arrangements of language as syntactical dislocation, the repetition of the same word or phrase or of similar sounds or cases, or the use of homonyms, etc. Alliterations, rhymes and puns are familiar examples of schemes. The function of these deviations is to enhance the beauty of the work. The second part of *The Figures of Rhetoric* deals with tropes. Bede defines a trope as 'an expression which, either for the sake of ornamentation or from necessity, has been transferred from its proper meaning and understood by analogy in a sense which it does not have' (ch. 2, p. 183). Among the thirteen tropes that Bede lists are allegory, metaphor, metonymy, synecdoche and periphrasis. In Bede's hands, allegory, which he defines simply as an expression 'which means something other than what it says', becomes the master trope (ch.2.12, p. 199). It is a fundamental tool for uncovering the hidden meanings that underlie the letter of the scriptural text, based on the assumption that its message is polyvalent and not immediately accessible to the untutored reader. Above all, Christian interpreters, beginning with Saint Paul (Galatians 4:22–6), read the 'Old' Testament allegorically in the belief that events narrated in it 'foreshadowed' the events of the 'New' Testament. In *The Figures of Rhetoric* Bede constructs his own version of 'fourfold' allegory. An allegory has meaning on the literal level, that is, the event depicted in the Old Testament really happened. But it also has meaning on one or more of three spiritual levels – typological (or 'allegorical'), in reference to Christ or the Church; tropological, in reference to the life of the individual Christian; and anagogical, in reference to the heavenly kingdom. As an example of an allegory in all four senses, Bede cites 'the temple of the Lord', which

> in the literal sense is the house which Solomon built; allegorically, it is the Lord's body, of which Christ said: 'Destroy this temple and in three days I will raise it up', or his Church, to whom the apostle Paul said: 'For the temple of the Lord is holy, which you are'; tropologically, it is each of the faithful, to whom the Apostle said: 'Know you not, that your bodies are the temple of the holy spirit, who is in you?'; anagogically, it is the joys of the heavenly mansion, for which the Psalmist sighed, when he said: 'Blessed are they that dwell in your house, O Lord; they shall praise you for ever and ever.'
>
> (*The Figures of Rhetoric*, ch. 2.12, p. 207)

In his commentaries on the books of the Bible, Bede wields the tool of allegory selectively; it was a flexible method, not a rigid system (see Chapter 9).

The other major branch of advanced studies, along with continued emphasis on music, was the *computus*, for which Bede composed three textbooks, *On Times*, *On the Nature of Things* and *The Reckoning of Time*. Discussion of this topic will be found in Chapter 8.

Educational facilities at Wearmouth-Jarrow

Something needs to be said of the physical facilities that Bede had at his disposal for schooling his charges. Archaeology reveals almost nothing about the layout of the monastic buildings at Wearmouth, but rather more about the plan at Jarrow. Beyond this, we must rely on scattered remarks in Bede and other Anglo-Saxon authors and on inferences from later practices in Carolingian schools that were heavily influenced by Jarrow. At the double monastery of Whitby, female novices were housed in separate quarters until they had completed their instruction in the regular way of life (*EH* IV. 23).

It seems likely that their schooling took place in the buildings where they were housed. On the (ideal) ninth-century continental Plan of St Gall, novices have their own separate chapel and claustral building where they would both live and be taught. Similar segregation may have been the case at Wearmouth-Jarrow, though we cannot be sure.

Rosemary Cramp's excavations in the cloister area south of the church of St Paul at Jarrow have revealed the foundations of two rectangular buildings, one of which Cramp interprets as the refectory. The second building measured 60 by 26 feet and had been divided into three rooms. The largest of the three rooms had internal measurements of 43 by 21 feet, with a place for a seat in the middle of the east wall. Among the finds in it were a stylus and a small whetstone. Of the two smaller rooms in the eastern end of the building, the one to the north measured 11 by 7 feet, and the one to the south 11 by 14 feet. There may have been an altar in the smaller northern room, and a sink or washbasin in the southern room. Cramp concludes:

> It would appear that this building could fulfil, in a later Benedictine monastery, the functions of the east range – the large room serving as a place for assembly and writing and the private suite perhaps used by the abbot or a senior monk.[13]

It is not out of the question that this was Bede's classroom and/or that it functioned as Jarrow's library or scriptorium. If it were Bede's classroom, it would be pleasant to imagine that the two smaller rooms made up Bede's private cell. The archaeology corresponds closely to Cuthbert's description of the physical setting of Bede's death-day (see below).

Jarrow's resources were extensive, but not unlimited. Supposing that the classroom (and perhaps the library) were housed in Cramp's second building, it seems unlikely that it could simultaneously have functioned as the scriptorium (unless it were two-storied). Charles Plummer interpreted a complaint of Bede's in the prologue to his *Commentary on the Gospel of Luke* to mean that 'he had to be his own amanuensis, shorthand writer, and copyist'.[14] Bede composed the commentary between 709 and 716. This coincides with the time (*c.* 692–716) that the Wearmouth-Jarrow scriptorium was producing the three great pandects of the Vulgate. The Codex Amiatinus alone was the work of nine scribes, which gives an idea of the massive effort and manpower required for this project.[15] Perhaps we should conclude that there were times during this extended period when Bede had to do his own copying because the Wearmouth-Jarrow scribes were otherwise engaged. The scriptorium may have been in another room as yet undiscovered.

Bede's impact on Western culture

Bede's influence was immediate and enormous. Archbishop Egbert of York was Bede's friend and probably his former pupil at Jarrow. Egbert and his successor Æthelbert built up the school of York into a great institution of learning on the model of Jarrow. Their pupil Alcuin ultimately became director of the Palace School of Charlemagne, from which the standards and practices of Anglo-Saxon schooling radiated throughout the Carolingian empire. Almost within his lifetime, Bede's writings were sought out on the continent (see Chapter 14). The Anglo-Saxon missionaries Boniface and Lull insistently demanded copies of his works. Similar requests followed in the ninth and tenth centuries. Though their popularity declined after the twelfth century, his textbooks, which were fundamental to the education of the Middle Ages, continued to be copied right up to the age of printing. Such was his reputation (he was sometimes referred to as the fifth Doctor of the Church) that, as long as they were known to be his, his works were transcribed with a degree of accuracy that was usually reserved for the Bible.

Bede's two Lives of Saint Cuthbert and the chapters in the *Ecclesiastical History* on Cuthbert and other saintly recluses are witnesses to the attractive power of the ascetic ideal of monasticism. But, again and again in Bede's writings, it is the active life that elicits his admiration.[16] In his portrait of Abbess Hild of Whitby, which includes the immortal tale of Cædmon, Bede emphasizes the stress that Hild put upon education and her training of five future bishops, as well as her indifference to the extremes of Irish asceticism (*EH* IV. 21–2). Equally instructive is his portrait of Benedict Biscop. He celebrates Benedict's practicality, his energy, his zeal for acquiring all that would be required to make his monasteries successful – books, buildings, pictures, craftsmen.

This was a decisive break from the ideals of Celtic monasticism. In his homily on Saint John the Evangelist, Bede sets up Saint Peter as the model for the active life and the beloved disciple John (whom Bede understood to be the author of the fourth Gospel, three Epistles and the Apocalypse) as the model for the contemplative life. The active life was open to every Christian, lay or clerical. It demanded keeping the self spotless from all impurities while devoting one's righteous labours to feeding the hungry, clothing the naked, visiting the sick, burying the dead and showing the erring the way of Truth. The reward of the active life was eternal salvation, but the labours that earned it ended at death, for there was no need for them in the life to come. The contemplative life, on the other hand, was open to very few, chiefly to celibate monks who, having over a long period of time practised all the precepts of the active life, were able to free themselves from the affairs of the world and to begin 'even in the present life to gain a foretaste of the joy of the perpetual blessedness ... by ardently desiring it, and even sometimes ... by contemplating it sublimely *in mental ecstasy* [Acts 11:5]' (*Homilies on the Gospels*, 1. 9, p. 91). Benedict Biscop is Bede's exemplar of the selfless ideal of the active life in the service of the contemplative:

> he strove to labor in so many ways in order that no necessity of our laboring would remain. He went away to so many places across the sea so that we would be plentifully supplied with all sorts of nourishment of saving knowledge, and we would be able to remain at rest within the cloister of the monastery to serve Christ with a liberty secure. (*Homilies*, 1. 13, p. 132)

For Bede, to 'serve Christ' was to engage in biblical scholarship. The fact that John, the beloved disciple, leaned on the breast of Jesus at the Last Supper 'prefigured that the gospel which this same disciple was going to write would include the hidden mysteries of divine majesty more copiously and profoundly than the rest of the pages of sacred scripture' (*Homilies*, 1. 9, p. 88). These are the mysteries that the advanced student of the Bible begins to uncover through the practice of allegorical exegesis. Bede concludes: '[John] gave testimony to the word of God by preaching, he gave it by writing, he gave it in turn by teaching the things which he had written' (*Homilies*, 1. 9, p. 93). Preaching, writing, teaching and exegesis – this was Bede's revised version of the contemplative life.

Bede was revered as a saint, but his fame was tied to his reputation as a teacher and scholar. His reputation was largely self-fashioned. He tells us of his love of learning and teaching in the autobiographical note he appended to the *Ecclesiastical History* (v. 24), quoted above. This was a role he chose for himself. It is how he *wanted* to be remembered. At the end of his life he did not aspire to retreat to an isolated cell. Instead he persisted in what he loved best – the practice of scholarship. His pupil Cuthbert recalls that, even in his final illness, he never omitted giving daily lessons to his students and chanting the Psalter. Nor did he put aside his project of translating a portion of the Gospel of Saint John into English. On the day he died, the boy Wilberht who was taking dictation reminded him that one chapter remained to be written, but worried that it might be too much for him. Bede urged him to sharpen his pen and write fast. Then in the evening, Wilberht said to him,

> 'There is still one sentence, dear master, that we have not written down.' And he said: 'Write it.' After a little the boy said: 'There! Now it is written.' And he replied: 'Good! It is finished [John 19:30]; you have spoken the truth. Hold my head in your hands, for it is a great delight to me to sit over against my holy place in which I used to pray, that as I sit there I may call upon my Father.' And so

upon the floor of his cell, singing 'Glory be to the Father and to the Son and to the Holy Spirit' and the rest, he breathed his last.[17]

The fact that Bede does not gesture in the direction of the life of the hermit suggests a paradigm shift – a complete reorientation of his mental map of the uses and purposes of life on earth. From this final perspective, Bede's importance as an educator is that he embodied an alternative model of Christian monasticism – the ideal of the educated, as opposed to the ascetic, Christian monk. In Bede's model, education – learning, teaching and scholarship – was an end, not merely a means to an end, since its reward was to go on practising these virtues eternally in the next life, in the enjoyment of the beatific vision (cf. *Homilies*, I. 9, p. 65). It is hardly an exaggeration to claim that, in validating the life of the mind and the importance of education, his model helped redirect the course of Western civilization.

NOTES

1. Primary sources for our knowledge of Bede and education in Anglo-Saxon England include Bede's *Ecclesiastical History* and his *History of the Abbots*; the *Life of Ceolfrith*; *Cuthbert's Letter on the Death of Bede*; and Eddius Stephanus, *Life of Bishop Wilfrid*. Important secondary sources, drawn upon but not cited in the following notes, include: G. H. Brown 1987; Irvine 1986; C. W. Jones 1975 and 1976; Kendall 1991; Lendinara 1991; Mayr-Harting 1991; Meyvaert 1976; Whitelock 1976; Wormald 1976.
2. Riché 1976: 361.
3. *Life of Ceolfrith*, chs. 2–5, in Farmer 2004: 213–15.
4. *Life of Ceolfrith*, ch. 33, p. 225.
5. Colgrave and Mynors 1969: xxxiv.
6. P. H. Blair 1970: 292–3.
7. *Cuthbert's Letter on the Death of Bede*, in Colgrave and Mynors 1969: 583. See also McCready 1995a.
8. See also *Life of Ceolfrith*, ch. 33, p. 226.
9. Laistner 1935: 263–6.
10. For Bede's firsthand knowledge of Vergil, see N. Wright 1981: 375–6. On the vexed question of his knowledge of Cicero, see Ray 2006: 27–9.
11. Riché 1976: 453–4.
12. *The Life of Bishop Wilfrid by Eddius Stephanus*, ed. and trans. B. Colgrave (Cambridge University Press, 1985), ch. 21, p. 45.
13. Cramp 1976: 239.
14. Plummer 1896: 1, xx.
15. Parkes 1982: 557.
16. DeGregorio 1999.
17. *Cuthbert's Letter on the Death of Bede*, in Colgrave and Mynors 1969: 585.

8

FAITH WALLIS

Bede and science

The parameters of Bede's science

Readers of the *Ecclesiastical History* may be tempted to skip the opening chapter, which seems to be more about obsolete geography than about history. Yet this prologue tells us much about Bede's conception of science and its place within his wider enterprises of learning. First, the island of Britain is carefully measured in its length, breadth and coastal circumference. Then there follows a catalogue of the island's natural endowments: its plant and animal life, its hot and salt springs and its minerals. Britain literally exudes health: its waters have medicinal properties, and the jet from its mines repels serpents. Finally, the northerly latitude of Britain makes for exceptionally long summer days and winter nights. One could say, then, that Bede frames his vision of English identity by measured space, measured time and an inventory of the natural world. These two signposts – nature and measurement – also mark off the frontiers of Bede's science. They are the substance of his two early treatises *On the Nature of Things* (*c.* 703) and *On Times* (703), and they are woven together in his magisterial *The Reckoning of Time* (725).[1]

The sections of the *Ecclesiastical History* that deal with the controversy over the calculation of Easter, such as the account of the meeting at Whitby (III. 25), are also likely to be skimmed. The dispute seems incomprehensibly technical, and rather unedifying. But here as well, Bede's narrative of history and identity is framed by measurement and nature – in this case, by the problem of how divinely instituted natural time and the injunctions of the Bible could be faithfully mirrored in the timekeeping practices of the Christian people. It is no accident that the timeline of the *Ecclesiastical History* begins with Julius Caesar, who created the solar calendar employed by the Church (cf. *The Reckoning of Time*, ch. 12), and ends with the adoption by the monastery of Iona of the Alexandrian Paschal table, as formulated by Dionysius Exiguus. Calendar and Paschal table are the core documents of what later writers came to call *computus*, the science of time-reckoning and fixing the dates of ecclesiastical feasts, and the subject of *On Times* and *The Reckoning of Time*.

These parameters alone might almost justify quarantining the word 'science' within inverted commas. More pertinently, modern readers of Bede's writings must bear in mind that nothing in his mental universe corresponds to the modern concept of science as a body of positive knowledge or as a method for discovering truths about the world. For Bede, *scientia* simply denoted 'knowledge'. His work on time was *ratio*, a word which embraces both 'reckoning' and 'reasoning'. In Bede's lexicon, *historia naturalis* was the title of a book by Pliny, not a term for a domain of knowledge. This was not because Bede was ignorant of the ancient categories of scientific learning: they are all laid out in Isidore of Seville's encyclopaedic *Etymologies*, for example. It was rather that he understood time-reckoning and the study of the natural world to be not self-contained and self-explanatory disciplines, but subordinate elements of *doctrina christiana* – 'Christian instruction' or erudition useful for Christian preachers and exegetes.

Doctrina christiana shaped the ways in which Bede understood both the natural world and the power of measurement and number to explain that world. When speaking about creation, Bede used the word 'nature' to denote the attributes of particular things, not the cosmos as a whole, let alone an abstract principle or law governing its operations. We might say that Bede recognized 'natures' but not 'Nature'. When he wrote about time, Bede used the term 'natural time' to mean 'time as God created it' – measured by the motions of the sun and moon, and hence based on a starting point at the vernal equinox, when the two luminaries were created. Natural time contrasts with conventional or human time, with its plethora of different calendars, and its discordant definitions of 'day', 'week', 'month' and so forth. The *natura* of natural time is *ratio* – 'reckoning' in the sense of both logical and mathematical congruence. Mathematics is thus not a tool to explain the physical world, but something closer to the allegorical meaning of the physical world.[2]

Given the circumscribed range of Bede's scientific interests, and the instrumental approach to secular knowledge implicit in *doctrina christiana*, it is easy to underestimate the originality and importance of Bede's scientific writings. This impression could be reinforced by the fact that *On the Nature of Things* and *On Times* were early works, strongly influenced by prior models and sources. Nonetheless, what Bede did with these sources was quite original, and in the case of *On Times*, revolutionary.

In science as in exegesis and history, Bede benefited from an exceptionally rich library at Wearmouth and Jarrow. His interest in the nature of things could be gratified, in the first instance, by patristic exegesis on the opening chapters of Genesis – Ambrose's and Basil's *hexaemera*, and the many commentaries by Augustine. These same works nourished Bede's own exposition of the biblical account of creation, namely Book 1 of *On Genesis*, which he began a decade later, in 717–18. He was also alert to scientific references in other biblical contexts as well: for example, the obscure Philippus Presbyter's exegesis of the Book of Job is cited in the analysis of tides in *The Reckoning of Time*, ch. 29. Besides Isidore of Seville (whom we shall consider in detail a little later) he also knew the Irish pioneers of Christian cosmography, Augustinus Hibernicus's *The Miracles of Holy Scripture* and the pseudo-Isidorean *Book of the Order of Creatures*.[3]

As a rule, Bede prefers not to name pagan sources if he can avoid it, and usually avoids praising them. But he makes an exception for Pliny the Elder, author of that 'delightful book, the *Natural History*', whose authority Bede rather boldly compares to that of Basil and Ambrose (*The Reckoning of Time*, ch. 31). Bede quotes from Books 2, 3–7, 28, 30, 35 and possibly 37. Solinus is also cited by name, and passages from Vegetius's *On the Art of War* appear (without ascription) in ch. 28 of *The Reckoning of Time*, in connection with the influence of the moon on terrestrial life, as well as in *On the Nature of Things*, chs. 19, 27 and 36. It is tempting to speculate that these classical writers might have been included in the magnificent *Book of the Cosmographers* which Benedict Biscop brought back from Rome, and which Ceolfrith gave to the learned King Aldfrith of Northumbria in exchange for eight hides of land by the River Fresca (*History of the Abbots*, ch. 15). Perhaps Ceolfrith prudently made a copy of this book before presenting the original to the king; or Aldfrith himself may have distributed copies of this anthology, as Bede tells us he did with Adomnán's *On the Holy Places*. Finally, Bede refers to medical literature in *The Reckoning of Time*. The *Letter to Pentadius* by the fourth-century North African physician Vindicianus furnishes him with an account of the four humours in their relationship to the seasons (*The Reckoning of Time*, ch. 35), while the pseudo-Hippocratic *Letter to King Antiochus* lays out the rules for maintaining health through the changing seasons (*The Reckoning of Time*, ch. 30). Bede was the first writer on *computus* to incorporate medical material.

Bede's familiarity with the literature of *computus* also shaped his overall approach to science. Much of this literature was in the form of polemical letters, or prologues attached to proposed tables of dates for Easter, arguing the merits of the principles on which they were constructed. Swimming in the wake of these controversial writings were short tracts, lists of formulae and didactic works. Album-like manuscript anthologies, some with distinctive transmission lineages, were the conventional vehicles of this material. C. W. Jones identified Bede's own *computus* anthology as a manuscript of the type represented by Oxford, Bodleian, Bodl. 309 (s. XI) and its affiliates. The core of this anthology was a group of letters and didactic dialogues assembled in southern Ireland. Bede's conception of the scope and significance of *computus* was deeply marked by these Irish works, which stretched the boundaries of *computus* to encompass philological and historical as well as mathematical erudition.[4] Macrobius's history of the Roman calendar from the *Saturnalia* was also conveyed (anonymously) to Bede through his Irish *computus*.

'On the Nature of Things'

As he lay dying, Bede was engaged in two projects: a vernacular translation of the Gospel of John, and the collection of excerpts from Isidore of Seville's *De natura rerum* (*The Nature of Things*), the latter undertaken lest 'my children [learn] what is not true, and [lose] their labour on this after I am gone'.[5] Bede was closing the circle of his life's labours, for one of his earliest books, *On the Nature of Things*, was both a reworking and a critique of Isidore's treatise of the same name.

Isidore's *The Nature of Things* was modelled on classical cosmographies created for classroom use. It falls into three thematic sections: the divisions of time in ascending order of size (chs. 1–8); the cosmos and astronomy (chs. 9–28); and 'meteorology' – the science of the region lying between sky and earth (chs. 29–48). Isidore included some discussion of problems which exercised Christian readers of the Bible, such as the waters above the firmament (ch. 14) and the possibility that the stars are living beings (ch. 27), but like the poet Lucretius whose title he borrowed, he saw his work as a tool for refuting popular superstition, paganism and heresy. Knowledge of nature was not an end in itself, but directed to knowledge of God. Hence Isidore always followed up naturalistic explanations with allegorical interpretations.

Bede agreed with Isidore that it was desirable to undercut belief in omens and in autonomous natural forces that could act with intent. The two authors may also have shared a desire to defuse apocalyptic expectations: Isidore wrote his *The Nature of Things* in an atmosphere of alarm about the eclipse of AD 612, and Bede's scientific writings, as we shall see, also had an anti-apocalyptic purpose. But Bede's *On the Nature of Things* also challenged Isidore's work in three ways. First, Bede abandoned Isidore's structure; he detached the chapters on time, and relocated them in *On Times*. Secondly, he corrected and improved Isidore with passages from Pliny. Thirdly, and most importantly, he reconceptualized the notion of Christian cosmography. Where Isidore was content to tack biblical parallels onto essentially Graeco-Roman material, Bede wanted to demonstrate how the Christian understanding of creation and classical science constituted a coherent account of a created cosmos.

Isidore of Seville's *The Nature of Things* was, in fact, the first non-exegetical literary treatment of the physical world to be written by a Latin Christian,[6] and it reflected a patristic consensus: Graeco-Roman concepts about the structure, contents and workings of the material world could be taken on board with few qualms and little modification, because the Bible presents no definitive portrait of the cosmos. With a few exceptions, most of the Fathers were content to understand the world as the ancients had understood it, except that they insisted on creation *ex nihilo*. Christian exegetes could expound Genesis using arguments from natural philosophy and facts from natural history, but there was little motivation to do the reverse, that is, to rewrite ancient science in a Christian register. The contrast with human history – an important ancient genre which Christians were determined to replace with their own ideology and distinctive literary forms – is very striking.[7]

Isidore's dependence on pagan school cosmographies is evident in his treatment of the universe itself as 'the totality of everything comprised by heaven and earth'. Isidore describes the zones of the celestial and terrestrial sphere and the four elements, and then launches into a top-down survey of the heavens. He threads biblical and patristic citations into this account, but there is nothing particularly Christian about the work's structure: the universe as Isidore describes it could as easily be the eternal cosmos of the pagans as the created universe of the Christians. The elements are simply 'parts' of this universe.

Bede's *On the Nature of Things* takes an approach which is quite different. Though he builds his text out of quotations from classical and Christian sources, which he flags by marginal references, his structure is novel. The opening chapter, 'The fourfold work of God' (p. 192), paints a sophisticated picture of the relationship between the physics of the material universe and God's creative action. From his reading of Augustine, Bede distilled a vision of four dimensions or levels of creation. Firstly, there are things which are *eternally created* 'before the ages began', not created through dispensation. Secondly, there are the *elements* which inhere in matter, and which were therefore created when primordial matter was created – that is, before the process described in Genesis was initiated. Thirdly, there was the creation described in Genesis, when the *causes*, created all at once, acted in temporal sequence to differentiate the elements into the contents of the material world. Finally, God's work of creation is extended into his post-creation *governance* of the world, in which these same causes operate to reproduce and replenish life. In sum, Bede begins not with the *universe* (as Isidore does), but with *creation*; and not with the narrative of Genesis, but with the wider metaphysical and theological context of creation itself as a divine action. The elements are not parts of the world, but properties of the matter from which God makes the world; the world is not self-existent, but encompassed by causes which direct its formation and assure its continued existence.

The world's status as product of divine creation is asserted in chapter 2, which is a summary of the Genesis narrative. Only in chapter 3 when the status of the created world is clarified does Bede turn from the act of creation to creation as the product of that act. Now he can cite Isidore's definition of the universe – and then transform it with the help of Pliny's *Natural History*:

> The world is the totality of the universe, which comprises heaven and earth [Isidore, *The Nature of Things*, 9.1], four elements *joined together in the form of a perfect sphere* [Pliny, *Natural History*, 2.4.10, 2.2.5] – [the elements] of *fire*, by which the stars *shine*; of air, by which *all* living things *breathe*; of *waters* which commune by encircling and penetrating the earth; and of *earth* itself, *the midmost and lowest point of the world* [Pliny, *Natural History*, 2.4.10–11]. Indeed, the heavens are designated by the term *mundus* because of their *perfect and absolute elegance*, for amongst *the Greeks it is called* 'cosmos' because of its *adornment* [Pliny, *Natural History*, 2.3.8].
>
> (*On the Nature of Things*, p. 194, lines 2–9; my translation)

Indeed, Pliny's definition of the world constitutes Bede's plan for *On the Nature of Things*. The four elements determine not only the qualities of material entities – their heat and cold, moisture and dryness – but also their location. Fire's nature is to go ever up towards the heavens, earth's to go always down. Water is lighter than earth, but heavier than air, so the rivers and oceans sit on the surface of the earth. Air, which is heavier than fire but lighter than water, constitutes the atmosphere between earth and heaven. The elements are the co-ordinates for a vertical map of the universe, a staircase on which the whole inventory of creation can be arranged. Bede's gradations are exquisitely precise. From the firmament (chs. 5–8), we descend through the fixed stars (ch. 11) to the planets, the sun and moon (chs. 12–20). When we finally stand beneath the moon, we can look upwards to consider the position of the moon in relation to the background of the zodiac (Bede provides a mathematical formula for finding the sign for a moon of any age in ch. 21, a telling departure from his authorities). From this vantage point, we can also experience solar and lunar eclipses (chs. 22–3). The changeable moon and the anomalies of eclipses form a suitable transition to the realm of air, and the zone of unpredictable, albeit natural, atmospheric phenomena, such as comets and pestilences (chs. 24–37).

The realm of water is divided into salt waters and fresh. Pliny and the Irish *Book of the Order of Creatures* helped Bede to sketch an analysis of the relationship between the moon and the tides (ch. 39), which he would expand in *The Reckoning of Time*.[8] This segment of *On the Nature of Things* seems to be a series of answers to questions: What causes the tides? Why does the sea not overflow with all the water that pours into it? Why is it salt, despite the fact that fresh waters empty into it? Is the Red Sea really red? When he turns to the earth itself, Bede shifts from answering questions to proving arguments. Earth is at the 'centre or pivot of the universe' (ch. 45), because the element of earth seeks the lowest point; earthquakes and volcanoes are caused by air trapped within the earth and struggling to escape to its natural place (chs. 49–50). The sphericity of the earth can be demonstrated by the fact that different constellations are visible in different locations (ch. 46), and by the variations in sundial shadows and length of daylight with latitude (ch. 47).

'On Times'

Given the close connection between the material world and time, we may wonder why Bede hived off the chapters on time in Isidore's *The Nature of Things* into a separate book, *On Times*. Bede offers no explanation, but possible motives emerge when we take into account his engagement with a subject to which Isidore paid scant attention, namely solving the problem of determining the date of Easter.

The problem can be summarized thus.[9] Easter commemorates the Passion and Resurrection of Christ, which took place during the Jewish feast of Passover. Therefore Easter is governed by the rules for scheduling Passover, which begins on the fourteenth day of the Jewish lunar month of Nisan, i.e. at the full moon. Nisan is the 'first month' of spring, a season governed by the sun. Finally, Christians in Bede's time celebrated Easter only on Sunday, which is the first day in the (non-astronomical) cycle of the week. Given all the above, what range of dates in the Roman solar calendar qualifies as possible dates for Easter? Can a formula be generated to find a date which satisfies all these conditions in any given year? Better yet, can a repeating cycle of Easters be devised? The problem was complicated by disputes over whether Easter commemorated the Passion or the Resurrection; whether the chronology of the Synoptic Gospels or the Gospel of John should be followed; whether spring began at the vernal equinox (and what the date of the equinox was) or at the sun's entry into Aries; and how to map lunar phases onto a solar calendar.

In 703 no Easter formula, table or cycle commanded universal acceptance in the Insular world. Dionysius's system competed with Victorius of Aquitaine's tables, and with the eighty-four-year cycle still used by the British and in areas influenced by Iona. Bede's personal interests, and his situation at the frontier of the Roman and 'Celtic' zones, motivated him to address time-reckoning as a discrete issue. Here again, Bede strikes out in a different direction from Isidore, who was under no such pressures, and whose account of time, in consequence, is fragmented. In the *Etymologies*, astronomical time, i.e. the movement of the sun and moon, is in Book 3 on cosmology; calendar time – that is, the units of time-reckoning from smallest to largest (as found in Isidore's *The Nature of Things*, but here including the world ages and their history) is in Book 5; and the rules for Easter *computus* are in Book 6, which is devoted to Scripture and liturgy. *On Times*, by contrast, is a concise, tightly focused survey of basic computistics, without any cosmological distractions.

The originality of *On Times* lies in its fusion of two traditions. First, Bede drew on the encyclopaedic tradition of Isidore and the innovative Irish didactic treatises by constructing his book around the units of time, ascending from the subdivisions of the hour up to the world ages. Secondly, he inserted the Paschal cycle between the year and the world age, and thus integrated *computus* into a comprehensive science of time. Chapters 11–15 are built up of computistical material derived from the polemical letters and prefaces, as well as from Irish treatises. They cover the Paschal cycle itself (chs. 11–12), the organization of the Paschal table, or table of projected dates for Easter (ch. 13), formulae for basic computistical data (ch. 14) and the symbolic meaning of the computistical criteria for Easter (ch. 15). *On Times* closes with a world chronicle – and here is where the bombshell fell.

The Christian world chronicle is a genre of historical writing born and bred in controversy. One of its aims was to refute pagan accusations that the Christian religion was a novelty by demonstrating that the Jewish roots of the faith predated Greece and Rome. It also conveyed a particular message about God's dominion over human time in the way it synchronized secular histories with the biblical narrative. Above all, world chronicles were arenas for disputes over the duration and approaching end of the world. A particular problem lay in the supposition that there were six ages of world history corresponding to the six days of creation, and that each of these ages was 1,000 years in length: the proof-text was 2 Peter 3:8 (echoing Psalm 90:4): 'with the Lord one day is as a thousand years, and a thousand years as one day'. This meant that the world would last 6,000 years; but if we know how long the world will last, we can use chronology to calculate the end of time. Bede was not the first to devise a world chronicle with a view to debunking this theory, but his results were exceptionally radical. By recalculating the lengths of the first two ages (Adam to Noah, Noah to Abraham) in accordance with Jerome's Vulgate translation, he shaved 1,247 years off the conventional age of the world, as propounded by Eusebius. Christ was born, not in *annus mundi* 5199, but in *annus mundi* 3952. If one believed in the thousand-year world ages, this put Christ's birth in the fourth age, not at the beginning of the sixth and last age.[10]

Whether seriously or in jest, someone in Bishop Wilfrid's entourage stated publicly that the chronology of *On Times* was heretical. Bede responded with a blistering critique of the thousand-year world ages theory: the *Letter to Plegwin* (709). Its arguments are for the most part exegetical, theological and philological in character, and as such are beyond the scope of this essay; but Bede seems to have worried that the episode cast a shadow over his work on *computus*, and perhaps the claims of the Alexandrian Paschal system as a whole. This is one plausible reason why he elected to bring out a revised textbook of *computus*, *The Reckoning of Time*. In his preface, Bede put the chronology controversy front and centre, and announced his intention to defend what he wrote in *On Times*. Yet *The Reckoning of Time* is much more than an elaborate response to charges of heresy which, if they were ever serious, had long since come to nothing. Bede had additional motives for writing a new treatise on time-reckoning – motives more closely tied to his science.

'The Reckoning of Time'

Bede claimed that *The Reckoning of Time* was composed at the request of his students, who found his two earlier textbooks too concise, and craved more ample explanations. Besides understating the book's originality, this explanation masks some of the urgency surrounding its creation. Though he completed the book in 725, internal evidence suggests that Bede started to write in 721 – the year when the last extension of Dionysius Exiguus's Easter table (ascribed to one Felix of Ghyllitanus) was due to expire. Dionysius's system needed to be explained and defended in a comprehensive manner. Indeed, attempts to codify the Dionysian *computus* were undertaken on the continent at exactly this time, though Bede was not aware of them, and they are not comparable in scope, sophistication or influence to *The Reckoning of Time*.

Bede's understanding of the scientific possibilities inherent in *computus* had also deepened between 703 and 721. When he came to write *The Reckoning of Time*, he knew he was breaking fresh ground by integrating *computus* with its astronomical and cosmological context. Moreover, the Plegwin episode inspired him to raise the stakes, so to speak, by articulating a vision of *computus* that actually accentuated its theological importance, and confronted the issue of eschatology squarely. The result was an impressively lucid, comprehensive and profound exposition that sealed the success of Dionysius's system in medieval Europe, and elevated *computus* to the status of Christian *scientia*. Bede accomplished this by fusing *On the Nature of Things*, *On Times* and the *Letter to Plegwin*, and by expounding their arguments in a more exhaustive and persuasive way.

The Reckoning of Time incorporates much of the information found in *On the Nature of Things*, but arranges the cosmology under computistical rubrics. Tide-lore, for example, which was filed under 'water' in *On the Nature of Things* (ch. 39), is here found within a discussion of the month, since the moon's monthly trajectory determines the pattern of the tides. On the other hand, Bede set aside material which is not pertinent to *computus* – atmospheric phenomena for example, or earthquakes and volcanoes. Nonetheless, *The Reckoning of Time* is the first treatment of *computus* to incorporate cosmography into its explanatory scope. It bears eloquent witness to Bede's broad scientific vision of a *computus* that encompassed issues about nature and time beyond the Paschal question.

Like *On Times*, *The Reckoning of Time* is arranged in ascending order of units of time, but in this case Bede layers his survey over a commentary on the computist's two fundamental documents: the solar calendar, and the Paschal table of Dionysius. After a technical prologue on calculation using finger reckoning and on fractions, Bede tackles the solar calendar, the frame of reference for all computistical calculation. The calendar covers the hierarchy of units of time from the day (chs. 5–7) through to the week (chs. 8–10) and the months (chs. 11–29) to the solar year itself (chs. 30–43). The next level, the luni-solar cycle, shifts our attention to the Paschal table. The backbone of this table is a vertical list of future years (numbered according to a prospective era, such as *annus Domini*), flanked by the projected date of Easter in each year; but most tables also include additional columns of computistical data. *The Reckoning of Time* reads Dionysius's table column by column, from left to right: *annus Domini* (ch. 47), indictions (chs. 48–9), lunar epacts (chs. 50–2), solar epacts or concurrents (chs. 53–5), the lunar cycle (chs. 56–8), the Easter terminus (chs. 59–60), Easter Sunday (ch. 61) and the age of the moon on Easter Sunday (ch. 62). The nineteen-year luni-solar cycles are compounded into a fully repeating Great Paschal Cycle of 532 years (ch. 65); arching above them are the Six Ages of world-historical time, chronicled in chapter 66. The Seventh Age (the time of the Church Expectant in heaven), and the Eighth Age of the world to come, take us into future time, and to the end of time itself (chs. 67–71). By guiding his readers upwards to the threshold of eternity, Bede raised the survey of units of time to a new level of imagination and meaning.

The Reckoning of Time also extends the scope of *computus* to include a wider range of theological and exegetical themes. In *On Times* Bede cautiously ventured into this liminal terrain by including an allegorical exposition of the computistical parameters of Easter (ch. 15). But in *The Reckoning of Time* he attempts even more daring conjunctions of computistics and biblical interpretation. In chapter 6 he brings astronomical logic to bear on the dating of the six days of creation, a subject initially broached by some Irish treatises. The sun and moon must have been created 'perfect', i.e. at a time when they could between the two of them illuminate the heavens for twenty-four hours. This can only happen at an equinox, when the moon is full, so the fourth day of creation must have been 21 March. In chapter 9, Bede offers to construe the seventy 'prophetic weeks' of Daniel 9:24 and their implications for Old Testament and intertestamental chronology; in chapter 27 he proves that the darkening of the sun at the Crucifixion must have been a miracle, as a solar eclipse would be impossible at the time of the Passover full moon. Bede's fusion of science and scriptural interpretation entails more than appropriating *computus* for apologetic purposes. Sacred texts are the keys to *computus*, but *computus* is itself a kind of text that can be subject to allegorical interpretation. Indeed, Bede's distinction between three types of time-reckoning according to nature, custom and authority (ch. 2) corresponds to the three criteria for judging proper *latinitas* – nature, custom and authority – adumbrated by Varro and Quintilian, and transmitted to the Middle Ages by Victorinus and Augustine. What Bede does in chapter 64 of *The Reckoning of Time*, 'The allegorical interpretation of Easter' (*Typica Paschae interpretatio*) is to read God's two texts – the biblical injunctions concerning Passover, and the astronomical phenomena of vernal equinox and full moon – as *figurae* which reveal the spiritual meaning of the feast.[11]

The *Reckoning of Time* is also more demanding as a scientific text than *On Times*. In the earlier work, Bede concentrated on laying out the core data and basic formulae of Alexandrian *computus*; in *The Reckoning of Time*, his goal is to prove the validity of the Alexandrian system exhaustively. This involves a detailed, systematic and explicit refutation of the errors of rival systems, and notably that of Victorius of Aquitaine. It also entails confronting some rather sensitive questions that might, if not satisfactorily answered, seriously jeopardize the credibility of the Dionysian *computus*. A good example is found in chapter 43, 'Why the moon sometimes appears older than its computed age'. Bede admits that the real moon in the sky is often older than the computed age of the moon in Dionysius's Paschal table; sometimes the difference can amount to two days. We know why, though Bede did not: the computed length of a lunation used by ancient astronomers and their Alexandrian followers was slightly shorter than the astronomical mean length. This produced a discrepancy which after 300 years would amount to a whole day. Assuming the ages of the moon in the Alexandrian tables were astronomically correct in the fourth century, there would have been a slippage of a day and a half by the time of Bede. This slippage was potentially embarrassing, because the theological arguments against rival cycles hinged on the acceptable limits of the age of the moon at Easter: for Dionysius, the moon had to be between fifteen and twenty-one days old. So if there were doubts about the moon's age, these could jeopardize the credibility of the system.

Bede offered some scientific reasons why the observer might be mistaken about the age of the moon: in spring, for example, distinguishing between the last crescent of the old moon and the first crescent of the new moon can be difficult. But he also frankly admitted that the mathematical artifice – the *ratio* – required to make a luni-solar calendar cycle will sometimes actually put the calculated age of the moon at odds with observed reality. Surely the Fathers at the Council of Nicaea knew about these adjustments, and endorsed them, since the Council approved the Alexandrian *computus*! Bede was speculating about the Council's intentions, and he knew it. But the fact that he addressed this problem, and the confidence he placed in *ratio*, speak well of his intellectual integrity and help us to grasp how he understood 'science'.[12]

Bede's concern to explain these problems exhaustively, and to close every avenue to error, has the unintentional but intriguing effect of revealing how he taught *computus* to his students. In *The Reckoning of Time*, he frequently complains that it is much easier to expound *computus* face to face than in writing (e.g. chs. 4, 16, 55), and his text often lets us hear his teaching voice. This suggests that he composed the work by consciously transcribing and editing his interactions with his students. For example, he explains formulae through worked examples, proceeding from simpler to more complicated applications, and capping the process by working backwards from the answer to the formula to demonstrate *why* the formula works. He anticipates that his students will have different levels of background preparation and mathematical aptitude, so he provides different methods for arriving at data such as the position of the moon in the zodiac, including reference tables (though he disapproves of these). He asks more advanced students to coach the less prepared (ch. 16). Finally, Bede found inventive ways to make scientific abstractions comprehensible through homely analogies and vivid thought experiments (chs. 7, 26, 34). Indeed, *The Reckoning of Time* might well be the first example of a scientific treatise designed as a manual for a *teacher*, complete with lesson plans, 'streamed' alternatives and object lessons. It is no wonder that it was so popular with Carolingian educators, who praised it as 'a most elegant and useful book'.[13]

But *The Reckoning of Time* also gives us teasing glimpses of what might plausibly be called 'research'. Details about the timing of the tides at various points along the British coast that allow Bede to enunciate the principle of 'port' (ch. 29) hint that he was part of a network of scientific information exchange, perhaps even involving a concerted survey. Casual instructions to consult a sundial to confirm the date of the equinox (ch. 30; cf. *Letter to Wicthed* and *EH* v. 21) suggest that astronomical observation employing an instrument was at least considered possible and praiseworthy, even if it is unlikely in this particular case that it could be carried out satisfactorily.

Conclusion

Bede's science is of a piece with the other learned activities he undertook in the cause of expounding and spreading the Christian faith. His curiosity about the natural world and the problems of the calendar was lively, but it was also disciplined by the demands of *doctrina christiana*. Though he claimed to 'seek for myself and for my people no better way of acting or speaking' than 'to follow the sure judgement of the most reverend Fathers' (*The Reckoning of Time*, ch. 43), he nonetheless substantially reshaped two crucial medieval scientific genres. He turned Isidore's treatment of the 'nature of things' into a genuinely Christian account of the universe; he forged a systematic, forcefully argued and theologically imaginative vision of time out of the motley array of didactic texts and polemics that had hitherto constituted the literature of *computus*. But his most significant achievement may have been an unintended one: to project through *computus* a vision of science as a problem-solving activity. Bede's writings made *computus* a core subject of clerical instruction well into the scholastic period, and its problems were matters of serious scientific debate until the Gregorian reform of 1582. New computistical problems sparked by astronomical issues that Bede knew nothing about made his treatises seem rather outmoded by the twelfth century. But by focusing on problems, as well as by the problems he focused on, Bede helped to define scientific literacy in medieval Europe.

NOTES

1. Stevens 1985 is the classic appraisal of Bede's science as a whole. Summary accounts are provided by C. W. Jones 1970b, Wallis 2005b and Eckenrode 1971 and 1976. On the relationship between Bede's cosmology and his theology, see Wallis 2007. Two excellent studies of the intellectual context of Bede's science are McCluskey 1998 and Contreni 2001. Finally, Bede's reputation as a scientific authority caused his name to be attached to many other works. These are catalogued by C. W. Jones 1939; see also Gorman 2001.
2. Wallis 2006 and 2005b.
3. Bede's use of these materials is discussed by Smyth 1996: see her index under 'Bede'.
4. C. W. Jones 1937; Ó Cróinín 1983.
5. *Cuthbert's Letter on the Death of Bede*, in Colgrave and Mynors 1969: 582–3. Most scholars hold that Bede become more hostile to Isidore over time (e.g. he

criticizes him by name in *The Reckoning of Time*, ch. 38); however, this assessment is challenged by McCready 1995a and 1995b.

6. Critical edition, with facing page French translation, by Fontaine 2002. The indispensable analysis is Fontaine 1983, esp. parts 3–5.

7. Inglebert 2001, part I.

8. Eckenrode 1974; P. Hughes 2003.

9. On *computus* and time-reckoning in Bede's time, the introduction to C. W. Jones 1943 provides an indispensable starting point, supplemented by the introduction to Wallis's translation of *The Reckoning of Time*. Declercq 2000 provides concise surveys of the wider historical context. For more detailed explanations of computistical problems and operations, see the essays in Stevens 1995 and C. W. Jones 1994, as well as Faith Wallis, *The Calendar and the Cloister: MS Oxford St John's College 17* at http://digital.library.mcgill.ca/ms-17. For the Irish background to Bede's *computus*, see the essays in Ó Cróinín 2003. The character of the Paschal controversy in the Insular world in Bede's day continues to be a matter of debate: see Ohashi 2005.

10. Landes 1988.

11. Rabin 2005.

12. Bede may have been motivated to raise this problem by the fact that there was a discrepancy between the date of a solar eclipse in May 664 recorded in annals available to him, and the age of the moon for that month according to the Dionysian tables: see Moreton 1998.

13. *Accessus ad auctorem Bedam*, ed. C. W. Jones, in *Bedae opera didascalica*, CCSL 123C (Turnhout: Brepols, 1980), vol. III, p. 70. On the reception of Bede's scientific writings, see C. W. Jones 1976 and Contreni 2005.

9

SCOTT DEGREGORIO

Bede and the Old Testament

Bede was the greatest biblical scholar of his age. Over forty works, all bound up in some way with understanding Christian Scripture, fill the catalogue at the end of the *Ecclesiastical History* (v. 24). But it is not merely that Bede was a prolific writer. It is also that his hermeneutic engagement with the Bible was so varied. Throughout his lifelong attempt to grasp its sacred meanings, he inhabited many authorial roles. As other chapters in this volume emphasize, he was a textual critic and linguist, a preacher and liturgist, a geographer and computist, an educator, a poet and a hagiographer in addition to being an exegete and a historian, the two roles for which he is best known today.

It is common to contrast Bede's fame as historian, which began in the twelfth century (see Chapter 16), with his renown as exegete, which began in his own lifetime and continued for centuries thereafter.[1] But equally germane is the contrast between the accessibility of the *Ecclesiastical History*, long available in translation and easy enough to comprehend, and the inaccessibility of the biblical commentaries, which hide in costly Latin editions, and whose theological content presents real interpretive challenges. Compared to the *Ecclesiastical History*, with its array of colourful personages and engaging narrative pace, the commentaries are bound to appear esoteric and isolated from the social world of their author. Fortunately, recent scholarship has countered such views, and now, thanks to the many English translations that have made these once inaccessible texts more widely available, readers without expertise in Latin may themselves apprehend what scholars have long proclaimed: that the commentaries are the foundational works of Bede's oeuvre, and that an understanding of them is crucial for understanding all he wrote, not least the *Ecclesiastical History*.[2]

Having entered the monastery at Wearmouth at age seven, Bede first encountered the Bible in those settings of worship that were fundamental to life as a monk: observing the rule, singing the Daily Office in choir, reading privately as a means to meditation and prayer. Here too he would have first heard the writings of the Church Fathers, perhaps in the morning office of

Matins which often featured readings from their commentaries.[3] Moreover, medieval Bible reading assumed that the text should be studied in concert with its established exegetical understandings. So Bede inevitably would have learned to view Scripture through the lens of interpretive commentary. In this connection he was enormously enabled by the Wearmouth-Jarrow library, which held many key patristic writings, not to mention various Latin (and some Greek) biblical manuscripts.[4] It is important to stress how unique a situation it was, for an eighth-century monk in the far north of Britain to have at hand virtually all the resources of Christian tradition, in addition to the ability and leisure to avail himself of them.

It is against this backdrop of sacred learning that Bede's oft-quoted description of his own life's work must be set:

> I have spent all my life in this monastery, applying myself entirely to the study of the Scriptures; and amid the observance of the discipline of the Rule and the daily task of singing in the church, it has always been my delight to learn or to teach or to write ... From the time I became a priest until the fifty-ninth year of my life I have made it my business, for my own benefit and that of my brothers, to make brief extracts from the works of the venerable fathers on the Holy Scriptures, or to add notes of my own to clarify their sense and interpretation. (*EH* v. 24, p. 567)

These words underline Bede's self-conception as a commentator on Scripture; his was a dual task: to unravel its multilayered senses in order to make them plain for others. They are also sometimes deemed a frank admission of the inferiority of his own work to that of the 'venerable fathers' before him, a notion expressed too, it would seem, in the memorable refrain of 'following in the footsteps of the fathers' (*patrum uestigia sequens*) that one encounters in his commentaries. But we might question whether such a view does justice to what Bede actually says, or for that matter to what he actually wrote. Would he really have sought 'to clarify their sense and interpretation', a phrase suggesting improvement was possible, if he saw himself as merely a transmitter of their words? And would he have written commentaries on the tabernacle, the temple, Ezra–Nehemiah, Proverbs, Tobit, Acts and the Seven Catholic Epistles, all portions of the Bible untouched by prior commentators, if he believed he was just their humble follower?

We shall have occasion to revisit these questions as we look in this chapter at Bede's commentaries on the Old Testament; subsequent chapters will take up his New Testament commentaries and Gospel homilies. Our first task should be to identify the texts relevant to our topic and establish some background for them. Then, because it is in his Old Testament commentaries that Bede expounds his exegetical method, we shall discuss the assumptions and aims of that method. Finally, we shall highlight the profound impact the story of ancient Israel had on Bede's thought and how his exegesis of that story in some of his Old Testament commentaries in turn intersects with the contemporary ecclesiastical concerns he expressed in the *Ecclesiastical History* and elsewhere.

Bede's Old Testament commentaries

For Bede the Christian Latin Old Testament[5] contained the twenty-four books of the Hebrew canon as well as those additional books labelled 'apocryphal' or 'deutero-canonical'. He devoted ten of his eighteen exegetical commentaries to this section of the Christian Bible. These ten works are of two kinds: either verse-by-verse interpretations of whole or near whole books, or discussions of just select verses or chapters. *On Genesis*, *On First Samuel*, *On the Song of Songs*, *On the Proverbs of Solomon*, *On Tobias* and *On Ezra and Nehemiah* all belong to the first category, while to the second belong *On the Tabernacle*, *On the Temple*, *Thirty Questions on the Book of Kings* and the *Commentary of Bede the Priest on the Canticle of Habakkuk*. In addition, Bede wrote two 'exegetical' letters on Old Testament topics. Entitled *On the Resting-Places* and *On What Isaiah Says*, both letters reply to questions posed by Acca bishop of Hexham, who shared Bede's interest in biblical interpretation and acted as a kind of patron. Another work, *On Eight Questions*, deals with both Old and New Testament themes. He also produced a shortened version of the Psalms, the *Abbreviated Psalter*, which presents select verses from each psalm as vehicles for meditation and personal prayer. In what follows, we are concerned with the ten exegetical commentaries.

Most of these commentaries lack specifics as to for whom, when and why they were composed; some include brief prefaces but they are hardly forthcoming. The prefaces to *On Genesis*, *On First Samuel* and *On Ezra and Nehemiah* are addressed to Acca, and all of them allude to his personally exhorting Bede to take up these books. The preface to *Thirty Questions on the Book of Kings* greets a different episcopal figure, Nothhelm archbishop of Canterbury, who also requested Bede's assistance, as its opening words make clear: 'With the Lord's help and to the best of my ability I have taken care to explain, dearest brother, the matters that you sent for personal clarification about the Book of Kings' (p. 89). In his *Commentary on Habakkuk*, Bede addresses a woman, a 'dearly beloved sister in Christ' (p. 65) who had asked his help in unveiling the spiritual meaning of the prophet's closing prayer (see Habakkuk 3), to which the entire commentary is devoted. Her identity is unknown, but that she was an abbess or nun of some nearby religious community is assured. The remaining works do not mention specific addressees. Yet there is general agreement about the larger audiences to which they and indeed all the commentaries were directed. We know Bede composed them for the spiritual enhancement of his monastic brothers at Wearmouth-Jarrow, for he tells us that himself: 'I have made it my business, for my own benefit and *that of my brothers*, to make brief extracts ...' (*EH* v. 24; full passage quoted above; emphasis mine). In addition, he no doubt sought a wider readership, namely people in positions of spiritual leadership anywhere whose charge it was to oversee the salvation and moral edification of the faithful. In Bede's usage, these are the *doctores* and *praedicatores*, the 'teachers' and 'preachers' of God's word, and all his commentaries abound with references to them and their all-important calling.[6] Even while discussing the body imagery employed in the Song of Songs, Bede could see fit to enumerate some of their more vital functions:

> They can rightly be called eyes, since they perceive the secrets of mysteries; rightly are they called teeth, since in reproving the ungodly it is as though they are chewing them and, once softened and humbled, transforming them into the body of the Church; rightly are they called a neck, since in preaching eternal joys it is as though they provide the whole body of the Church with the breath of life and prepare the doctrinal food with which she is nourished unto salvation; and they are also quite aptly referred to as breasts, since they supply the milk of the saving word to those who are still infants in Christ.
>
> (*On the Song of Songs*, p. 251; my translation)

The many passages like this on the pastoral responsibilities of those appointed to such roles in the Church underline the deeply didactic, pastoral orientation of Bede's exegetical writings. It is an orientation born not of unoriginality or unsophistication, but, in Alan Thacker's words, of a programme 'increasingly tailored to the needs of his own society'.[7]

The question of when in his career Bede composed these commentaries is less easily resolved since the works themselves contain no dates; unlike modern authors, Bede had no interest in this aspect of publication. Yet there are some clear indications to go on. In the preface to the fourth and final book of *On First Samuel*, Bede explains that he had completed the first three books when Ceolfrith, his abbot, suddenly announced his intention to depart for Rome, an event dated 4 June 716. Bede admits that this troubling incident interrupted his work on the commentary, which evidently he finished by the following year, in 717 (p. 212). *On the Temple*, meanwhile, was completed around 731, for in his letter to Abbot Albinus of Canterbury Bede speaks of it as having been completed around the same time as the *Ecclesiastical History*.[8] But for the other commentaries we not only lack such clues but also face certain difficulties: for example, the possibility that writing a commentary could take Bede several years, as in the case of *On Genesis*, whose composition spanned the years 717–25;[9] or the possibility that Bede might have had several projects going at once, as is also implied by *On Genesis*, which relates in its preface that Bede suspended work on the commentary to begin writing on the Book of Ezra (pp. 66–7). Nevertheless, attempts to date these works have not been entirely fruitless: recent suggestions put *On Ezra and Nehemiah* either early (*c.* 715) or late (post-725) in Bede's career; *Thirty Questions on the Book of Kings* around 715; *On the Song of Songs* around 716; and *On the Proverbs of Solomon* sometime between 709 and 716.[10] The other Old Testament commentaries remain undated.

Nor do we know everything about why Bede chose these portions of the Old Testament. But there is evidence of simultaneous objectives. As we saw, in some cases he was directed by the requests of others. The preface to *On Genesis* is revealing in this regard. Bede notes that many illustrious exegetes have taken up the Genesis story but to little avail for most readers, either because their commentaries are too difficult to understand or too costly to acquire. And so, meeting his bishop's request, he explains that he has combed through them, extracted what is useful, and at times even summarized their words so that both 'a still inexperienced reader' and 'a scholar' might benefit in turn (p. 66). On the other hand, to the six books of his *On the Song of Songs* he added a seventh comprising comments from Gregory the Great's works, 'thinking that it would be pleasing to readers if we would put together as it were in one volume those things which in the explanation of this book he discussed piecemeal throughout all his works, because his remarks are very many and lengthy' (p. 359; my translation).

In these instances, Bede may appear to us as a compiler, that is, a transmitter of what others before him had said. But we should not assume that was his exegetical role. Indeed, for many of his Old Testament selections, there were no patristic predecessors to follow, no earlier commentaries to transmit. Here Bede's role was altogether different: he was breaking new ground. Such is the case with *On the Proverbs of Solomon*, *On Tobias*, *On the Tabernacle*, *On the Temple* and *On Ezra and Nehemiah*. In these commentaries he forged a path with his own footsteps, and his concerns are often telling, as we shall see. Meanwhile, even in those cases where patristic sources existed Bede did not abandon his own ideas. For he still had to decide what portions of those sources to transmit verbatim, what to paraphrase, what to modify or correct, and what to omit altogether. Such decisions also involve critical work, and they provided no less an occasion for ingenuity.[11] And so in the case of his *Commentary on Habakkuk*, where Bede had access to a commentary of

Jerome, his use of it was more critical than subservient, for he had purposes of his own to fulfil quite apart from those of his earlier exegetical counterpart.[12] Examples such as this drive us towards a bold conclusion: that the tag 'following in the footsteps of the Fathers' heralds not a programme of slavish imitation, but reflects instead Bede's attempt to join the tradition of the Fathers by writing alongside them as a collaborator and partner – that is, as one of their own.[13]

Bede's exegetical method

Bede's fluency in the interpretive methods of the Fathers is one clear measure of his status as their equal. It is on full display in his Old Testament commentaries, where like so many exegetes before him he faced the question of the old covenant's relationship to the new. Of course, that question was pressing even in the earliest Christian centuries. Responses to it had been formulated already in the New Testament writings. The underlying premise at work there, which would become so determinative for the earliest Fathers as for Bede, is that the story of Israel is actually a story about Christ. The Old Testament was no ordinary chronicling of the past. Israel's was a 'living history', in the sense that its many ancient narratives – every event, person, place, every minute colouring detail – could be read as 'types' or 'figures' of what Christ did and continues to do for all who compose his Church.[14] Indeed, according to this view, Christian society represents a 'new Israel', the 'spiritual Israel', to use Saint Augustine's formulation,[15] in which the promises of the old covenant will come steadily to pass.

All this demanded special reading strategies designed to harmonize the two testaments. Here too, Bede and the Fathers inherited methods already applied by New Testament writers. In his Epistle to the Galatians, Paul employed the word 'allegory' to interpret the story of Abraham's two sons, one born from his wife Sarah, the other from his slave Hagar: 'There is an allegory here: these women stand for the two covenants' (4:24–5). Paul did not invent the term or its literary applications. Scholars in pre-Christian antiquity relied on allegorical interpretation to explain Homeric poetry and the Greek myths, and Paul's near contemporary, the Jewish writer and philosopher Philo of Alexandria (20 BC–AD 50), wrote several allegorical treatises on the Jewish Scriptures. Yet it was from Paul that subsequent Christian allegorizers received their impetus.[16] The tradition began to flower with the Church Fathers of the third and fourth century associated with Philo's Alexandria, so much so that such allegorical exegesis is often termed 'Alexandrian' as opposed to 'Antiochene', a more literal-historical mode of biblical analysis developed in the fourth century in the rival Syrian city of Antioch.[17] The writings of Origen of Alexandria in the third century, Tyconius and Augustine in the fourth and fifth, and Gregory the Great in the sixth – which were all available in the Wearmouth-Jarrow library – form the main literary channel through which the Alexandrian hermeneutical method would reach Bede, who almost alone was its chief exponent in his own immediate age.[18]

Fundamental to Origen's influential application of that method was the distinguishing of various levels of meaning or 'senses' within a given Old Testament verse or passage. Typically he spoke of three: as human beings have bodies, souls and spirits, so Old Testament stories can be analysed in terms of their literal, moral and spiritual meanings. Though later tradition would deem some of his teachings heretical, Origen's idea of discerning multiple senses within Scripture passed into the patristic mainstream, where through John Cassian and others a fourfold distinction came to be used. In Bede we find evidence of a variety of such approaches. Often he enumerates a fourfold scheme comprising historical, allegorical, tropological and anagogical meanings.[19] Such is the teaching in his guidebook to scriptural interpretation, *The Figures of Rhetoric*. Citing the Jerusalem of Psalm 147:12–13, Bede writes, 'This trope can rightly be taken as referring literally to the citizens of the earthly Jerusalem, allegorically to the Church of Christ, tropologically to each saved soul, and anagogically to the celestial homeland' (p. 207). In *On the Song of Songs*, he argued via the same psalm verses that so many levels of signification can be wrung out of any given verse if, like a honeycomb dripping with honey, it is squeezed 'by careful examination to see how much sweetness of spiritual understanding it contains inside' (p. 260; my translation). And the tabernacle's structure as described in Exodus 25:26 afforded no less fitting an occasion to make the point: 'The table of the tabernacle has four feet because the words of the celestial oracle are customarily taken in either a historical, or an allegorical, or a tropological (that is, moral), or even an anagogical sense' (*On the Tabernacle*, p. 25). But nowhere in his own interpretive practice did Bede rigidly or consistently apply this fourfold scheme.[20] He could speak just as contentedly of three or two senses, and indeed it is the basic twofold distinction between a literal/historical meaning on the one hand and some kind of spiritual meaning on the other – variously termed 'allegorical', 'figurative', 'mystical' or 'hidden' – that informs the hermeneutical procedure most often followed in his Old Testament commentaries.[21]

Bede, following Paul's injunction in 1 Corinthians 10:4 ('Now these things were done as an example for us'), constantly urged his readers to elicit the deeper spiritual meaning from the sacred writings of the Jews – something he believed the Jews themselves had failed to do.[22] Thus he began his reading of the apocryphal Book of Tobit by admitting that, while the literal story had value since it offered 'lessons for the moral life', yet 'anyone who knows how to interpret it not just historically, but also allegorically, sees that just as fruits surpass their leaves this book's inner sense surpasses its literal simplicity' (*On Tobias*, p. 57). In *On the Tabernacle* he noted that there was a time when the Jews, like burning lamps, were rightly afire with observing their laws literally, but once it became clear that 'all these things were to be kept in the Church spiritually rather than according to the letter, it was as if the wicks of the lampstand were being snuffed out, so that after being repaired they might give better light. For they supplied the Holy Church with the light of saving doctrine more sublimely once they began to be understood in the Spirit' (p. 40). In just that vein he warned his monastic readers in *On First Samuel* about the danger of following 'the literal meaning in the Jewish manner'; to illustrate the point, he continued with some rather blunt questions: 'What do we acquire of correction, consolation or of doctrine if, on opening the Book of Samuel, we discover that the one man Elkanah had two wives – especially in the case of ourselves, who aim to be celibate – unless at the same time we have learned how to extract from these and similar texts an allegorical sense such as may refresh us inwardly in a lively way by chastising, instructing or consoling?' (p. 9; my translation). Bede even went so far as to insist that the poetry of the Song of Songs, with its potentially deleterious content, was devoid of any literal meaning, and that 'the whole of it be understood spiritually and typically' (*On the Song of Songs*, p. 337; my translation).

If such comments, coupled with the strong allegorizing tendency at work in most of his commentaries, suggest that Bede had little interest in Scripture's historical-literal aspects, it must be countered that he did not apply the techniques of allegory haphazardly or even exclusively. It is true that his commentaries are the product of methods unlike those favoured by the famous Canterbury school of exegesis associated with Archbishop Theodore and Abbot Hadrian, which flourished in the south of Anglo-Saxon England around 700 and adopted the literal and historical approach of the fourth-century Antiochene exegetes.[23] But Bede's interests in the Bible were exceedingly wide-ranging; they encompassed every imaginable facet of the text and there is no doubting that they included an abiding fascination with its literal reading. In such works as *Thirty Questions on the Book of Kings*, *On the Resting-Places* and *On Eight Questions*, his approach in fact is predominantly literal, intent as it is on resolving a number of chronological and geographical problems. Moreover, even in the allegorical commentaries his attentiveness to the text as text remains apparent. Thus in *On First Samuel*, one of his most strongly allegorical works, he includes an appendix entitled

'Names of the Places' (*Nomina locorum*), in which he discusses the names and historical significance of places mentioned in the Book of Kings (pp. 273–87); and elsewhere he worried aloud about the extent to which an interpreter 'may have forsaken the manifest truth of history by allegorical interpretation' (*On Genesis*, p. 69). To avoid such pitfalls, Bede's usual practice follows a definitive sequence: first explain the literal meaning, then explore the spiritual import. And so we catch him saying even in *On the Song of Songs*, 'But since we have already drawn a few things together from the surface meaning of the text, now let us turn to write of the meanings that can be extracted from the allegory' (p. 221; my translation).[24]

Interpreting Israel's history

Bede's mind was immersed in the biblical past and there can be no doubt, given how much he wrote about it, that Israel's history especially captivated him.[25] He engaged that history not as a historian but as a theologian for whom history was the history of salvation, presented originally to the biblical Israelites and now bestowed on the Church as Israel's successor. Hence when he turned to history it was 'ecclesiastical' history that preoccupied him, his concern being to show how the story of Israel could be read figuratively as the story of the Church in general and of the Anglo-Saxon Church in particular.[26] Israel's chronicled experiences with its God provided a fertile source for much he wished to convey in the *Ecclesiastical History* about the *ecclesia gentis Anglorum*, the Church of the English people. As one scholar has observed, 'Bede's mind was already attuned to the moral lessons of one people's past. In turning to instruct his own "little ones" … through their own history, he naturally understood it in similar terms.'[27] Obviously the *Ecclesiastical History* is a splendid achievement in this regard. But what made it possible was the many years Bede devoted to studying the Old Testament in his commentaries.

Collectively, Bede's Old Testament commentaries survey much of Israel's sacred history, moving from the origins in the Genesis saga up through the exile in Babylon to the attempts at repatriation that followed. And here they sample not only from the historical books but from Israel's prophetic, wisdom and apocryphal traditions as well. But one stretch of that history dominated Bede's attention, especially in terms of its relevance to contemporary Anglo-Saxon society. In *On the Tabernacle*, *On the Temple* and *On Ezra and Nehemiah*, he devoted long works of exegesis to three Jewish sanctuaries: the tabernacle built under the aegis of Moses and Aaron during the exodus from Egypt; the first temple constructed during the reign of King Solomon; and the second temple rebuilt by the Jews who returned from

Babylon with Ezra and Nehemiah. Bede was the first Christian exegete to produce complete verse-by-verse commentaries on these subjects. And so it is important to ask why he chose to expend so much interpretive energy on them.

In the narrative of the Old Testament, the tabernacle and the temple mark a critical phase of development in God's covenantal relationship with Israel. For these structures – the former a small tent made of wood and coloured fabrics, the latter a large building constructed of hewn stone – were dwelling places for God, thus revealing his desire to live amongst his people and be their deity. They housed Israel's most holy artefact, the Ark of the Covenant, which contained the tablets of the Law and itself was the locus for theophanies of the divine presence (see Exodus 25:22). The tabernacle, a portable structure, held the Ark while the people wandered in the wilderness en route to the Promised Land; once there, it was moved to the temple, built in Jerusalem as a permanent dwelling place for God. Already in the New Testament these sacred sanctuaries were taken as figures of both Christ's body (John 2:13–18) and a celestial residence, a house 'not made by human hands but everlasting, in the heavens' (2 Corinthians 5:1). In *On the Tabernacle* and *On the Temple*, Bede develops these figurative associations, with particular attention to the Church as the temple's successor, the new 'building' in which God dwells: 'The tabernacle that Moses made for the Lord in the wilderness, like the temple that Solomon made in Jerusalem, designates the state of the Holy Church universal, part of which already reigns with the Lord in heaven, while part is still journeying in this present life away from the Lord, until its members die and follow one another' (*On the Tabernacle*, p. 45). Bede's technique in both commentaries is ruminative and associative, so that each spiritual meaning can acquire multiple layers of signification. Thus he distinguishes the tabernacle from the temple in two ways: on one level, the tabernacle designates 'the present Church, which is daily employed in its labours', whereas the temple signifies 'the repose of the future Church' in heaven (*On the Tabernacle*, p. 45); on the other hand, the tabernacle can stand too for 'the time of the synagogue', since it was built by 'the Hebrew people alone', with the temple representing the Church since 'its builders came from the Gentiles as well' (p. 46).

Now the idea of building a house for God parallels Bede's historical account of the foundation of the *ecclesia gentis Anglorum* in the *Ecclesiastical History*. The resonance intensifies when it is recalled that the tabernacle and temple commentaries (and probably *On Ezra and Nehemiah* as well) and the *Ecclesiastical History* are contemporaneous works, suggesting Bede may have envisioned a massive exegetical-historical project on a set of interrelated themes which he deemed particularly pressing. Noteworthy here is his concern for unity-in-diversity.[28] Just as the curtains of the tabernacle consist of multicoloured fabrics, so Bede explains that 'the Holy Church universal is built from many elect persons, from many churches throughout the world, and from flowers of diverse virtues' (*On the Tabernacle*, p. 48). Hence the reason King Solomon sought the help of foreigners in building the Jerusalem temple (which was thus the collaboration of Jews and Gentiles), for 'every kind of person by whom the Church was to be built had already gone before in the building of the temple' (*On the Temple*, p. 14). In the Anglo-Saxon present, such co-operation amongst different peoples (Latin *gentes*) found its own typological fulfilment in the many difference races (Roman and Irish above all) who conspired to build the English Church through their missionary efforts, and then again in that Church itself, composed as it was of the various Germanic and Celtic peoples who had settled in Britain.[29] Like the work of the apostles begun in Acts, the conversion of these barbarian *gentes* is seen by Bede as a continuation of the mission to evangelize all Gentile nations, of whom the English are the latest instance, thereby placing their conversion within the providential scheme of world (and biblical) history.

Connected with this is a second prominent theme: the need to provide such newcomers to the faith with instruction in doctrine and morals. Here what the *Ecclesiastical History* dramatizes in its many tales of saintly teachers such as Aidan and Cuthbert (see III. 3–5, 13–17 and IV. 27–31) finds its theoretical undergirding in the treatment of the tabernacle and temple priesthoods, which furnished a set of images Bede could use to admonish the spiritual leaders of his day. Thus to each of the priestly vestments worn by Aaron and his sons he assigns a deeper spiritual message: to the superhumerale, the need for good works; to the rational, the virtue of discernment; to the tunic, confidence in speaking and teaching, and so on (*On the Tabernacle*, pp. 113–44). Any doubt that Bede had in mind an English audience when discussing such priestly virtues is erased by his topical remarks on the destruction by fire of Aaron's first two sons, which he is quick to read as 'a sign of our unhappy time, in which some who have attained positions as priests and teachers – merely to mention it is both distressing and sad enough – are consumed by the fire of heavenly vengeance because they prefer the fire of cupidity to the fire of heavenly love' (p. 110).

Although also found in the *Ecclesiastical History* (see III. 5), references to contemporary conditions are less expected in a biblical commentary, where they may reveal something about the ends Bede thought that genre could serve.[30] Indeed, in *On Ezra and Nehemiah*, which I have argued constitutes Bede's third entry in a trilogy of commentaries on the tabernacle–temple theme,[31] such references are especially conspicuous, as they anticipate the views on ecclesiastical reform outlined in his last known work, the *Letter to*

Bishop Egbert. Written just months before his death in 735, this letter decries the secular and ecclesiastical ills Bede believed were corrupting his native Northumbrian Church and demands their swift reform.[32] But *On Ezra and Nehemiah* in particular shows that his thinking on the subject was no mere deathbed reflection.[33] Indeed, as the First Book of Samuel guided his judgements on kingship,[34] so his ideas on reform owe much to his careful reading of Ezra–Nehemiah, whose contents, he perceived, were markedly different from the portions of Scripture he treated in *On the Tabernacle* and *On the Temple*. Where Exodus 24–30 and 1 Kings 5–7 concentrate mainly on architectural details, Ezra–Nehemiah's focus is the restoration and reform of the Jewish people themselves, now that they had returned to their homeland and, through the aid of their secular and religious leaders, were attempting to reconstitute themselves as a community before God. The analogy to the present was evident and Bede was keen to make the most of it.

The commentary's opening pages sketch the envisaged allegorical scheme: '... the rebuilding of the Lord's house after it was burnt down, the restoration of Jerusalem after its destruction, the return of the people to their homeland after their captivity, and the recovery of the holy stolen vessels to their house all typologically denote this one and the same return of penitents to the Church' (*On Ezra and Nehemiah*, p. 9). On the figurative level, then, Bede aligns the story's controlling images – exile and repatriation, destruction and reconstruction, loss and recovery – with the common spiritual condition of being separated from the community of the Church through sin but returning to it through repentance. But the need to allegorize these Old Testament books was less pressing; their literal sense was just as efficacious to a Northumbrian Church in need of reform. Here Bede's skill as a discriminating reader takes centre stage as he exploits the setting, characters and other formal elements of the plot for their bearing on the present. So when he comes to Ezra 6:18 ('And they appointed the priests in their orders and the Levites in their divisions to supervise the services of God in Jerusalem'), the newly reconstructed temple with its full cast of religious functionaries suggests to him by contrast the pitiful situation of his contemporaries 'who, though founding monasteries with splendid workmanship, in no way appoint teachers in them to exhort the people to God's work but rather those who will serve their own pleasures and desires there' (p. 102; cf. *Letter to Bishop Egbert*, pp. 349–53). Striking an equally contemporary note, he relates the unfair taxation that some Jews imposed on their less well-off brethren (see Nehemiah 5:1–4) to those clerics in his own day 'who exact an immense tax and weight of worldly goods from those whom they claim to be in charge of while in return giving nothing for their eternal salvation either by teaching them or by providing them with examples of good living' (*On Ezra and*

Nehemiah, p. 184) – thus anticipating another burning issue of his letter, episcopal greed and simony (cf. *Letter to Bishop Egbert*, p. 347). Tellingly, the passage concludes with an appeal for a Northumbrian Nehemiah: 'Would that some Nehemiah ... might come in our own days and restrain our errors, kindle our breasts to love of the divine, and strengthen our hands by turning them away from our own pleasures to establishing Christ's city!' (p. 184).

But it is Ezra the priest and scribe whom Bede especially utilizes as a vehicle for his reform programme. For Ezra's dual status made him exceptionally relevant to present-day English clergy. Thus Bede emphasizes that Ezra's task as scribe was not only the preservation and transmission of Holy Writ but also its learned dissemination through preaching and teaching (*On Ezra and Nehemiah*, pp. 108–9). Hence Bede's Ezra is something like a Bedan exegetical *doctor* who reforms others through the interpretation of sacred texts! Concerning Ezra's priesthood, Bede calls him *pontifex* or 'high priest', a role not assigned to him in the biblical story. His purpose in doing so emerges in his exegesis of a key episode of the biblical narrative, Ezra's reprimand of the returnees for mingling with foreign women (see Ezra 9):

> And it should be carefully noted and used as an example of good works that while some leaders sinned and caused the common people who were entrusted to them to sin, other leaders who were of more wholesome view for their part did their best to correct those sins; but because they cannot do this themselves they refer the matter to their *pontifex* (i.e. their archbishop) through whose authority so grave, so manifold, and so long-lasting a sin can be expiated. (*On Ezra and Nehemiah*, pp. 138–9)

The equation of Jewish pontifical and Anglo-Saxon episcopal authority is an ingenious touch. For it transforms the actions of the Old Testament character into a paradigm for contemporary bishops like Egbert of York, to whose authority Bede directly appealed for solutions to the present dilemma outlined in his letter. It is a stunning example of Bede's highly original appropriation of Old Testament narrative and his desire to make it speak to the needs of his own society.

Conclusion

Bede's Old Testament commentaries rank highly amongst his literary achievements, and not only because their pages bulk so largely. They testify to his ability to step into a tradition – and an enormously storied one at that – and master its conventions as capably as did its first practitioners, while at the same time making some very real contributions of his own, be it in covering books neglected by prior interpreters, or in adapting the texts interpreted to the circumstances of his own time. In both cases, what emerges is something rather different from the seemingly humble depiction of his exegetical endeavours he offers us at the end of the *Ecclesiastical History*. As much as those remarks underline – as was only proper for a monk[35] – his subservience to those great authorities who preceded him, the commentaries themselves reveal the extent to which he succeeded in forging such an identity for himself as he laboured for the spiritual welfare of his own people and the many others who would read his commentaries for centuries to come.

NOTES

1. G. H. Brown 1987: 42.
2. DeGregorio 2004 and 2006b; Ray 1982.
3. Ward 1990: 41–6.
4. Laistner 1935; Lapidge 2006.
5. Bede did not read the Jewish Scriptures in the original Hebrew; what little knowledge he had of Hebrew he appears to have drawn mainly from the writings of Jerome. See Sutcliffe 1935.
6. Thacker 1983, 1992 and 2006.
7. Thacker 2006: 38.
8. Meyvaert 1999: 278.
9. Kendall 2008: 45–53.
10. DeGregorio 2004; Holder 2005a; Meyvaert 1999 and 2005.
11. Ray 1982; Stansbury 1999a.
12. Ward 1993. On Bede's disagreements with Jerome, see also Ray 1987 and Thacker 2006: 45.
13. Ray 2006.
14. Auerbach 1973; O'Keefe and Reno 2005: 24–44.
15. Saint Augustine, *On Christian Teaching*, trans. R. Green, Oxford's World Classics (Oxford University Press, 1999), 3.34.48, pp. 93–4.
16. de Lubac 2000: vol. II, pp. 1–8.
17. Young 2003.
18. Holder 1990: 405; C. W. Jones 1970a: 132.
19. Thus the word 'allegorical' applies broadly to this whole reading method and narrowly to one of the 'senses' thereby discerned: see Kendall 2006: 107–9.
20. Ray 1982; Robinson 1994.
21. C. W. Jones 1970a; Kendall 2006.
22. *On the Proverbs of Solomon*, pp. 95–6: 'What does it profit the unfaithful Jewish people to have the riches of the Scriptures when they cannot understand Christ in them?' For discussion of the theme, see Scheil 2004: 35–9.
23. Bischoff and Lapidge 1994.
24. Cf. *On the Tabernacle*, p. 47: 'But first we must reflect for a little while upon the text of the material letter itself, so that we shall be able to discuss the spiritual sense with greater certainty.'
25. For a recent discussion of the subject, see Scheil 2004: 30–110.
26. On the continuities between Israel and the Church, see Carroll 1946: 67–98.
27. Wormald 1992: 23.

28. Carroll 1946: 77–80; Holder 1991: 145–50.
29. On the meaning of the Latin word *gens* in this connection, see Yorke 2000.
30. DeGregorio 2002.
31. DeGregorio 2004 and 2006d.
32. J. Blair 2005: 100–8.
33. DeGregorio 2004, 2005, 2006c and 2006d.
34. McClure 1983; Wallace-Hadrill 1971: 76–8.
35. Cf. Ray 2006: 12–18, who reads Bede's humble self-presentation as a calculated act of rhetorical modesty.

10

ARTHUR G. HOLDER

Bede and the New Testament

One of the best-known stories in Bede's *Ecclesiastical History* tells of a council meeting at the court of King Edwin of Northumbria around 627 (II. 13). The king had been listening to the preaching of a missionary bishop from Canterbury named Paulinus and had nearly made up his mind to accept baptism and become a Christian. But first he wanted to confer with his chief counsellors in order to ask their opinion of this unfamiliar doctrine and new form of worship. The chief priest of the old religion, whose name was Coifi, wryly observed that, although he had been the most loyal servant of the pagan gods, he had not received as much honour and wealth from the king as others who were less devout. 'So it follows that if, on examination, these new doctrines which have now been explained to us are found to be better and more effectual, let us accept them without any delay' (p. 183). Another one of Edwin's counsellors agreed, but for somewhat different reasons. This unnamed advisor compared a human being's life on earth to the flight of a sparrow that flies into the king's banquet hall in winter. For a brief span of time, the sparrow is warmed by the fire and protected from the storm outside, but then it flies out again into the cold. 'So this life of man appears but for a moment; what follows or indeed what went before, we know not at all. If this new doctrine brings us more certain information, it seems right that we should accept it' (p. 185). Soon afterwards, the king was baptized along with several members of his family and many of the people.

What did Bede think Christianity had to offer by way of both temporal and eternal rewards? What information about human life and destiny did he believe this new faith had to offer the English people? And on what authority did he base his convictions? The answers to these questions are bound up with Bede's view of Holy Scripture, as we learn in another famous story from the *Ecclesiastical History*. After Abbess Hild and the learned men of her monastery at Whitby discovered that the cowherd Cædmon had received the miraculous gift of turning Christian doctrine into song, they instructed him in the story of salvation by teaching him from the Bible. The topics of

142

Cædmon's verse compositions are indicative of Bede's understanding of the Christian message as found in Scripture:

> He sang about the creation of the world, the origin of the human race, and the whole history of Genesis, of the departure of Israel from Egypt and the entry into the promised land and of many other of the stories taken from the sacred Scriptures: of the incarnation, passion, and resurrection of the Lord, of His ascension into heaven, of the coming of the Holy Spirit and the teaching of the apostles. He also made songs about the terrors of future judgement, the horrors of the pains of hell, and the joys of the heavenly kingdom.   (IV. 24, p. 419)

In sum, Christianity offered the English people the promise of heavenly delights and the avoidance of the fires of hell. The truth revealed in Scripture was the great history of human salvation, and the authority behind that truth was the Holy Spirit that inspired the authors of the Bible as well as its interpreters throughout the ages.

For Bede, it was axiomatic that this sacred story had two distinct but complementary acts: the Old Testament and the New Testament, which he often identified as 'the law' and 'the gospel'. But the relationship between the two biblical testaments was more complicated than merely chronological or supersessionist (as though the New simply replaced or contradicted the Old). As Bede explained in his interpretation of the book held in God's right hand as he sits on the heavenly throne in Apocalypse 5:1: 'This vision represents the mysteries of Holy Scripture, as laid open to us through the Incarnation of the Lord. And its concordant unity contains, so to say, the Old Testament without, and the New within' (*Commentary on the Apocalypse*, p. 34). As he had learned from Augustine and the other Church Fathers, both testaments testify to Jesus Christ as the Redeemer of humankind, but from different perspectives. What the Old Testament anticipated has been fulfilled in the New; what the New Testament reveals was veiled in shadowy types and figures in the Old.[1] From his boyhood on, Bede would have been exposed to visual depictions of this relationship between the two testaments whenever he entered the monastery church of St Paul at Jarrow, where Abbot Benedict Biscop had installed complementary pictures of Old and New Testament scenes such as 'Isaac carrying the wood on which he was to be burned as a sacrifice ... below that of Christ carrying the cross' and 'the Son of Man lifted up on the Cross ... paired with the serpent raised up by Moses in the desert' (*History of the Abbots*, ch. 9, p. 194).[2]

Since Bede saw the two testaments as offering their common message in different modes of presentation, we might expect his exegesis of the New Testament to make little if any use of allegorical interpretation, at least outside of the visionary symbolism of the Book of Revelation. After all, if the

Gospel message is openly revealed in the New Testament, what need is there for the exegete to uncover hidden mysteries? But again following the tradition he had received, Bede found it necessary not only to explain the historical references in the New Testament books and to draw out their moral implications for Christian living, but also to interpret them 'spiritually' or 'mystically'. For example, Bede says that when the Syrophoenician woman in Mark 7:24–30 tells Jesus that even the dogs eat the crumbs from the children's table, she represents the entire Church of the Gentiles and the table stands for the Holy Scriptures that provide believers with the bread of life (*Commentary on the Gospel of Mark*, pp. 523–4). Similarly, when the disciples in Luke 24:2 find the stone rolled away from the tomb and the body of Jesus missing, Bede explains that the stone represented the Mosaic law which had been written on stone tablets but has now been unsealed to reveal not the dead body of the Lord but the living Christ (*Commentary on the Gospel of Luke*, p. 411). Even the detail given in Acts 20:8 that there were several lamps burning in the upper room where Paul was teaching prompts Bede to give the text a spiritual reading: 'We can speak allegorically here, for the upper room is the loftiness of spiritual gifts; night is the obscurity of the scriptures; the abundance of lamps is the explanation of the more enigmatic sayings' (*Commentary on the Acts of the Apostles*, p. 159). In his commentaries on the New Testament, Bede was just as eager as he was in those on the Old Testament 'to shed light on those things which seemed to be treated mystically or stated somewhat obscurely' (*Commentary on Acts*, p. 3).

Bede's New Testament commentaries

The corpus of Bede's works includes seven major commentaries on New Testament books. Apparently the first to be composed (*c.* 703–9) was the *Commentary on the Apocalypse* dealing with the last book in the Bible, also known as the Book of Revelation. In a dedicatory letter addressed to his fellow monk 'Eusebius' (actually Hwætberht, later abbot of Jarrow), Bede noted that he had divided the work into three short books and kept the exposition brief on account of 'the indolence of our nation, I mean of the English', which had only recently received the seed of faith at the time of Pope Gregory and had not yet perfected the art of reading (p. 9). The same letter contains seven rules for exegesis composed by the fourth-century Donatist theologian Tyconius, which Bede had taken from Augustine's *On Christian Doctrine*. Particularly useful to Bede was the sixth rule, which states that the events narrated in Scripture did not always occur in the order in which they are recorded but are sometimes repeated or 'recapitulated' for the sake of exposition or emphasis. This rule allowed Bede to argue, following his patristic sources Victorinus and Primasius in addition to Tyconius, that the Apocalypse is not actually a prophetic timetable for the end of the world but rather a symbolic and cyclical account of the Church's struggles against heresy and persecution throughout the world's sixth age – which is certainly the last age, but of indeterminate length.[3] Bede expected Christ to come again in glory to judge the living and the dead, but he had no patience with those who claimed to be able to calculate the precise date of his arrival. His eschatological hope was summed up in his comment on Apocalypse 2:28, which now serves as a memorial inscription above his tomb in the Galilee Chapel in Durham Cathedral: 'Christ is the morning star who when the night of this world is past brings to his saints the promise of the light of life and opens everlasting day.'

The only direct Latin precursor for Bede's *Commentary on the Acts of the Apostles* (*c.* 709) was a verse commentary by the sixth-century poet Arator, but he also drew on works by Augustine, Eusebius, Gregory, Isidore and Jerome, as well as the Jewish historian Josephus and the Latin natural historian Pliny. Sometimes he quoted his sources at length; other times he merely drew on them for particular points or allusions. If he was derivative as an author, it was not the result of any lack of industry or knowledge; on the contrary, only an assiduous and extremely well-read scholar could have produced a synthetic and readable commentary from so many widely scattered sources. Like much of Bede's exegetical work, this commentary on Acts was written at the behest of Bishop Acca of Hexham, who had originally asked the monk of Jarrow for a commentary on the Gospel of Luke but did not receive that more complex work until several years later. The *Commentary on Acts* is notable for Bede's beginning forays into textual criticism (the comparison of different biblical manuscripts in order to establish the authoritative version) and his occasional reference to a Greek text in addition to the Vulgate and several Old Latin versions. But many years later (*c.* 725–31), probably inspired by Augustine's similarly titled example, Bede wrote a second commentary (*Retraction on the Acts of the Apostles*) in which he made use of his more highly developed facility with the Greek language to correct some of his own earlier errors, respond to some objections voiced by critics, and expand his work on establishing the best Latin text of this biblical book.

Bede's next exegetical project (*c.* 709–16) was a commentary on the seven New Testament epistles attributed to James, Peter, John and Jude, 'which church tradition calls catholic, that is, universal' because they are not addressed to particular churches (*Commentary on the Seven Catholic Epistles*, p. 3). His only predecessor in this field was Augustine, from whose work on the First Epistle of John he quoted fairly extensively; for the other six epistles he was for the most part working without direct sources to follow. Since these epistles contain so much doctrinal instruction and moral exhortation, Bede's commentary is mostly literal and historical rather than allegorical in nature. A recurrent theme in the commentary (as in the epistles themselves) is the refutation of heretics and schismatics, but whereas the biblical authors seem mostly to have been concerned about early Christian Gnostics, Docetists and libertines, Bede applied their strictures against such later alleged opponents of orthodoxy as the Manicheans, Arians, chiliasts and especially the Pelagians who (as Bede saw it) denied the need for God's grace. Although there were no admitted adherents of these heretical groups in Anglo-Saxon England at the time of Bede, he feared that English Christians might fall into doctrinal error as a result of ignorance or be led astray by reading heretical texts unawares. Moreover, throughout his life he was deeply involved in the debates between his own 'Romanist' party and various 'Celtic' (Irish or British) groups over the dating of Easter and the proper form of monastic tonsure. While he would not have thought of Christians who persisted in the Irish observance as heretics in the strict sense, he was certainly aware that some Romanists had accused them of Pelagianism because they were thought to celebrate Easter during the Jewish Passover and thus symbolically deny the need for Christ's resurrection.[4]

The other major collection of epistles in the New Testament is comprised of those attributed to Saint Paul. For Bede, this included not only all those bearing Paul's name (some of which are considered pseudonymous by modern scholarship) but also the Epistle to the Hebrews, about which there was dispute over authorship even in ancient times. Although he was obviously devoted to 'the Apostle' who was the patron of his own monastery at Jarrow, Bede never wrote a commentary of his own on the Pauline epistles. Instead, as he says in his autobiographical statement in the *Ecclesiastical History*, 'I have transcribed in order whatever I found in the works of St Augustine' (v. 24, p. 569). For the most part, Bede actually took the material in his *Excerpts from the Works of Saint Augustine on the Letters of the Blessed Apostle Paul* from a collection compiled by Eugippius in the sixth century. But whereas Eugippius had arranged his collection thematically, Bede's was in the order of the Pauline texts themselves, making the *Excerpts* much more accessible as a commentary and certainly contributing to its subsequent popularity.[5]

The longest of Bede's New Testament commentaries are those he composed on the Gospel of Luke (*c.* 709–16) and on the Gospel of Mark (*c.* 725–30); the second commentary repeats much of the exegesis from the first since the two Gospels have a good deal of material in common. Both were written at the request of Bishop Acca and prefaced with letters in which Bede described a system of marginal notation that he had invented in order to indicate borrowings from his four principal patristic sources.[6] As he explained to Acca in the prologue to the *Commentary on the Gospel of Luke*:

> Having gathered together the works of the Fathers as if they were the most eminent and most worthy craftsmen of such a great gift, I diligently undertook to examine what blessed Ambrose, what Augustine, and then what Gregory, the apostle of our nation who was 'most watchful' in accordance with his [Greek] name, what Jerome the interpreter of sacred history, [and] what the rest of the Fathers thought and said about the words of blessed Luke ... Because it was laborious to insert their names every time and to indicate by name what had been said by which author, I found it convenient to note the first letters of their names in the margin and in this way to show where the discourse I have transcribed from each of the Fathers individually begins and where it ends. [This I have done] carefully throughout, lest it be said that I was stealing the words of my predecessors and putting them forth as my own. I very much pray and beseech my readers through the Lord that if anyone should perhaps judge these works of ours to be in any way worthy of transcription, they might remember also to add the aforementioned signs of the names as they find them in our exemplar. (p. 7; my translation)

Even with the aid of Bede's source marks, the currently available critical editions of these two commentaries do not identify all of the material taken from other authors. Many of the ideas and much of the language are drawn from the works of the Fathers, but Bede has put his own stamp on the material. As one scholar has noted, he 'subjected his sources to an endless series of adaptation, condensing and amplifying, reorganizing and explaining'.[7] Nor was he afraid to contradict a traditional authority on occasion, or to exercise his own independent judgement by choosing one Father's position over that of another. As a result of one such determination, Bede had to defend himself (in the same prologue to the *Commentary on the Gospel of Luke* quoted above) against criticism that he had been a theological innovator in an earlier work. In his *Commentary on the Apocalypse*, Bede had followed Augustine's identification of the four beasts in Apocalypse 4:7 by saying that the evangelist Matthew was represented by the lion, Mark by the man, Luke by the ox and John by the eagle. The conventional interpretation in Anglo-Saxon England, however, instead followed Jerome in linking Mark with the lion and Matthew with the man. Bede's lengthy rejoinder quoted Augustine's *On the Consensus of the Evangelists* extensively in order to prove that his own view was not without precedent, but he was well aware that he was taking a controversial and unpopular position. In any case, it is certain that Bede saw both his selections from the Fathers and the interpretations he offered to supplement and extend their labours as serving the same purpose: the instruction of pastors and teachers in the faith 'once delivered to the saints' (Jude 3).

Bede's exegetical method in practice

All of Bede's New Testament commentaries proceed through the biblical text following Jerome's arrangement of the Vulgate *per cola et commata* (that is, divided into lines according to phrases in order to facilitate reading aloud). There are certainly recurrent themes and patterns in Bede's exegesis, and his exposition retains a sense of the overall structure of the biblical narratives or the epistolary frameworks. Nevertheless, he tends to treat each verse (or sometimes a group of two or three verses) as a discrete unit to be analysed, interpreted and appropriated by the Christian reader. On occasion he did not hesitate to offer two or more interpretations of a single verse, in accordance with Augustine's dictum that there is nothing wrong with a variety of interpretations as long as all of them can be confirmed with reference to other scriptural passages and are in harmony with the truth.[8] In moving from literal text to spiritual meaning, Bede employed all the exegetical techniques he had learned from the Church Fathers: the etymology of words (especially from the Hebrew and Greek), number symbolism, the interpretation of images drawn from nature and history, and elucidation according to the principle of 'concordance' by which a particular verse is linked to other biblical verses.

Bede uses all of these techniques together in his usual eclectic fashion in the course of commenting on the first chapter of the Book of Acts. For example, a Greek etymology taken from Jerome explains that the name of the book's addressee, Theophilus, means 'lover of God, or beloved of God' in Greek. 'Therefore, anyone who is a lover of God may believe that this [work] was written for him, because the physician Luke wrote it in order that he [the reader] might find health for his soul' (*Commentary on Acts*, p. 9). Number symbolism as applied to the forty days that Jesus spent with his disciples after the resurrection shows that the number forty 'designates this temporal earthly life, either on account of the four seasons of the year, or on account of the four winds of the heavens' (p. 10). The familiar natural association of height with exaltation and merit allows Bede to say that the presence of the apostles in an upper room shows that 'having already been raised up from an earthly way of life, they [the apostles] had mounted up to greater heights of knowledge and virtue' (p. 15). The principle of concordance is applied in a rather complicated way in Bede's discussion of Acts 1:26, where the apostles cast lots to choose between two candidates to replace Judas Iscariot who betrayed Jesus. Bede recalls two other places in the Bible where lots were cast: in Jonah 1:7 when sailors identified Jonah as the cause of a storm at sea, and in Luke 1:9 when Zechariah the priestly father of John the Baptist was chosen to offer incense in the temple. Quoting Jerome's comment on the Jonah passage, Bede observes that 'the prerogative of individuals ... can in no way make a general law'

(p. 20), so these biblical precedents cannot be used to support the casting of lots by Christians in later times. Indeed, all three of these incidents came before Pentecost, when the Old Covenant with its sacrifices and offerings gave way to the New Covenant made perfect in the fire of the Holy Spirit. After Pentecost, no lots were cast when the apostles appointed seven deacons as related in Acts 6:1–6; therefore, Christians 'should see that these same apostles needed only the assembly of the brethren gathered together and prayers poured forth to God' (p. 21).

Scholars have noted, with good reason, that Bede's approach to theology and exegesis was more practical and ethical, less psychological and mystical, than that of his mentor Gregory the Great; in modern terms, Bede played the extrovert to Gregory's introvert.[9] Nevertheless, Bede's commentaries – like his homilies – often utilize what has been called 'the Gregorian method of the interiorisation of exterior details'.[10] A typical example is Bede's interpretation (drawn largely from Ambrose, Augustine and Gregory) of Luke 15:22, where the forgiving father orders his servants to clothe the repentant prodigal son with a robe, ring and sandals (*Commentary on the Gospel of Luke*, p. 291). Taking each element of the biblical passage in turn, Bede draws theological and moral meanings from the text. Thus he explains that the robe is the garment of innocence and immortality that humanity received at creation but lost at the fall. The servants are the preachers who proclaim reconciliation with God and promise mortals that they will become not only citizens of heaven but also heirs of God and co-heirs with Christ (Romans 8:17). A ring symbolizing pure faith is given to the Church when she is married to Christ, and it is put on her finger so that her faith may shine with works and her works be strengthened with faith. The sandals on the prodigal's feet represent the office of preaching the Gospel, by which the course of one's mind is turned from earthly things and enabled to tread safely upon serpents and scorpions (Luke 10:19). 'Therefore hands and feet (that is, deeds and thoughts) are both adorned: deeds, so that we may live rightly; thoughts, so that we may hurry to eternal joys' (*Commentary on the Gospel of Luke*, p. 291; my translation). It is characteristic of Bede's exegesis that his exposition of particular details in the biblical text should end with a general moral application: Christians should be adorned with pure thoughts and good deeds. Thus the internalization of exterior details brings the reader step by step towards a transformation of earthly behaviour in anticipation of heavenly delights.

Some favourite themes

Until recently, biblical scholars since the Enlightenment have been most interested in trying to determine the 'original meaning' of a text in the mind of its human author. This has been changing to some extent with the advent of postmodern approaches to the Bible such as deconstruction, postcolonial reading and reader-response criticism. Interestingly enough, in some ways the postmodern approaches bring us closer to biblical interpretation as practised by Bede and other patristic and medieval commentators. As Paul Meyvaert has suggested, their exegetical work

> should be viewed as a grand exercise in the use of the imagination, and we should not be overly concerned with the particular text of Scripture which is being commented on. Figures like Bede and Gregory were concerned to make certain doctrinal points and to pass on some of the lessons they had drawn from their own spiritual experience. They are constantly on the watch for scriptural verses on which they can peg this or that idea. What ultimately counts is less the incongruity of some of the pegs than the insistence and frequency with which we find this or that theme being repeated. This is what furnishes a real key to the inner preoccupations of the writer.[11]

Bede was more interested in what the scriptural text might mean in the lives of contemporary readers than in what was in the minds of the human authors. The goal is inspired reading and appropriation of the text, not just critical analysis. Reading Bede's New Testament commentaries as such a 'grand exercise in the use of the imagination', we discover some recurrent topics such as the ideal of the 'primitive Church', apostles as models for Christian pastors and teachers, miracles as revelatory of spiritual growth, action and contemplation, and in one instance reference to a 'true law of history'. It will be instructive to consider each of these briefly in order to trace some favourite themes in Bede's approach to theology, spirituality and history.

The primitive Church

In the *Ecclesiastical History*, Bede praised the monastic communities established by Augustine at Canterbury (I. 26) and by Hild at Whitby (IV. 23) because they had imitated the example of the 'primitive Church'. When Bede employed this term, he was usually referring to the early Christian community in Jerusalem as depicted in Acts 4:32: 'Now the multitude of believers were of one heart and soul; neither did any of them say that any of the things they possessed were their own, but all things were common to them.' Following a long patristic tradition, Bede saw this community as representing the ideal pattern for monks, as his comment on this same verse suggests: 'Those who had completely left the world behind by no means pushed themselves forward, one over the other, glorying in the nobility of their birth. Rather, as born from the womb of the same mother, the church, they all rejoiced in one and the same love of brotherhood' (*Commentary on Acts*, p. 52). Leaving the world behind was integral to the monastic vocation in Bede's view, and the rejection of preferential status based on noble birth was a particular hallmark of the Benedictine Rule as strongly advocated by Benedict Biscop, the founder of Bede's own monastic community at Wearmouth-Jarrow (*History of the Abbots*, ch. 11, p. 196).[12] So here and in many other places in Bede's exegetical and historical works, the 'primitive Church' represents a model of perfection. But sometimes the emphasis falls rather on the inchoate and imperfect character of the Christian community during the time before the admission of Gentiles, when the Church was still a group of Jewish believers following the Old Testament law (e.g. Bede's comment on Acts 15:21 in the *Commentary on Acts*, p. 131, where he refers to 'the primitive Church, still practicing Jewish ways'). When Bede considers the early Church from this perspective, he traces a historical development from infancy to maturity, from intolerant narrowness to missionary inclusion, and from a mono-ethnic community to a pluralistic one.[13] In this trajectory it is possible to see a parallel with the *Ecclesiastical History*'s account of the supplanting of the allegedly insular and ingrown British Church by Bede's own Anglo-Saxon Church, which he depicts as being more mission-minded, expansive and in touch with the rest of the Christian world.

Apostles, pastors and teachers

The vision of the New Jerusalem recorded in Apocalypse 21:9–14 speaks of a heavenly city with twelve gates inscribed with the names of the twelve tribes of Israel, twelve angels at the gates and twelve foundations bearing the names of the twelve apostles. Naturally Bede's *Commentary on the Apocalypse* identifies both the gates and the foundations as the apostles of Christ who 'either by writing, or by work, laid open to all nations an entrance into the Church' (p. 146). But it comes as something of a surprise that he sees the angels as those *doctores* (teachers) 'who follow the footsteps of the Apostles in the mystery of the faith and word' (p. 146). Bede knew that the Greek word *angelos* means 'messengers' or 'heralds', so he readily associated the angels of the New Jerusalem with the pastors and teachers who were his primary audience. For their sake, in his commentaries on both testaments he frequently admonished Christian pastors to study the Scriptures so they might learn the truth themselves before teaching it to others, to practise all the virtues that they preached, and to proclaim the Gospel both willingly and without expectation of temporal gain. 'For just as someone who performs his ministry well wins for himself a good station [1 Timothy 3:13], so he who tries to grab the responsibility of teaching for himself without being taught, who proclaims Christ from mixed motives [Philippians 1:15–17], deserves judgment of condemnation more than if he should perish alone in his wicked deed' (*Commentary on the Seven Catholic Epistles*, p. 35). We see the same high pastoral ideal in Bede's depictions of Aidan, Cuthbert, Hild and other teachers who appear in the pages of the *Ecclesiastical History*. Bede often compares these saintly religious leaders with the apostles, as in the encomium of Cuthbert's episcopal ministry found in the *Ecclesiastical History* (IV. 28).

Miracles

Like other Christians of his time, Bede accepted the miracle stories in the New Testament as historically true. His comments on the miracles performed by Christ and the apostles were therefore not intended to defend their authenticity but to interpret their meaning for believers. Following Gregory the Great, Bede saw the primary purpose of biblical miracles as apologetic: they were 'signs' that strengthened faith by establishing the authority of Christ's teachings and revealing the power of his divine nature.[14] His interpretation of New Testament miracles emphasized inner spiritual conversion more than physical transformation, as in his comment on Mark 8:22: 'All the maladies cured by the Lord are signs of spiritual maladies to which the soul draws near through sin to eternal death ... so in the gradual healing of this blind man by the Lord is designated the illumination of the hearts of those who are foolish and wandering far from the way of truth' (*Commentary on the Gospel of Mark*, p. 534; my translation). But emphasis on the spiritual dimension was often even stronger in his treatment of modern miracles: 'In the earliest times the Holy Spirit fell upon believers and they spoke in tongues which they had never studied. But nowadays, because the holy Church does not need external signs, whoever believes in the name of Jesus Christ and has love for his brother gives witness to the Holy Spirit abiding in him' (*Commentary on the Seven Catholic Epistles*, pp. 198–9). Bede certainly believed that miraculous healings and portentous events continued to his own day; indeed, many of the miracle stories in his historical works appear to have been based on scriptural models. But Bede agreed with Augustine and Gregory that modern miracles were both less frequent and less spectacular than those in biblical times.[15] Quoting Gregory, Bede explained that numerous miracles had been necessary at the beginning of the Church when its faith was young and tender, just as we must water a new plant extensively until its roots are established, after which irrigation is no longer required (*Commentary on the Gospel of Mark*, p. 645).

Action and contemplation

Anglo-Saxon monasteries like Wearmouth-Jarrow were centres of preaching, teaching and pastoral ministry as well as prayer. So it is not surprising that Bede should understand the active and contemplative lives not as opposites or alternative lifestyle options but as complementary movements in the Christian life.[16] This theme appears frequently in the Old Testament commentaries and in the homilies, but it is also pervasive in Bede's works on the New Testament. Jesus himself provided the best model of the 'mixed life', as Bede explained (once again quoting Gregory) in his comment on Luke 5:16: 'That he performed miracles in the city but spent the night praying in the desert or on the mountain ... shows us the examples of both lives – that is, the active and the contemplative' (*Commentary on the Gospel of Luke*, p. 119; my translation). Although contemplation is 'higher' than action because the former pertains to the love of God and the latter to love of neighbour, the two lives are inseparably joined together in a Christian's obedience to the commandments of the Decalogue, which includes them both. Action is dominant here in this earthly life, where the vision of God is always fleeting and imperfect. Contemplation, however, will reign in heaven where there will be no hungry people to feed or sick people to nurse, but only God's beauty to be adored. 'But because this vision is hoped for in the future ... what consolation must we make use of when we are not yet allowed to enjoy the divine sight? ... Therefore, if we love one another with a sincere and intelligent charity, God remains in us, manifested by the works of that charity, although not yet visibly appearing' (*Commentary on the Seven Catholic Epistles*, p. 207). The need to pursue the contemplative vision without neglecting active service to the neighbour is also a prominent theme in Bede's historical works, where he depicts bishops such as Cuthbert in accordance with the Gregorian ideal of the pastor who repeatedly leaves monastic seclusion in order to minister to his flock.[17]

'True law of history'

Near the end of the preface to the *Ecclesiastical History*, Bede declares that his accounts of the life of Saint Cuthbert are based on earlier writings from Lindisfarne and the testimony of reliable witnesses. In accordance with *uera lex historiae* ('a true law of history'), he says, 'I have simply sought to commit to writing what I have collected from common report, for the instruction of posterity' (preface, p. 7). Some years earlier, Bede had borrowed the phrase 'true law of history' from Jerome in order to explain that when the evangelist Luke referred to Joseph as the father of Jesus, he was simply expressing vulgar opinion, not contradicting his previous testimony to the virgin birth

(*Commentary on the Gospel of Luke*, p. 67). Scholars have sometimes engaged in passionate debates about what Bede could have meant by applying this phrase to his own writing of history.[18] Was he merely warning his readers that his narrative was only as reliable as his sources? Or was he justifying the inclusion of popular tales that he knew to be doubtful or even patently untrue? Or was he perhaps suggesting that factual veracity was not as important as theological truth? Did he appeal to this 'law' as a general principle of historiography, or just a specific rule governing the particular situation of a historian dealing with common beliefs that are contrary to fact? Without further elaboration from Bede himself, much about this 'true law of history' is bound to remain unclear. What we can say with confidence is that he obviously thought of Luke and the other evangelists as fellow historians who had collected documents, interviewed witnesses and crafted rhetorically effective narratives in order to tell the story of God's providential work in the early days of the Christian Church. Surely Bede thought that he was justified in using similar methods to tell the 'ecclesiastical history' of his own English people. Indeed, scholars have discerned a variety of ways in which his study of the Gospels and the patristic commentaries on those books influenced the vocabulary, literary style and narrative structure of his historical works.[19]

Biblical scholar to the end

The affecting account of Bede's death written by his pupil Cuthbert reports that the master's final days were filled with Scripture in various forms. During the day he taught his students and chanted the Psalter; at night he woke periodically from sleep and 'would at once take up again the familiar melodies of Scripture, not ceasing to spread out his hands in thanksgiving to God'.[20] In addition to reciting prayers and exhortations from the Bible, Bede on his deathbed was engaged in two literary projects: correcting errors he found in Isidore's *On the Nature of Things*, and translating the Gospel of John into English. Apart from his homilies, Bede had not devoted much exegetical attention to the Fourth Gospel – probably because he considered Augustine's commentary accessible enough to be understood by most English pastors and teachers. But the translation of John was presumably intended not for the audience of Bede's commentaries, who could read Latin well enough but were sometimes distracted or confused by the topical references and sophisticated allusions in the works of the Fathers, but rather for those 'uneducated priests' in the countryside for whom he had been compelled to translate such basic catechetical texts as the Creed and the Lord's Prayer (*Letter to Bishop Egbert*, p. 346). It is remarkable to think that Bede, so often recognized both then and now as the greatest scholar of his age, did not consider it beneath his station to translate this fundamental New Testament text into English for the benefit of those whose Latin was so poor that they could not understand the relatively simple language of the Gospel of John.

Even Bede's last words (at least according to Cuthbert's hagiographical account) were suffused with quotations from Scripture. 'The time of my departure is at hand [2 Timothy 4:6], and my soul longs to see Christ my King in all His beauty [Isaiah 33:17].' Then after dictating a final sentence and being told that it had been written down, he said to the boy Wilberht who was acting as his scribe: 'Good! It is finished [John 19:30]; you have spoken the truth.'[21] Finally Bede asked to be placed on the floor of the cell where he used to pray; there he sang the *Gloria Patri* one last time, and breathed his last. Thus he was remembered as having died just as he had lived, a devoted and energetic biblical scholar who found in Holy Scripture all the food he needed for his soul.

NOTES

1. de Lubac 1998: vol. I, pp. 225–68.
2. Meyvaert 1979.
3. Bonner 1966; Landes 1988: 174–8.
4. Holder 2005a: 100–2; Holder 2005c: 57–8.
5. Fransen 1961 and 1987; Hurst 1999: 8–10; Thacker 2006: 53–4.
6. J. Hill 1998; Stansbury 1999b; Gorman 2002.
7. Kaczynski 2001: 21. For Bede's use of patristic sources in these commentaries, see Hart-Hasler 1993 and Kelly 1993.
8. Augustine, *On Christian Teaching*, 3.27.38, trans. R. Green, Oxford World's Classics (Oxford University Press, 1999), pp. 86–7.
9. Meyvaert 1976: 47; DeGregorio 1999: 11–14; DeGregorio 2010.
10. de Margerie 1990: 197.
11. Meyvaert 1976: 45–6.
12. Mayr-Harting 1976.
13. Olsen 1982.
14. McCready 1994: 105–6.
15. *Ibid.*, 85.
16. See DeGregorio 1999: 26–34; Thacker 1992.
17. For example, see *EH* IV. 28, for Bede's account of Cuthbert's election as bishop of Lindisfarne and his reluctant return to active ministry from his hermitage on the Inner Farne. For more on this theme, see Thacker 1983 and DeGregorio 1999: 34–5.
18. Ray 1980; McCready 1994: 195–213; Goffart 2005.
19. Ray 1976 and 1985.
20. *Cuthbert's Letter on the Death of Bede*, in Colgrave and Mynors 1969: 581.
21. *Ibid.*, 585.

11

LAWRENCE T. MARTIN

Bede and preaching

Bede's *Ecclesiastical History of the English People* is, to a large extent, the story of the conversion of England, brought about by a series of preachers, most of them monks, some coming from Rome, others from Ireland. Pope Gregory the Great sent Augustine and his monastic companions 'to preach the word of God to the English race' (I. 23, p. 69), and when Bede summarizes the accomplishments of Gregory's life, he says 'he snatched our race from the teeth of the ancient foe and made them partakers of everlasting freedom by sending us preachers' (II. 1, p. 131). Bede incorporates a letter from Pope Honorius to King Edwin of Northumbria which refers to Gregory himself as 'your preacher' (II. 17, p. 195).[1] Paulinus is sent to Northumbria 'not only, with the Lord's help, to prevent those who had come with him from lapsing from the faith, but also to convert some of the heathen, if he could, to grace and faith by his preaching' (II. 9, p. 165). Aidan and other Irish monks came to Lindisfarne 'preaching the word of faith with great devotion' (III. 3, p. 221), and Columba, also an Irishman, 'came to Britain to preach the word of God to the kingdoms of the northern Picts', while the southern Picts 'received the true faith through the preaching of the Word' by Ninian (III. 4, p. 223). Bede speaks of the preaching work of many others who had a role in the conversion of various regions of Britain, such as Birinus (III. 7), Fursa (III. 19), Cedd (III. 21–3), and Wilfrid (IV. 13).

Even after conversion had been largely accomplished, preachers had to nourish believers' faith and combat backsliding, as Cuthbert did in frequent trips from his monastery to neighbouring villages, where he 'preached the way of truth to those who had gone astray' (IV. 27, p. 433). Bede also describes the work of English monk-preachers like Willibrord, who took the Christian message to unconverted Germanic areas on the continent (V. 10–11). And Bede incorporates a letter from Abbot Ceolfrith, which gives a detailed exposition regarding the correct dating of Easter and tells how Adamnan, who had visited Northumbria, 'proved how much he had profited by seeing the observances of our churches, because afterwards, when he had returned to Ireland, he led large numbers of that race to the catholic observance of Easter by his preaching' (v. 21, p. 551).

Bede's theory of preaching

Bede wrote many works designed to aid the work of preachers. These include not only his many scriptural commentaries but also rhetorical treatises like *The Figures of Rhetoric*. Though he did not compose a treatise which systematically lays out his theory of preaching, it is possible to discover in his writings various aspects of what he thought about preaching. In one of his earliest exegetical works, the *Commentary on the Acts of the Apostles*, Bede looks beyond the surface meaning of several details in a story in order to discover some fundamental truths about the role of the preacher in the Church. Acts 10 tells how Peter was brought, through divine intervention, to change his thinking and realize that the good news about Jesus was to be preached not only to Jews but to the whole world. In this story, Cornelius, a Roman centurion, is granted a vision in which an angel tells him to send someone to fetch Peter. Cornelius sends two of his servants and one soldier. In the meantime, Peter himself, while praying on his roof, is given a vision of something like a great sheet being let down from heaven to earth by its four corners, and it contains 'all kinds of four-legged animals, and serpents of the earth and birds of the air', as Peter hears a voice saying 'Arise, Peter, kill and eat.' In the vision Peter refuses, saying that he has never eaten anything common or unclean, and the voice responds, 'What God has made pure you should not call common' (Acts 10:15).

Concerning the voice that Peter heard in his vision, saying, 'Arise, Peter, kill and eat', Bede offers a reading which underscores the dual role of preaching in the Church: to spread the Gospel to the unconverted world and to provide correction against errors in the Church. The voice, says Bede, told Peter:

> Arise to make ready to preach the gospel. Kill in the gentiles what they had been, and make them what you are, for whoever eats food lying outside of himself turns it into his own body. Therefore [the voice] taught that the nations, which had formerly lain outside through their lack of belief, would, once their former life had been put to death, be incorporated within the society of the Church ... Those who are taken in by heretics are as though devoured by death while they are still alive. (*Commentary on Acts*, p. 98)

The fact that Cornelius sent two of his household servants and one of his soldiers to fetch Peter signifies for Bede the preacher's special vocation within the Church: 'Cornelius sent three people to Peter because the gentile world, which was to come to believe in the faith of the apostles, had subjugated Europe, Asia, and Africa, which were to be taken over partly by military zeal (that is by urgent preaching), and partly by domestic business dealings.' And the sending of two household servants but only one soldier indicates the specialness of the preaching vocation, for in the Church 'there are more who know how to hear the word than those who know how to speak it' (*Commentary on Acts*, p. 96).

Finally, the voice of the Spirit that told Peter to come down from his rooftop and to go with Cornelius' emissaries is interpreted by Bede in a way which seems to affirm that the preacher's role in the Church can be appropriately exercised by a monk:

> He was ordered to descend from the roof and to go to preach in order to show that the church should not only watch for the Lord by climbing to the heights, but, returning to the active life as if rising from her bed, she should preach this same Lord to all the lowliest and to those still situated outside, as it were, but who are nevertheless knocking at the door of Simon.
>
> (*Commentary on Acts*, pp. 99–100)

Many, but not all, of the monks whose preaching Bede describes in his *Ecclesiastical History* were bishops. The monks who accompanied their bishop Augustine shared his preaching task (II. 23; I. 26). At times Bede seems to suggest that even monks who had not been ordained to the priesthood may have done some preaching: 'Many came from the country of the Irish into Britain and to those English kingdoms over which Oswald reigned, preaching the word of faith with great devotion. Those of them who held the rank of priest administered the grace of baptism to those who believed' (III. 3, p. 221).

Bede was convinced that good preaching must be solidly grounded in the sacred Scriptures. This is seen not only in the strongly biblical focus of his own homilies, which will be discussed below, but also in the terminology Bede uses to describe the work of preachers. Relatively seldom in his *Ecclesiastical History* does Bede use 'preach' (*praedicare*) by itself (e.g. III. 26, p. 310; V. 15, p. 506). He prefers the construction 'preach the Word' (*uerbum praedicare*: III. 21, p. 281), sometimes further specifying: 'the word of God' (*uerbum Dei*: I. 23, p. 69; III. 4, p. 223), 'the word of life' (*uerbum uitae*: I. 26, p. 77; II. 15, p. 191) or 'the word of faith' (*uerbum fidei*: III. 3, p. 221; V. 11, p. 487). Bede also speaks of 'preaching Christ' (*Christum praedicare*: V. 19, p. 523). Occasionally he uses a different verb with these constructions, as in *uerbum Dei adnuntiare* (III. 19, p. 275, which Colgrave and Mynors translate 'preached the word of God'), or *uerbum ministrare* (IV. 16, p. 383, which they translate 'teach the word', although the context here too is one of preaching). At times he uses *euangelizare* by itself, meaning 'to preach the gospel' (III. 3, p. 221; IV. 13, p. 373). Occasionally Bede omits a verb of preaching altogether, using simply a noun construction which points to the scriptural content of preaching, as, for example, *opus Verbi* (I. 25, p. 73, which Colgrave and Mynors translate 'the task of preaching the Word'), or 'the ministry of the Word' (*Verbi ministerium*, v. 11, p. 485), or simply *uerbum* by itself, as in the description of Paulinus, who 'toiled hard and long in preaching the word' (*multo tempore illo laborante in uerbo*: II. 9, p. 165). Very seldom does Bede use an object for *praedicare* that does not clearly indicate scriptural content – he refers to Cuthbert preaching 'the way of truth' (*uiam ueritatis praedicabat*), but here the context is preaching 'to those who had gone astray', to country people who 'in times of plague would forget the sacred mysteries of the faith into which they had been initiated and take to the false remedies of idolatry, as though they could ward off a blow inflicted by God the Creator by means of incantations or amulets or any other mysteries of devilish art' (IV. 27, p. 433). In his *Letter to Bishop Egbert*, Bede recommends preaching 'the beliefs of the Church, as set out in the Apostles' Creed, and also the Lord's Prayer, which a reading of the holy Gospel teaches us' (p. 345). Bede's favourite metaphor for preaching in his *Ecclesiastical History* is agricultural – Felix, for example, was sent to 'preach the word of life' to the Angles, and 'the devoted husbandman reaped an abundant harvest of believers in this spiritual field' (II. 15, p. 191; see also III. 7, p. 233; V. 9, pp. 479–81). It is very likely that Bede's preference for this metaphor is based on the Gospel parable of the sower, where, in Luke's version, Jesus explicitly says, 'the seed is the Word of God' (Luke 8:11). In his commentary *On the Song of Songs*, Bede develops a related metaphor in which the parts of the body involved in converting food to nutrition are compared to the role of preachers and teachers in the Church (passage quoted above in Chapter 9, p. 130).

What does Bede regard as the criteria for good preaching? The qualities of good and successful preaching which are mentioned most often in his *Ecclesiastical History* are the preacher's learning and good character. For example, when Egbert was planning to take the Gospel message to unconverted areas on the continent, he chose companions 'who were outstanding both by their lives and learning and so most suitable for preaching the Word' (V. 9, p. 477), and the four priests whose preaching converted many of the Middle Angles were chosen by Bishop Finan because of 'their learning and their character' (III. 21, p. 279). Oftfor, a monk of Whitby, is put forth as an exemplar of both of these qualities. He was very learned in the Scriptures, having studied at both of Hild's monasteries, and then, anxious for greater knowledge, he went to Kent to study with Archbishop Theodore, and then to

Rome. Later, he returned to the kingdom of Hwicce, where he served for many years, 'preaching the word of faith and setting an example of holy life to all who saw and heard him' (IV. 23, pp. 409–11). Cuthbert's preaching was very successful because of his holiness of life. He undertook preaching tours to the remote villages near his monastery, 'calling the peasants to heavenly things both by the words he said and by his virtuous deeds' (IV. 27, p. 435), and after he became a bishop he continued to teach the people 'what should be done but first showed them how to do it by his own example, as it is most helpful for a teacher to do. He was before all things fired with divine love, sober-minded and patient, diligent and urgent in devotion and prayer, and friendly to all who came to him for comfort' (IV. 28, p. 439).[2] In his *Letter to Bishop Egbert*, Bede says that a bishop's teaching role and personal holiness must go together, and that neither is complete without the other, 'for the bishop who lives a holy life should not neglect the duty of teaching, and he would be condemned if he gave good instruction but failed to follow it in practice' (p. 343).

In *On Ezra and Nehemiah*, Bede emphasizes the preacher's responsibility to live a life of greater perfection and imitation of Christ than is required of other Christians. In Nehemiah 8:4–5, Ezra ceremoniously reads the Torah publicly, standing 'above all the people' and 'on a wooden step that he had made to speak upon'. Bede's commentary focuses on these spatial details, from which he draws criteria of a good preacher – namely, a good life and imitation of Christ's suffering:

> The *pontifex*, therefore, stands out 'above all the people' when he who receives the rank of teacher rises above the activity of the crowd by the merit of a more perfect life; but he stands 'on a wooden step that he had made to speak upon' when he makes himself higher than the rest through exceptional imitation of the Lord's passion. Hence he deservedly obtains the trust to preach God's word freely; for he who disdains to imitate the Lord's passion in his own modest way has not yet mounted the wooden step from where he can stand above the weak.[3] (*On Ezra and Nehemiah*, p. 194)

Bede clearly valued rhetorical effectiveness, as is evident from his little handbook of rhetorical devices, *The Figures of Rhetoric*, and from the quality of his own highly polished syntax in his own homilies. It is therefore surprising that Bede says little about eloquence as a qualification of a good preacher. In his *Ecclesiastical History* he does attribute the success of Fursa's preaching to the 'persuasiveness of his teaching' (*incitamento sermonis*) as well as the example of his virtues (III. 19, p. 269). He also says 'so great was Cuthbert's eloquence, so keen his desire to drive home what he had begun to teach' that his listeners could not help but respond with repentance for their sins (IV. 27,

p. 433). Although Bede does not emphasize eloquence as a qualification for a preacher, he does recognize that an effective preacher must be fluent in the language of his listeners. Bishop Agilbert was a Gaul who came by way of Ireland to preach to the West Saxons, and he was extremely learned in the Scriptures and anxious to preach, but the king became so impatient with Agilbert's 'barbarous speech' that he split his kingdom into two dioceses and gave the see of Winchester to another Gaulish bishop who could better speak the Saxon language (III. 7, p. 235). King Oswald of Northumbria had spent time in Ireland as an exile, and later, when he became king, many Irish missionaries, upon Oswald's request, came to Northumbria 'preaching the word of faith with great devotion'. One of these Irish monks was Aidan, who, though distinguished by many qualities that should have made him an effective preacher, lacked fluency in the language of his Northumbrian listeners. In this case, however, the king, instead of replacing the preacher, offered his own assistance as interpreter: 'It was indeed a beautiful sight when the bishop was preaching the gospel, to see the king acting as interpreter of the heavenly word for his ealdormen and thegns, for the bishop was not completely at home in the English tongue, while the king had gained a perfect knowledge of Irish during the long period of his exile' (III. 3, p. 221).

For Bede, Aidan was also an exemplar of another important qualification of a good preacher, namely discretion, which involves both not talking over the heads of one's listeners and not being too negative or harsh. An unnamed Irish bishop had preceded Aidan in coming to Oswald's kingdom, but this man was 'of harsher disposition' than Aidan, and his preaching to the English was unsuccessful, so he returned to Ireland, complaining that the English were 'intractable, obstinate, and uncivilized'. Aidan, who was present, responded:

> It seems to me, brother, that you have been unreasonably harsh upon your ignorant hearers: you did not first offer them the milk of simpler teaching, as the apostle recommends [1 Corinthians 3:2], until little by little, as they grew strong on the food of God's word, they were capable of receiving more elaborate instruction and of carrying out the more transcendent commandments of God.
>
> (*EH* III. 5, p. 229)

Those who were present realized that Aidan was 'pre-eminently endowed with the grace of discretion, which is the mother of all virtues', and he was therefore sent to preach to the English, where he showed himself remarkable for 'moderation and good sense' (III. 5, p. 229). Also in *On Ezra and Nehemiah*, Bede makes the point that a good preacher will balance chastisement with more joyful tidings. Nehemiah 8:9 reads 'All the people were weeping when they heard the words of the law', as read out by Ezra, and

Bede comments that 'because the same holy teachers who move the minds of their hearers to tears both with holy readings and with their devout exhortations also assuage those tears when they promise their hearers that eternal joys are to follow', it is right that Ezra then says (in Nehemiah 8:10) 'Go and eat fat food and drink sweet drink, and send portions to him who did not prepare anything for himself, because it is the holy day of the Lord, and do not be saddened' (p. 195).

Bede's *Homilies on the Gospels*

Let us turn now to Bede's own contribution to the preaching genre, his collection of fifty *Homilies on the Gospels*, arranged in two books. It does not cover the entire liturgical year but instead focuses attention on the two major liturgical seasons of Advent–Christmas and Lent–Easter–Pentecost. There are also a few homilies provided for some important saints' days, and two homilies for the dedication of a church.

In terms of their Gospel pericopes, there is almost no overlap between Bede's fifty homilies and Gregory the Great's *Forty Gospel Homilies*. Only one pericope is found in both collections, Luke 2:1–14, the story of the birth of Jesus, and interestingly in this case Gregory begins his homily with a sort of apology for not being able to do justice to this text: 'Because [by the Lord's bounty] I am going to celebrate the Eucharist three times today, I can comment only briefly on the Gospel lesson.'[4] Such a statement could easily have prompted Bede to offer a fuller exposition of such an important story. The general lack of overlap in Gospel texts between Gregory and Bede suggests that Bede chose to compose his homilies only on pericopes that Gregory had not addressed, and to treat his own texts in the spirit of Gregory's homilies. In other words, Bede may have conceived of his own *Homilies on the Gospels* as a supplement to Gregory's *Forty Gospel Homilies*.

An interesting but probably unanswerable question is whether Bede actually first preached his homilies orally, or whether they were from the beginning literary compositions. At Bede's time, most monastic preaching was done by the abbot, but since Bede was a priest, he could have preached, especially during one of his abbot's lengthy journeys away from the monastery. Benedicta Ward imagines Bede's homilies as 'given in his own monastery and in the context of the liturgy, most probably after the reading of the Gospel either at the Eucharist or at the preceding vigil'.[5]

However, neither in Bede's other works nor in the writings of his contemporaries are there any clear references to Bede himself preaching. The homilies do include passages of direct address, such as 'dearly beloved brothers', but these may be merely conventional, and if Bede did originally deliver the homilies orally, in their present form they are surely literary works intended to be read and reread as part of the annual cycle of the Church year. The homilies lack any topical references to specific events or issues that would have caused them to become dated, and the themes addressed have such a universal quality that they spoke to monastic audiences throughout Europe. The one homily which includes specific local references, Homily i. 13, on Benedict Biscop, was universalized in some manuscripts by replacing the local material with references to Benedict of Nursia.

Bede may have intended his homilies to be used for private devotional reading – the *lectio divina* called for in *The Rule of St Benedict* – or for public reading to the brethren which Benedict calls for at meals and between Vespers and Compline,[6] or perhaps at a daily chapter meeting, which at least by the time of the tenth-century monastic reform in England had come to include, on feast days, a reading of the Gospel of the day and an explanation of the reading by the prior.[7]

It is also possible that Bede intended his homilies to be read within the liturgical setting of the Divine Office itself. The description of the night office in Benedict's Rule prescribes readings from the books of the Old and New Testaments, as well as 'explanations of Scripture by reputable and orthodox catholic Fathers'.[8] Dom Pierre Salmon, in his history of the Divine Office, asserts that Bede's homilies were 'intended to provide readings at the celebration of the divine office',[9] but it seems unlikely that Bede would have regarded himself as one of the 'reputable and orthodox catholic Fathers'. He frequently described himself as 'following in the footsteps of the Fathers' and in his scriptural commentaries Bede often incorporated lengthy direct quotations from the works of the Fathers. If in composing his homilies, therefore, Bede had thought of himself as providing texts for the night office, it seems likely that he would have collected passages from writers who were generally recognized as Fathers of the Church. However, perhaps the most distinctive difference between Bede's Gospel homilies and his commentaries on the Gospels of Mark and Luke is the almost total lack of direct quotations from the Fathers in the homilies, and the abundance of such patristic quoted material in the commentaries. This feature of Bede's homilies might therefore point to an original setting which was non-liturgical or para-liturgical, or, on the other hand, it might be evidence that Bede did first preach his homilies orally and later wrote them down for private or public reading, revising them perhaps for the sake of a wider reading audience.

Whatever Bede's intended use of his homilies may have been, in fact less than a hundred years after his death, these works did become an important part of the monastic night office through a homiliary prepared by Paul the Deacon, a monk of Monte Cassino, who was commissioned by Charlemagne to collect 'certain flowers from the wide-flung fields of the Catholic fathers'.[10] While Paul the Deacon's collection includes a wide range of works by both Greek and Latin Fathers of the Church, the writer who supplied the greatest number of selections is Bede. There are thirty-four selections from Bede's homilies, as well as twenty-three excerpts from his commentaries, making Bede's work account for almost a quarter of the total homiliary. Cyril Smetana, reflecting upon these statistics, says that Paul the Deacon 'could not have found more admirable instruction and inspiration for the monks and clerics who attended the night offices [than] Bede's work, [which] was wholesomely orthodox and stylistically correct'.[11] Through its incorporation in the monastic and Roman breviaries, Paul the Deacon's homiliary became the standard collection of readings for the night office, and in this way Bede's homilies have had immeasurable influence on generations of clergy and monks, who have listened to or read the Matins lessons for Sundays and feast days.

Bede's homilies are, generally speaking, fairly uniform in length, and they follow the same basic structure, beginning with a brief introduction touching on the general theme of the reading. Then there is a verse-by-verse explanation, though Bede does not necessarily comment on every verse of the reading. He focuses on the characters of the story, the setting and the narrative details, giving the symbolic meaning of all of these elements, and making general applications to the lives of his brethren. Finally, there is a conclusion, which is often a passage of direct address, a series of 'let us' clauses, or sometimes a sort of doxology.

One of the Lenten homilies is a good example of this structure. The Gospel pericope is the story of the miracle of the multiplication of loaves and fishes (John 6:1–14). Bede's introduction is a general reminder of how to relate to stories of Jesus' miracles, namely that listeners should not 'pay attention to what in them produces outward astonishment', but rather they should 'consider what they themselves ought to be doing inwardly, following the example of these [signs], and what mystical truths they ought to be pondering in these [stories]' (*Homilies* ii. 2, p. 13). Bede expands upon this theme for several lines, and then says: 'Having said this much by way of brief introduction, I would like to examine more diligently the whole sequence of this sacred reading and to indicate to you dear ones whatever mystical meaning I am capable of pointing out in it' (*Homilies* ii. 2, p. 14). He then works his way through the story, beginning with the setting, for which he provides some background geographical information on the place, derived from Pliny, and a symbolic reading based on Jerome's work *On Hebrew Names*. Next, he turns to the time of the story, just before the feast of Passover, which, he explains, represents the 'passing over' or 'transcending' by the Lord's chosen of 'the lustful concupiscences of the flesh by the loftiness of their minds' (*Homilies* II. 2, p. 16). He then turns to the symbolic meaning of various details of the story, such as the fact that there were five barley loaves and two fish – the number of loaves signifying the five books of Moses, and the fact that they were barley loaves 'because of the stricter ordinances of the law, and the thicker outer husks of its literal [interpretation] which, as it were, cover the inner pith of its spiritual sense', while the number of fish signifies the Psalms and prophets, and 'it is also appropriate that it was animals that live in the water that prefigured the heralds of that age in which faithful people could in no way live without the waters of baptism' (*Homilies* II. 2, pp. 17–18). Bede next makes some observations about the comparable story in the Synoptic Gospels, and he then returns to a consideration of the symbolism of other details in John's account, including some fairly complex number symbolism regarding the five thousand who were fed and the twelve baskets of fragments which were collected after all had eaten. The conclusion is a fairly brief general summation ending in a doxology.

Bede's main concern in his exposition of a Gospel text is the spiritual meaning of the story for his monastic brethren. He does not, however, indulge in the sort of excessive allegorizing or moralizing which simply uses the biblical text as a springboard for the preacher's own pet themes. For example, in one of his Eastertide homilies, on Luke 24:1–9, the story of the women at the empty tomb, the text mentions that the women found the stone rolled away from the tomb, and Bede says this:

> Mystically, the rolling away of the stone implies the disclosure of the divine sacraments, which were formerly hidden and closed up by the letter of the law. The law was written on stone. Indeed in the case of each of us, when we acknowledge our faith in the Lord's passion and resurrection, his tomb, which had been closed, is opened up. We enter the tomb, but do not find the body of the Lord, when in our hearts we carefully think back over the order [of events] of his incarnation and his passion, and recall that he has risen from the dead and is no longer to be seen in his mortal flesh. (*Homilies* II. 10, p. 90)

Later in the homily, however, Bede turns to the historical sense, giving a long and detailed discussion of tomb construction in Palestine, based on a pilgrim's account of a visit to the holy places.[12]

Bede's homilies are filled with echoes and quotations from places in the Bible other than the Gospel text being explained. Bede is often led by a process of association to another place in Scripture where a word or idea occurs. Jean Leclercq refers to this as 'exegesis through reminiscence' and he regards it as 'specifically monastic', though it 'approaches rabbinic exegesis.'[13] Bede is a particular master of this technique, and he often brings texts together in a way that illumines the spiritual meaning of the Gospel text under discussion. At times Bede does not merely make a brief allusion to another scriptural passage, but he 'takes considerable time to explore the riches of the two passages that he connects, relishing certain words and phrases, repeating them in fugue-like patterns of allusion, and using them as a sort of bridge between the historical world of the Gospel story and the present world of his listeners' or readers' own spiritual experience',[14] and a full appreciation of his meaning sometimes depends upon the listener knowing the Bible well enough to be aware of the full context of the passage to which Bede alludes.

Although Bede's homilies are full of quotations from other places in the Bible, quotations from other writers are conspicuously absent, a feature of the homilies which, as mentioned above, distinguishes them from Bede's commentaries, which are filled with lengthy quotations from the Fathers of the Church. However, by no means does the lack of direct quotation from the Fathers in Bede's homilies mean that Bede was not influenced by his predecessors.[15] O. C. Edwards points out that it is 'obvious that Bede had read Augustine's *On Christian Doctrine* and followed its precepts both in the interpretation of Scripture and in the use of rhetoric',[16] and Bede's syntactic patterns, for example, his fondness for juxtaposing parallel constructions to express some striking contrast, shows the influence of Augustine's Latin style.[17] Bede is indebted to Gregory the Great for his basic approach to the Gospel text in his homilies, avoiding digressions and sticking close to the Gospel story, focusing on the symbolic meaning of the narrative details.

In addition, although Bede seldom in his homilies directly quotes the Fathers, he often borrows ideas and themes from their works. Often he paraphrases or summarizes, interpreting a passage in essentially the same way as did an earlier writer. At other times there is only a rather general resemblance between Bede's interpretation and that of one of the Fathers. The most interesting cases, however, are those where Bede clearly draws on an earlier writer but exhibits great creativity and originality in the way in which he reworks that writer's interpretation, adapting it to his own homiletic purposes. Bede's homily for the Feast of the Purification, on Luke 2:22–35, the story of the Presentation of Jesus in the Temple, includes a long passage devoted to the spiritual symbolism of the 'two turtle doves or two young pigeons' offered by the holy family. In Bede's reading, 'a pigeon indicates simplicity, and a turtle-dove indicates chastity' (*Homilies* 1. 18, p. 181). In his development of the symbolism, Bede quite clearly draws on two passages – one from Augustine's *Fifth Tractate on John's Gospel* for the symbolic meaning of the pigeon as simplicity, and the other from Jerome's *Against Jovinian* for the turtle dove as a symbol of chastity, based on this bird's supposed habit of not seeking another mate if it loses its first one. However, the discussion in

Augustine concerns a different passage where one of these birds appears, namely, the story of Jesus' baptism in the Jordan, and more importantly, the kind of 'simplicity' which the bird represents for Augustine is not the spiritual quality of simplicity of soul which Bede recommends to his monastic listeners, but rather simplicity in the sense of the unrepeatable uniqueness of baptism which the Donatist heretics had denied. As for the symbolism of the dove, Bede has in mind chastity as a virtue which is demanded of all Christians but has special significance for the monk. The passage in Jerome which is Bede's source concerns the controversy between Jerome and Jovinian over the question of the relative value of marriage and the state of consecrated virginity, and also the question concerning whether widows should remarry. Later in the same homily, Bede recapitulates the meaning of the two birds as 'sobriety, simplicity and compunction of our heart' (*Homilies* 1. 18, p. 185), a much more general spiritual state of virtue than Jerome had in mind. Near the end of the same homily, Bede returns once more to the symbolism of the two birds in the story of the Purification. This time he ponders the question of why the law of Leviticus (12:8) required that these two particular birds be offered as part of the ritual for purification of a woman after childbirth, and his response is: 'There are two kinds of compunction by which the faithful immolate themselves to the Lord on the altar of the heart, for undoubtedly, as we have received from the sayings of the Fathers, the soul experiencing God is first moved to compunction by fear, and afterwards by love' (*Homilies* 1. 18, p. 185). Bede's 'from the sayings of the Fathers' most likely refers to the influence of a passage in Gregory's *Morals on Job*, a work Bede often quoted in his exegetical works. Gregory's comment, however, concerns Leviticus 5:6–8, which does not concern the purification of a woman after childbirth, but rather a more general purification ritual which involved the sacrifice of the same two birds. More importantly, Gregory's interpretation sees these birds as symbols of the sorrow of repentance for two things, sins committed and good works not done. While Bede acknowledges Gregory's influence for his general approach to the law of bird sacrifice in Leviticus, Bede's own interpretation of the ritual as symbolizing two stages in the psychological process of repentance is quite different from Gregory's reading of the law. These passages on the symbolism of birds in Bede's homily for the Purification, therefore, illustrate Bede's creative use of his predecessors' work, freely adapting their words and ideas to enrich and ornament his own homiletic themes.

Conclusion

Bede was an extremely important figure in the history of preaching. He recognized the importance of good preaching in the life of the Church and was himself a master of rhetoric in his own homilies, which, especially through their incorporation in the homiliary of Paul the Deacon, greatly influenced medieval Latin homily writers as well as vernacular homilists like Ælfric (see Chapter 15). They not only incorporated ideas and wording from Bede's *Homilies*, but also learned from Bede a general approach to the Gospel pericope, providing a more or less continuous gloss which elucidates the spiritual meaning underlying the surface details of the narrative. Few of Bede's successors, however, exhibited his discipline in anchoring the spiritual meaning firmly in the literal historical sense of the Gospel passage under discussion.

The most important influence of the *Homilies*, however, is to be found in the way in which Bede, like the homilists he admired in his *Ecclesiastical History*, succeeded in preaching 'the beliefs of the Church, as set out in the Apostles' Creed, and also the Lord's Prayer, which a reading of the holy Gospel teaches us', as he wrote in his *Letter to Bishop Egbert* (p. 345). The great doctrines of the Christian Church, like the Incarnation, the Redemption and the sacramental life, are based on biblical stories which were told to believers annually through the course of the liturgical year, and homilies were a necessary complement to these stories. Bede's homilies excel in this complementary role, for they point out in a generally clear and simple way the doctrinal significance of the Gospel stories and their implications for the life of a Christian. Some of those who benefited from Bede's *Homilies* in this way became preachers and teachers themselves, passing on great doctrines of the Church to others. This general sort of influence of the *Homilies* extended beyond preaching to other forms of verbal art as well, such as hymns and drama, and also to visual arts which taught the doctrinal meaning of the biblical stories through painting, stained glass and sculpture. Adolf Katzenellenbogen, speaking of the programme of sculpture at the cathedral of Chartres, points out that the dogmas taught by the artists had been developed over many centuries – determined by Church councils after controversies and struggles with heretics, and reiterated in theological writings – but that fundamentally it was homilies (especially those which had become a part of the standard homiliary used in the night office, which relied heavily on Bede's homilies) that were the primary influence on the relief sculpture of Chartres:

> The meaning of the reliefs corresponds to homilies used in the office, homilies in which certain dogmatic concepts are concentrated and related to the very events represented in the tympanum and the lintels. These sermons, therefore, may provide a more specific key for an understanding of the meaning than the dogmas at large.[18]

Katzenellenbogen offers several examples of the influence of Bede's homilies on specific aspects of the sculptural reliefs above the right portal of the west side at Chartres. It presents convincing evidence that two of Bede's homilies, one for Christmas Day (I. 8) and the other for the Feast of the Purification (I. 18), guided the iconographic representation of the doctrine of Christ's divine and human natures, the doctrine of Mary as mother of God, and the essential connection between the doctrine of the Incarnation and the sacrament of the Mass.[19] From the time of the building of the great cathedral until today, thousands of pilgrims, as they arrive at Chartres, have been reminded of the interrelated significance of these foundational doctrines as Bede expressed them in his *Homilies on the Gospels*.

NOTES

1. *praedicatoris uestri*, which Colgrave and Mynors translate as 'your evangelist', though *praedicare* is generally translated by them as 'preach'.
2. Cf. *Life of Saint Cuthbert*, ch. 26. Chapters 30, 32 and 33 of this work also contain brief references to Cuthbert's preaching tours through the villages of his bishopric.
3. For the significance of the title *pontifex* here, see DeGregorio in *Ezra and Nehemiah*, p. 113, n. 7.
4. Gregory the Great, *Forty Gospel Homilies*, trans. D. Hurst (Kalamazoo, MI: Cistercian Publications, 1990), p. 50.
5. Ward 1991: vol. I, p. v.
6. *The Rule of St Benedict*, ed. T. Fry (Collegeville, MN: The Liturgical Press, 1981), chs. 38, 42 and 48 (pp. 236–7, 242–3, 248–53).
7. Gatch 1977: 40–1.
8. *Rule of St Benedict*, ch. 9, pp. 204–5.
9. Salmon 1962: 67.
10. Smetana 1978: 79.
11. *Ibid.*, p. 80.
12. *Homilies* II. 2, pp. 94–6, drawing on Adomnán's *De locis sanctis*.
13. Leclercq 1961: 95.
14. Martin 2006: 191–2.
15. See the source notes in *Homilies on the Gospels* and the index of sources and parallels in vol. 2, pp. 271–4.
16. Edwards 2004: 147.
17. Martin 1989: 35.
18. Katzenellenbogen 1959: 11.
19. *Ibid.*, 7–15 and 115, n. 95.

12

ALAN THACKER

Bede and history

Bede was in many ways a natural historian. He was deeply interested in the past. He liked to sort things out, get things right. Indeed he was so good at this that he has been viewed as a modern scholar *avant la lettre*. But that interest in accurate information is deceptive. Bede had an agenda. He was above all a Christian scholar and exegete, and for him, history, although unquestionably interesting for its own sake, had moral purpose. To study and to write history was to participate in a dynamic process: the unfolding of God's purposes for mankind as the world moved towards final judgement and the end of time. Such an approach linked history with hagiography, the lives of the saints, which told of men and women through whom God had worked his purposes on earth.

To the modern mind, these two disciplines might seem at odds. History is about particularity, about the specificity of the past, albeit searching out patterns in the flow of events. Hagiography as a genre is dominated by *topoi*, by models and conventions, for it seeks to show through the surface detail of particular and individual human lives the underlying quality common to the saints in their service to God. It is also much concerned with miracles, with God's interventions in the natural world to demonstrate the holiness and power of his elect. The narration of miracles has not of course been regarded as appropriate subject matter for historians since the Renaissance if not before. To Bede and his contemporaries, however, wonders were wholly appropriate to historical narrative, although, as we shall see, Bede's own approach to such material was complex.

Bede's historical and hagiographical writings spanned his entire working life. All in Latin, they form a group of related entries within the list of his works which he appended to the *Ecclesiastical History* (v. 24, pp. 569–71). That grouping is revealing. It begins with hagiography, termed 'histories of the saints', among which Bede includes a *Life* of the Italian confessor Felix (died *c.* 260), in prose but based on poems by Paulinus of Nola; a revised *Passion* of the Persian martyr Anastasius (d. 627/8), the text of which had been collected from the original Greek; and finally 'the life of the holy father Cuthbert [bishop of Lindisfarne, d. 687], first in heroic verse and then in prose'. All except the prose *Life of Saint Cuthbert*, written by 721, are early works. From hagiography, Bede moves seamlessly to his 'history of the abbots' of his own monastery and then to what most would regard as his masterpiece – the *Ecclesiastical History*, defined as 'a history of the Church of our island and people', written in the early 730s. He concludes with his 'martyrology of the festivals of the holy martyrs', an innovative compilation, the first of its kind to enliven the customary bare record of name and calendar with historical detail, also probably a late work.

It is worth bearing in mind that there is much history elsewhere in Bede's writings. His great computistical work, *The Reckoning of Time*, for example, ends with a chronicle of world events (see Chapter 8). And his biblical exegesis is saturated in history: for Bede was intensely interested in the Old Testament account of the people of Israel, a narrative he regarded as of particular significance for his own time (see Chapter 9). While all this material informs our view of the importance of history to Bede and the way in which he worked as a historian, this chapter will focus primarily upon his most important works in the genre, the *Ecclesiastical History*, the *Lives* of Saint Cuthbert and the *History of the Abbots*.

Bede's view of history

Early medieval history and hagiography looked back to a classical tradition. In the Roman world, history was primarily the telling of public events – the doings of rulers, wars, the administration of justice. It was a rhetorical narrative, often dramatic, with speeches put into the mouths of the principal protagonists. Although supposed to be non-partisan, it could involve 'both polemic and apologia',[1] and might often deal with contemporary or near contemporary events. It also had a biographical element, apparent, for example, in the imperial obituaries which the fourth-century historian Ammianus Marcellinus intrudes at appropriate points into his narrative. Closely allied to history was a tradition of biography or autobiography of public figures such as generals and politicians.

With the establishment of Christianity as the favoured religion of the Roman empire under Constantine (306–37), new models of history and biography were developed. Most importantly, Eusebius produced his *Ecclesiastical History*. For Eusebius as a Christian bishop, political affairs were no longer primary subject matter, although the Roman state, through the succession of its emperors, provided an organizing principle for his text. History was now sacred history, focused upon the people of God, the

Christian Church. As was the case with the classical pagan historians, it was a chronologically determined narrative, but one that was more archival than rhetorical in character. The ancients on the whole had avoided the insertion of documents into their text, lest they interrupt the desired 'elevated stylistic tone'.[2] Eusebius, however, used documents extensively and avoided placing speeches in the mouths of his protagonists. His themes in the *History* reflected these preoccupations. He sought to trace the succession of bishops in the principal Christian sees and to record important events and outstanding heroes in the history of the Church, the names and dates of heretics, and the persecutions and martyrdoms of the faithful 'down to my own time'.

Alongside Eusebius's innovations in the writing of history may be set the transformation of biography into hagiography, the lives of the saints. Athanasius's *Life of Saint Anthony*, written c. 360, is perhaps the earliest example of the new genre. Again, we move away from public affairs to focus upon a holy man whose pattern of life, teachings, miracles and visions provided a model for a life lived in detachment from the political world. Anthony's warfare was with the devil and his demons; his arena of conflict was the tombs and the inner mountain deep in the desert; his weapons were prayer and asceticism. Although indifferent to the communications of emperors and kings, through the spiritual power of his hidden life he attained great fame and influence.

The formative works of Eusebius and Athanasius were written in Greek and disseminated in the West in Latin translations. Bede read Eusebius's *Ecclesiastical History* in the version produced by Rufinus of Aquileia in the early fifth century and Athanasius's *Life of Saint Anthony* in the elegant paraphrase of Evagrius of Antioch made shortly after its composition. Both left their mark. The structure and many of the themes of Bede's *Ecclesiastical History* derive from Eusebius: in particular, its broadly chronological arrangement, the tracing of episcopal succession within the English kingdoms, the concern with heresy. But Bede also looks back to the older classical tradition – in his employment of obituary notices at appropriate points in his narrative (e.g. *EH* II. 1; V. 19), and in his use of direct speech, as in his account of the proceedings at the synod of Whitby (III. 25).

Unlike Eusebius, Bede was concerned not with the universal Church but with a particular section of it. His territory was Britain, rather than the Roman empire, and within that territory he focused upon a single people: he sought to chart how the English became part of the universal Church and to establish their particular role in the economy of salvation. In thus confining himself, Bede was joining a select group of 'narrators of barbarian history'.[3] Among these, he certainly knew the ten books of the *Histories of the Franks*, produced by Gregory, bishop of Tours, in the later sixth century.

Although very different in tone from anything produced by Bede, Gregory's work may have inspired the novel restriction of the *Ecclesiastical History* to a single people.

Athanasius's *Life of Saint Anthony* provided a crucial model for Bede's depiction of Cuthbert, a central figure in his historical writings. By Bede's time, however, although celebrated, it was one saint's life among many: the library at Wearmouth-Jarrow had a vast hagiographical literature to draw upon. Bede was well aware of the conventions governing this burgeoning genre, but here, as elsewhere, he transcended his models. That is particularly apparent in his merging of hagiography and history. Just as in his biblical commentaries he gave emphasis both to the surface nature of the text and to its inner meaning, so in his hagiography as in his histories, he remained governed by an underlying moral purpose while concerned with the accuracy and particularity of the narrative. Bede's hagiography, his 'histories of the saints', contains much precise historical detail. His holy protagonists lived specific earthly lives, as well as being actors in the cosmic drama of salvation. The *Ecclesiastical History*, Bede's greatest historical work, has been memorably characterized as 'a gallery of good examples',[4] and is full of miracles. As such, it is in part at least hagiography. Bede's high seriousness enhances its character in this respect. Although Gregory of Tours is much concerned with wonders in his *Histories*, he interweaves them with highly unedifying (and entertaining) material satirizing the depravity of this fallen world. Bede, by contrast, rarely if ever allows satire or irony to detract from his consciously elevated tone; when evil-doing is allowed into his exemplary world, it is for an obvious didactic purpose, to demonstrate the terrible punishments which are its ineluctable fruit.

One crucial inspiration for Bede in his development of these genres was the historical narratives in the Bible. In particular, the Pentateuch, the first five books of the Old Testament, influenced both structure and content. It told the history of the Jews from creation to the death of Moses, under whom they had received and adopted God's laws and were at the point of entering Canaan, the Promised Land. Like the Pentateuch (but unlike Eusebius), the *Ecclesiastical History* is divided into five books. It begins with a laudatory description of Britain and Ireland, implicitly equating them with the Promised Land; Bede draws attention to the parallel by noting that five languages were spoken in Britain just as the divine law was divided into five books (I. I). The point is made again at the end of Book v, where Bede's references to the *Ecclesiastical History* make plain that it deals both with a chosen people, the English, and with a promised land, Britain, which that people had come to occupy.[5]

Bede seems to have got the idea of a providential, biblically based, historical narrative from a sixth-century British work, Gildas's *On the Ruin of Britain*, freely quoted verbatim in the first book of the *Ecclesiastical History*, although only named once (see I. 22). Gildas wrote like an Old Testament prophet, presenting the Britons as a people of God, who had fallen away from their allotted role; he deplored their depravity, which had brought down upon them the wrath of God, and ended in despairing prayer for the few remaining good pastors among them. Bede took over this narrative and subtly reshaped it; he followed Gildas in depicting the Britons as a new Israel occupying a promised land, but differed from him in concluding that they had been supplanted by a new people, the English, who heard God's word and obeyed it (see v. 22). Later, Bede's concern that the contemporary English, like Gildas's Britons, were threatened by evil pastors clearly emerges as a driving element in the narrative.[6]

The Bible influenced the *Ecclesiastical History* in other ways. Bede's exegesis, especially in his later years when he was writing his great work, was dominated by the historical books of the Old Testament. Like Augustine, greatest of Latin exegetes and a formative influence, Bede emphasized the concrete historical reality of the sacred text before going on to elucidate its hidden spiritual significance. History had value in itself. Bede's concern with the accurate recording of events is especially evident in the prefatory material to both the *Ecclesiastical History* and the prose *Life of Saint Cuthbert*. In his dedicatory letter to the Northumbrian king Ceolwulf, after noting that he had submitted a preliminary draft of the *Ecclesiastical History* to the king for critical assessment, Bede provided an unusually detailed and specific account of his researchers and informants, of the archives which they consulted and the traditions which they transmitted. In the preface to the *Life of Saint Cuthbert*, he was even more exacting. He claimed that he had not presumed to write anything down without the 'most rigorous investigation of the facts' or to publish the text 'without the scrupulous examination of credible witnesses' (p. 143). When the book was in note-form he had shown it to former companions of Cuthbert himself for them to read and revise. The ensuing text, a 'rigorous investigation of the truth' (p. 145), had been read over a period of two days to senior and learned members of the community and been found worthy of publication without a single alteration.

Such rigour had, however, to be combined with a not entirely happy bedfellow. In his letter to Ceolwulf Bede draws attention to the driving force behind the *Ecclesiastical History*:

> Should history tell of good men and their good estate, the thoughtful listener is
> spurred on to imitate the good; should it record the evil ends of wicked men, no
> less effectually the devout and earnest listener or reader is kindled to eschew

what is harmful and perverse and with greater care to pursue those things which he has learned to be good and pleasing in the sight of God. (*EH*, preface, p. 3; translation modified)

The methods by which such edification could be achieved were then spelled out in a famous passage which deals with Bede's sources in his native Northumbria; he had relied, he says, not only upon personal knowledge but upon 'innumerable witnesses' and he implores the reader not to impute any error to him:

> For, in accordance with a true law of history, I have simply sought to commit to writing what I have collected from common report, for the instruction of posterity. (*EH*, preface, p. 7; translation modified)

The meaning of this statement, which in some ways seems to subvert the preceding critique of sources, has been much discussed.[7] Clearly, by 'common report' (*fama vulgans*) Bede meant not vulgar rumour but rather the common perception of men of his own background and learning. The phrase 'true law of history', which he derived from Jerome, is especially problematic. Interestingly, Bede had already used it in his *Commentary on the Gospel of Luke*, to justify the evangelist's description of Joseph as the (natural) father of Jesus. Luke had not, Bede says, forgotten that Mary conceived and gave birth as a virgin, but was rather heedful of the fact that Joseph was universally regarded as the true father to preserve Mary's good name. In thus recording common belief, Luke was following the (or a) true law of history. That, however, Bede was rather uneasy about this is suggested by his adoption of Augustine's argument that there was a degree of literal truth in Luke's statement: since Jesus was the son of Joseph's wife, Joseph stood in a much more fatherly relation to him than if he had been adopted from some other party (*Commentary on Luke*, p. 67). All this suggests that, in his justification of reliance on common report as a governing principle of history (although not necessarily the only one), Bede was thinking more as exegete and hagiographer than as historian. Emphasis was placed on 'simple faith', on relating things straightforwardly (*simpliciter*); in the end it was not the historian's job to probe deeper, to look beneath the surface of the edifying narrative. It was in this spirit, it seems, that Bede received his source material for the life of Cuthbert with its innumerable miracles.

We have here then something of a paradox. On the one hand, in the preface to the *Ecclesiastical History* Bede offers us as a governing principle the straightforward faith of the hagiographer in the stories offered by his trustworthy witnesses. On the other, in the prose *Life of Saint Cuthbert* he offers a wholly exceptional assertion of rigour in pursuit of historical truth. While in the *Ecclesiastical History* Bede offers a hagiographer's perception of history, in the prose *Life* he presents a historian's methodology for hagiography. It is interesting to note, however, that the prose *Life* was no mere collection of edifying facts; it was, Bede claimed, 'planned and complete' (*deliberatus ac confectus*, p. 145). New material, as opposed to the correction or refinement of what was there already, could not be included. In other words, Bede's historical account of Cuthbert had a specific purpose.

It is revealing to consider the *History of the Abbots* alongside these works. Here we have a text based on the traditions of Bede's own monastery. From the historiographical viewpoint, the interesting thing is that when Bede sifts the evidence for an institution which he had known almost since its inception, he does not, apparently, follow the 'law of history' as presented to King Ceolwulf. In some ways, although this is perhaps deceptive, the *History of the Abbots* is the most purely historical work of all Bede's oeuvre. There is no evidence here of him accepting miracle stories 'in simple faith'. Is this because, at least in the matter of wonders, Bede is applying standards he does not choose to apply elsewhere? That, however, does not mean that he sought to be objective; as we shall see, in the *History of the Abbots* as in the prose *Life of Saint Cuthbert* Bede wrote to prove a point.

Content and sources of the major historical works

The 'Ecclesiastical History'

Almost certainly Bede regarded this great work as of especial importance, since, uniquely, he appended to it details of his life and writings. The five books of the *Ecclesiastical History* span the period from the invasion of Julius Caesar, incorrectly dated to 60 BC, to the author's own day. Bede drew the line at 731, an eventful year in Northumbrian history, during which King Ceolwulf, the *Ecclesiastical History*'s dedicatee, was temporarily deposed and Bede's diocesan, Bishop Acca of Hexham, was driven from his see. But that does not necessarily mean the work was finished then. Bede worked on the text over a long period and it went through more than one revision; indeed, there are indications that he may still have been adding to it and amending it as late as 734. A draft was sent to Ceolwulf for his approval (perhaps in 731) and the completed text, presumably revised in accordance with the king's prescriptions, seems to have been published some three years later.[8]

The *Ecclesiastical History* is notable for its treatment of the English as, in some sense, a single people or *gens*, albeit one divided into separate kingdoms whose inhabitants are also termed *gentes*. It focuses upon the conversion of these kingdoms and the establishment and development of the Church within them. Although it takes the story right up to Bede's own day, it concentrates on the seventh century rather than the earlier eighth, in particular on the heroic period between the 620s and 690, which saw the initial conversion of Northumbria by the Roman missionary Paulinus, and the subsequent development of the Church there.

Book I opens with a description of *Britannia*, the island of Britain, setting the scene for the providential narrative which follows. The failure of the British to preach to the pagan English incomers leads to the eventual loss of their promised land. The first book culminates in Pope Gregory's dispatch of a mission to the English, the envoys' arrival in King Æthelberht's Kent, and the establishment of the see of Canterbury. It concludes with the pagan Northumbrian king Æthelfrith's conquests in *Britannia* and in particular his defeat of the Irish of Dál Riada (in what is now Scotland).

After an opening panegyric of Gregory I, Book II describes the pope's plan for dividing the English Church into two provinces each led by a metropolitan bishop, one based in the south, in London, the other in the north, in York. It then chronicles the establishment of the see of London, quickly vitiated by the South East's relapse into paganism, before moving on to the mission to Northumbria, its initial success and the establishment of a see at York. After a chapter devoted to the conversion of the East Angles, Bede returns to Northumbria and the Roman mission's failure, after the defeat and death of its patron, King Edwin, in 633 at the hands of the barbarous British king, Cædwalla of Gwynedd, and his pagan ally, Penda of Mercia.

Book III recounts the apostasy of Edwin's successors in Northumbria and focuses mainly upon the establishment of a fresh mission to the kingdom, from the Irish of Iona, not Canterbury, and based at the island monastery of Lindisfarne rather than at York. It presents the patron of the mission, the Northumbrian king Oswald (634–42), as an exemplary Christian warrior-ruler and the community at Lindisfarne as equally exemplary monks and pastors, who unlike their modern counterparts followed Pope Gregory's precepts. The book is much concerned with the Irish mission's differences from current Roman practice in matters of Church discipline, principally the style of the clerical tonsure and the calculation of the date of Easter. The abandonment of those differences at the synod of Whitby in 664 forms a climax, representing the adoption of fully Roman observance by the mother Church of Bede's native Northumbria. The book ends with the dispatch of a bishop-elect of Canterbury to Rome by the kings of Northumbria and Kent, a prelude to the revitalization of the role of that see.

The appointment of Theodore to Canterbury in 668 forms the opening to Book IV. Bede recounts his remarkable rise to dominance as sole archbishop of the entire English Church – both north and south of the Humber. Disregarding the Gregorian scheme (a matter on which Bede makes no comment), Theodore embarked upon a radical subdivision of the English dioceses, hitherto very large and often coincident with an entire kingdom. In Northumbria, his ultimately successful attempts to partition the kingdom's vast diocese brought him into conflict with its incumbent, Bishop Wilfrid. Bede deals with this unedifying strife within the English ecclesiastical establishment in a very discreet way; his careful shaping of the story is apparent because, unusually, we can compare it to another account, in Stephen of Ripon's *Life of Bishop Wilfrid* (below). Book IV also charts the flourishing of the Northumbrian Church after 664 in the wake of the reconciliation at Whitby, but then strikes a rather gloomier note, telling of the Northumbrian king Ecgfrith's ill-omened attack on the Picts in 685, an event resulting in the king's own death and characterized as the moment that 'the hope and strength of the English kingdom (i.e. Northumbria) began to ebb and fall away' (IV. 26, p. 429). The book nevertheless concludes triumphantly with the life and miracles of Cuthbert, bishop of Lindisfarne. Irish-trained, but exhibiting Roman virtues commended by Pope Gregory, he represents the fruit of the concord achieved at Whitby.

In Book V, as he approaches his own times, Bede moves the focus from the internal affairs of the English kingdoms (in which there was much that he disliked) to the activities of the English overseas. He concentrates especially upon the mission of the Northumbrians to the Irish of Iona and to the continental Germans. There follows a careful account of the career of the controversial Wilfrid (d. 710), edited to present him as ardent catholic, missionary and authentic bishop. We then return to the theme of mission, first with an account of an initiative from the Picts of northern Britain on the Easter question, which ended with the Picts' adoption of current Roman custom. The next chapter, the penultimate of the narrative, is in effect the climax of Book V and in some ways of the entire work. It describes the final yielding of Iona in 716 to the inexorable progress of Roman custom in the matter of Easter. Bede spells out the message: the Irish, who unlike the British had 'willingly and ungrudgingly' (v. 22, p. 555) taken care to communicate the Christian faith to the English, had now in turn been brought by those same English to the observance of more perfect norms. In a final chapter, Bede surveys the state of the English Church and of Britain in his own time. As noted, his narrative ends in the year 731, mentioning the death of Archbishop Berhtwald and the appointment of his Mercian successor, but not the deposition and restoration of Ceolwulf and the expulsion of Bishop Acca of Hexham. These events, which were followed by the (probably enforced) resignation of the bishop of York and his replacement by Bede's correspondent Egbert, almost certainly represent the inauguration of a new regime. Bede, it seems, deliberately chose to draw a veil over the presumably unseemly manoeuvrings of a period of significant change.

The *Ecclesiastical History* thus has a strong driving narrative. Bede's skill in constructing this is all the more remarkable, given the complex and varied nature of his sources. For although he drew on valuable written text, both archival and hagiographical, some now lost, much of his material seems to have been hitherto unrecorded traditions, transmitted either orally or by letter and mostly emanating from grand ecclesiastics such as Abbot Albinus at Canterbury and the priest Nothhelm (later archbishop of Canterbury). Material from such disparate sources, however authoritative, must have been extremely difficult to date and arrange into a coherent chronological narrative. Bede managed this task superbly. Above all, he organized events around the single governing principle of dating the years of the world from the birth of Christ. Although he did not invent this, he was the first to use it in such a complex work.

The 'History of the Abbots'

This work, which Bede describes as being in two books (*EH* v. 24,), tells the story of the early years of the monasteries of Wearmouth and Jarrow, from their foundation in 673/4 and 681/2 respectively, up to the departure and death in 716 of Abbot Ceolfrith, under whom they had been formally united. Perhaps written very shortly after that event, it opens with the building of Wearmouth, and an account of Biscop's origins and early life, expressly comparing him with Pope Gregory's monastic hero, Benedict of Nursia, whose name he had adopted when he became a monk. Bede then recounts Biscop's journeys to Rome, his association with Theodore, his early collecting of relics and books, and his return to his native Northumbria in the early 670s when he so impressed Ecgfrith that the king granted him an extensive estate on which to found a monastery. A further journey to Gaul and Italy is one of the few events relating to the monastery also to be mentioned in the *Ecclesiastical History*. This expedition was notable for its rich haul of relics, books, sacred pictures and icons, the papal privilege exempting Wearmouth from outside interference, and – perhaps most crucial of all – the ensuing visit of the archcantor of St Peter's in Rome, sent by the pope among other things to teach Biscop's monks the most authoritative current liturgical practice in music and worship.

Bede moves on to recount Ecgfrith's endowment of a second monastery, at Jarrow, to which, he says, Biscop sent his deputy, Ceolfrith, and seventeen monks from Wearmouth. Rather uneasily, it might be thought, Bede adds here Biscop's highly unusual nomination of his cousin Eosterwine as his fellow abbot at Wearmouth, justified on the ground that Biscop was often away on journeys 'for the good of the monastery' (ch. 7, p. 194) and by the specious claim that it accorded with best monastic practice. Bede provides a glowing character sketch of the new abbot. He then describes Eosterwine's death from plague, the mortal sickness of Biscop himself and of Sigfrith, Eosterwine's successor as co-abbot, the appointment of Ceolfrith of Jarrow as abbot of both communities, and Biscop's deathbed admonition to preserve the union in harmony and peace. The fact that Bede chose to end Book I with these events rather than, as might be expected, with the deaths of Biscop and Sigfrith, which followed hard on Ceolfrith's elevation, highlights their importance in his eyes.

Book II (chs. 14–22) opens with the two abbots' deaths and an account of Ceolfrith's stewardship of the united monasteries before moving on to its central theme: Ceolfrith's resignation and replacement by Hwætbehrt, canonically elected by the brethren of the two monasteries according to the prescription of the Rule of Saint Benedict and the papal privilege of protection. To emphasize the solemnity of the former abbot's departure for Rome, Bede, as was proper for history (but unconventional in hagiography), includes a letter by Hwætberht recommending him to the newly elected pope, Gregory II. The work then continues with a short chapter recounting Hwætberht's elevation and reburial of the remains of Eosterwine and Sigfrith next to the high altar of Wearmouth church, an action which at that date amounted to canonization. The final chapters are devoted to Ceolfrith's final journey and death in September 716 at Langres.

A vexed but crucial question is the relationship of the *History of the Abbots* to another hagiographical work produced at Wearmouth or Jarrow, in or probably shortly after 716. The anonymous *Life of Abbot Ceolfrith* is closely related to the *History of the Abbots* (although there are a few significant differences in factual information), but is more focused upon Ceolfrith, and in particular concentrates on his early life and training. It is generally thought to have been written before the *History of the Abbots* and therefore to have been Bede's source.[9] It has even been suggested that it was also by Bede, that it was an earlier version of the text eventually finalized as the *History of the Abbots*.[10] But in fact there is no certain way of establishing the chronology of the two works and, as is explained elsewhere in this volume, reasons can be adduced to support the view that the *History of the Abbots* was written first (see Chapter 6).

Given such uncertainty, it is perhaps best to look elsewhere for Bede's models in compiling the *History of the Abbots*. While the *Life of Ceolfrith* is more focused on a single protagonist, Bede's work is highly unusual in that it is a history of a community. Although no close parallels can be adduced, one remarkable feature accords with hagiography which Biscop himself may have encountered in Gaul. Works such as Hilary of Arles's *Life of Honoratus*, though in many ways remote from the productions of eighth-century Jarrow, nevertheless share with the *History of the Abbots* an almost complete neglect of miracles. There are also Gallic histories of twinned or interconnected communities, such as the *Life of the Fathers of Jura*. It is thus possible that Bede was encouraged in his distinctive presentation of the abbots of his own community by his reading of material brought back from the area where Biscop himself had been received into the monastic life.

The 'Lives' of Saint Cuthbert

The most important of Bede's hagiographies are the two *Lives* of Cuthbert. The earlier, metrical *Life* was probably written fairly soon after the accession of the Northumbrian king Osred in 705/6, while the prose *Life* was compiled some years later, probably around 720. Both drew much of their material from an earlier *Life* of the saint, a monumental work in four books, written by an anonymous monk of Lindisfarne at the request of Bishop Eadfrith, shortly after Cuthbert's translation in 698.

The main outlines of the anonymous *Life* are clear. Book I is concerned with the birth and childhood of the saint, above all with the signs which foretell his holy status before birth and demonstrate his holiness as a boy; Book II relates his entry into monastic life in Melrose, his rise to the office of prior and the miracles which confirm his status there; Book III deals with his transference to Lindisfarne and his withdrawal to live a life of extreme austerity as a hermit on the island of Farne; and Book IV recounts his reluctant acceptance of the see of Lindisfarne, his life and miracles as a bishop, his holy death, burial enshrinement and posthumous wonders.

In terms of content, Bede's metrical *Life* follows this quite closely, apart from omitting one or two miracles and making a few important additions, particularly about Cuthbert's last days and death. A notable structural change, however, was the replacement of the division into four books by a single succession of forty-six chapters, an arrangement whose high symbolic significance will be discussed below. The metrical *Life* is not an easy text. Its 'allusiveness and compression'[11] required it to be read in conjunction with its prose companion, and it has been convincingly suggested that it belonged to a specific genre, that of the 'paired work' (*opus geminatum*), a literary form which goes back to the fifth-century poet Sedulius and was certainly known and admired in eighth-century Northumbria.[12] In such pairings, according to the English scholar Alcuin (d. 804), the poetic work was designed to be 'meditated upon in the privacy of one's room', while the more straightforward narrative of the prose work was meant to be heard publicly by the brethren in church.[13] Certainly, the metrical *Life* seems to have had a very restricted, private distribution. Produced at the request of some of Bede's own brethren, evidently it was initially unknown at Lindisfarne. Its meditative purpose is apparent from the prologue, in which Bede expressed the hope that it would provide the addressee, an otherwise unknown priest called John, with consolation on his projected pilgrimage to Rome.

The prose *Life* by contrast was addressed, like the anonymous work, to Eadfrith and the monks of Lindisfarne, the public guardians of the cult. Clearly intended for a wider audience, it represents a more radical departure from the anonymous author's picture of Cuthbert. Like the metrical *Life* in forty-six chapters, it sought to make more explicit, to bring into focus, the saint's activity as prior, hermit and bishop (see chs. 9, 17 and 24). This reshaping was attempted primarily in chapters which describe Cuthbert's mode of life at various stages in his career, passages which have no obvious counterparts in the anonymous *Life* and are scarcely present in Bede's poem (see chs. 16 and 26). Scattered too throughout the work are shorter comments setting the miracles within the context of Cuthbert's exemplary pastorate (see chs. 10–15). In all this material, Bede highlighted some important paradigms of pastoral, monastic and ascetic behaviour, as exemplified by protagonists of Gregory the Great's *Dialogues* and Athanasius's heroic Anthony. Cuthbert was intended to appear as in every sense the equal of these famous and admired figures. Above all, Bede re-presents the saint as an exemplar of the pastoral and contemplative ideals of Gregory the Great, on a par with the monastic rule-giver Benedict of Nursia, one of the great heroes of the *Dialogues*.

Bede also added new narrative material to the anonymous *Life*, largely the product of conversations with Herefrith, abbot of Lindisfarne in Cuthbert's time. In these discursive passages he contrives to present Cuthbert as protective patron of Northumbria, if not of the English as a whole, resplendent in miracles and thronged by pilgrims from both near and far. Even more important is the elaborate account of Cuthbert's last days and death (chs. 37–40), an episode treated quite briefly by the anonymous author. In this new text, Cuthbert is given a final speech in his retreat on Farne in which he insists that the brethren have no communion with those who do not keep the proper Easter or who indulge in evil living, and that they should leave Lindisfarne, taking his bones with them, rather than fall under the power of schismatics. He adds that, although in life he seemed contemptible to some, after his death he and his teaching would be vindicated (ch. 39). The succeeding narrative suggests that these words were meant to be seen as prophetic. When Herefrith announced Cuthbert's death to his companions, they were singing Psalm 59, which begins 'O God, thou hast cast us off and hast broken us down; thou hast been angry and hast had compassion on us' (ch. 40, p. 287). This text, which formed part of the office of Lauds, was also being sung when the saint's death was made known to the brethren on the main island of Lindisfarne. All this looked forward to the 'blast of trial' (ch. 40, p. 287) which came upon the brethren after Cuthbert's death, causing many to leave rather than be in the midst of such dangers. God's compassion – and Cuthbert's vindication – was embodied in the person of Eadberht, who after a year became bishop and restored peace.

Agenda and audience

Bede's reforming agenda in his late works

By 716, Bede was developing a programme of moral and spiritual reform. He was of the opinion that the spiritual leaders, pastors and preachers of his own age and people were by and large idle, venal, ignorant and corrupt. His commentaries, addressed primarily to the Church's elite teachers and preachers, make frequent reference to the need for spiritual improvement, and in 734 he elaborates a practical programme as to how this might be achieved in his *Letter to Bishop Egbert*.[14] These concerns have a crucial importance for his later hagiography and histories, addressed to a wider, if still elite, audience. Bede's Cuthbert, the ideal pastor and contemplative, illustrates the moral teaching of the commentaries. The *Ecclesiastical History* fleshes out that picture with numerous other examples of similar teachers and preachers. The historical and hagiographical works of Bede's maturity, though in form, language and content a distinct genre, cannot be divorced from his exegetical works of the same period. They are all informed by the same overriding moral and spiritual concerns; they are all driven by the same agenda.

While such imperatives dictated the providential scheme of the *Ecclesiastical History*, it is worth noting that more contingent concerns also inflected the narrative. Bede expected this work to reach out beyond the monastery or episcopal household to an educated political elite who, if they did not read, at least had the resources to be read to. For them he had some very specific messages. The concluding chapters of the *Ecclesiastical History*, for example, were clearly written in part to pave the way for the restoration of metropolitan status to the see of York and with it the Gregorian plan for two provinces, voluntarily suspended by the Northumbrians when they consented to obey Theodore as archbishop of Britain (*EH* IV. 2).

Bede and the English in the 'Ecclesiastical History'

Although Bede wrote 'for always and for everywhere', his teaching is directed especially towards his own people, the English, and in particular the Northumbrians. The English had their allotted place in salvation history. The island of Britannia is crucial to that providential role and provides Bede's epic with an apocalyptic dimension. Presented as remote, far from the rest of mankind, it represents the isles of the uttermost west whose conversion in Christian eschatology would herald the Second Coming of Christ. The *Ecclesiastical History* thus formed a fitting counterpoint to Eusebius, chronicling the inauguration of the final phases in Christian salvation, just as Eusebius had chronicled the first.[15]

Bede is with some justice regarded as the father of English history, and as one who in the *Ecclesiastical History*, in particular, elaborated a concept of Englishness – of a single English people – and gave it new impetus.[16] Whether or not that was his intention is another matter. The classic exposition of the view that it was is that of Patrick Wormald in two famous articles.[17] Wormald argued that Bede's was the view from Canterbury, derived ultimately from Gregory the Great, who thought of the English as a single people inhabiting the Roman province of Britannia under the leadership of a dominant king. Canterbury, especially under Theodore and his immediate successors, when it was the sole metropolitan and archiepiscopal see, had a strong interest in 'imparting a sense of unity to diverse and feuding peoples … reminding them that they were all, as Englishmen, represented in Heaven by the same saints'.[18]

Now it is very clear that Bede did indeed use English (*Angli*) inclusively, to designate all the Germanic groups or peoples (*gentes*) in Britain. But this is often not so much to stress their unity under God as to distinguish them from their non-Germanic neighbours, or from those who spoke a different language.[19] It is noticeable that where the *Angli* referred to in the *Ecclesiastical History* can be localized, they are almost always Northumbrians, or men of Kent, or both. The *Ecclesiastical History* has a lot to say about these two peoples. That, of course, is partly a matter of sources: Bede knew most about his native Northumbria and had excellent informants in Kent. But as we have seen, Bede did not always choose to say most about what he knew most about. Almost certainly, this focus has deeper roots. Wormald thought that Bede was driven by Canterbury's wish to establish a single English Church within *Britannia*, according to the papal blueprint.[20] There is much in this view, but it is also possible to see matters from a more Northumbrian perspective.

This brings us to the question of Bede's loyalties. Bede was patriotic in the sense that he identified strongly with his home province of Bernicia, its

Church and its royal house, and with the wider realm of Northumbria which that house had come to rule. The Northumbrian Church's credentials, however, were not entirely satisfactory. The Roman mission had failed there and the work of conversion had been taken up by the Irish of Iona, exemplary pastors but imperfect spiritual forebears in that their observance of Easter was based upon rules not in accord with those of Rome. Bede's stress on the oneness of the English flows from a need to connect up the somewhat unsatisfactory history of the origins of his own people's Church with the blue-chip catholicity of the Church in Kent.

As a proud Northumbrian, Bede sought to demonstrate that his *gens* was central to the unfolding of Pope Gregory's mission. The best way to do this was to highlight the role of the universal Gregory rather than the geographically specific Augustine of Canterbury. Emphasis is laid on the pope as apostolic evangelist and on his mission to the English as a whole rather than to King Æthelberht and his dominions in particular. Bede also offered a carefully constructed account of the role of the Church of Canterbury, emphasizing that the Gregorian and therefore apostolic plan was for two co-equal ecclesiastical authorities – a southern province based at London/Canterbury and a northern province based at York. His problem was that the northern province had failed, leaving a single figure of authority based in the south. One way to render this palatable to Northumbrian sensibilities was to present that remaining figure not as focused upon Canterbury but as archbishop of the island of Britain – a pastor as much for the Northumbrians as for the men of Kent. Bede was able to do this most successfully in his depiction of Archbishop Theodore, whom he presented (correctly) as embodying a new start. The axis between the Northumbrians and the men of Kent thus lay at the heart of Bede's concept of Englishness. It is a view which implicitly excludes other Anglo-Saxons, above all the Mercians, the inhabitants of the great Midland kingdom which in Bede's day was the most powerful entity south of the Humber and a bitter rival of Northumbria. They are almost never expressly included by name within the *Angli*.

Rewriting Cuthbert

Bede's rewriting of the anonymous *Life of Saint Cuthbert* can only have been occasioned by urgent and exceptional requirements. One driving force was the restructuring of the text. That is apparent from Bede's reference to his prose *Life* as a 'planned and complete work' (p. 145), similarly arranged to the metrical one – presumably an allusion to the forty-six chapters, retained in the prose *Life* even though new material had been added. Forty-six was a number laden with high exegetical significance. According to the evangelist John the number of the years that it took to rebuild the Temple, it was interpreted by Augustine and, following him, by Bede as a figure for Christ's human body. The planned and perfect work which was the prose *Life* thus presented Cuthbert by implication as a Christ-like rebuilder of the Church, an especially appropriate way of viewing the saint who embodied the best of both traditions reconciled at Whitby.[21]

Another key factor is the publication, probably in 712 or 713, of Stephen of Ripon's biography of Bishop Wilfrid. Stephen's work presented something of a challenge to the Cuthbert cult.[22] Although modelled, through direct quotation, upon the anonymous author's Cuthbert, his hero is subtly presented as an improvement on the original; Wilfrid emerges as the champion of Roman orthodoxy endowed with the episcopal virtues of Cuthbert but without his dubious non-Roman past. Bede's reshaping of Cuthbert's image in the prose *Life* responded by presenting the saint as truly Roman, in that he represented the values championed by Gregory the Great.

That Bede had Wilfrid much in mind when he compiled the prose *Life* is suggested by his inclusion of Herefrith's account of Cuthbert's last days and their aftermath. There can be only one explanation of the turmoil following Cuthbert's death: Wilfrid's year-long rule at Lindisfarne, 687–8 (see *EH* IV. 29). Cuthbert's reference to fleeing schismatics perhaps represents a covert allusion to the bishop, who according to Stephen had been excommunicated in 702–3. Herefrith's narrative shows Cuthbert foreseeing the danger posed by Wilfrid and, ultimately, providing for his community through the latter's replacement by Eadberht. As the saint predicted, his teaching had been vindicated. The prose *Life* carried that message, already implicit in Bede's poem, to a wider audience, located not only in the monastic choir or refectory but in Northumbria's educated aristocratic milieux.

Defending the rule at Wearmouth and Jarrow

The *History of the Abbots* is primarily concerned with the internal life and institutions of Wearmouth and Jarrow. Bede is thus very specific about the foundation endowment of both monasteries and its origin as King Ecgfrith's gift from his personal property (chs. 4 and 7); he is also careful to add details of later acquisitions, hardly of interest to anyone outside the two communities. Another inward-looking theme is the emphasis on the authority and pedigree of Wearmouth and Jarrow's monastic observance. Benedict Biscop's role is to underwrite this as founder (ch. 6). He is presented as seeking the best authorities in Rome and elsewhere for the monastic rule, liturgy and buildings; above all, he is made to emphasize the need to follow the Benedictine Rule in excluding all considerations of hereditary right in choosing an abbot (ch. 11). Alongside this theme must be set an almost obsessive emphasis on unity – both on the unity of the twin foundations and on the need for unity among the brethren themselves (chs. 13 and 15). Much of this finds expression in the long and moving account of Ceolfrith's resignation and departure for Rome (ch. 17).

Although Bede was anxious to present Wearmouth and Jarrow as conforming to the highest norms of Gregorian and Benedictine observance, they were perhaps in many ways closer to the more worldly communities he so vigorously condemned than he might have wished. In particular, some of the brethren apparently expected the abbacy to remain within the founder's kin and resented Biscop's exclusion of his brother in favour of more distant relatives (of whom Ceolfrith may have been one). It is clear that the brethren were divided – and the abbatial succession and the continuance of the two communities under a single abbot (itself scarcely a canonical arrangement) were probably at the root of these divisions. Ceolfrith's resignation and departure brought these issues to a head and hence received disproportionate attention in the *History of the Abbots*.

Any assessment of this work must take account of the differences in emphasis between it and the anonymous *Life of Ceolfrith*. The most obvious is that, in comparison with the anonymous text, Bede says very little about Ceolfrith's early career; he awards Biscop more prominence, especially in the foundation of Jarrow, where Ceolfrith's role, evident in the dedicatory inscription, is played down.[23] That may be because Bede saw things more from a Wearmouth perspective: certainly he stresses that it was the senior community. It is interesting too that Bede makes no mention of a revolt against Ceolfrith's rule as prior of Wearmouth and that he entirely omits Ceolfrith's important links with Wilfrid. Wilfrid after all had invited the young Ceolfrith to his monastery at Ripon, ordained him priest, and released him, at Biscop's behest, to go to Wearmouth. Bede's silence on these matters is presumably another example of his unspoken reserve about the bishop's role within the Northumbrian Church.[24] Tensions (also evident in the *Life of Ceolfrith*) lurk beneath the calm and scholarly surface of the *History of the Abbots*. It is likely that in 716 the two monasteries were troubled institutions and that this had some connection with Ceolfrith's departure. The febrile atmosphere is reflected in the generation of two texts within a short period of each other both addressing similar issues but presenting them with different emphases.

Although it is now greatly admired, the *History of the Abbots* was in some ways a more private, less universal text than either the *Ecclesiastical History* or the *Life of Saint Cuthbert*, composed primarily for a highly restricted group, the brethren of Wearmouth-Jarrow. Bede writes warmly of his holy abbots but, unlike Cuthbert, they are not presented as subjects, or even potential subjects, of a widespread public cult. The absence of miracles is evidence that here, Bede was not, as in the *Ecclesiastical History*, seeking to engage with a wide audience. It is curious too how little is said abut the two monasteries in the latter work.

Conclusion

What is the place of history, and its sister discipline hagiography, within Bede's oeuvre as a whole? On the one hand they were subordinate to his overall agenda: to advance through teaching and exegesis the work of the Church on earth. But he also had more contingent concerns, among them the state of the contemporary English Church and the position of Northumbrian saints, bishops and monasteries within that Church. That is especially apparent in the shorter hagiographical works, which seem often to have been elicited by contemporary events and may have been expected to have quite a short shelf life. Although such concerns are also apparent in the *Ecclesiastical History*, in that much more ambitious text such contingent matters were clearly subordinated to Bede's wider providential vision.

That history should be edifying and teach through its portrayal of holy example undoubtedly affected its content in Bede's hands. Bede had in some ways a very historical cast of mind and his approach to exegesis, for all its use of allegory, resembled Augustine's in giving full weight to the literal, historical meaning. Bede liked to edit and codify complex and confusing information into an orderly structure. He was fastidious in his endeavour to assess his sources and to represent accurate and truthful information. He did not make things up. But he had formulated a view of history which allowed him to record received opinion (of an informed and educated kind) without necessarily believing it. It was one at least of the historian's jobs truthfully to set down what he had received from trustworthy witnesses. So wonders about which Bede might well have had doubts, of the kind he most certainly did not record in his home environment, he could retell in the *Ecclesiastical History* and the prose *Life of Saint Cuthbert* if he thought they would advance his underlying purpose. Conversely, information which he knew to be true could, if he deemed it unhelpful or unedifying, be suppressed. Bede then was a complex figure. Undoubtedly supremely well-equipped to research and write history and hagiography, he presented a carefully crafted picture. Such was his skill that we can identify with him very easily; thus for Plummer, he was 'the very model of the saintly scholar priest'.[25] Yet in the end Bede was a man of his time. He did not aspire to academic objectivity; he was a man with a vision which underpinned all that he wrote.

NOTES

1. Badian 1966: 9.
2. Wallace-Hadrill 1986: 24.
3. Goffart 1988.
4. Campbell 1986: 25.
5. Brooks 1999.
6. Hanning 1966.
7. Ray 1976 and 1980; Goffart 2005; Campbell 1986: 25–6.
8. Kirby 1992: 2–6; Goffart 1988: 242.
9. Goffart 1988: 277, 279; Wood 1995: 2, 8–10.
10. McClure 1984.
11. Lapidge 1988: 93.
12. Godman 1982: lxxviii–lxxxviii.
13. Lapidge 1988: 93.
14. Thacker 1983; DeGregorio 2002 and 2004.
15. Scully 1997: 33–5; O'Reilly 2005.
16. Brooks 1999: esp. p. 5.
17. Wormald 1983 and 1992.
18. Wormald 1983: 121.
19. Brooks 1999: 11.
20. Wormald 1983: 125–9.
21. Eby 1997.
22. Goffart, 1988; Thacker 1989.
23. Wood 1995: 9.
24. *Ibid.*, 8–9; Goffart 1988: 278.
25. Plummer 1896: lxxviii–lxxix.

PART III

Reception and influence

13

DAVID ROLLASON

The cult of Bede

The aim of this chapter is to explore when, where and to what extent Bede was treated as a saint in the medieval period. In the early Middle Ages, there existed no generally agreed process for recognizing saints. Not until the twelfth century did the popes take control of the process of canonization, based on evidence of the saint's posthumous miracles and, in the case of a martyr, manner of death, or, in the case of a confessor, outstandingly virtuous life. This process, however, did not apply to those who were already being treated as saints.[1] Bede was certainly never canonized in the formal sense. In 836, the Council of Aachen called him 'venerable', but not so much as a title as in the context of a description of him as 'the priest Bede, in these modern times a venerable and admirable teacher'.[2] Only in 1899 did the pope give him the title of Doctor of the Church, with his feast being formally adopted into the Roman Catholic Church but placed since 1969 on 25 May, rather than 26 or 27 May, on which it was generally celebrated in the Middle Ages.[3]

If Bede was treated as a saint in earlier periods, it must have been in the vaguer, more local, more informal way by which saints were recognized before the advent of papal canonization. There seem to have been several parts to this process. Firstly, someone had to compose texts that described the saint's life, death and miracles, working from a variety of sources, including oral tradition, possibly with a strong local flavour (that is, such a tradition would be strongest in areas invested in Bede's reputation). Secondly, liturgical commemoration of the saint would have been introduced into the services of a particular church or churches; this process would probably have begun with the church of which the saint had been a member. Thirdly, the guardians of the cult would have encouraged devotion to the saint's relics as an assured means of procuring his or her intervention in earthly affairs on behalf of his petitioners. The most notable of such relics were the entombed physical remains, but there were also so-called secondary relics, which might be either corporeal (hair or nail clippings etc.) or created by contact with the saint or with the tomb. The primary means of promoting a saint's relics was translation, the removal of the corporeal remains to a new shrine, but the distribution of secondary relics was also important. Let us examine these processes in turn as they concern Bede.[4]

Hagiographical evidence

The only text of any sort definitely written at Wearmouth-Jarrow following Bede's death in 735 was the letter of Cuthbert, future abbot of Wearmouth-Jarrow, addressed to his fellow teacher (*conlector*) Cuthwin, and describing Bede's last illness and death.[5] Can this be regarded as having been written in some sense to secure Bede's recognition as a saint? At first glance, it appears to be an item in normal correspondence between Cuthbert and Cuthwin, since in the first sentence the former acknowledges receipt of a letter and a present from Cuthwin. It then emerges, however, that the letter in question contained the information that Cuthbert most wanted to find – that is, that Cuthwin's religious community was 'regularly offering masses and devout prayers for the benefit of God's chosen servant Bede' (pp. 580–1). It would, of course, have been quite normal throughout the Middle Ages for the religious community of a dead person to have requested masses and prayers for him from other communities; but, in the grey area which was early medieval saint-making, it is not impossible that Cuthbert had been taking the first steps in spreading liturgical commemoration of Bede as a saint. Moreover, the letter lays great emphasis on the holiness of Bede's last hours and, while it does not emphasize his sufferings in his last illness, it does note that he was 'found worthy' (p. 583) to be scourged by his sickness; it emphasizes his devotion to God to the last, including the famous story of how he finished his translation into English of Saint John's Gospel with the words 'consummatum est' (p. 585); and more particularly it observes that it seemed to those watching him 'that he knew very well when his end should be' (p. 585). Foreknowledge of the time of death, denied to most, was a mark of proximity to God and therefore potentially an element of sainthood. Moreover, Cuthbert remarks that many other things could have been written about Bede, and he will write a 'fuller account' (p. 587); if he did so, this account does not survive. Together with the wide diffusion of the letter,[6] these aspects suggest the possibility that it was a first step in the recognition of Bede as a saint.

There is evidence (discussed below) that in the later eighth century Bede was indeed venerated as a saint at Wearmouth-Jarrow and at various Carolingian centres, especially those associated with the English missionaries Boniface and Lull. By *c.* 800 Alcuin could write to the boys of Jarrow describing Bede as 'blessed' (*beatus*) and recommending him to them as their patron.[7] He was also referred to as *beatus* and *sanctus* by a number of Carolingian authors.

Nevertheless, after Cuthbert's letter, we find nothing of a hagiographical nature relating to Bede until he became the subject of a life which was copied in the late eleventh century into the manuscript of his *Ecclesiastical History* given to Durham Cathedral Priory by Bishop William of Saint Calais (1080–96),[8] and in the period *c.* 1115 to *c.* 1130 into a booklet, which was in part the work of the historian and cantor, Symeon of Durham.[9] This life contains little that is not in Bede's own account of himself in his *Ecclesiastical History* and in Cuthbert's letter on his death, but Fiona Gameson notes that it lays greater emphasis than does the latter text on the physical pain he endured during his last illness, which is more consistent with his position as a saint specially cleansed of sin by God. Gameson argues that the life is unlikely to have been written at Jarrow following Bede's death, since it does not mention the miracle referred to by Alcuin, and its Northumbrian patriotism seems to rule out composition on the continent. She concludes that it could either have been written in Durham in the late eleventh century, although it does not refer to the presence of Bede's relics there (on which, see below), or, perhaps more likely, at Wearmouth or Jarrow after they had been restored as Benedictine monasteries by Aldwin and his colleagues in the 1070s.[10]

In his *History of the English Kings* of 1125, William of Malmesbury wrote about Bede, chiefly commenting on his work, but noting a tradition that he had visited Rome, and asserting that he had certainly been invited to advise the pope. This was supported by extracts from a purported letter of Pope Sergius, pressing Bede's abbot to send him to Rome. In addition, Malmesbury seems to have added to the account of Bede's death that there arose a paradisiacal fragrance, another indication of the deceased's status as a saint.[11]

These elements were included in a later medieval life of Bede in the sixteenth-century compilation *Nova Legenda Angliae*, based on John of Tynemouth's fourteenth-century collection of saints' lives.[12] This adds two explanations of why Bede was called 'venerable', one being that he was tricked into preaching to stones which miraculously applauded him as 'venerable father', another that the cleric deputed to write his epitaph was unable to make the words 'the bones of St Bede' scan, and was prompted by an angel to substitute 'the bones of the venerable Bede' which did scan.[13]

Liturgical commemoration

Bede's feast does not appear in the metrical martyrology thought to have been composed at York in the 760s or in the earliest English liturgical calendar, which is probably from northern England in the ninth century.[14] Indeed it only appears in English liturgical calendars in the eleventh century, suggesting that it was probably not of importance before then.[15] After the Norman Conquest, it still does not appear in English calendars with any consistency, and is not even found in a twelfth-century Durham calendar.[16]

In the eight and ninth centuries Bede's reputation was in some ways more highly developed abroad, above all in Germany, than in England itself. Bede was clearly much admired by the English missionary Boniface, who repeatedly requested copies of his works and referred to him as 'a lantern of the church'.[17] Lull, Boniface's close associate and successor as archbishop of Mainz, went further and, in correspondence with Bede's disciple Cuthbert, by then abbot of Wearmouth-Jarrow, referred to Bede as 'of blessed memory'.[18] Several Carolingian writers term Bede 'blessed' or a saint.[19] That Bede was indeed commemorated as a saint in Carolingian Frankia is suggested by an entry recording his feast day (here termed his 'deposition') on 26 May in an early ninth-century calendar from Auxerre or Fleury. Although he does not appear in the earliest, roughly contemporary calendar from Fulda, he is entered in a later calendar from that monastery, dating from c. 980, as 'St Bede the priest'. He also appears in a few later eleventh- and early twelfth-century calendars and martyrologies compiled in the imperial territories, including Germany, Italy and Utrecht.[20] Other evidence of liturgical cult is his inclusion among the saints invoked in Carolingian litanies, including one of the early ninth century from Cologne and another of the early tenth from St Gall.[21]

Relics

We do not know for certain where Bede was originally buried; later tradition (see below) suggests that it was most probably at Jarrow, but a case could also be made for Wearmouth, where other revered figures, including the early abbots Benedict Biscop and Eosterwine, were enshrined. Nor is there any evidence that Bede was translated (as Biscop and Eosterwine had been) during this early period. What we do know, however, is that by the mid eighth century, under Abbot Cuthbert, Bede's remains were promoted as an object of devotion; for in 764 Cuthbert wrote to Archbishop Lull, thanking him for the gift of a silk wrapping sent 'for the relics of Bede, in remembrance and veneration of our master of blessed memory'.[22] In the late eighth century Alcuin, who had been educated at York, wrote about a healing miracle worked by these relics.[23] At some point too, in this early period, perhaps under Abbot Cuthbert, Wearmouth-Jarrow had apparently distributed secondary relics of Bede: in the ninth century the Carolingian scholar Hrabanus

Maurus (d. 856), who was successively abbot of Fulda and archbishop of Mainz, mentions such a relic at Boniface's church at Fulda.[24]

The Viking invasions brought to an end the early monastic communities at Wearmouth and Jarrow, and with it presumably any incipient Bedan tomb-cult in his home monastery. But English interest in Bede's relics seems to have revived by the early eleventh century.[25] Symeon of Durham, writing a century later, tells a story of how Alfred Westou, sacrist of Durham in the 1030s, had stolen Bede's remains from Jarrow and placed them, contained in a linen bag, with the relics of Saint Cuthbert.[26] There are good reasons for accepting this account. The relics are located at Durham in the Old English poem on the saints of that city,[27] and the monks who opened Cuthbert's tomb in 1104 are reported to have found them in the linen bag mentioned by Symeon.[28]

Symeon's account is thus our first evidence of the location of Bede's burial. It may even suggest that memory of Bede's interment had been preserved from 735. Symeon tells of a memorial chapel which existed in his time on the north side of St Paul's Jarrow,[29] a church which, although restored in the 1070s, retained its seventh-century fabric;[30] so this chapel may have been early in date, and indeed on the actual site of the grave, which was presumably, like the graves of the early abbots at Wearmouth, housed within the church.[31] At all events, all this is certainly evidence that the cult continued to be sponsored by the post-Conquest cathedral community at Durham. By Symeon's time it was even possible to see Bede's cell, although the excavations at Jarrow show it is unlikely that this latter was an authentic survival.[32]

In 1104 Bede's relics were not restored to their position beside those of Cuthbert. We hear nothing more of them until the time of Bishop Hugh of Le Puiset (1153–95), who created a shrine for them, apparently in connection with his largely abortive attempt to reshape the east end of the cathedral.[33] In the context of another reshaping of the eastern limb, this shrine was removed in 1370 to the Galilee Chapel at the west end of the cathedral.[34] This might be seen as a downgrading, but the shrine was clearly still important at Durham, and it was the responsibility of the subprior to unlock it so that it could be carried in procession on important festival days.[35] The cathedral's continuing interest in the cult is also apparent from its relic lists, four of which refer to relics of Bede, including his clothes. Bede's relics occur also in a thirteenth-century list from Waltham, a church closely associated with Durham.[36] The shrine was defaced along with Saint Cuthbert's in 1541,[37] and the existing tomb was built following the excavation of a skeleton, believed to be that of Bede, in 1831.[38]

Durham was not the only English church with an interest in Bede's remains during the Middle Ages. In the twelfth century, Glastonbury asserted that it had the entire relics of Bede, together with those of other northern saints, a claim which may go back to the tenth century.[39] Three later medieval lists from the abbey also include relics of Bede, as does a fifteenth-century list from Salisbury.[40]

Conclusion

Bede's relics never obtained the currency of those of his fellow Northumbrian, Saint Oswald, either in England or on the continent.[41] Throughout the Middle Ages, his appearance in the calendars was fluctuating and uncertain. Yet there is clear evidence that, in the decades immediately after his death, an informal cult was sponsored at Wearmouth-Jarrow by his pupil Cuthbert and diffused on the continent by English missionaries, who admired Bede's writings. Indeed, Bede appears in calendars from Frankia well before any of those surviving from England, where the Viking invasions disrupted the cult, which in any case may have faded after the death of Abbot Cuthbert. In the later tenth and early eleventh century interest in Bede revived among English monastic reformers, alongside interest in the *Ecclesiastical History* and its depiction of the golden age of the English Church, and by the eleventh century Bede was again the object of informal cult at Durham. There veneration for him was to continue until the Reformation. Outside Durham, his cult was clearly a modest one, and even in Durham it could not compete with that of Saint Cuthbert.[42]

NOTES

1. Rollason 1989: 3; Thacker and Sharpe 2002: esp. 45–73.
2. *Concilia Aevi Karolini*, ed. A. Werminghoff, 2 vols., Monumenta Germaniae Historica 2, Parts 1–2: Concilia (Legum Sectio 3) (Hannover: Hahn, 1906–8), vol. i.ii, p. 759: 'venerabilis et modernis temporibus doctor admirabilis Beda presbiter'.
3. Holweck 1924: under Bede, pp. 144–5.
4. See also Blair 2002: 514.
5. *Cuthbert's Letter on the Death of Bede*, in Colgrave and Mynors 1969: 579–87.
6. Dobbie 1937: 49–105; Rollason 2000: lxix, n. 287 (for revisions and additions to Dobbie's work).
7. See Carroll 1946: 58.
8. Durham, Cathedral Library, MS B.II.35, ff. 119–23; *Bibliotheca Hagiographica Latina*, 2 vols. (Brussels: Society of Bollandists, 1898–1901), no. 1,069. The text is printed in J. P. Migne (ed.), *Patrologiae cursus completus*, Series latina, 221 vols. (Paris, 1844–64), vol. XC, cols. 41–54; for commentary, see Hardy 1862–71: no. 985.
9. London, British Library, MS Harley 526, ff. 28–37, on which see Gullick 1998: 28.

10. F. Gameson, 'The *Vita Bedae* in Durham, Cathedral Library, MS B.II.35', unpublished paper delivered at the Manuscripts of Bede workshop, Durham, August 2008. I am very grateful to Dr Gameson for permission to use her forthcoming work. On the restoration of Monkwearmouth-Jarrow, see, for example, Baker 1970.

11. William of Malmesbury, *The History of the English Kings*, ed. and trans. R. A. B. Mynors, R. M. Thomson and M. Winterbottom, 2 vols., Oxford Medieval Texts (Oxford: Clarendon Press, 1998–9), vol. I, sects. 54–62, esp. 58, 61.

12. *Nova Legenda Anglie as Collected by John of Tynemouth, John Capgrave, and Others, and First Printed, with New Lives, by Wynkyn de Worde AD MDXVI*, ed. C. Horstman, 2 vols. (Oxford: Clarendon Press, 1901), vol. I, pp. 107–11.

13. For other lives of Bede, which are mostly mere confections from other sources, some made in the early modern period, see Hardy 1862–71: 451–4 (nos. 986–91); and *Bibliotheca Hagiographica Latina*, nos. 1,070–6b.

14. *English Benedictine Kalendars before A.D. 1100*, ed. F. Wormald, Henry Bradshaw Society 72 (London: Harrison and Sons, 1934), no. 1.

15. *Saints in English Kalendars before A.D. 1100*, ed. R. Rushforth, Henry Bradshaw Society 117 (Woodbridge: The Boydell Press, 2008): table V (May).

16. *English Benedictine Kalendars after A.D. 1100*, ed. F. Wormald, 2 vols., Henry Bradshaw Society 77 and 81 (London: Harrison and Sons, 1939–46), esp. vol. II, p. 172.

17. Boniface, Letter 76, in *The Letters of Saint Boniface*, trans. E. Emerton (New York: Columbia University Press, 2000), p. 112 (no. 59).

18. Whitelock 1979: 832 (no. 185).

19. Carroll 1946: 58–9.

20. *Der Karolingische Reichskalender*, ed. A. Borst, Monumenta Germaniae Historica, Antiquitates, vol. II: Libri Memoriales (Hannover: Hahn, 2001), p. 920.

21. Carroll 1946: 58–9.

22. Whitelock 1979: 831 (no. 185).

23. Alcuin, *The Bishops, Kings and Saints of York*, ed. and trans. P. Godman (Oxford: Clarendon Press, 1982), lines 1,315–18, pp. 103–5.

24. Hrabanus Maurus, 'Denotatio dedicationis ecclesiae sancti Salvatoris constructae in monasterio Fuldae', in *Poetae Latini aevi Carolini*, ed. E. Dümmler, Monumenta Germaniae Historica, Poetarum Latinorum Medii Aevi 2 (Berlin: Weidmann, 1884), p. 208.

25. Carroll 1946: 60–2.

26. Symeon of Durham, *Libellus de exordio atque procursu istius hoc est Dunhelmensis ecclesie*, ed. D. Rollason, Oxford Medieval Texts (Oxford: Clarendon Press, 2000), III. 7, pp. 164–7. See also Kendall 1984.

27. Howlett 1994.

28. *Symeonis Monachi Opera Omnia*, ed. T. Arnold, 2 vols., Roll Series 75 (London: Longman, 1882–5), vol. I, pp. 152–3. Rollason 2000: 167, n. 37 is in error in this respect.

29. Symeon of Durham, *Libellus de exordio*, I. 14., pp. 68–9.

30. Taylor and Taylor 1965–78: s.n. Jarrow.

31. Rollason 1989: 37.

32. Cramp, Bettess, Bettess, Anderson and Lowther 2005–6.

33. Symeon of Durham, *Libellus de exordio*, pp. 322–3; Snape 1980: 23; Halsey 1980: 61.
34. Fowler 1903: 44–6; Snape 1980: 27–8.
35. Fowler 1903: 96; McKinnell 1998: 24.
36. Thomas 1974; and Symeon of Durham, *Libellus de exordio*, III. 23, pp. 210–13 (on Waltham).
37. Raine 1828: 178.
38. Fowler 1903: 286–7.
39. William of Malmesbury, *History of the English Kings*, vol. II, pp. 49–50; Rollason 1989: 152; Scott 1981: 68.
40. Thomas 1974.
41. Thacker 1995; Clemoes 1983.
42. Marner 2000.

14

JOSHUA A. WESTGARD

Bede and the continent in the Carolingian age and beyond

When the Venerable Bede composed the literary autobiography that closes the final chapter of his *Ecclesiastical History of the English People*, he wrote out of concern for his legacy and for the benefit of future readers of his works. According to his own humble description, the primary purpose of his literary endeavours had been to clarify the Holy Scriptures and their interpretation 'for [his] own benefit and for that of [his] brothers' (v. 24, p. 567). Taken at face value, these words suggest that Bede wrote mainly for his fellow monks, the present and future members of his own twin community of Wearmouth-Jarrow. Indeed, there can be little doubt that the local brethren were a concern of his, but at the same time there is ample evidence that he thought his works would reach a much wider audience. After all, if he truly had thought that his works were going to remain within his own monastic family – among those who knew him well and who could be relied upon to keep his memory alive – why would he have composed an autobiographical sketch in the first place, and especially one in which he speaks of his brethren in the third person? The autobiographical sketch itself demonstrates that he envisioned his works reaching a wider audience.

In the centuries after his death, Bede's audience was indeed much wider than his fellow monks, wider even than the English people. In fact, his audience was ultimately more widespread both in time and space than he himself probably ever imagined it would be. Within a few generations of his death, not only were his works known throughout Britain and in Ireland, but they also had made their way to continental Europe, where they became a central component of the educational and literary flowering under the Carolingians. It was among the Carolingians that Bede's reputation as an authority figure was firmly and permanently established, and ultimately it was in Carolingian scriptoria and libraries that his works were carefully copied and preserved, and from which some of them were re-imported into Britain in the wake of the ninth century, when disruption and neglect appear to have led to the loss of many of the manuscripts of his works that must have been present in the libraries of eighth-century Northumbria.

The wide availability of Bedan works in the Carolingian period in turn made possible their even greater multiplication and spread during the course of the twelfth century, when they continued to be copied frequently for both new and established monastic libraries, and when their popularity peaked. To judge by their prominence in surviving medieval library catalogues, Bede's writings ranked with the works of the Latin Fathers in importance in a typical twelfth-century book collection. Numerous copies of his works that had been made in the twelfth century, moreover, must still have been in circulation as copying slowed in the thirteenth and fourteenth centuries. In the late Middle Ages, Bede's scientific works fell into neglect, but his exegetical works and the *Ecclesiastical History* continued to be copied, though less frequently, right up to the arrival of printing.

Bede's audience

Before turning to the question of the transmission and reception of Bede's works and the audience that they ultimately would reach, it is worth pausing for a moment to consider the audience that he had in mind when he set about writing his works.[1] The works themselves, and especially the prefatory letters he attached to them, often give us clues to the immediate context of their composition. As noted above, in his autobiographical sketch Bede described his writings as having been undertaken for his fellow monks; this characterization is confirmed by the preface to *The Reckoning of Time* (p. 3), where he writes of having undertaken the project at the behest of his brethren, who had not found the earlier scientific writings he had presented to them, *On Times* and *On the Nature of Things*, sufficiently detailed. That monastic students were his intended audience is further supported by both the content and form of the work.[2] *The Art of Poetry* and *The Figures of Rhetoric*, conceived by Bede as two halves of a single work, were also composed for the local community, as is demonstrated by its being addressed to his pupil Cuthbert. Similarly, Bede's fellow monk Hwætberht, whom he affectionately nicknamed Eusebius, and who would later become abbot of Wearmouth-Jarrow, was the addressee of his *Commentary on the Apocalypse*; Bede also mentions him in the preface to the *Commentary on the Acts of the Apostles*.

Bede's statement that he was writing for his fellow monks is, therefore, clearly more than just a rhetorical affectation, and yet at the same time it does not tell the whole story of his ultimate literary aspirations. This humble statement, it would seem, masks a grander conception of his intended audience, just as his characterizing his own works as simple 'extracts from the works of the venerable fathers' (*EH* v. 24, p. 567) masks what was likely a grander understanding of their importance and originality.[3] In addition to the works mentioned above addressed to his fellow monks, a number of his writings were addressed to Northumbrian authority figures. For example, *On Genesis*, *On First Samuel* and both of his Gospel commentaries were addressed to his bishop, Acca of Hexham, as were two letters dealing with exegetical themes, *On the Resting-Places of the Children of Israel* and *On What Isaiah Says*. But Bede's connection to the hierarchy of the Northumbrian Church was not only by way of his diocesan. The preface to the prose *Life of Saint Cuthbert* was addressed to Bishop Eadfrith of Lindisfarne, and was written first and foremost for the monastic community there, though Bede goes on to explain that he had also composed a metrical version of the life of the same saint for his own community. Bede clearly saw the Northumbrian ecclesiastical establishment as part of his wider audience, and we furthermore have confirmation that he did in fact reach that audience from early in his literary career. In the *Letter to Plegwin*, written in 708, Bede defends himself against a charge of heresy that had been levelled against him in the presence of Wilfrid, Acca's predecessor as bishop of Hexham.[4] Thus, from the outset of his literary career, Bede seems to have been aware that his writings were going to be scrutinized within the upper echelons of the Northumbrian Church.

Perhaps Bede's most famous addressee, however, was not an ecclesiastic, but rather a king, albeit a rather well-educated one who would himself eventually take the tonsure. Ceolwulf of Northumbria (r. 729–37) was the recipient of an early draft of the *Ecclesiastical History*, as well as a final draft with a prefatory letter addressed to him. The letter was clearly intended to be an open letter to the king, since it seems to have been attached to the house copy of the work, as well as to copies made and sent to other places, but there is no reason to doubt that Ceolwulf received a copy sent directly from the author. Given the content of the *Ecclesiastical History*, it is perhaps not surprising that this, of all Bede's works, would be addressed to a secular figure. There may have been other contemporary laypersons who also took an interest in the work, as subsequent English kings undoubtedly did, but because Bede was writing in Latin – although in a less elaborate style than that of the exegetical works, still a learned language – we have to conclude that here too he probably envisioned his audience as primarily learned ecclesiastics.

Early distribution

The famous prefatory epistle to Ceolwulf, together with the letter that Bede sent to another early recipient of the *Ecclesiastical History* – namely his friend and mentor Albinus (d. 732), abbot of the monastery of Saint Peter and Saint Paul in Canterbury – provide an image of the mechanism by which Bede's works, and especially the longer works, are likely to have been 'published' during his lifetime.[5] In both the Albinus and Ceolwulf letters, Bede notes that he is sending his correspondent copies of his works 'for transcription' (*ad transscribendum*). His expectation appears to have been that these copies would be returned, in order that they might subsequently be sent to other correspondents in a similar fashion, and the process of transcription repeated. In sending out copies in this way – and especially when sending copies to major scriptoria such as Canterbury – Bede was presumably fully aware, and indeed probably hoped, that the house copies thereby created would themselves be copied and disseminated to additional libraries. Bede says as much in his letter to Albinus, when he asks Albinus and the monks of Canterbury to pray for him, and to 'ask those to whom you send copies of my work to do the same' (p. 278). Indeed, this process of secondhand publication was probably the only way that some of Bede's longer works could have been disseminated widely in a relatively short period of time.

When it came to international distribution, however, the situation was quite different. The distances were great, and travel dangerous and uncertain – uncertain enough to preclude any expectation that copies sent out for transcription could be returned. This was, perhaps, especially true when sending books to correspondents in the mission field, who might not be in a position to arrange for the copying themselves, even if long distances and uncertainty of travel were not obstacle enough. In such cases, copies had to be completed locally for export as outright gifts, and the large demand for Bede's works made this a burden on the local scriptorium, as evidenced by Abbot Cuthbert's reply to Archbishop Lull of Mainz's request for copies of Bede's works:

> I have sent in accordance with your wishes the books about the man of God, Cuthbert, composed in verse and prose. And if I could have done more, I would gladly have done so. For the conditions of the past winter oppressed the island of our race very horribly with cold and ice and long and widespread storms of wind and rain, so that the hand of the scribe was hindered from producing a great number of books.[6]

According to Malcolm Parkes, the demands placed on Wearmouth-Jarrow for copies of Bede's works in the generations after his death were so great that the scriptorium was driven to adopt a quick and economical script, the so-called Insular minuscule, in order to keep up (see Figure 5).[7]

It was therefore fortunate both for the overworked scribes of Wearmouth-Jarrow and for those seeking copies of Bede's works that there were other sources that could be relied upon to supply them. Hexham and York, and probably other Northumbrian libraries as well, almost certainly possessed collections of Bede's works in the generation after his death. As early as 746 or 747, the Anglo-Saxon missionary Boniface (*c.* 675–754), papal legate and missionary to Germany, wrote to Egbert, archbishop of York from 732 to 766 and a former pupil of Bede's, to ask that he send copies of Bedan works.[8] A few years later, Boniface would write to York again with another, more specific request, this time for copies of the *Homilies on the Gospels* and *On the Proverbs of Solomon*, and in the 760s or 770s his successor Lull would also turn to York for copies of works, as previously he had turned to Wearmouth-Jarrow.[9]

But these missionaries' letters are not the only evidence that York may have exported Bede's works to the continent. George Hardin Brown has suggested that Alcuin may have been responsible for arranging for the Moore Bede (Cambridge University Library, Kk.5.16), today the oldest surviving copy of the *Ecclesiastical History*, to be brought to the court library of Charlemagne, and if that is so then the chances are good that the volume was brought from Alcuin's community at York.[10] The missionary Liudger, moreover, spent time as a student in York in the 760s, and returned from there to his mission field in Saxony well supplied with books.[11] Among the books he may have carried with him was a copy of the *Ecclesiastical History*, a copy which today survives in only a single-leaf fragment (Münster in Westfalen, Universitäts- und Landesbibliothek, Fragmentensammlung Kaps. 1,3), and which is likely to have been the copy from which are derived the manuscripts of the *Ecclesiastical History* containing the so-called *Continuatio Bedae*, a set of largely Northumbrian-centred annals covering the years 732–66.[12]

We know from Bede's letter to Albinus that he had sent at least two of his works, the *Ecclesiastical History* and *On the Temple*, to Canterbury during his lifetime. In addition, he must have sent copies of his *Thirty Questions on the Book of Kings* and *On Eight Questions* to their addressee, Nothhelm, shortly after their completion. Though Nothhelm was a priest of London, he was also a close associate of Albinus of Canterbury, and would become archbishop of Canterbury in 735, so presumably by that date, if not before, these two works would also have been known and available in Canterbury. Michael Lapidge has recently argued that the archetype of the so-called *c*-type recension of the *Ecclesiastical History* is a redaction made at Canterbury, perhaps by Albinus or Nothhelm, on the basis of the copy that Bede had sent there in 731 or 732.[13] If Lapidge's hypothesis is correct, then it is from that single Canterbury copy that most of the later medieval English copies (most of which are of the *c*-type) are ultimately derived. An early descendant of this Canterbury copy is London, British Library, Cotton Tiberius c.ii (see Figure 6). The copy of *On the Temple* that Bede sent to Albinus may also have been distributed more widely; it is in continental copies of *On the Temple* that the Albinus letter itself has been preserved into modern times, which suggests that these copies are derived from the copy that Bede sent to Canterbury with the letter.[14] We know that *On the Temple* was also exported to the continent from Wearmouth-Jarrow, but it seems unlikely that the Albinus letter, even if a copy of it were preserved at Wearmouth-Jarrow, would have been included in a manuscript made there for export.[15]

As might be expected, the evidence suggests that, once a work had been exported, continental scriptoria took the leading role in the local dissemination of the work. As a result, a single exported copy might eventually populate an entire region with its descendants. This was the case with the *Ecclesiastical History*; the vast majority of later continental copies of this text appear to be descended from a handful of early migrants. For example, the Moore Bede was, as noted above, almost certainly in Charlemagne's court library at Aachen by sometime around 800. At the court, a tract on the prohibited degrees of consanguinity in marriage (*De consanguinitate*) was added to the manuscript before multiple copies of the whole volume, including the supplement, were made for distribution to the libraries of western Frankia.[16] This process of supplementation, mass reproduction and dissemination of the *Ecclesiastical History* would seem to indicate that Bede's works were not only considered useful by the missionaries themselves (as is shown by their letters), but also that the *Ecclesiastical History* was considered a particularly salutary work for the reform of the Frankish Church, even within established Christian areas, which is where the direct copies of the Moore manuscript were sent.[17]

Bede's works among the Carolingians

The early interest in Bede's works on the part of the Anglo-Saxon missionaries and others who had a hand in their export to the continent would subsequently bear much fruit. During the course of the ninth century, Bede's works reached an audience greater in both numbers and extent than any that the author may have imagined for himself. It was during the Carolingian era that his works came to be found in the majority of European libraries, where they served as an important component of the programme of education established under Charlemagne (see Map 5). While Bede's reputation may have been growing already in eighth-century Northumbria, it was in Carolingian Frankia that his works were ultimately preserved for posterity and his fame was truly made. As will be seen, there is some evidence to suggest that only those works that already had been established as basic texts in the

Carolingian literary landscape would go on to achieve a wide readership later in the Middle Ages.[18]

Bede was a prolific author, and quite a large proportion of his works gained a measure of popularity in the Middle Ages, but it goes without saying that some of his works were more widely read than others. It has often been stated that Bede was first and foremost an exegetical writer, and this is certainly a reasonable conclusion from his description of his own literary efforts, where the exegetical works are given prominence. It is equally true, however, judging by the surviving manuscripts of his works, that a medieval reader, particularly in the Carolingian period, was as likely to know one of Bede's scientific, historical or didactic works. To judge by the surviving continental manuscripts dating from the ninth century, Bede's eight most popular works among the Carolingians were as follows: *Commentary on the Gospel of Luke* (forty-one copies), *The Reckoning of Time* (thirty-four), *Commentary on the Gospel of Mark* (thirty), *Commentary on the Apocalypse* (twenty-five), *Commentary on the Seven Catholic Epistles* (twenty-five), *Commentary on the Acts of the Apostles* (twenty-five), *On the Nature of Things* (twenty-three) and the *Ecclesiastical History* (twenty).[19] Since Bede wrote more works of exegesis than of any other single genre, it is noteworthy that three of the most popular works among the Carolingians were not biblical commentaries, but rather works of science and history.[20] It is also significant to note that all five exegetical works on this list are commentaries on books of the New Testament. To judge by the number of surviving copies, his most popular Old Testament commentary in the ninth century was *On the Proverbs of Solomon* (eighteen copies). Since survival of manuscripts is not perfectly random, these numbers are merely impressionistic. The Gospel commentaries, for example, were frequently excerpted for homiletic use, and so not all surviving fragments of those commentaries necessarily represent what were once complete ninth-century copies. Nonetheless, the numbers do offer us at least a rough sketch of which works were being read most widely in the early period.

It is also instructive to consider just how many of Bede's various works might have been available in a single library. Here, too, the surviving evidence is only suggestive, but the general impression made by what does survive is that his works could be very well represented in major libraries from an early date. The Benedictine abbey of St Gall was founded in the early eighth century (though its origins date back to the early seventh), near the upper Rhine in what is today Switzerland, and boasts perhaps the best preserved of all medieval libraries. In the ninth century it already housed an impressive book collection, including an excellent selection of Bede's works. Its earliest booklist dates from the later ninth century and contains the following works of Bede: both of the Gospel commentaries, the *Homilies on the Gospels*, the *Commentary on Acts* together with the *Commentary on the Apocalypse* in a single volume, the *Commentary on the Seven Catholic Epistles*, *The Reckoning of Time* (and possibly *On Times* as well), *On Genesis*, *On the Proverbs of Solomon*, *On the Temple*, *On Tobias* together with *On Ezra and Nehemiah* in a single volume, the *Martyrology*, *Commentary on the Canticle of Habakkuk* and the *Ecclesiastical History*; a later hand adds copies of *On the Song of Songs* and (perhaps) the *Life of Saint Cuthbert*.[21] *The Art of Poetry* and *On Orthography* are listed apart from Bede's other works, among grammatical texts; altogether, *The Art of Poetry* is listed seven times, which could indicate that there were seven copies of the work.[22] One mention of *The Art of Poetry*, along with *On the Proverbs of Solomon*, comes in a later addition to the booklist, under the heading 'books written in Irish [script]' (*libri scottice scripti*). This might be taken as evidence that some of the early copies of Bede's works had made their way to St Gall by way of Irish *peregrini*, if not from Ireland itself.[23] Even if we were to conclude that the scribe who added the list of Irish books might have referred to any early Insular book as 'Irish', there is other evidence that Irish *peregrini* did play a role in the dissemination of Bede's works, including early manuscripts of the *Ecclesiastical History* and *The Reckoning of Time* that were made by *peregrini*, and other manuscripts of *The Reckoning of Time* with Irish glosses.[24]

A single booklist, of course, cannot tell the whole story. In addition to the works found in the St Gall list, we also have ample evidence that *On the Tabernacle* and *Thirty Questions on the Book of Kings* were available, and reasonably well-known, in the libraries of Carolingian Europe. Even though the library at St Gall was probably exceptionally well supplied with copies of Bede's works, this booklist does offer striking evidence of just how many of his works had made their way across the Channel from an early date. Evidence from other important Carolingian centres, moreover – such as Corbie, Fleury, Lorsch, Reichenau and St Emmeram – suggests that St Gall was not unique in being well supplied with Bedan works. Thus, we may safely conclude that not only were many of Bede's works common in ninth-century Frankia, but a good library such as that of St Gall might be well supplied with the wide range of Bede's writings, possessing copies of nearly all his major works.

Subsequently, the fact that Bede's works enjoyed such wide diffusion and popularity in Carolingian Europe would be particularly important for their long-term survival, especially because they were not well preserved in Northumbria itself. A particularly striking contrast emerges if one compares the evidence for copies of Bede's works among the Carolingians with that for copies among the Anglo-Saxons themselves. As Dorothy Whitelock has rightly pointed out, the conditions for the survival of manuscripts in early medieval Britain were not favourable, and we should not be misled by the lack of early English copies into thinking that there was no interest in Bede's works among the Anglo-Saxons.[25] And while we acknowledge that a lack of institutional continuity, especially in Northumbria, must have led to the demise of many early copies, including most of Bede's own library at Wearmouth-Jarrow, it is nonetheless striking to observe that access to many of Bede's works in later Anglo-Saxon England seems to have been limited at best. Of the approximately 100 manuscripts of Bedan works listed by Helmut Gneuss in his *Handlist of Anglo-Saxon Manuscripts*, the vast majority were written on the continent, date from the late eleventh century, or both. Notable exceptions are the early manuscripts of the *Ecclesiastical History*, which – between the manuscripts of the Latin and Old English versions, both complete and fragmentary – constitute nearly one-third of the total number of surviving pre-1100 English Bede manuscripts.

On the other hand, there survive but six manuscripts of *On the Tabernacle* known to have been present in Britain prior to 1100, and all six were written after the Conquest, several of them probably on the continent.[26] A similar fate met the *Commentary on the Apocalypse*, of which three of the four surviving pre-1100 English copies date from after the Conquest; the fourth is a late-tenth-century Anglo-Saxon copy from Exeter. In those cases where early English copies of Bedan works have survived, moreover, more often than not they have been preserved on the continent. This is true of the most famous early copies of the *Ecclesiastical History* (the Moore and St Petersburg manuscripts; for the latter, see Figure 5), the fragmentary remains of two early copies of *The Reckoning of Time* and the fragments of an early Anglo-Saxon copy of the *Commentary on the Gospel of Luke*.[27] An early fragment of the *Commentary on the Acts of the Apostles* was probably written at an Anglo-Saxon centre on the continent.[28]

One might be tempted to conclude from these examples that the Conquest itself contributed to the loss of Anglo-Saxon copies of Bede's works, that is, that the manuscript record is the product of a post-Conquest effort to replace Anglo-Saxon copies, perceived to be poorly legible, with 'modern' copies. Certainly this may have been a factor contributing to the loss of some early copies, but on the other hand there is some evidence that the process of re-importation of Bedan works from the continent was already under way before the Conquest. Though the precise dates of migration of manuscripts are difficult to establish, there is reasonably clear evidence that at least six manuscripts of Bedan works were imported from the continent in the pre-Conquest period, including copies of *The Reckoning of Time*, *The Art of Poetry* (excerpt), *Commentary on the Gospel of Luke*, *Commentary on the Seven Catholic Epistles* and two copies of the *Metrical Life of Saint*

Cuthbert.[29] An additional four manuscripts were imported in the second half of the eleventh century, perhaps prior to 1066, including copies of the *Commentary on the Gospel of Luke, The Reckoning of Time, Commentary on the Seven Catholic Epistles* and a single manuscript containing *On the Temple, Thirty Questions on the Book of Kings* and *Commentary on the Canticle of Habakkuk.*[30]

Beyond the Carolingians

If it was the Carolingian age that served to establish Bede's place in the landscape of medieval libraries and learning, it was during the twelfth century that the copying of his works truly exploded. Statistics drawn from the dates of surviving manuscripts must, of course, be treated with caution, since survival rates, which can be influenced by many factors, are not necessarily equivalent to actual rates of copying, let alone to levels of interest during a given period. Nonetheless, a comparison of the numbers of surviving manuscripts over time is instructive in establishing some sense of the relative popularity of Bede's many works. The following chart tabulates the numbers of surviving manuscripts of Bede's most frequently copied works from the eighth to the fifteenth centuries. For the purpose of this chart, manuscripts containing epitomes or extracts from a text have been excluded, though fragments (however small) that may once have been complete copies have been retained. Composite manuscripts with parts originating in different centuries and those dated around the turn of a century have been divided equally between the centuries in question. The transmission histories of Bede's various works have received widely divergent degrees of scholarly attention, and hence the numbers provided here should be treated only as rough estimates.

It is clear from these figures that many works were already widely available by the ninth century. In the tenth century, copying of all of Bede's works slowed down, but in the eleventh century it began to pick up again, and continued vigorously into the twelfth. To judge by the number of surviving copies, the twelfth century marks the peak of popularity for most of Bede's works, with the exception of his scientific (*The Reckoning of Time, On Times* and *On the Nature of Things*) and didactic works (*The Art of Poetry/The Figures of Rhetoric*), which were never again as popular as they had been among the Carolingians, although some interest in the last of these seems to have re-emerged in the fifteenth century. The *Martyrology*, which was never particularly widely disseminated, surviving in some nineteen copies, is another work that declined steadily in popularity after peaking in the ninth century. Bede's exegetical works, and the *Ecclesiastical History* as well, were

Table 1 *Surviving manuscripts of Bede's works, by date of origin*[31]

Work	s. 8–9	s. 10	s. 11	s. 12	s. 13	s. 14	s. 15–	Total
Ecclesiastical History (Latin)	25.5	1	21	58.5	6	26	26	164
The Reckoning of Time	57.5	24.5	17.5	30.5	7	5	4	146
Comm. on Cath. Epist.	14	10.5	15	38.5	17	4	15	114
On the Nature of Things	43	13	11	28.5	8.5	4.5	4.5	113
Comm. on Apoc.	28.5	7.5	16.5	21.5	2.5	4.5	15	96
Comm. on Acts	17	7.5	8	34.5	7.5	2.5	18	95
On Proverbs	11.5	9	5.5	38.5	13.5	6	9	93
Comm. on Mark	19.5	8	10	33	11.5	3.5	6.5	92
Comm. on Luke	15.5	16	8.5	28	6.5	3.5	12	90
Art of Poetry/Figures of Rhetoric	18.5	10.5	14.5	3.5	13	10	16	86
On Tobias	7.5	3	4	41.5	13.5	3.5	5	78
On the Tabernacle	8.5	2.5	9.5	31.5	10.5	1	5.5	69
On Times	26.5	11.5	12	12	1	2	2	67
On the Song of Songs	6	1	8.5	35	7.5	4	0	62
On the Temple	4	3	4	20.5	12	1.5	5	50
On the Holy Places	2	2.5	4.5	14.5	13	4	6.5	47
Thirty Questions on Kings	11.5	4	2.5	15	7	2	3	45
Life of Cuthbert (prose)	0	2	3	23.5	7.5	2	3	41
On Ezra and Nehemiah	6	2.5	1.5	19	4	1	1	35
Homilies	5	2.5	3	6.5	1.5	1.5	1	21

most popular in the twelfth century, and continued to attract interest in the thirteenth, but were largely neglected in the fourteenth. The fifteenth century saw a revival of interest in certain works. Over the course of the Middle Ages, the *Ecclesiastical History* enjoyed the greatest level of sustained interest.

Reception and influence

It remains to explore how Bede's works were received by their many readers over the course of the Middle Ages. Some clues about the early missionaries' interest in his works can be gleaned from their letters. Boniface wrote of Bede as a 'lantern of the Church' endowed with 'spiritual intelligence'.[32] He was also an 'inspired ... student of the Sacred Scriptures', whose homilies 'would form a convenient and useful manual for us in our preaching'.[33] In the early ninth century, Bede was cited as an authority in a number of Carolingian Reform councils.[34] For Notker of St Gall (*c.* 840–912), Bede was a 'new sun' who rose as a teacher for the non-Roman *barbari*, and who could transmit the learning of the Fathers to them with lucidity.[35] These are but a few representative examples of how the Carolingians revered Bede.[36]

Another indicator of the reverence shown for Bede is the treatment of his works themselves. For the most part, Bede's works seem to have been transmitted remarkably faithfully through the generations. With the exception of the *Homilies on the Gospels*, which were excerpted by Paul the Deacon for his homiliary and subsequently were most commonly found out of their original arrangement and context, Bede's works were treated with a respect that precluded tampering. Admittedly, excerpts from his works were often made for separate circulation, but excerpting is something different from the revising, interpolating and other forms of 'improvement' to which the works of many medieval authors were subjected by later scribes. More often than not, Bede's works circulated complete and unabridged, in copies seemingly not far removed from the author's own, not only textually, but often also in their layout and apparatus. Eventually, elements of Bede's exegetical works, for example parts of the *Commentary on the Seven Catholic Epistles* and *On Ezra and Nehemiah*, were incorporated into the so-called *Ordinary Gloss* on the Bible, and thereby many of his biblical interpretations achieved an additional measure of canonicity and an even wider audience.[37] At the same time, other works simply never achieved a particularly wide audience, such as his *On First Samuel*, or his *Excerpts from the Works of Saint Augustine on the Letters of the Blessed Apostle Paul*.[38]

To do justice to the topic of the reception and influence of Bede's oeuvre would require a study many times the length of the present overview, but it is possible, in a relatively brief space, to say something about the appeal of what was arguably his most important single work, the *Ecclesiastical History* (on the reception of this work specifically in England, see Chapter 16). The *Ecclesiastical History*, as has been noted, was transmitted to the continent early on, and enjoyed a wide readership throughout the Middle Ages. Its appeal for English audiences needs little explanation, but its appeal to continental audiences is less immediately apparent. And yet the fact remains that it was widely copied and read by audiences throughout Germany, France, the Low Countries and Italy over the course of the Middle Ages. Why were these readers interested in the conversion and early history of the Anglo-Saxons?

Some clues are offered by the excerpts that were taken from the text and circulated separately.[39] Similarly, marginal notations are reflections of reader interest. Together, this evidence suggests several reasons for the success of Bede's work. First of all, saints' lives, miracles and otherworld visions seem to have attracted the most interest. Saint Oswald, in particular, was much venerated in medieval Germany, and the historical information about him that was provided by Bede was valued in that context, even though Oswald's cult in Germany soon became fused with layers of local legend unconnected to Bede's text.[40] Another focal point for readers of the *Ecclesiastical History* was otherworld visions, which were not only excerpted and circulated separately from the main text, but also were frequently marked off in the margins of the manuscripts, sometimes with brief descriptions of their salutary message for unrepentant sinners. In this way, the evidence of the work's continental reception seems to coincide with the interests of the Old English translator of Bede (see Chapter 15), who also preserved nearly all the miracles and information about saints, even while omitting much other material he deemed extraneous.[41]

Similarly, just as the Old English translator treats Bede's preface with a measure of disregard, so also a group of Latin *Ecclesiastical History* manuscripts from twelfth-century Austria shows a later scribe's failure to appreciate the preface. These manuscripts preserve a deliberately truncated version of the preface that omits nearly the entire discussion of sources.[42] At the same time, it is clear from certain marginalia that there was frequent interest in the original letters and documents that Bede inserted verbatim into his text. For example, the *Libellus responsionum*, the collection of Gregory the Great's replies to the questions of the missionary Augustine concerning the process of conversion, attracted the attention of many readers, to judge by both the marginal notations and the circulation of this section of the text on its own.[43] In that sense, the readers of the Latin Bede seem to have had somewhat different priorities from the Old English translator, who omitted many of the documents, but who retained the *Libellus*.[44]

Conclusion

These examples have only just scratched the surface of the vast reception and influence of Bede's writings in the later Middle Ages, but the outlines are clear. Many of his works enjoyed a significant measure of success from an early date. The Carolingians read the entire range of his writing, including his didactic works, science, exegesis and the *Ecclesiastical History*. The copies of his works that were made in Carolingian scriptoria not only served as the exemplars from which the later continental copies would be made, but they also provided copies for re-importation into later Anglo-Saxon and post-Conquest England. In the later Middle Ages, Bede's science fell out of fashion, but his exegetical works and historical writing continued to be copied widely in the twelfth century, when his overall popularity as an author peaked. No doubt Bede would have been pleased to know that his works were prized by so many readers in lands so far from his home. It is only through an examination of that readership that we can begin to appreciate the nature and significance of his achievement.

NOTES

1. A masterful account of the early circulation of Bede's works, to which the present survey owes much, is Whitelock 1960. For the longer view of Bede's legacy, see G. H. Brown 1987: ch. 6.
2. Wallis 1999: xxxi–xxxiv.
3. On Bede's literary aspirations, see Ray 2006 and Thacker 2006.
4. For the context of the letter, see Wallis 1999: xxx–xxxi.
5. Meyvaert 2002.
6. Whitelock 1979: 831–2 (no. 185).
7. Parkes 1982.
8. *The Letters of Saint Boniface*, Letter 75, trans. E. Emerton (New York: Columbia University Press, 2000), pp. 110–11 (no. 59).
9. *Letters of Boniface*, Letter 91, pp. 145–7 (no. 75); Whitelock 1979: 831–2 (no. 185), and 834–5 (no. 188).
10. G. H. Brown 1997: 168. The Moore Bede traditionally has been dated AD 737, but this dating is questioned in Dumville 2007; the traditional view is outlined in Lapidge and Chiesa 2008–9: xc–xcii.
11. Altfrid, *Life of Liudger*, chs. 10–12 (trans. Whitelock 1979: 787–90 [no. 160]).
12. The fragment contains a number of variants that are preserved almost perfectly in the manuscripts containing the *Continuatio Bedae*. This point will be discussed in detail in my edition of the *Continuatio* (forthcoming).
13. Lapidge and Chiesa 2008–9: civ–cxv.
14. At least two continental copies of *On the Temple* – London, British Library, Additional 18329; and Göttweig, Stiftsbibliothek 37 (rot) – preserve the Albinus letter. The lost manuscript Metz, Bibliothèque municipale, 400 (s. x, St-Arnoul, Metz) was probably the source from which Jean Mabillon's text of the letter was derived.
15. Whitelock 1960: 7.
16. Bischoff 1994: 67–8.
17. Rollason 2001.
18. This is also the hypothesis put forth by G. H. Brown to explain *On First Samuel*'s relative lack of success; see G. H. Brown 2006: 140–2.
19. These figures are based on Bischoff 1998–2004, and Laistner and King 1943, but they are merely rough estimates and should be used with caution. These figures include manuscripts containing excerpts, which have been excluded from Table 1 below. For a detailed overview of the manuscript evidence for the presence of Bede's works among the Carolingians, see McKitterick 2002.
20. See also Contreni 2005.
21. The catalogue lists a volume 'on computus and times', which could refer to a volume containing both *The Reckoning of Time* and *On Times*; and another 'on the miracles of St Cuthbert' which may refer to Bede's *Life of Saint Cuthbert* (in verse or in prose).

22. Lehmann 1918: 68–75 (no. 16).
23. *Ibid.*
24. The manuscripts are, respectively, Bern, Stadtbibliothek, 207 and 363; Karlsruhe, Badische Landesbibliothek, Aug. 167; and Vienna, Österreichische Nationalbibliothek, 15298. On Irish readers of Bede, see Kershaw 2008.
25. Whitelock 1960: 6.
26. Gneuss 2001: nos. 571, 578.5, 580, 690, 749 and 875.4.
27. Respectively, nos. 25, 846, 818, 856 and 831.2 in Gneuss 2001.
28. Lapidge 2006: Appendix C, no. 11; Gneuss 2001 omits this manuscript.
29. Lapidge 2006: Appendix D, nos. 32, 44, 55, 61, 38 and 67. These are, respectively, nos. 384, 489, 557, 607, 419 and 882 in Gneuss 2001.
30. Nos. 134, 492, 681 and 133 in Gneuss 2001. Lapidge 2006, Appendix D, includes only ninth-century manuscripts, and thus omits Gneuss's 681 (s. x); the others are, respectively, nos. 13, 46 and 12.
31. The data in this chart are based on Laistner and King 1943, with corrections drawn from subsequent reviews, editions and other studies of Bedan works, as well as original research in manuscripts and manuscript catalogues. Calvin Kendall and George Hardin Brown generously supplied unpublished materials that allowed me to improve my figures, but of course they are not responsible for any omissions and errors that may remain.
32. *Letters of Saint Boniface*, pp. 110–11 (no. 59).
33. *Ibid.*, pp. 145–7 (no. 75).
34. J. Hill 2006: 236–9.
35. Allen 1996: 65–6.
36. For a fuller study of Bede's authority among the Carolingians, see J. Hill 2006.
37. Gibson 1989: 239–40; for an introduction to twelfth-century glossed Bibles, see Gibson 1992.
38. On the former, see G. H. Brown 2006; the latter survives in fewer than ten manuscripts.
39. Laistner and King 1943: 103–13.
40. On the diffusion of Oswald's cult in general, see Thacker 1995; on the cult in Germany in particular, see Clemoes 1983 and Jansen 1995.
41. Whitelock 1962: 75.
42. *Ibid.*
43. Meyvaert 1971.
44. Whitelock 1962: 70.

15

SHARON M. ROWLEY

Bede in later Anglo-Saxon England

'It is not hard. Take your pen and mend it, and then write fast.'[1]
– Bede

The epigraph comes from a story related by Bede's student, Cuthbert, in a letter he wrote to a fellow student describing their teacher's death. In the story, young Wilberht asks Bede, who is on his deathbed, if it would be too hard to finish dictating the book he is writing. Bede replies as above. According to the story, he finishes his task before his peaceful death. Cuthbert's letter, which includes the short English poem known as 'Bede's Death Song', was widely circulated in England and the continent in the early Middle Ages; it survives in over forty manuscripts from the ninth to the twelfth centuries. Whether the story recounts the truth about Bede's dying words and actions is imponderable, but the letter, its circulation and the story it contains reveal how Bede's students revered him. His students, including Cuthbert and Egbert (archbishop of York, 735–66), played a crucial role in popularizing and preserving Bede's writings. They spread his books, reputation and teaching style into the later Anglo-Saxon period. Egbert's student, Alcuin (c. 735–804), abbot of Tours, took many of Bede's writings to the court of Charlemagne, where they were incorporated into the Carolingian Reform, a channel via which they later returned to England.

Cuthbert's portrait of a man so dedicated to writing that he finished dictating a book on his deathbed is borne out by textual evidence. Bede was a prolific writer; he composed over forty different books, ranging from his *Ecclesiastical History of the English People* to hymns, poems, commentaries and textbooks on grammar and the calculation of Easter. We can better understand how influential Bede's work became by considering the number of surviving manuscripts that contain his works, and by looking at the work of other writers, such as Ælfric of Eynsham (c. 955–1010) and Byrhtferth of Ramsey (c. 970–1020), who drew on Bede's writings in their own. Around thirty-five named or anonymous Old English authors either translated Bede's works into English or used Bede as a source of knowledge. They did so in texts ranging from the early sections of the *Anglo-Saxon Chronicle* to charters, homilies, hymns, saints' lives and poetry, including the poems known as *Judgement Day II*, *Genesis A* and *Christ II*. Letters requesting copies of

Bede's works and medieval library inventories provide further evidence of his influence. Although not all of the manuscripts mentioned in such sources survive, over ninety manuscripts that were written or owned in Anglo-Saxon England, and which contain works by Bede, do. While ninety may not seem like much, it is about ten per cent of all manuscripts surviving from England from this period. After a discussion of the historical contexts of the reception of Bede's works in the later Anglo-Saxon period, this chapter examines the translation of his writings, especially the *Ecclesiastical History*, into English. Because Bede's works also had a profound influence on Ælfric, who was the most prolific writer of the later Anglo-Saxon period, this chapter also discusses the ways in which Ælfric transmits Bede's writings – especially his homilies – to wider vernacular audiences. Finally, Ælfric and Byrhtferth translated Bede's textbook, *The Reckoning of Time*, into English. These works, while lesser known than the *Ecclesiastical History* or homilies, forms a crucial part of Bede's legacy.

From early to late Anglo-Saxon England

Addressing Bede's legacy first requires thinking about the historical and political changes that took place between Bede's day (*c.* 673–735) and the later Anglo-Saxon period. As Patrick Wormald observes, the Anglo-Saxon period is usually thought to be one long period, but it should be divided into two parts, on either side of the divide of the ninth-century Scandinavian raids and settlements.[2] But larger, more powerful kingdoms had already begun to absorb smaller ones in Bede's day. While Bede was alive, Northumbria was the dominant political power in Britain, though it was one kingdom amongst many. Towards the end of the *Ecclesiastical History*, Bede describes how the power of the Northumbrian king, Ecgfrith, began to 'ebb and fall away' (IV. 26, p. 429). Later, he lists the bishops of eleven different kingdoms in England (V. 23). By *c.* 800, these were consolidated into four kingdoms: Northumbria, East Anglia, Wessex and Mercia.[3] The centre of power, culture and learning had begun to shift south and west since Bede's day, first to Mercia, then even further south to Wessex under King Alfred (871–99). William of Malmesbury (d. 1143?), a historian based in Wessex, drew extensively on Bede's *Ecclesiastical History*. William considered Northumbria's greatest achievement to be cultural rather than political, largely because of Bede. Whereas Northumbrian power structures left little trace on later history, those of Wessex can be traced in England today. But as William already recognized, Bede's intellectual, historical and theological achievements had a lasting impact on learning, culture and the way we understand English history.

External pressures combined with internal hostilities in England to foster change on several levels from the late eighth century onwards. Vikings sacked the great monasteries of Lindisfarne in 793, then Jarrow in 794, destroying the world-class library that inspired and informed Bede's writings. Such attacks remained sporadic until the arrival of the 'Great Army' in 865, after which followed years of invasion in force. Settlement and co-existence followed; in some areas, this corresponded with continuing raids. Because the borrowing of words or place names from one language to another rarely occurs in highly stratified societies or warlike circumstances, the large number of Scandinavian place names in the eastern and northern parts of England lends weight to the theory that Scandinavian settlement also played a complex role in the changing, composite face of the island. For a period, Britain was even divided into separate political entities by the creation of the Danelaw. This was a region of Danish settlement created in a treaty between King Alfred and Guthrum, leader of the Danes, after the Battle of Edington (878).

While King Alfred was the first to rule a 'Kingdom of the Anglo-Saxons' and to initiate a series of administrative and educational reforms, the consolidation and stabilization of such a kingdom was a process that continued across the reigns of Edward the Elder (899–924), Æthelstan (924–39) and Edmund (939–46). These kings ruled ethnically diverse kingdoms; none of them rose to power unopposed or reigned without internal problems. For example, although Edward reconquered part of the Danelaw from 910 to 920, he had lost control over areas in the north and east by the time of his death in 939. It was Æthelstan who eventually became the 'first King of England', using great councils, laws and coinage to '"weld together" newly subjugated territories' and extend his control beyond that of his grandfather.[4] Æthelstan's reign, in turn, helped set the stage for the peaceful reign of Edgar (959–75) and the Benedictine Reform of the later tenth century. Nevertheless, power struggles and resettlement continued. The territories in the north and east remained especially contested throughout most of this era, and by 1016 the Danish King Cnut became 'King of all England'.

All of these changes had an impact on the development of intellectual and religious culture in later Anglo-Saxon England, because they affected the resources that were available for learning in England. King Alfred played a crucial role in reviving learning and fostering book production in the wake of the Scandinavian raids and the destruction of many of the great libraries. For teachers and books, Alfred turned westward to parts of Mercia and Wales – where a few libraries and centres of learning had survived – and to the continent. Famously, Alfred brought Asser from Wales to his court at Winchester. Plegmund and Wærferth came from Mercia; John the Old Saxon, from Saxony; and Grimbald of Bertin joined them from Gaul.[5]

With the help of these last two teachers, the Carolingian Reform provided an important model for learning, as well as a channel for the return of some of Bede's books, many of which were stolen or destroyed in the raids, into England. Again, patterns of manuscript production and survival provide evidence. While five copies of Bede's *Ecclesiastical History* survive from eighth-century England, none survive from ninth- or tenth-century England. In contrast, eleven copies survive from ninth-century France and Germany.[6]

Importantly, the only manuscripts containing the *Ecclesiastical History* that survive from the tenth century are two copies and three short excerpts of the Old English translation of Bede's *Ecclesiastical History* (OEHE). Translation played a key role in the transmission of Bede's ideas and writings into later Anglo-Saxon England. Monks, nuns and priests who learned Latin could read Bede's works as he wrote them, but laymen (even nobles) did not necessarily learn to read at all until the late ninth century. Alfred instituted a school at his court wherein his noblemen and their sons could learn to read English. Those who intended to enter the Church went on to learn Latin. Translation and the teaching of Latin, tasks in which Bede himself engaged, played key roles in Alfred's court school, as well as in the later educational programmes of the tenth-century Benedictine Reform. Alfred's plan to translate 'certain books which are the most necessary for all men to know' led to several important works of Old English prose.[7] Alfred himself translated Gregory the Great's *Pastoral Care*, with help from his advisors. Asser tells us that Wærferth translated Gregory's *Dialogues*. Boethius's *Consolation of Philosophy*, the prose translation of the first fifty psalms, and the Preface to Alfred's laws, which are also in English, complete the list of the vernacular texts clearly associated with Alfred's programme.[8] English translations from the late ninth and early tenth century also include a martyrology and Orosius's *History against the Pagans*.

Bede in Old English

The use of English not only as a vehicle of learning and instruction, but also as the language of government and preaching, was unprecedented in Europe at the time. Although Alfred lamented the decline of Latin learning, and although later scholars like Byrhtferth complain about the poor skills of some clerics or students, the role of translation in education should not be looked upon as one of mere simplification. Speakers of English, Welsh and Irish were among the first to grapple with the problem of learning Latin as a foreign language. Until the tenth century, vernacular languages on the continent were closely related to Latin; speakers of these languages did not face the challenges to comprehension or learning faced by those whose native languages were Germanic or Celtic.[9] Bede's influence on the process of learning Latin was crucial. It went on to have a profound effect on Latin instruction on the continent in the ninth century, via Alcuin and his student Hrabanus Maurus, when changes to spoken forms of vulgar Latin made different forms of instruction necessary.[10] Bede's work in this area has some precedent in the teachings of Theodore of Tarsus (archbishop of Canterbury, 669–90). Theodore and his associate Abbot Hadrian, who was originally from Africa and who became an abbot in Naples before travelling to England with Theodore, provided early training in Latin as a foreign language in Britain. However, the surviving textual tradition starts with Bede. According to Roger Wright,

> [t]he linguistic works that survive from the pen of Insular scholars attest to a pedagogical and scholarly tradition that began with Bede ... Bede kept what seem to be a teacher's notebook, in which he progressively noted down all kinds of useful details valuable to the teacher of Latin.[11]

It might be tempting to underestimate the importance of Bede's influence on grammar and the study of Latin as a language. But Latin was the language of Christianity in the later Middle Ages; it was also the language of learning, government and philosophy. Bede's explanations of pronunciation, which were transmitted via his writings and his students, laid part of the groundwork for Latin as the *lingua franca* in the later medieval period.

In a sense, Bede's grammatical teachings helped students learn to read his other works in Latin. For those who did not learn Latin, however, translations were an important resource, which is something that teachers across the period recognized. While Bede's own translations do not survive (he was said to be translating the Gospel of John when he died), other teachers translated his major works and many of his homilies into English. These translations allowed his influence to reach all levels of Anglo-Saxon society, not just monks or the nobles at Alfred's schools. Bede's homilies and saints' lives, along with his martyrology and exegetical writings, reached lay folk who attended church to hear Ælfric, or any priest who used copies of his homilies. Bede's writings about Scripture, grammar, the natural world and the calculation of Easter constituted much of the early English curriculum. Byrhtferth and Ælfric both made translations themselves, following Bede's example by becoming bilingual, monastic teachers who were deeply invested in the connection between spirituality and education.

Bede's masterwork, his *Ecclesiastical History*, not only became a key source for the early parts of the *Anglo-Saxon Chronicle*, but was also translated into English in its own right.[12] Both of these translations helped popularize his account of the arrival and conversion of the Angles, Saxons and

Jutes. The OEHE also brought his accounts of important early English saints like Oswald, Æthelthryth and Cuthbert to wider audiences. The OEHE was translated anonymously sometime between 883 and 930. Because so little comparative evidence survives from this period, there is no sound basis for dating the text with greater precision. Because the OEHE was translated around the time of Alfred's reign, scholars generally assume that it was part of his programme. Whether it actually was remains unclear. As Janet Bately points out, 'the fact that Bede's [*Ecclesiastical History*] is a text whose translation might well have been desired by Alfred is not proof that the surviving translation was made at the king's request'.[13] There is no contemporary documentary evidence connecting the translation with the king; Alfred does not claim it, nor does his biographer, Asser, mention it. Ælfric attributed the OEHE to the king about a hundred years later, so the association between the two, though unproven, is longstanding. However, because the OEHE was originally written in a Mercian dialect of Old English, scholars have long been aware that Alfred did not translate the text himself. One of the reasons the OEHE continues to be associated with Alfred's programme is the king's claim that 'Learning had declined so thoroughly in England that there were very few men on this side of the Humber who could ... even translate a single letter from Latin into English.'[14] Clearly, the fact that his teachers Plegmund and Wærferth came from Mercia demonstrates that Latin learning was not entirely gone, but we do not know what other English centre might have produced someone capable of translating Bede's *Ecclesiastical History* with such accuracy. It is possible that the king's programme prepared or inspired the translators who produced the other anonymous translations. It is also possible that these texts were translated independently. If the OEHE was not part of the king's programme, then it provides evidence that Latin learning survived in unknown pockets in England at the time. But none of these scenarios can be definitively proven.

Asking the question, 'Who made this translation?' is akin to asking 'Why did someone make this translation?' If the OEHE was part of Alfred's programme, then we know it was translated for educational purposes. Although we have no incontrovertible evidence as to who made the OEHE, looking more closely at the text and its manuscripts can shed light on the role it played in later Anglo-Saxon England. Five substantial manuscripts of the OEHE survive in England. We do not know where all of these were written, but we have some idea where they were housed. Library catalogues confirm the existence of copies of the text in Canterbury and Durham; we know that Ælfric was aware of the translation, and probably used it at Cerne Abbey (*c.* 990–5). Consequently, we can place copies of the OEHE all around England – from Durham in the north to Canterbury in the southeast, Exeter in the southwest, and towns more centrally located, such as Burton-on-Trent. Because scholars have been unable to determine the exact relationship between all of the surviving copies of the OEHE, we may also conclude that some of the manuscripts that we have were copied from other manuscripts that no longer survive. So, the manuscripts (surviving, mentioned and suggested), teamed with their wide geographical dispersal, indicate that the OEHE was popular and readily available in later Anglo-Saxon England.

Analysis of the OEHE, its contents, vocabulary and style, provides further information. Based on the vocabulary, Dorothy Whitelock concludes that the translation as we have it is the work of at least three people, though one translator did most of the work.[15] This translator revises Bede's *Ecclesiastical History*, shortening it by about a third. He trims Bede's descriptions of England and Ireland, cuts most of the Roman history and removes many of the details of Bede's account of the controversy over the dating of Easter. He entirely eliminates Bede's account of the Pelagian heresy. He also omits or radically summarizes fourteen of the fifteen papal letters that Bede includes, and moves the letter in which Gregory the Great replies to a series of Augustine of Canterbury's questions (the *Libellus responsionum*) from Book I to a place after the end of Book III. The translator rearranges many chapter divisions and omits Bede's excerpts from Adomnán's *On the Holy Places*, as well as most poems and epitaphs. While he cuts Books I and V the most drastically, he presents Books III and IV, which contain the stories of early English saints, Christian kings and visionaries, almost in their entirety.

Whether the translator sought to create a simplified teaching text, failed to understand Bede's almost modern sense of documentary historical evidence, or abridged his text for another reason altogether has been the subject of debate. Whatever his motivation, the translator's editing was remarkably consistent; he leaves no stray references to persons or events that he edits out. If one of the purposes of ecclesiastical history as a genre is to refute heresy (a task in which Bede clearly engaged), it seems possible that the translator of the OEHE was less concerned with such an agenda. He seems more concerned with representing the lives and works of the people who helped found and develop the English Church. In the end, the vernacular history that the translator produces is a streamlined account of the arrival and conversion of the peoples who become the English, along with the tales of their early saints, kings and visionaries. Although the translator adds very little, the overall effect of the changes he makes is to render the OEHE more hagiographical and eschatological than Bede's original.

Although some scholars see the fact that the translator abridged the *Ecclesiastical History* as evidence of his failure to understand the importance of documentary evidence, in some instances his changes improve the story. For example, by removing the papal letters from Book II, he transforms Bede's account of King Edwin's conversion into a concise, dramatic narrative. In the Latin original, Edwin and his wife Æthelburh receive three papal letters, two from Pope Boniface (II. 10–11) and one from Honorius (II. 17). The letters consist of long exhortations encouraging the king to convert and the queen to help him do so, so that 'the unbelieving husband shall be saved by the believing wife' (II. 11, p. 175, quoting 1 Corinthians 7:14). These letters inform Bede's account of Edwin's conversion with papal authority. Because the OEHE eliminates this material, however, audiences of the vernacular version read (or heard) a concise, symbolic tale of death and (re)birth at Easter.

Initially, Æthelburh's brother Eadbald, the king of Kent, refused to marry his Christian sister to the pagan Edwin, for fear that he would profane her. When Edwin agrees to allow her to continue practising Christianity, they arrange the marriage. Bede reports that Bishop Paulinus accompanies Æthelburh as an attendant to her marriage; however, Paulinus's real intention is to convert the Northumbrians. These intentions notwithstanding, Paulinus's efforts to convert the king remain unsuccessful until a famous assassination attempt on Edwin's life. When the assassin from Wessex leaps for the king with his dagger, Lothere, Edwin's thane, uses his body as a shield to protect the king. Lothere dies, but saves his lord, who is merely wounded. Notably, this scene occurs at Easter, the same day on which Æthelburh gives birth to their daughter, Eanflæd. At the moment when Edwin receives the news of his daughter's safe delivery, he promises to convert. In the same breath, Edwin gives the baby to be consecrated to God; Eanflæd becomes the first person in Northumbria to be baptized. Although Edwin delays his own baptism, both Bede and his translator assert that he ceased to sacrifice to idols at the moment of this promise (II. 9; OEHE, p. 124). The rapid succession of events, including the assassination attempt, the substitute death of Lothere, the birth of Eanflæd and Edwin's conversion, resonate with Christian symbolism, especially the sacrificial death–rebirth symbolism of Easter. Lothere's death, combined with Eanflæd's birth and consecration, literalizes the symbolic rebirth of Edwin in the moment of his conversion. Although Queen Æthelburh seems to fade into the background, giving birth to Eanflæd reasserts the Pauline idea that the believing wife sanctifies both husband and child. For Edwin's essential moment of conversion to centre on the birth of his daughter, which intrudes rather spectacularly into a scene of Anglo-Saxon feud at Edwin's court, is symbolically powerful. By shortening and streamlining the story, the OE translator heightens the dramatic tension of the episode. While it would be inaccurate to claim that all the differences between the *Ecclesiastical History* and the OEHE improve the stories, the translation brought a clear, accurate and sometimes exciting version of Bede's *Ecclesiastical History* to vernacular audiences.

Other episodes from the *Ecclesiastical History*, especially the episodes concerning important English saints, such as Cuthbert, Æthelthryth and King Oswald, also reached a wider vernacular audience via homilies and saints' lives and in manuscripts compiled to honour individual saints. In such manuscripts, episodes from the *Ecclesiastical History* accompanied *vitae*, prayers, hymns and poems. Putting excerpts from a history into prayer books may seem odd to modern audiences, but it serves as a reminder that we should keep Bede's title, the 'ecclesiastical history', firmly in mind. Ælfric and other homilists, especially Paul the Deacon, drew on Bede's *Ecclesiastical History* and his homiliary as a source, in Latin and in English. They brought a wide range of Bede's accounts of early English saints, along with his analyses of Scripture, to a significant portion of early medieval society: from monks, nuns, priests and bishops to literate lay nobles and the men and women who attended the church services in which Bede's homilies (or parts of them) were read.

Charlemagne himself commissioned Paul the Deacon (*c.* 790 to *c.* 797), a monk from Monte Cassino, to compile homilies, sermons and readings for the Divine Office. The resulting collection, which includes passages from thirty-four of Bede's homilies, survives in multiple manuscripts, sixteen of which come from Anglo-Saxon England. It provides another example of Bede's writings returning from the continent transformed for new audiences. Importantly, this homiliary became a seminal text of the Benedictine Reform, a movement in which Ælfric played a key role. In this context, Bede's ideas were sometimes transmitted anonymously, as patristic orthodoxy, rather than as his ideas *per se*.

Bede, the Benedictine Reform and learning in later Anglo-Saxon England

The Benedictine Reform brought about a third efflorescence of learning and ecclesiastical culture in Anglo-Saxon England, at the same time as it helped foster and extend Bede's legacy.[16] Because of the continued military strife through the reigns of Alfred and his successors, levels of learning, access to books and the stability of ecclesiastical life varied across time and place. Noble men and women continued to establish and inhabit monasteries, but even in Bede's day, the structure and governance of these institutions were not always in keeping with monastic ideals. Aristocrats, some of whom had little inclination to practise the strict observances of the monks, occupied some of the monasteries. Other monasteries housed members of secular orders, some of whom were married. The principal leaders of the Benedictine Reform were Dunstan (archbishop of Canterbury, 959–88), Æthelwold (bishop of Winchester, 963–84) and Oswald (archbishop of York, 971–92). These leaders worked under the patronage of King Edgar to reform existing monasteries. They founded (or refounded) about fifty additional Benedictine monasteries, including those at Glastonbury, Abingdon, Peterborough and Ramsey. The process took almost half a century. The reformers expelled secular priests from monasteries in 964, and instituted a uniform system of observances for all monks in England with the *Regularis Concordia* (*c.* 970).

Æthelwold also founded an important school in Winchester, where he not only engaged in translation and teaching, but also oversaw a larger, longer-lasting revival of learning in Latin and Old English than Alfred had been able to organize in his troubled times. Æthelwold admired and imitated the writing of Aldhelm (bishop of Sherborne, *c.* 630 to *c.* 710). His style, called the hermeneutic style, was complex and difficult. Bede also used this style for his *Metrical Life of Saint Cuthbert*, one manuscript of which returned to England from the continent, most likely for use at Æthelwold's school. This manuscript (now Paris, Bibliothèque Nationale, lat. 2825) contains syntactical glosses, which aided students in identifying the proper word order when reading or translating.

Ælfric of Eynsham was one of Æthelwold's students in Winchester, where he benefited from Æthelwold's learning – and what must have been a wonderfully deep library containing most, if not all, of the works of Bede. According to the *Fontes Anglo-Saxonici* database, Ælfric makes over eight hundred references to Bede's writings.[17] In addition to quoting Bede's homilies, saints' lives and *Ecclesiastical History*, Ælfric makes extensive use of Bede's commentaries and scientific writings. Ælfric himself wrote about 130 homilies, along with an extensive collection of saints' lives and translations of Old Testament texts. These became invaluable resources for religious education in the vernacular over the course of the next two hundred years. Bede provided both inspiration and often the sources for Ælfric, who regularly acknowledged this debt. However, Ælfric's writings were not slavish copies. In his homily on the 'Life of Oswald', for example, Ælfric streamlines Bede's account of that saint using strategies almost identical to those used by the translator of the OEHE. In other homilies, Ælfric combines Bede with other sources to address his own concerns.

For example, Ælfric considered the popular *Vision of Saint Paul* to be heretical because it held that 'Paul was not allowed to make his vision known to men'.[18] Ælfric addressed this problem in a pair of homilies, in which he recounts two visions included in Bede's *Ecclesiastical History*. One is of Saint Fursey, the other of Dryhthelm, a thane who dies for a night, tours heaven and hell, then awakens to live out his life in penance. This is appropriate to the occasion, because these homilies are for the Tuesday before Ascension Day, which is traditionally a time of penance. Although Ælfric uses Bede's account of Dryhthelm, he turns to Bede's own source, the continental Latin *Life of Fursey*, possibly because it includes details of Fursey's trial in heaven that Bede omits. These details allow Ælfric to clarify the difference between *digelan* ('hidden') words, and words that should be made known – a concern that surfaces in his other writings, such as the preface to his translation of Genesis.

Although Ælfric adapts his source, the fact that Bede includes Fursey's vision in the *Ecclesiastical History* nevertheless adds authority to Ælfric's homilies, and weight to his argument against the *Vision of Saint Paul*. All three versions recount how Fursey ascends to heaven, passing through the fires of human sin (which burn only those who kindle them) with the help of angels. Drawing on the continental source, Ælfric includes more details of Fursey's trial and instruction in heaven than Bede. During the visionary's descent, the fires unexpectedly scorch Fursey, because he had accepted clothing from a sinful man. While both Bede and Ælfric exploit the ambiguity of this 'sin' to encourage penance, Ælfric develops a contrast between Fursey's divinely sanctioned revelation – made visible by his scar – and Paul's silence. Whereas Bede reports that Fursey only told his vision to people who sought him because they 'desired to repent' (III. 19, p. 275), Ælfric's version emphasizes that Fursey was commanded to reveal his vision. Ælfric repeats three times that Paul refused to reveal what should be hidden, but that the angels instructed Fursey to tell his vision and to encourage men to confess and do penance. Ælfric's account of Dryhthelm reiterates this message. He shortens Bede's account, and has Dryhthelm report his vision freely as soon as he awakens. Later, Dryhthelm also tells his vision 'to the king of the people, Alfred, and to all devout men' (*Alio Visio*, p. 199). In addition to reiterating that (unlike Paul) Dryhthelm willingly told people his vision, Ælfric adds the authority of King Alfred to the transmission of the miracle. In doing so, he updates his source, referring to a king not only more recent, but also better known than Bede's Northumbrian king, Æthelred. Clearly, Ælfric combines and adapts his sources to masterful effect for tenth-century audiences and issues. He draws on Bede's authority to exhort his audience to penance, to provide valid examples and to enhance his warnings against the popular but problematic *Vision of Saint Paul*.

Ælfric also drew on Bede as a source in other areas of teaching. He wrote an English treatise entitled *On the Seasons of the Year* based on Bede's scientific books, *On Times* and *The Reckoning of Time*.[19] These textbooks on grammar, nature and the calculation of Easter (known as the *computus*) may be less well-known now, but they were important resources in the early Middle Ages. In addition to being used in monastic classrooms, Bede's scientific writings had a wider, though sometimes subtle, impact on society. His observations of the tides, for example, and his clarification of the dating of Easter influenced everyday life, travel and even trade in ways so practical as to go unnoticed. As Faith Wallis discusses in Chapter 8, Bede solved the longstanding dilemma of calculating the date of Easter. He explains this solution in *The Reckoning of Time*, which was actually a manual for teaching the *computus*. It circulated immediately and almost as widely as the *Ecclesiastical History*. Later monastic teachers, Ælfric and Byrhtferth, also wrote treatises on the *computus* in the late tenth and early eleventh centuries; their versions, like the OEHE, adapted Bede's source materials to later audiences, who had different needs and different levels of Latin learning.

Byrhtferth also wrote a bilingual commentary, or *Enchiridion*, for his students at Ramsey.[20] Bede was one of Byrhtferth's main sources, though he also used Ælfric's vernacular version and discussed poetic metre and other issues along with *computus*. While this combination might seem odd to modern audiences, Easter was the principal feast of the Christian calendar, and the task of figuring the correct date involved accommodating the lunar Hebrew calendar to the solar Roman one. For teachers like Bede, Ælfric and Byrthferth, this task involved more than just astronomy and arithmetic. It reflected the order of the universe, and the higher language through which God organized that universe; reckoning time was intimately connected with interpreting Scripture and understanding salvation history. Easter marked the birth of Christ as feast of light, demonstrating the victory of light over darkness, good over evil. According to Bede's world view, the full moon following the vernal equinox embodied this light, demonstrating the harmony of the cosmos with the light of the Resurrection. Understanding *computus*, then, was a way of understanding the order of God's universe and the position of human time within that unified whole. The story of Edwin's conversion (discussed above) taps into this cosmological Easter symbolism. Bede's treatises explaining the mechanics of calculating Easter and the scriptural importance of doing so properly had a profound influence on how the Anglo-Saxons understood their place in Christian time. Both Ælfric and Byrhtferth acknowledge Bede as the 'wisest teacher', and helped transmit his knowledge and ideas.

Bede also explains the basics of *computus* in the *Ecclesiastical History*, not simply because the controversy over the calculation of Easter was a part of early English history, but also because the task of positioning humanity in time is part of the task of history in general from Bede's catholic perspective.

This task also accounts for Bede's interest in the end of time, the visions he includes in his *Ecclesiastical History*, and his poem 'On the Day of Judgement'. Preparation for 'The End' was a crucial issue, and Bede's eschatological writings influenced later poems, such as 'Judgement Day II' and several other apocalyptic homilies. Cuthbert's letter (with which I opened this chapter) includes Bede's 'Death Song', which reiterates this theme with its warning that death is certain, but the time of death uncertain. This letter can be read as a reflection and product of Bede's teachings. From language learning, to history, to understanding and interpreting Scripture, time and the order of the universe, Bede's thought and writings had a profound influence on the intellectual and religious cultures of later Anglo-Saxon England. Because of translation and preaching in English, Bede's influence extended well beyond the cloister, possibly to all levels of society, although to what precise extent we cannot measure.

NOTES

1. *Cuthbert's Letter on the Death of Bede*, in Colgrave and Mynors 1969: 585.
2. Wormald 1991.
3. *Ibid.*, 2.
4. Dumville 1992: 147–8.
5. Keynes and Lapidge 1983: 26.
6. Davis 1989: 104.
7. Alfred, 'Prose Preface to Gregory's *Pastoral Care*', in *Alfred the Great: Asser's 'Life of King Alfred' and Other Contemporary Sources*, trans. S. Keynes and M. Lapidge (London: Penguin Books, 1983), p. 126.
8. Bately 2003: 109.
9. J. Hill 2003.
10. R. Wright 2002: 14.
11. *Ibid.*, 12.
12. Miller 1890–8.
13. Bately 1988: 103–4.
14. Alfred, 'Prose Preface to *Pastoral Care*', in *Alfred the Great*, p. 125.
15. Whitelock 1962 and 1974.
16. J. Hill 1998.
17. *Fontes Anglo-Saxonici* 2008.
18. Ælfric, *Item in Letania maiore. Feria tertia* and *Alio Visio*, in Ælfric's *Catholic Homilies: The Second Series*, ed. M. Godden, Early English Text Society, s.s. 5 (Oxford University Press, 1979), pp. 190–203, at 190.
19. *Aelfric's De Temporibus Anni*, ed. H. Henel, Early English Text Society, o.s. 213 (Oxford University Press, 1942).
20. *Byrhtferth's Enchiridion*, ed. P. Baker and M. Lapidge, Early English Text Society, s.s. 15 (Oxford University Press, 1995).

16

ALLEN J. FRANTZEN

The Englishness of Bede, from then to now

Shakespeare and Chaucer are more famous English authors than Bede, who wrote nothing in the English language that has survived. But his place in English culture is, like theirs, a lasting one, if only because his account of the cowherd Cædmon in the *Ecclesiastical History of the English People* supplies an iconic narrative for the origins of vernacular poetry (IV. 24). Even though his fame, for many readers, hangs on this slender thread, Bede has long been recognized not only as a great author but also as a distinctively English writer.

Bede did not think of himself as English, however, and those who admiringly refer to him as English risk the error of implying either that Bede wrote in English or that his sense of the English people corresponds to theirs. The last two words in the title of Bede's most famous work – *Historia ecclesiastica gentis Anglorum* – are ambiguous. A *gens* is a people as opposed to a nation or tribe, but all three ethnic units are notoriously difficult to describe.[1] *Anglorum* could refer to the continental Angles, a people named by Bede among the foreign settlers of Britain; to those who lived in Northumbria in his own time, or to Mercians; to all those tribes that eventually became the 'English', an inclusive term for Angles, Saxons and several other ethnic groups; or to those who spoke English.[2] Yet, as if these specific meanings did not exist, generations of readers after the Old English period have found their own views mirrored in Bede's and have seen him as English in the same way they see themselves.

In this chapter I explain Bede's Englishness as a function of his ambivalent sense of insularity. Bede thought that he lived in an isolated and unique world; he also believed that his place and time were, in their isolation, especially blessed.[3] This view, related to the classical trope of the *locus amoenus* (the happy or fortunate place), carries with it a sense of difference, even exclusivity. Thus, for Bede, difference was balanced against identity and alterity against sameness. Bede's readers were drawn to these attitudes, which were easily detached from both the man and his works. Like Bede himself, some readers believed that they lived in a different kind of place – an *alter orbis* – and used this sense of happy separation to imagine a world they shared with Bede, an *orbis idem* ('same world'). *Alter orbis* is a phrase first used to describe Bede's world by the twelfth-century writer William of Malmesbury, who wrote that Bede lived 'in the most distant corner of the world, on the furthest shore of an island which some call another world'.[4] The *alter orbis* for later writers was defined not by physical isolation but rather by spiritual and intellectual integrity and set apart by piety, learning and reverence for the nation and its Church. This world was also the *orbis idem*; writers who occupied it believed that they carried on Bede's work, whether as historians, as spiritual guides or as both. Those who believe that they live in a world that is set apart form bonds of shared understanding: the *alter orbis* supports the *orbis idem* and the *orbis idem* the *alter orbis*. Together, I propose, these two components describe the English world of Bede.

Bede's life was circumscribed by the monastery of Wearmouth and Jarrow (see Chapter 6). Having been raised 'on an island of the ocean far outside the world', as he put it when he defended his bookishness in his commentary *On the Song of Songs*, he observed that he could know about remote worlds only through the writings of the ancients. In his commentary *On First Samuel*, Bede compared the security of geographical boundaries to spiritual strength.[5] But his most famous expression of the *locus amoenus* opens the *Ecclesiastical History*. Although this description, quoted by many later historians, borrows from Pliny's *Natural History*, the *Polyhistor* of Solinus and other ancient sources, the catalogue of the land's features is Bede's own. 'The island is rich in crops and in trees, and has good pasturage for cattle and beasts of burden,' Bede wrote. 'It also produces vines in certain districts, and has plenty of both land- and waterfowl of various kinds' (I. 1, p. 15). He described kinds of fish and the waters where they are found and gave details about the climate. How Bede knew so much about Britain's geography and economics is not clear, for he rarely travelled. He is said to have gone once to Lindisfarne and once to York, both journeys undertaken in the last fifteen years of his life.[6]

His geographical world might have been limited, but Bede's intellectual horizons were vast. His reputation as an English writer rested on many strengths and was understood variously by the scores of writers who drew on his life and work. For many of them, Bede represented an English identity that they wished to cultivate for themselves and adapt to their own ends. I divide my survey into four phases, reaching from the end of the Old English period to about 1200; then to the end of the fourteenth century, the time of Chaucer and the Lollards; then to the establishment of the Church of England in the mid-sixteenth century; and from there to the modern period.

Anglo-Norman England

From the reign of Edward the Confessor (1042–66) to the end of the reign of Henry II (1154–89), the first Angevin king of England, Bede's name was invoked continuously by chroniclers. But Antonia Gransden noted that Bede's historical writings were seen 'merely as one element in his total achievement'. Equally important was Bede's 'venerability and learning in the scriptures'.[7] That renown owed much to Bede's exegetical writings, and especially to his prominent place in the *Glossa ordinaria*, a twelfth- to thirteenth-century collection of commentaries that illuminated levels of meaning in Scripture. In that work Bede was quoted along with Augustine, Gregory and other authorities of the early Church; later writers, including Peter Lombard (d. 1160) and Thomas Aquinas (d. 1274), incorporated Bede's exegesis into their own. There is no better marker of Bede's status as an exegete than the tenth canto of Dante's *Paradiso*, where Aquinas himself includes Bede in the blessed wreath of the wise, the *sapienti*, that encircles Dante's guide, Beatrice.[8]

On a less exalted plane, Bede served as an inspiration for revivals when eleventh-century religious leaders looked back to his age as the high point of English learning and attempted to recreate that world. In 1077 Aldwin, the prior of Winchcombe, wanted to refound Bede's own monastery of Saint Paul at Jarrow, and Walcher, the bishop of Durham, wanted to refound a monastery in Saint Cuthbert's see; Walcher failed, but his successor, William of Saint Carilef, also a Norman, succeeded in doing so in 1083.[9] Elsewhere Bede's work figured in Anglo-Norman attempts to document institutional continuity after the Conquest of 1066. Lanfranc, for example, the first Norman archbishop of Canterbury, cited the *Ecclesiastical History* at the Council of Winchester in 1072 to argue for the historical precedence of Canterbury over York.[10] But at the same time, Lanfranc roused the ire of his Anglo-Saxon contemporaries by suppressing the prominence of several Anglo-Saxon saints, including Wilfrid and others admired by Bede.[11]

The Normans were eager to demonstrate what Gransden calls the 'intellectual stagnation' of Anglo-Saxon England in the period of the Conquest and to emphasize, by way of damning contrast, the glorious state of the Church in earlier periods. William of Malmesbury was foremost among those who argued that Anglo-Saxon monasticism had flourished in Bede's time, subsequently declined, been revived in the tenth century, and lapsed again into a condition from which the Normans rescued it. William's *Gesta regum*, written between 1135 and 1140, was planned as a continuation of Bede's *Ecclesiastical History*.[12] William borrowed the most durable trope of the *Ecclesiastical History*, the idea that conquest by a foreign people is a nation's punishment for falling into sin, which Bede had borrowed from the British author Gildas (1. 15–16). Thus, for William, the Conquest punished the sins of the Anglo-Saxons. 'They consumed their whole fortune in mean and despicable houses, unlike the Normans and the French who in noble and splendid mansions live with frugality,' William wrote. William also claimed to be the successor to Bede in that, like Bede, he wrote in Latin, leaving the vernacular to lesser authors.[13] Another imitator was Orderic Vitalis, who is thought to have titled his *Historia Ecclesiastica* (1123–41) after Bede and who is known to have made a copy of the entire work in his own hand.[14] Contemporary with William and Orderic, Henry of Huntingdon (1110–54) wrote the *Historia Anglorum* at the behest of Bishop Alexander, who told Henry to follow Bede and then use the chronicles up to the point at which Henry had his own materials; Henry drew on 132 of the 140 chapters of Bede's book.[15] Like William, he began with Bede's celebrated description of Britain but, unlike William, acknowledged his source; according to Nancy F. Partner, Bede is 'the only author mentioned by name in the prologue'.[16]

These and other authors used Bede to describe the early Anglo-Saxon Church as an *orbis idem*, a centre of learning whose standards they themselves would restore; they eulogized Bede to 'add glory to the Northumbrian renaissance'.[17] But it is only in retrospect that golden ages are called into being. As we see in his *Letter to Bishop Egbert*, Bede had no illusions that he lived in one. He was concerned about ecclesiastical corruption, advocated monastic reform and wanted pastoral texts to be available in the vernacular.[18]

Imitations and continuations of Bede's *Ecclesiastical History* were not the only historical mode in which Bede was known. The first departure from this model, contemporary with the works of Bede's closest followers, came when Geoffrey of Monmouth published the *Historia regum Britanniae* in 1136. Geoffrey did not refer to Bede by name, but he began his work as Bede began the *Ecclesiastical History*, with a description of the island of Britain. Geoffrey also borrowed Bede's list of the five languages of Britain (English, British, Irish, Pictish and Latin) but altered the list to include Normans, Britons, Saxons, Picts and Scots, perhaps trusting readers familiar with the *Ecclesiastical History* to recognize the echo (1. 15).[19]

Geoffrey neither eulogized Bede nor confirmed Bede's paradigms (e.g. of chosen or condemned peoples) because Geoffrey had a different origin in mind. He was, as Partner has written, in search of a new national hero to set up in opposition to Henry II. This new figure was King Arthur, someone Bede did not mention. Geoffrey's interest was the oldest and most western area of Britain and its people, not the Anglo-Saxons but rather the British who occupied the island before them. Bede had set the pattern for viewing the early British as apostate Christians and made no mention of King Arthur (*EH* I. 15–16). Seeing an opportunity, Geoffrey created a golden age prior to the golden age others saw in Bede's Northumbria. The political aim of the *Historia regum Britanniae* was apparently to use Arthur to establish a narrative to counter the Angevin dynasty of Henry and to reach beyond the Conquest to an originary point older than what twelfth-century readers could find in Bede. In 1191 monks at Glastonbury exhumed what they claimed were the bodies of Arthur and Guinevere. Gransden suggests that Henry II was behind this event, since the king was not eager to support the myth of an ancient British king whose hoped-for return would add 'zest to the rebellions of the Welsh and Bretons against the Angevin kings'.[20]

As this attempt to defuse the myth of Arthur shows, Geoffrey's history was widely believed. Only readers in the north – readers who were more conscious than most of Bede's work – seem to have doubted the *Historia regum Britanniae*. Ailred of Rievaulx first challenged Geoffrey, commenting on the success of his 'fables and lies' and 'fictitious tales'. William of Newburgh, Geoffrey's most explicit opponent, did not write until Geoffrey's book was half a century old. William cited Bede and one of Bede's sources, Gildas, seeking to expose Geoffrey's fictions. Yet Gransden finds only three writers – all of them writing in the fourteenth and fifteenth centuries – who validated William's criticism of the *Historia regum Britanniae*. Indeed, so uncritical was historical writing and the use of sources in the period that Bede's work and Geoffrey's were sometimes conflated and Bede's authority extended to some of Geoffrey's claims, confounding differences in these writers' accounts of English origins.[21]

The later Middle Ages: Bede as translator

As his authority as a historian became clouded by Geoffrey's influence, Bede's reputation as a translator grew. Bede's lasting association with the vernacular is rooted in the eighth-century text, *Cuthbert's Letter on the Death of Bede*, which reports at his death that Bede was translating the Gospel of Saint John 'into our mother tongue to the profit of the Church'.[22] As Sharon Rowley notes in Chapter 15, it was erroneously assumed already in the tenth century that Bede had written the *Ecclesiastical History* in the vernacular, although the work was not translated until the late ninth or early tenth century.[23] In the early thirteenth century, Bede's standing as an author of works in England was clearly represented by Layamon, a parish priest working near Worcester, in the west Midlands. Layamon's *Historia Brutonum*, usually known as *Brut*, was probably composed in the first half of the thirteenth century, after the death of Henry II in 1189.[24] *Brut* is an English translation of the *Roman de*

Brut by the Norman poet Wace, which was completed about 1155; Wace's work, in turn, is a paraphrase and expansion in French of Geoffrey's *Historia regum Britanniae*. Layamon's *Brut* neatly expresses Bede's identity as a champion of the vernacular. As he set out to tell the story of England's nobles, Layamon writes, he chose three books: 'the English book that Bede composed', the book in French by Wace, and a book in Latin by Saint Alban and Saint Augustine.[25]

Layamon had reason for associating Bede with writing in English. The cathedral library at Worcester owned a number of Anglo-Saxon manuscripts, including a copy of the Old English version of Bede's *Ecclesiastical History* glossed by a scribe who left his mark on many Old English manuscripts and who, by virtue of his difficult script, is known as the Tremulous Hand.[26] An early thirteenth-century poem known as the *First Worcester Fragment* (formerly called *Sanctus Beda*) also survives, thanks to this scribe. The work laments that English is no longer the language used to instruct the people and mourns deaths of famous men who taught in English, including Bede. 'Sanctus Beda was iboren her on Breotene mid us, / and he wisliche [bec] awende / þet þeo Englise leoden þurh weren ilerde' ('Saint Bede was born here in Britain with us, and wisely he translated books so that the English people were taught by them').[27]

There is some validity to the claim that Bede was the precursor of writers who translated sacred texts into English, since Bede's *Letter to Bishop Egbert* urged the use of the vernacular in this way. Indeed, it is fortunate for Bede that his reputation had acquired this dimension, for the *Ecclesiastical History* had ceased to speak to the literary interests and narrative forms of the later period. Geoffrey of Monmouth had successfully supplanted Anglo-Saxon origins with Arthurian legends, and history itself had escaped the confines of chronicles and historical narratives like Bede's for the realms of poetry and romance. No better barometer of Bede's reputation exists, perhaps, than the work of Geoffrey Chaucer (d. 1400), in which Bede's name, his texts and his characters pass unknown. Chaucer rarely focused on the Old English period. When he did so in 'The Man of Law's Tale', he derived his knowledge from a French source, the *Chronicle* of Nicholas Trivet, written in the early fourteenth century, which in turn drew on Bede. Trivet seems to have known Bede's *Ecclesiastical History* and derived the name of one of his major characters, Alla, from the Northumbrian king Bede calls Ælle.[28]

Yet when he conjures a world of religious persecution and intolerance in 'The Man of Law's Tale', a world where both the true faith and law are in danger, it is just possible that Chaucer was thinking of a group of his contemporaries with a stronger connection to Bede than his own. Custance, the heroine, enters the dark Northumbrian world from Rome by way of Syria, speaking '[a] maner Latyn corrupt'.[29] In Chaucer's time, the end of the fourteenth century, Wycliffe and his followers were insisting that Scripture be available in the vernacular. In the *General Prologue* to the Wycliffite Bible, the phrase 'Latyn corrupt' is identified not as a learned language but as a vernacular, as the speech of Italians: 'Latyn corrupt, as trewe men seyn, that ben in Italie'.[30] The Lollards advocated broad use of the vernacular. They knew of Bede's reputation as a translator and mistakenly thought he had turned the Bible into English, citing this work as a precedent for their own wish for a vernacular Bible.[31] According to the *General Prologue* of the Wycliffite Bible preface, 'Bede translatide the bible, and expounide myche in Saxon, that was English, either comoun langage of this lond, in his tyme.' In this Bede was not alone, for King Alfred, Frenchmen and Britons 'han the bible, and othere bokis of deuocioun and of exposicioiun, translatid in here modir langage'.[32] Another tract noted that 'Also venerabile Bede lede be þe spirit of God translatid þe Bible or a grete part of þe Bible into Englishe.' The author commented that the text was written in 'so oolde Englische þat vnneþe can any Englishe man rede hem, ffor þis Bede regnede an hooly doctor after þe Incarnation seuene hundred yeer and xxxij'.[33]

To these writers, Bede is 'like us' in providing books of devotion in the 'comoun langage of this lond'. As he was in the twelfth century, Bede was once again an example for reformers who believed in the *orbis idem*, which was also an *orbis alter*, an alternative to the world of those who opposed the diffusion of sacred works in the vernacular. Although the 'Oolde Englische' is said in the Wycliffite Prologue to be so remote that 'scarcely anyone is able to read it', some authors could do so. Thomas Rudborne, a monk at Winchester in the middle of the fifteenth century, read the Old English translation of Bede's *Ecclesiastical History* written 'in lingua Saxonica'.[34] But Rudborne's knowledge of Old English was not typical, and Bede's work continued to be better known in its Latin than in its vernacular. The Lollards' desire for a vernacular Bible kept alive Bede's identity; what was truly 'English' about Bede in their eyes was that, like them, he thought the people should be able to pray in their own language.

Bede in early modern England

Late-fourteenth-century ecclesiastical controversies intensified in the fifteenth century, contributing to what Anne Hudson has called 'the premature reformation'.[35] For writers with heterodox views like those of the Lollards, England became a much more dangerous place with the heresy and treason statutes of Henry VIII, strictures that were not relaxed until Edward VI was crowned in 1547.[36] By that point, Bede's *Ecclesiastical History* had come to be seen as a theological work; during Henry's reign (1509–47) such texts were unwelcome. Hence the text was printed for the first time in Strasbourg (1475–82). It was not until 1565 that the work was translated into English a second time (the Old English translation being the first), and no edition appeared in England until 1643.[37] During this time Bede played a small but distinctive role in representing what came to be seen as the medieval heritage of newly Protestant England and its Church. Among the early reformers, John Bale and John Foxe were especially important in advancing Bede's reputation as a vernacular writer.

Bale (1495–1563) was a collector of ancient manuscripts of English historical works and a historian himself.[38] His most important work, *The Image of Bothe Churches*, was published in Antwerp in 1545 or 1546. Bale argued that the Church had been corrupted in the early Christian period and that subsequently the Church had two forms, a corrupt See of Saint Peter and an isolated community of those few who retained belief in the true Church.[39] Bede was one of Bale's chief witnesses to the survival of the latter group, just as he had been, to the Anglo-Normans, a witness to the integrity of the early Anglo-Saxon Church. Bale's use of Bede supplies a splendid example of difference paired with identity – difference from the hated Church of Rome constituting the sameness of English identity. For Bale, Bede's Church was not Roman but English.[40]

Foxe (1516–87) popularized Bale's theological and historical arguments in his much reprinted *Acts and Monuments*, which appeared first in Latin in 1563 and in English in 1570 and which was reissued in 1576 and 1583. Bede figures in Foxe's list of good teachers who persisted in the truth faith amidst corruption.[41] Foxe also knew about books in Old English and listed several he thought to have been translated by King Alfred, including Bede's *Ecclesiastical History*.[42] But Bede remains a remote figure in this work. The most that could be said for him was said when Foxe listed him along with Alcuin, Aidan and John of Beverley as a good teacher who struggled to defend the truth in a time of corruption. Foxe sought to enlighten the unlearned, 'long led in ignoraunce, and wrapt in blindnesse for lacke especially of Gods word, and partly also for wanting the light of history'.[43] Publication in the vernacular was fundamental to Foxe, who believed that it had also been important to Bede.

As we have seen, Bede's work in the Anglo-Norman period was used both to support and to contradict the claims of Geoffrey of Monmouth. Likewise, in the sixteenth century, Bede figured in arguments on both the Catholic and Protestant sides. Unlike Anglo-Norman historians, Bale and Foxe lacked a deep knowledge of Bede's works. Such knowledge emerged again only in 1565, when Thomas Stapleton published the first translation of the

Ecclesiastical History into modern English. He dedicated it to Queen Elizabeth, hoping that she would find in Bede a clear view of matters that the 'pretended refourmers' had falsified (Foxe had done the same with *Acts and Monuments*). Stapleton intended to juxtapose 'a number of diuersities between the pretended religion of Protestants, and the primitive faith of the english Church', and contrasted the authority of Bede, who wrote without prejudice, with that of Bale, Foxe and others.[44] Stapleton saw himself, like Bede, as a writer on the right side of controversy; Bale and Foxe, of course, held the same view, but to an opposite conclusion. Stapleton was, in the long run, correct, but as the voice of an endangered minority he could not remain in England. He had a distinguished career as a theologian in the English community in exile at Douai, in northern France.[45]

In the work of Bale, Foxe and Stapleton – and in the history of Anglo-Saxon studies in the early modern period more generally – Bede is a minor figure. That is because the study of Anglo-Saxon history and language during this period was dominated by Matthew Parker and his circle, and to them Bede meant less than King Alfred and the abbot Ælfric. Parker (1504–75) was chaplain to Anne Boleyn and, in 1559, was consecrated by Elizabeth as the first Anglican archbishop of Canterbury. Elizabeth required a full argument of the doctrinal principles of the English Church and used Parker 'to justify the independence of the national church from the papacy and to claim antiquity for their departure from the consensus of late medieval theology in such matters as the nature of Christ's presence in the Eucharist'.[46] Parker supervised a group of scholars who collected and edited Anglo-Saxon manuscripts useful to this cause. Their most famous publication, *A Testimonie of Antiquitie*, appeared in 1566, and contained the first Anglo-Saxon texts set in type. The purpose of this collection of Old English homilies and prayers was to supply precedents for the Anglican view of the sacramental, clerical conduct and other matters. An edition of Anglo-Saxon laws by Lambarde, *Archaionomia*, appeared in 1568. Foxe's edition of the Anglo-Saxon translation of the Gospels appeared in 1571, and *Alfredie Regis res gestae*, containing the life of King Alfred by Asser and the famous preface to Alfred's translation of Gregory the Great's *Pastoral Care*, in 1574.[47]

Although marginal to Parker's publication scheme, Bede was not ignored entirely. One of those on whose work Parker depended was Robert Talbot, prebendary of Norwich, who died in 1558, before Parker had published any Old English texts. Talbot is said to have been the first serious collector of Old English manuscripts since the dissolution of the monasteries under Henry VIII. Talbot had a copy of Bede's *Ecclesiastical History* (although the manuscript is unknown); he lent manuscripts of Ælfric's *Grammar* and Ælfric's translation of the *Heptateuch* to Bale, and manuscripts of the *World History* of Orosius and the *Anglo-Saxon Chronicle* to Leland.[48] Another reader of Bede was Ben Jonson, who borrowed a copy of Ælfric's *Grammar* from Robert Cotton (and also had a copy of the *Ecclesiastical History*). Laurence Nowell compiled the first dictionary in Old English, transcribed important and since destroyed manuscripts and acquired the *Beowulf* manuscript. In 1562, while in William Cecil's service, he transcribed a manuscript containing Bede's *Ecclesiastical History* in Old English, the *Anglo-Saxon Chronicle*, the poem known as 'The Seasons for Fasting' and others.[49]

English scholars also made excerpts from Bede's works, but no editions of Bede appeared in England during the sixteenth century, making Stapleton's translation of the *Ecclesiastical History* (1565) all the more remarkable. Already in the late fifteenth century the first partial edition of the *Ecclesiastical History* was published around 1475–80 in Strasbourg (it was completed in 1500). Another edition appeared in Antwerp in 1550; an eight-volume edition of Bede's collected works appeared in Basel in 1563; and the *Ecclesiastical History* appeared in collections of the Latin Fathers in 1583 and 1587. The first English contribution is made in 1643, when Abraham Wheelock, a professor at Cambridge, published an edition of the *Ecclesiastical History* in Latin and Old English. Wheelock's edition is remarkable not only for its parallel Latin and Old English texts but for a translation of the Old English into Latin supplied by Wheelock himself.[50] Wheelock injected an entirely new academic note into the discussion. His knowledge of Old English was much better than that of the earlier generation; he also had access to multiple manuscripts. When writing about Bede's account of matters that had become controversial, Wheelock supported the views of Parker and his circle. It has been said that his motives were 'almost identical' to those of Parker, but his carefully annotated work has also justly been called a 'remarkable scholarly achievement'.[51]

Bede in the modern era

It might seem unusual to begin the modern phase of Bede's reputation as an English writer in 1722, when George Smith's edition appeared, but there are three reasons to do so. Firstly, Smith is credited with establishing an authoritative version of the Latin text, and his work held the field until Charles Plummer's edition of 1896.[52] He was the first editor to use the earliest Latin manuscript of Bede (the 'Moore' manuscript) and to make a critical study of the text's Latin tradition. Secondly, Smith printed several of Bede's texts, not only the *Ecclesiastical History* but also the *Life of Saint Cuthbert*, *On the Holy Places* and the *Martyrology*. He printed both the Latin and Old English versions of the *Ecclesiastical History* but significantly separated them by hundreds of pages. Thirdly, Smith compiled appendices concerning the ecclesiastical controversies in which Bede had figured in earlier periods, summing up this history rather than expressing his own views – even though Smith had written a pamphlet entitled 'British and Saxons not converted to Popery', suggesting that his sympathies lay with Wheelock and Parker.[53] Smith's edition manifests an interest in English geography and monuments related to Bede. He included several illustrations, among them an engraving of the east window of Durham Cathedral, Bede's tomb and his epitaph. For Smith, Bede's life and work were not the focus of controversy but rather matter for study and historical observation.[54] Smith's work represents Bede as a distinctly English historical figure, not in order to exploit his views but rather in order to set them into English place and time. Smith's modernity can be seen in a reduced sense of the *orbis idem* and a greater sense of the *alter orbis*: Bede's world is an artefact, and not the same world as Smith's.

At the end of the nineteenth century, however, when Bede's historical works were re-edited by Plummer, the century's greatest scholar of Bede, the dichotomy of the *alter orbis* and the *orbis idem* retained its power. Like many important medieval authors, Bede was credited with the authorship of works he did not write. The Old English version of the *Ecclesiastical History* is one example. Bede's name was also attached to a handbook of penance, a book for priests to use in confession; such texts list all manner of sins, ranging from improper treatment of the Eucharist to sexual sins. Adamantly opposed to the suggestion that Bede wrote a penitential, Plummer observed, 'The penitential literature is in truth a deplorable feature of the medieval church. Evil deeds, the imagination of which may perhaps have dimly floated through our minds in the darkest moments, are here tabulated and reduced to system. It is hard to see how anyone could busy himself with such literature and not be the worse for it.'[55] John McNeill and Helena Gamer suggested that Bede might well have been acquainted with the sins listed in the penitential, only to prompt M. L. W. Laistner to reply that Bede was too good a Latinist to have written the text.[56] Handbooks of penance belonged to the mundane world, not the elevated *alter orbis* of Bede's learning. Moreover, such texts would dissolve the *orbis idem* shared by these scholars and Bede: he could not have worked with penitentials, it seems, because scholars who admired him would have nothing to do with such texts themselves.

Whether they emphasize their identity with Bede or their distance from a world like the one Bede regarded as remote from his own, scholars like Plummer echo the proud insularity and quiet superiority that distinguishes the personal voice in Bede's work. William Wordsworth's admiration for Bede – which Laistner noticed – sounds a different note.[57] In his *Ecclesiastical Sonnets*, which reflect on the origins and growth of Christianity in Anglo-

Saxon England, Wordsworth described a 'care-worn Chieftain' who 'quits the world' and exchanges his sword for 'penitential cogitations' in a monastery (Sonnet 21). Wordsworth suggests in the following sonnet that one who is 'tired of the world and all its industry' might retire instead to a 'vacant hermitage' where even a cock's crow would not disturb him (the cock's crow being a common medieval image of the preacher rousing sinners to repent; Sonnet 22). But the peace of that escape would soon be troubled by the 'hovering Shade' of 'venerable Bede' that appears in the following sonnet: 'The saint, the scholar, from a circle freed / Of toil stupendous'. Reproving the 'recreant soul' of Sonnet 22 who shunned 'the debt / Imposed on human kind', Bede exemplified diligence and the 'unrelaxing use of a long life' – up to, as the *Ecclesiastical History* attests, the holy man's dying breath (Sonnet 23).[58] Wordsworth's sonnet seems encrusted with idealism and romanticism. Yet it is a fitting reminder that Bede's *alter orbis* was not an escape into scholarship untroubled by the cares of the Northumbrian Church, and, correspondingly, that admission to Bede's *orbis idem* must be earned by sincerity of purpose and hard work.

NOTES

1. Harris 2003: 9–16.
2. Colgrave and Mynors 1969: 596. The concept of 'the English people' emerges in the ninth-century translation of Bede's History; see Scragg 2000: 4–5.
3. For a concise account of Bede's isolation, see P. H. Blair 1970: 3–9; Blair's introduction, 'Orbis alter', inspired the theme of the present essay.
4. William of Malmesbury, *Gesta regum*, quoted in P. H. Blair 1970: 9.
5. Bede's commentaries are quoted in P. H. Blair 1970: 7.
6. Mayr-Harting 1991: 40. See Laistner 1933: 92 for reservations about this point.
7. Gransden 1992a: 2.
8. Dante Alighieri, *Paradiso*, canto 10, in *The Divine Comedy*, trans. C. S. Singleton, 6 vols. (Princeton University Press, 1975), pp. 112–15. Dante died in 1321.
9. Gransden 1992b: 74–5.
10. Gransden 1992a: 14.
11. Brehe 1990: 534.
12. Gransden 1992a: 10.
13. William of Malmesbury, *The Deeds of the Kings of the English*, in D. Douglas and G. Greenaway (eds.), *English Historical Documents, 1042–1189*, 2nd edn (London: Eyre Methuen, 1981), p. 315.
14. Gransden 1992a: 11, citing Colgrave and Mynors 1969: lxi.
15. Bartlett 2000: 623.
16. Partner 1977: 20.
17. Gransden 1992a: 16, see also Gransden 1992b: 72–5.
18. DeGregorio 2002 and 2004. See also DeGregorio's comments in Chapter 9.
19. Geoffrey of Monmouth, *History of the Kings of Britain*, trans. Sebastian Evans, rev. Charles W. Dunn (New York: Dutton, 1958), ch. 2, pp. 4–50.

20. Gransden 1992a: pp. 2–21, quoting Treharne 1967: 105–6, and Tatlock 1933: 122.
21. Gransden 1992a: 19–24.
22. *Cuthbert's Letter on the Death of Bede*, in Colgrave and Mynors 1969: 582–3.
23. Miller 1890–8.
24. Kennedy 1989.
25. Layamon, *Brut*, ed. G. L. Brook and R. R. Leslie, 2 vols., Early English Text Society, o.s 250, 277 (Oxford University Press, 1963, 1978), vol. I, p. 3.
26. Franzen 1991: 59.
27. Brehe 1990: 521–36.
28. Frankis 2000.
29. Chaucer, 'The Man of Law's Tale', from *The Canterbury Tales*, ed. L. D. Benson, in *The Riverside Chaucer* (Boston: Houghton Mifflin, 1987), p. 94, line 519.
30. *The Holy Bible, Containing the Old and New Testaments, with the Apocryphal Books, Made from the Latin by John Wycliffe and His Followers*, ed. Josiah Forshall and Sir Frederic Madden, 4 vols. (Oxford University Press, 1850), vol. I, p. 59.
31. Watson 1995.
32. *The Holy Bible*, ed. Forshall and Madden, vol. IV, p. 59. Hudson 1988: 237–8, 243–7.
33. Bühler 1938: 174, lines 131–40.
34. Ker 1957: xlix.
35. Hudson 1988: 390–445.
36. King 1982: 3–9.
37. Colgrave and Mynors 1969: lxxi–lxxii.
38. Fairfield 1976; McKisack 1971: 11–20. See also Graham 2000 and 2001.
39. Fairfield 1976: 75–7.
40. J. Bale, *Illustrium Maioris Brittaniae scriptorum* (Wesel, 1548), which includes Bede in a list of British authors whose names Bale took from Geoffrey of Monmouth. See Fairfield 1976: 98.
41. John Foxe, first preface to *Actes and Monuments of Matters Most Speciall and Memorable* (London, 1570), p. 3.
42. Foxe, *Actes and Monuments*, Book 3, p. 190.
43. Foxe, dedication to Queen Elizabeth, *Acts and Monuments* (London, 1583), p. 5.
44. *The History of the Church of England Compiled by Venerable Bede, Englishman*, ed. Thomas Stapleton (Antwerp, 1565), p. 3b.
45. Levy 1967: 110–12.
46. Berkhout and Gatch 1982: ix.
47. Leinbaugh 1982.
48. Ker 1957: l–li and 188–9.
49. Flower 1935.
50. Leinbaugh 1982: 62.
51. Murphy 1967: 50; Leinbaugh 1982: 62.
52. Colgrave and Mynors 1969: lxxii–lxxiii.
53. *Baedae Historia Ecclesiastica Latine et Saxonice*, ed. Johannis Smith (Cambridge: Typis Academicis, 1722), pp. 168 and 170–1.
54. *Baedae Historia Ecclesiastica*, sig. b2ᵛ–b4ʳ; the first engraving is opposite the first page, the second opposite p. 805.

55. Plummer, 1896: vol. I, pp. clvii–clviii. For commentary, see Frantzen 1983: 1–4.
56. McNeill and Gamer 1990: 217; see the reply by Laistner 1957: 166–70.
57. Laistner 1933: 93.
58. *Cuthbert's Letter on the Death of Bede*, in Colgrave and Mynors 1969: 580–7. The sonnets are quoted from *The Complete Poetical Works of William Wordsworth*, ed. A. J. George (Boston: Houghton, Mifflin & Co., 1904), pp. 609–10.

Introductory studies

Brown, G. H. *Bede the Venerable*. Twayne's English Authors Series. Boston: Twayne Publishers, 1987.

Carroll, Sister M. T. A. *The Venerable Bede: His Spiritual Teachings*. Studies in Medieval History, New Series, IX. Washington, DC: Catholic University of America Press, 1946.

Ward, B. *The Venerable Bede*. Outstanding Christian Thinkers Series. London: Continuum, 1990; republished Cistercian Studies Series 169. Kalamazoo, MI: Cistercian Publications, 1998.

Collections of critical essays

Bonner, G. (ed.). *Famulus Christi: Essays in Commemoration of the Thirteenth Centenary of the Birth of the Venerable Bede*. London: SPCK, 1976.

DeGregorio, S. (ed.). *Innovation and Tradition in the Writings of the Venerable Bede*. Medieval European Studies 7. Morgantown: West Virginia University Press, 2006.

Farrell, R. (ed.). *Bede and Anglo-Saxon England: Papers in Honour of the 1300th Anniversary of the Birth of Bede, Given at Cornell University in 1973 and 1974*. British Archaeological Reports 46. Oxford: BAR, 1978.

Frantzen, A. and J. Hines (eds.). *Cædmon's Hymn and Material Culture in the World of Bede: Six Essays*. Medieval European Studies 10. Morgantown: West Virginia University Press, 2007.

Houwen, L. A. J. R. and A. A. MacDonald (eds.). *Beda Venerabilis: Historian, Monk, & Northumbrian*. Groningen: Egbert Forsten, 1996.

Lebecq, S., M. Perrin and O. Szerwiniack (eds.). *Bède le Vénérable entre tradition et postérité*. Lille: CEGES, 2005.

Thompson, A. H. (ed.). *Bede: His Life, Times, and Writings: Essays in Commemoration of the Twelfth Centenary of his Death*. Oxford: Clarendon Press, 1935; reissued New York: Russell & Russell, 1966.

Backgrounds

Blair, J. *The Church in Anglo-Saxon Society*. Oxford University Press, 2005.
Blair, P. H. *The World of Bede*. Cambridge University Press, 1970; reprinted 1990.
Northumbria in the Days of Bede. London: St Martin's Press, 1976.
An Introduction to Anglo-Saxon England. 3rd edn. Cambridge University Press, 2003.
Foot, S. *Monastic Life in Anglo-Saxon England c. 600–900*. Cambridge University Press, 2006.
Hawkes, J. and S. Mills (eds.). *Northumbria's Golden Age*. Stroud: Sutton, 1999.
Rollason, D. *Northumbria, 500–1100: Creation and Destruction of a Kingdom*. Cambridge University Press, 2003.
Stenton, F. M. *Anglo-Saxon England*. 3rd edn. Oxford University Press, 1971.
Thacker, A. 'England in the Seventh Century' in P. Fouracre (ed.), *The New Cambridge Medieval History. Volume I: c. 500–c. 700*. Cambridge University Press, 2005, pp. 462–95.
Yorke, B. *The Conversion of Britain: Religion, Politics and Society in Britain, c. 600–800*. Harlow: Pearson Education, 2006.

The Ecclesiastical History

Campbell, J. 'Bede II' in *Essays in Anglo-Saxon History*. London: Hambleton Press, 1986, pp. 29–48.
Gofffart, W. 'Bede and the Ghost of Bishop Wilfrid' in *The Narrators of Barbarian History (A.D. 550–800): Jordanes, Gregory of Tour, Bede, and Paul the Deacon*. Princeton University Press, 1988; reprinted University of Notre Dame Press, 2005, pp. 235–328.
Higham, N. J. *(Re-)Reading Bede: The Ecclesiastical History in Context*. London: Routledge, 2006.
Wallace-Hadrill, J. M. *Bede's Ecclesiastical History of the English People: A Historical Commentary*. Oxford Medieval Texts. Oxford: Clarendon Press, 1988; reprinted 1991.
Wright, J. Robert. *A Companion to Bede: A Reader's Commentary on The Ecclesiastical History of the English People*. Grand Rapids, MI: Eerdmans, 2008.

Biblical exegesis

DeGregorio, S. 'The Reforming Impulse of Bede's Later Exegesis.' *Early Medieval Europe*, 11 (2002): 107–22.
Holder, A. 'Bede and the Tradition of Patristic Exegesis.' *Anglican Theological Review*, 72 (1990): 399–411.
Jenkins, C. 'Bede as Exegete and Theologian' in Thompson (ed.), *Bede: His Life, Times, and Writings*, pp. 152–200.
Laistner, M. L. W. 'Bede as a Classical and a Patristic Scholar.' *Transactions of the Royal Historical Society*, 16 (1933): 69–93.
Martin, L. T. 'The Two Worlds in Bede's Homilies: The Biblical Event and the Listeners' Experience' in T. Amos, E. Green and B. Mayne Kienzle (eds.), *De

Ore Domini: Preacher and Word in the Middle Ages. Kalamazoo, MI: The Medieval Institute, 1989, pp. 27–40.

Meyvaert, P. 'Bede the Scholar' in Bonner (ed.), *Famulus Christi*, pp. 40–69.

Ray, R. 'What Do We Know about Bede's Biblical Commentaries?' *Recherches de théologie ancienne et médiévale*, 49 (1982): 1–20.

Robinson, B. 'The Venerable Bede as Exegete.' *The Downside Review*, 112 (1994): 201–26.

West, P. 'Liturgical Style and Structure in Bede's Homily for the Easter Vigil.' *American Benedictine Review*, 23 (1972): 1–8.

*In addition, the introductions to the English translations of his commentaries contain much fine discussion of Bede; these are listed in the Bibliography, pp. 247–8.

Hagiography

Bonner, G., D. Rollason and C. Stancliffe (eds.). *St Cuthbert, His Cult and His Community*. Woodbridge: The Boydell Press, 1989.

Coates, S. 'Ceolfrith: History, Hagiography and Memory in Seventh- and Eighth-Century Wearmouth-Jarrow.' *Journal of Medieval History*, 25 (1999): 69–86.

Colgrave, B. 'The Earliest Saints' Lives Written in England.' *Proceedings of the British Academy*, 44 (1958): 35–60.

Eby, J. 'Bringing the *Vita* to Life: Bede's Symbolic Structure of the Life of St Cuthbert.' *American Benedictine Review*, 48 (1997): 316–38.

Thacker, A. 'Bede's Ideal of Reform' in P. Wormald, D. Bullough and R. Collins (eds.), *Ideal and Reality in Frankish and Anglo-Saxon Society: Studies Presented to J. M. Wallace-Hadrill*. Oxford: Basil Blackwell, 1983, pp. 130–53.

Educational, poetic and scientific writings

Irvine, M. 'Bede the Grammarian and the Scope of Grammatical Studies in Eighth-Century Northumbria.' *Anglo-Saxon England*, 15 (1986): 15–44.

Jones, C. W. 'Bede's Place in Medieval Schools' in Bonner (ed.), *Famulus Christi*, pp. 261–85.

Kendall, C. B. 'Introduction' to *Bede: Libri II De arte metrica et De schematibus et tropis: The Art of Poetry and Rhetoric*. Saarbrücken: AQ-Verlag, 1991, pp. 15–33.

Lapidge, M. (ed.). *Bede's Latin Poetry*. Oxford Medieval Texts. Oxford University Press, forthcoming.

Palmer, R. B. 'Bede as Text-Book Writer: A Study of his *De arte metrica*.' *Speculum*, 34 (1959): 573–84.

Wallis, F. 'Introduction' to *Bede: The Reckoning of Time*. Translated Texts for Historians 29. Liverpool University Press, 1999, esp. pp. xv–xxxiv, lxiii–lxxi.

BIBLIOGRAPHY

Bede's writings

a) Latin editions

(NB: CCSL = Corpus Christianorum, Series latina / PL = Patrologia Latina)

Bedae Vita Sancti Cuthberti, in *Two Lives of Saint Cuthbert*, ed. B. Colgrave. Cambridge University Press, 1940; first paperback edn 1985.

Bedas metrische Vita sankti Cuthberti, ed. W. Jaager. Leipzig: Mayer & Müller, 1935.

Collectio Psalterii Bedae Venerabili adscripta, ed. G. M. Browne. Bibliotheca scriptorum Graecorum et Romanorum Teubneriana Monachii. K. G. Saur, 2001.

De arte metrica et de schematibus et tropis, ed. C. B. Kendall. CCSL 123A. Turnhout: Brepols, 1975.

De locis sanctis, ed. F. Fraipont, in *Itineraria et alia geographica*. CCSL 175. Turnhout: Brepols, 1965.

De natura rerum liber, ed. C. W. Jones. CCSL 123A. Turnhout: Brepols, 1975.

De octo quaestionibus, ed. in PL 93.

De orthographia, ed. C. W. Jones. CCSL 123A. Turnhout: Brepols, 1975.

De tabernaculo, ed. D. Hurst. CCSL 119A. Turnhout: Brepols, 1969.

De templo, ed. D. Hurst. CCSL 119A. Turnhout: Brepols, 1969.

De temporum ratione, ed. C. W. Jones. CCSL 123B. Turnhout: Brepols, 1977.

Édition pratique des martyrologes de Bède, de l'anonyme lyonnais et de Florus, ed. J. DuBois and G. Renaud. Paris: Éditions du Centre national de la recherche scientifique, 1976.

Epistola ad Ecgbertum Episcopum, in *Venerabilis Baedae opera historica*, ed. C. Plummer. 2 vols. Oxford: Clarendon Press, 1896; reprinted as 1 vol., 1946.

Epistola ad Helmuualdum, ed. C. W. Jones. CCSL 123C. Turnhout: Brepols, 1980.

Epistola ad Pleguinam, ed. C. W. Jones. CCSL 123C. Turnhout: Brepols, 1980.

Epistola ad VVicthedum, ed. C. W. Jones. CCSL 123C. Turnhout: Brepols, 1980.

Expositio Actuum Apostolorum, ed. M. L. W. Laistner. CCSL 121. Turnhout: Brepols, 1983.

Expositio Apocalypseos, ed. R. Gyrson. CCSL 121A. Turnhout: Brepols, 2001.

Expositio Bedae presbyteri in Canticum Habacuc, ed. J. E. Hudson. CCSL 119B. Turnhout: Brepols, 1983.

Historia Abbatum auctore Baeda, in *Baedae Opera Historica*, ed. C. Plummer. 2 vols. Oxford: Clarendon Press, 1896; reprinted as 1 vol., 1946. Also prints the Latin text of Bede's letter to Albinus of Canterbury.

Historia ecclesiastica gentis Anglorum, ed. B. Colgrave and R. A. B. Mynors. Oxford Medieval Texts. Oxford: Clarendon Press, 1969; reprinted 2001.

Homiliae euangelii, ed. D. Hurst, in *Opera homiletica*. CCSL 122. Turnhout: Brepols, 1955.

In Cantica Canticorum, ed. D. Hurst. CCSL 119B. Turnhout: Brepols, 1983.

In epistolas VII catholicas, ed. D. Hurst. CCSL 121. Turnhout: Brepols, 1983.

In Ezram et Neemiam, ed. D. Hurst. CCSL 119A. Turnhout: Brepols, 1969.

In Lucae euangelium expositio, ed. D. Hurst. CCSL 120. Turnhout: Brepols, 1960.

In Marci euangelium expositio, ed. D. Hurst. CCSL 120. Turnhout: Brepols, 1960.

In primam partem Samuhelis, ed. D. Hurst. CCSL 119. Turnhout: Brepols, 1962.

In principium Genesim, ed. C. W. Jones. CCSL 118. Turnhout: Brepols, 1967.

In prouerbia Salomonis, ed. D. Hurst. CCSL 119B. Turnhout: Brepols, 1983.

In Regum librum XXX quaestiones, ed. D. Hurst. CCSL 119. Turnhout: Brepols, 1962.

In Tobiam, ed. D. Hurst. CCSL 119B. Turnhout: Brepols, 1983.

Nomina locorum ex Beati Hieronimi et Flaui Iosephi collecta opusculis, ed. D. Hurst. CCSL 119. Turnhout: Brepols, 1962.

Opera rhythmica, ed J. Fraipont, in *Opera homiletica*, ed. D Hurst. CCSL 122. Turnhout: Brepols, 1955.

Passio S. Anastasii, in *The Latin Dossier of Anastasius the Persian: Hagiographic Translations and Transformations*, ed. C. Vircillo Franklin. Toronto: Pontifical Institute of Mediaeval Studies, 2004.

Rectractatio in Actus Apostolorum, ed. M. L. W. Laistner. CCSL 121. Turnhout: Brepols, 1960.

Versus de die judicii, ed. J. Fraipont, in *Opera rhythmica*. CCSL 122. Turnhout: Brepols, 1955.

Vita Sancti Felicis, ed. T. Mackay. 'Critical Edition of Bede's *Vita Felicis*'. PhD thesis, Stanford University, 1971.

b) English translations

(NB: CSS = Cistercian Studies Series / TTH = Translated Texts for Historians)

The Abbreviated Psalter of the Venerable Bede, trans. G. M. Browne. Grand Rapids: Eerdmans, 2002.

The Age of Bede, trans. J. F. Webb and D. H. Farmer. London: Penguin Books, 1965; reprinted 2004. Contains English translations of Bede's prose *Life of Saint Cuthbert* and his *Lives of the Abbots of Wearmouth and Jarrow* (also known as *History of the Abbots*), as well as the *Anonymous History of Abbot Ceolfrith* (also known as *Life of Ceolfrith*) and Stephanus's *Life of Bishop Wilfrid*.

Bede: A Biblical Miscellany, trans. W. T. Foley and A. G. Holder. TTH 28. Liverpool University Press, 1999. Contains English translations of the following six works: *On the Holy Places*, *On the Resting-Places*, *On What Isaiah Says*, *On Tobias*, *Thirty Questions on the Book of Kings*, *On Eight Questions*.

Bede: Libri II De Arte metrica et De schematibus et tropis: The Art of Poetry and Rhetoric, trans. C. B. Kendall. Saarbrücken: AQ-Verlag, 1991.

Bede: On Ezra and Nehemiah, trans. S. DeGregorio. TTH 47. Liverpool University Press, 2006.

Bede: On Genesis, trans. C. B. Kendall. TTH 48. Liverpool University Press, 2008.

Bede: On the Tabernacle, trans. A. G. Holder. TTH 18. Liverpool University Press, 1994.

Bede: On the Temple, trans. S. Connolly. TTH 21. Liverpool University Press, 1995.

Bede: On Tobit and On the Canticle of Habakkuk, trans. S. Connolly. Dublin: Four Courts, 1997.

Bede: The Reckoning of Time, trans. F. Wallis. TTH 29. Liverpool University Press, 1999. Also contains English translations of three letters: the *Letter to Plegwin*, the *Letter to Helmwald* and the *Letter to Wicthed*.

Bede the Venerable: Excerpts from the Works of Saint Augustine on the Letters of the Blessed Apostle Paul, trans. D. Hurst. CSS 183. Kalamazoo, MI: Cistercian Publications, 1999.

Bede the Venerable: Homilies on the Gospels, trans. L. T. Martin and D. Hurst. 2 vols. CSS 110–11. Kalamazoo, MI: Cistercian Publications, 1991.

Ecclesiastical History of the English People, ed. and trans. B. Colgrave and R. A. B. Mynors. Oxford Medieval Texts. Oxford: Clarendon Press, 1969; reprinted 2001.

Ecclesiastical History of the English People, trans. J. McClure and R. Collins. Oxford University Press, 1994. Also contains English translations of *The Greater Chronicle*, the *Letter to Bishop Egbert* and *Cuthbert's Letter on the Death of Bede*.

Ecclesiastical History of the English People, trans. L. Sherley-Price. London: Penguin Books, 1955; reprinted with revisions, 1990. Also contains English translations of the *Letter to Bishop Egbert* and *Cuthbert's Letter on the Death of Bede*.

The Explanation of the Apocalypse by Venerable Beda, trans. Rev. Edward Marshall. Oxford: James Parker and Co., 1878.

Letter to Albinus, trans. P. Meyvaert, in Meyvaert 1999: 278.

Martyrology, trans. F. Lifshitz, in *Medieval Hagiography: An Anthology*, ed. T. Head. New York and London: Routledge, 2001.

Two Lives of Saint Cuthbert, ed. and trans. B. Colgrave. Cambridge University Press, 1940; first paperback edn 1985. Contains an English translation of Bede's prose *Life of Saint Cuthbert*.

The Venerable Bede: Commentary on the Acts of the Apostles, trans. L. T. Martin. CSS 117. Kalamazoo, MI: Cistercian Publications, 1989.

The Venerable Bede: Commentary on the Seven Catholic Epistles of the Venerable Bede, trans. D. Hurst. CSS 82. Kalamazoo, MI: Cistercian Publications, 1985.

Secondary literature

Alexander, J. J. G. 1978. *Insular Manuscripts, 6th to the 9th Century*. London: Harvey Miller.

Allen, M. I. 1996. 'Bede and Frechulf at Medieval St Gallen' in Houwen and MacDonald (eds.), *Beda Venerabilis*, pp. 61–80.

Auerbach, E. 1973. '"Figura"', trans. R. Manheim, in *Scenes From the Drama of European Literature: Six Essays*. St Paul: University of Minnesota Press, pp. 11–76.

Badian, E. 1966. 'The Early Historians' in T. A. Dorey (ed.), *Latin Historians*. New York: Basic Books, pp. 1–38.

Baker, L. G. D. 1970. 'The Desert in the North.' *Northern History*, 5: 1–11.

Bartlett, R. 2000. *England under the Norman and Angevin Kings 1075–1225*. Oxford: Clarendon Press.

Bassett, S. 1992. 'Church and Diocese in the West Midlands: The Transition from British to Anglo-Saxon Control' in Blair and Sharpe (eds.), *Pastoral Care Before the Parish*, pp. 13–40.

Bately, J. 1988. 'Old English Prose Before and During the Reign of Alfred.' *Anglo-Saxon England*, 17: 93–138.

2003. 'The Alfredian Canon Revisited: One Hundred Years On' in T. Reuter (ed.), *Alfred the Great: Papers from the Eleventh-Centenary Conferences*. Aldershot: Ashgate, pp. 107–20.

Baxter, S. *et al.* (eds.). 2008. *Early Medieval Studies in Memory of Patrick Wormald*. Aldershot: Ashgate.

Berkhout, C. T. and M. McC. Gatch (eds.). 1982. *Anglo-Saxon Scholarship: The First Three Centuries*. Boston: G. K. Hall.

Bischoff, B. 1954. 'Wendepunkte in der Geschichte der lateinischen Exegese im Frühmittelalter.' *Sacris Eruditi*, 6: 189–281.

1994. 'The Court Library of Charlemagne' in *Manuscripts and Libraries in the Age of Charlemagne*, trans. M. Gorman. Cambridge Studies in Palaeography and Codicology 1. Cambridge University Press, pp. 56–75. Originally published as 'Die Hofbibliothek Karls des Großen' in *Karl der Große: Lebenswerk und Nachleben*, vol. 2 (Düsseldorf: L. Schwann, 1965), pp. 42–62.

1998–2004. *Katalog der festländischen Handschriften des neunten Jahrhunderts (mit Ausnahme der wisigotischen)*, ed. B. Ebersperger. 2 vols. (to date). Wiesbaden: Harrassowitz.

and M. Lapidge. 1994. *Biblical Commentaries from the Canterbury School of Theodore and Hadrian*. Cambridge University Press.

Blair, J. 2002. 'A Handlist of Anglo-Saxon Saints' in A. Thacker and R. Sharpe (eds.), *Local Saints and Local Churches in the Early Medieval West*. Oxford University Press, pp. 495–565.

2005. *The Church in Anglo-Saxon Society*. Oxford University Press.

and R. Sharpe (eds.). 1992. *Pastoral Care Before the Parish*. London: Leicester University Press.

Blair, P. H. 1970, reprinted 1990. *The World of Bede*. Cambridge University Press.

Bodden, M. C. 1988. 'Evidence for the Knowledge of Greek in Anglo-Saxon England.' *Anglo-Saxon England*, 17: 217–46.

Bonner, G. 1966. *Saint Bede in the Tradition of Western Apocalyptic Commentary*. Jarrow Lecture. Jarrow: Jarrow Parish Council. Reprinted in Lapidge, *Bede and His World*, vol. 1, pp. 153–83.

(ed.). 1976. *Famulus Christi: Essays in Commemoration of the Thirteenth Centenary of the Birth of the Venerable Bede*. London: SPCK.

and D. Rollason and C. Stancliffe (eds.). 1989. *St Cuthbert, His Cult and His Community to AD 1200*. Woodbridge: The Boydell Press.

Bracken, D. 2006. 'Virgil the Grammarian and Bede: A Preliminary Study.' *Anglo-Saxon England*, 35: 7–21.

Brehe, S. K. 1990. 'Reassembling the *First Worcester Fragment*.' *Speculum*, 65.3: 521–36.

Brooks, N. 1999. *Bede and the English*. Jarrow Lecture. Jarrow: Jarrow Parish Council.

Brown, G. H. 1987. *Bede the Venerable*. Boston: Twayne Publishers.

  1997. 'The Preservation and Transmission of Northumbrian Culture on the Continent: Alcuin's Debt to Bede' in P. E. Szarmach and J. T. Rosenthal (eds.), *The Preservation and Transmission of Anglo-Saxon Culture*. Kalamazoo, MI: Medieval Institute Publications, pp. 159–75.

  2006. 'Bede's Neglected Commentary on Samuel' in DeGregorio (ed.), *Innovation and Tradition*, pp. 121–42.

Brown, M. P. 1996. *The Book of Cerne*. London and Toronto: British Library and Toronto University Press.

  2000. '*In the beginning was the Word*': *Books and Faith in the Age of Bede*. Jarrow Lecture. Jarrow: Jarrow Parish Council.

  2003a. *The Lindisfarne Gospels*. London and Toronto: British Library and Toronto University Press.

  2003b. 'House-Style in the Scriptorium: Scribal Reality and Scholarly Myth' in C. Karkov and G. H. Brown (eds.), *Anglo-Saxon Styles*. Albany: State University of New York Press, pp. 131–50.

  2008. *Manuscripts from the Anglo-Saxon Age*. London and Toronto: British Library and Toronto University Press.

Brown, T. J. *et al.* (eds.). 1969. *The Stonyhurst Gospel of St John*. Oxford: Roxburghe Club.

  1993. *A Palaeographer's View: The Selected Writings of Julian Brown*, ed. J. Bately, M. Brown and J. Roberts. London: Harvey Miller Publishers.

Bruce-Mitford, R. L. S. 1967. *The Art of the Codex Amiatinus*. Jarrow Lecture. Jarrow: Jarrow Parish Council. Reprinted in Lapidge (ed.), *Bede and His World*, vol. I, pp. 186–234.

Bühler, C. F. (ed.). 1938. 'A Lollard Tract: On Translating the Bible into English.' *Medium Aevum*, 7: 167–83.

Bullough, D. 1981. 'Hagiography as Patriotism: Alcuin's "York Poem" and the Early Northumbrian Vitae sanctorum' in E. Patlagean and P. Riché (eds.), *Hagiographie, cultures, et sociétés: IVe–XIIe siècles*. Paris: Études Augustiniennes, pp. 339–59.

Campbell, J. 1986. *Essays in Anglo-Saxon History*. London and Ronceverte: Hambledon.

  2004. 'Bede' in H. C. G. Matthew and B. Harrison (eds.), *Oxford Dictionary of National Biography*. 60 vols. Oxford University Press, vol. IV, pp. 758–65.

  2007. 'Some Considerations on Religion in Early England' in M. Henig and T. J. Smith (eds.), *Collectanea Antiqua: Essays in Memory of Sonia Chadwick Hawkes*. Oxford: Archaeopress, pp. 67–74.

Carroll, Sister M. T. A. 1946. *The Venerable Bede: His Spiritual Teachings*. Washington, DC: Catholic University of America Press.

Charles-Edwards, T. 2000. *Early Christian Ireland*. Cambridge University Press.

Clemoes, P. 1983. *The Cult of St Oswald on the Continent*. Jarrow Lecture. Jarrow: Jarrow Parish Council. Reprinted in Lapidge (ed.), *Bede and His World*, vol. II, pp. 587–610.

and K. Hughes (eds.). 1971. *England Before the Conquest: Studies in Primary Sources Presented to Dorothy Whitelock*. Cambridge University Press.

Coates, S. 1999. 'Ceolfrith: History, Hagiography and Memory in Seventh- and Eighth-Century Wearmouth-Jarrow.' *Journal of Medieval History*, 25: 69–86.

Colgrave, B. (ed.). 1940, reprinted 1985. *Two Lives of Saint Cuthbert: A Life by an Anonymous Monk of Lindisfarne and Bede's Prose Life*. Cambridge University Press.

and R. A. B. Mynors (eds.). 1969, reprinted 2001. *Bede's Ecclesiastical History of the English People*. Oxford Medieval Texts. Oxford: Clarendon Press.

Contreni, J. 2001. 'Counting, Calendars, and Cosmology: Numeracy in the Early Middle Ages' in J. Contreni and S. Casciani (eds.), *Word, Image, Number: Communication in the Middle Ages*. Florence: SISMEL – Edizioni del Galluzzo, pp. 43–84.

2005. 'Bede's Scientific Works in the Carolingian Age' in Lebecq *et al.* (eds.), *Bède le Vénérable*, pp. 247–59.

Corbett, W. J. 1900. 'The Tribal Hidage.' *Transactions of the Royal Historical Society*, New Series, 14: 187–230.

1913. 'England (to c. 800) and English Institutions' in J. B. Bury (ed.), *The Cambridge Medieval History*, vol II. Cambridge University Press, pp. 43–74.

Cramp, R. 1976. 'Monastic Sites' in D. M. Wilson (ed.), *The Archaeology of Anglo-Saxon England*. London: Methuen, pp. 201–52.

and G. Bettess, F. Bettess, S. Anderson and P. Lowther. 2005-6. *Wearmouth and Jarrow Monastic Sites*. Swindon: English Heritage.

Cubitt, C. 1989. 'Wilfrid's "Usurping Bishops": Episcopal Elections in Anglo-Saxon England, *c.* 600–*c.* 800.' *Northern History*, 25: 18–38.

1992. 'Pastoral Care and Conciliar Canons: the Provisions of the 747 Council of *Clofesho*' in Blair and Sharpe (eds.), *Pastoral Care Before the Parish*, pp. 193–211.

1995. *Anglo-Saxon Church Councils c. 650–c.850*. London: Leicester University Press.

Davis, R. H. C. 1989. 'Bede After Bede' in C. Harper-Bill (ed.), *Studies in Medieval History Presented to R. Allen Brown*. Woodbridge: Boydell and Brewer, pp. 103–16.

Declercq, Georges. 2000. *Anno Domini: The Origins of the Christian Era*. Turnhout: Brepols.

DeGregorio, S. 1999. 'The Venerable Bede on Prayer and Contemplation.' *Traditio*, 54: 1–39.

2002. 'The Reforming Impulse of Bede's Later Exegesis.' *Early Medieval Europe*, 11: 107–22.

2004. 'Bede's *In Ezram et Neemiam* and the Reform of the Northumbrian Church.' *Speculum*, 79: 1–25.

2005. 'Bede's *In Ezram et Neemiam*: A Document in Church Reform?' in Lebecq *et al.* (eds.), *Bède le Vénérable*, pp. 97–107.

(ed.) 2006a. *Innovation and Tradition in the Writings of the Venerable Bede*. Morgantown: West Virginia University Press.

2006b. 'Introduction: The New Bede' in DeGregorio (ed.), *Innovation and Tradition*, pp. 1–10.

2006c. 'Footsteps of His Own: Bede's Commentary on Ezra-Nehemiah' in DeGregorio (ed.), *Innovation and Tradition*, pp. 143–68.

2006d. 'Introduction' to *Bede: On Ezra and Nehemiah*. Translated Texts for Historians 47. Liverpool University Press, pp. xiii–xliv.

2008. 'Bede and Benedict of Nursia' in Stephen Baxter *et al.* (eds.), *Early Medieval Studies*, pp. 149–63.

2010. 'The Venerable Bede and Gregory the Great: Exegetical Connections, Spiritual Departures.' *Early Medieval Europe*, 18: 43–60.

de Lubac, H. 1998, reprinted 2000. *Medieval Exegesis: The Four Senses of Scripture*, vol. I (1998), trans. M. Sebanc, vol. II (2000), trans. E. M. Macierowski. Grand Rapids, MI: Eerdmans. Originally published as *Exégèse médiévale: Les quatre sens de l'écriture*. Paris: Éditions Montaigne, 1959.

de Margerie, B. 1990. 'Bède le Vénérable, commentateur original du Nouveau Testament' in *Introduction à l'histoire de l'exégèse*, vol. IV: *L'Occident latin de Léon le Grand à Bernard de Clairvaux*. Paris: Cerf, pp. 187–228.

de Rossi, G. B. 1888. *La Bibbia offerta da Ceolfrido Abbate al Sepolchro di S. Pietro. Al Sommo Pontefice Leone XIII omaggio giubilare della Biblioteca Vaticana*. Vatican City: Vatican.

Dionisotti, C. 1982 'On Bede, Grammars, and Greek.' *Revue bénédictine*, 92: 111–41.

Dobbie, E. v. K. 1937. *The Manuscripts of Caedmon's Hymn and Bede's Death Song*. New York: Columbia University Press.

Draper, P. and N. Coldstream (eds.). 1980. *Medieval Art and Architecture at Durham Cathedral*. London: British Archaeological Association.

Dumville, D. 1976. 'The Anglian Collection of Royal Genealogies and Regnal Lists.' *Anglo-Saxon England*, 5: 23–50.

1992. *Wessex and England from Alfred to Edgar: Six Essays on Political, Cultural, and Ecclesiastical Revival*. Woodbridge, Suffolk: The Boydell Press.

2007. 'The Two Earliest Manuscripts of Bede's Ecclesiastical History?' *Anglo-Saxon*, 1: 55–108. Reprinted in Dumville, *Anglo-Saxon Essays, 2001–2007*. Aberdeen: Centre for Anglo-Saxon Studies, 2007 pp. 55–108.

Eby, John. 1997. 'Bring the *Vita* to Life: Bede's Symbolic Structure of the *Life of Saint Cuthbert*.' *American Benedictine Review*, 48: 316–48.

Eckenrode, T. 1971. 'Venerable Bede as a Scientist.' *American Benedictine Review*, 22: 486–507.

1974. 'Venerable Bede's Theory of Ocean Tides.' *American Benedictine Review*, 25: 56–74.

1976. 'The Growth of a Scientific Mind: Bede's Early and Late Scientific Writings.' *Downside Review*, 94: 197–212.

Edwards, O. C., Jr. 2004. *A History of Preaching*. Nashville: Abingdon Press.

Fairfield, L. P. 1976. *John Bale: Mythmaker for the English Reformation*. West Lafayette, IN: Purdue University Press.

Faith, R. 1997. *The English Peasantry and the Growth of Lordship*. London: Leicester University Press.

Farmer, D. H. (ed.). 2004. *The Age of Bede*. Rev. edn. London: Penguin Books.

Farr, C. 1999. 'The Shape of Learning at Wearmouth-Jarrow: The Diagram Pages in the Codex Amiatinus' in Hawkes and Mills (eds.), *Norhumbria's Golden Age*, pp. 336–44.

Fichtenau, H. 1957. *Arenga: Spätantike und Mittelalter im Spiegel der Urkundenformen*. Mitteilungen des Instituts für Österreichische Geschichtsforschung, Erganzungsband 18. Graz: Oldeburg.

Flower, R. 1935. 'Laurence Nowell and the Discovery of England in Tudor Times.' *Publications of the British Academy*, 21: 46–73.

Fontaine, Jacques. 1983. *Isidore de Seville et la culture classique dans l'Espagne visigothique.* 2nd edn. Paris: Études augustiniennes.

2002. *Isidore de Seville: Traité de la nature.* Paris: Études augustiniennes.

Fontes Anglo-Saxonici Project (ed.), *Fontes Anglo-Saxonici: World Wide Web Register,* http://fontes.english.ox.ac.uk/, accessed July 2008.

Foot, S. 2006. *Monastic Life in Anglo-Saxon England c. 600–900.* Cambridge University Press.

Fowler, J. (ed.). 1903. *Rites of Durham, being a Description or Brief Declaration of All the Ancient Monuments, Rites, and Customs belonging or being within the Monastical Church of Durham before the Suppression.* Durham: Andrews and Co.

Frankis, J. 2000. 'King Ælle and the Conversion of the English: The Development of a Legend from Bede to Chaucer' in Scragg and Weinberg (eds.), *Literary Appropriations of the Anglo-Saxons,* pp. 74–92.

Fransen, P.-I. 1961. 'Description de la collection de Bède le Vénérable sur l'Apôtre.' *Revue bénédictine,* 71: 22–70.

1987. 'D'Eugippius à Bède le Vénérable.' *Revue bénédictine,* 97: 187–94.

Frantzen, A. J. 1983. *The Literature of Penance in Anglo-Saxon England.* New Brunswick, NJ: Rutgers University Press.

Franzen, C. 1991. *The Tremulous Hand of Worcester: A Study of Old English in the Thirteenth Century.* Oxford University Press.

Gatch, M. McC. 1977. *Preaching and Theology in Anglo-Saxon England: Aelfric and Wulfstan.* University of Toronto Press.

Gibson, M. T. 1989. 'The Twelfth-Century Glossed Bible.' *Studia Patristica,* 23: 232–44. Reprinted in Gibson, '*Artes' and Bible,* no. XIV.

1992. 'The Place of the *Glossa ordinaria* in Medieval Exegesis' in K. Emery, Jr and M. Jordan (eds.), *Ad Litteram: Authoritative Texts and their Medieval Readers.* University of Notre Dame Press, pp. 5–27. Reprinted in Gibson, '*Artes' and Bible,* no. XV.

1993. '*Artes' and Bible in the Medieval West.* Aldershot: Variorum.

Gneuss, H. 2001. *Handlist of Anglo-Saxon Manuscripts: A List of Manuscripts and Manuscript Fragments Written or Owned in England up to 1100.* Tempe, AZ: ACMRS.

Godden, M. and M. Lapidge (eds.). 1991. *The Cambridge Companion to Old English Literature.* Cambridge University Press.

Godman, P. 1982. 'Introduction' to Alcuin, *The Bishops, Kings and Saints of York.* Oxford University Press.

Goffart, W. 1988. *The Narrators of Barbarian History (A.D. 550–800): Jordanes, Gregory of Tour, Bede, and Paul the Deacon.* Princeton University Press; reprinted University of Notre Dame Press, 2005.

2005. 'Bede's *vera lex historiae* Explained.' *Anglo-Saxon England,* 34: 111–16.

Gorman, M. 2001. 'The Canon of Bede's Works and the World of Ps.-Bede.' *Revue bénédictine,* 111: 399–445.

2002. 'Source Marks and Chapter Divisions in Bede's Commentary on Luke.' *Revue bénédictine,* 112: 246–90.

Graham, T. 2000. *The Recovery of Old English: Anglo-Saxon Studies in the Sixteenth and Seventeenth Centuries.* Kalamazoo, MI: The Medieval Institute.

2001. 'Anglo-Saxon Studies: Sixteenth to Eighteenth Centuries' in P. Pulsiano and E. Treharne (eds.), *A Companion to Anglo-Saxon Literature*. Oxford: Blackwell, pp. 415–33.

Gransden, A. 1992a. 'Bede's Reputation as an Historian in Medieval England' in Gransden, *Legends, Traditions and History in Medieval England*. London: Hambledon Press, pp. 1–29.

1992b. 'Tradition and Continuity in Late Anglo-Saxon Monasticism' in Gransden, *Legends, Traditions and History in Medieval England*. London: Hambledon Press, pp. 31–79.

Grosjean, P. 1955. 'Sur quelques exégètes irlandais du viie siècle.' *Sacris Eruderi*, 7: 67–98.

Gullick, M. 1998. 'The Hand of Symeon of Durham: Further Observations on the Durham Martyrology Scribe' in D. Rollason (ed.), *Symeon of Durham: Historian of Durham and the North*. Stamford: Shaun Tyas, pp. 14–31.

Halsey, R. 1980. 'The Galilee Chapel' in Draper and Coldstream (eds.), *Medieval Art and Architecture*, pp. 59–73.

Hanning, R. W. 1966. *The Vision of History in Early Britain from Gildas to Geoffrey of Monmouth*. New York: Columbia University Press.

Hardy, T. D. 1862–71. *Descriptive Catalogue of Materials Relating to the History of Great Britain and Ireland to the End of the Reign of Henry VII*. 3 vols. Rolls Series 26. London: Longman, Green, Longman and Roberts.

Harris, S. J. 2003. *Race and Ethnicity in Anglo-Saxon Literature*. New York: Routledge.

Hart-Hasler, J. N. 1993. 'Bede's Use of Patristic Sources: The Transfiguration.' *Studia Patristica*, 28: 197–204.

Hawkes, J. and S. Mills (eds.). 1999. *Northumbria's Golden Age*. Stroud: Sutton.

Henderson, G. 1980. *Bede and the Visual Arts*. Jarrow Lecture. Jarrow: Jarrow Parish Council. Reprinted in Lapidge (ed.), *Bede and His World*, vol. 1, pp. 507–38.

1993. 'Cassiodorus and Eadfrith Once Again' in R. Spearman and J. Higgitt (eds.), *The Age of Migrating Ideas*. National Museums of Scotland: Edinburgh, pp. 82–91.

Higham, N. J. 2006. *(Re-)Reading Bede: The Ecclesiastical History in Context*. London: Routledge.

Hill, J. 1998. *Bede and the Benedictine Reform*. Jarrow Lecture. Jarrow: Jarrow Parish Council.

2003. 'Learning Latin in ASE: Traditions, Texts and Techniques' in S. R. Jones (ed.), *Learning and Literacy in Medieval England and Abroad*. Turnhout: Brepols, pp. 7–30.

2006. 'Carolingian Perspectives on the Authority of Bede' in DeGregorio (ed.), *Innovation and Tradition*, pp. 227–49.

Holder, A. G. 1990. 'Bede and the Tradition of Patristic Exegesis.' *Anglican Theological Review*, 72: 399–411.

1991. 'The Venerable Bede on the Mysteries of Our Salvation.' *American Benedictine Review*, 42: 140–62.

1999. 'The Patristic Sources of Bede's Commentary on the Song of Songs.' *Studia Patristica*, 34: 370–5.

2005a. 'The Anti-Pelagian Character of Bede's Commentary on the Song of Songs' in C. Leonardi and G. Orlandi (eds.), *Biblical Studies in the Early Middle Ages*. Florence: SISMEL – Edizioni del Galluzzo, pp. 91–103.

2005b. 'The Feminine Christ in Bede's Biblical Commentaries' in Lebecq (ed.), *Bède le Vénérable*, pp. 109–118.

2005c. 'Using Philosophers to Think With: The Venerable Bede on Christian Life and Practice' in R. Valantasis *et al.* (eds.), *The Subjective Eye: Essays in Culture, Religion, and Gender in Honor of Margaret R. Miles*. Eugene, OR: Pickwick Publications, pp. 48–58.

2006. 'Christ as Incarnate Wisdom in Bede's Commentary on the Song of Songs' in DeGregorio (ed.), *Innovation and Tradition*, pp. 169–88.

Holtz, L. 1981. 'Irish Grammarians and the Continent in the Seventh Century' in H. B. Clarke and M. Brennan (eds.), *Columbanus and Merovingian Monasticism.* Oxford: BAR, pp. 135–52.

Holweck, F. G. 1924. *A Biographical Dictionary of the Saints: With a General Introduction on Hagiology*. St Louis: Herder; reprinted Detroit: Gale Research Co., 1969.

Houwen, L. A. J. R. and A. A. MacDonald (eds.). 1996. *Beda Venerabilis: Historian, Monk & Northumbrian*. Mediaevalia Groningana 19. Groningen: Egbert Forsten.

Howlett, D. R. 1994. 'The Shape and Meaning of the Old English Poem "Durham"' in D. Rollason, M. Harvey and M. Prestwich (eds.), *Anglo-Norman Durham 1093–1193*. Woodbridge, Suffolk: The Boydell Press, pp. 485–95.

Hudson, A. 1988. *The Premature Reformation: Wycliffite Texts and Lollard History*. Oxford: Clarendon Press.

Hughes, K. 1971. 'Evidence for Contacts Between the Churches of the Irish and English from the Synod of Whitby to the Viking Age' in Clemoes and Hughes (eds.), *England Before the Conquest*, pp. 49–67.

Hughes, P. 2003. 'Implicit Carolingian Tidal Data.' *Early Science and Medicine*, 8: 1–24.

Hurst, D. 1999. 'Translator's Introduction' to Bede, *Excerpts from the Works of Saint Augustine on the Letters of the Blessed Apostle Paul*, pp. 7–11.

Inglebert, H. 2001. *Interpretatio christiana: Les mutations des savoirs (cosmographie, géographie, ethnographie, histoire) dans l'Antiquité chrétienne (30–630 après J.-C.)*. Paris: Études augustiniennes.

Irvine, M. 1986. 'Bede the Grammarian and the Scope of Grammatical Studies in Eighth-Century Northumbria.' *Anglo-Saxon England*, 15: 15–44.

Jansen, A. 1995. 'The Development of the St Oswald Legends on the Continent' in Stancliffe and Cambridge (eds.), *Oswald*, pp. 230–40.

Jones, C. W. 1937. 'The "Lost" Sirmond Manuscript of Bede's Computus.' *English Historical Review*, 51: 204–19.

1939. *Bedae Pseudepigrapha: Scientific Writings Falsely Attributed to Bede*. Ithaca, NY: Cornell University Press.

1943. *Bedae opera de temporibus*. Cambridge, MA: Mediaeval Academy of America.

1970a. 'Some Introductory Remarks on Bede's Commentary on Genesis.' *Sacris Erudiri*, 19: 115–98.

1970b. 'Bede, the Venerable' in *Dictionary of Scientific Biography*. 16 vols. New York: Scribner, vol. I, pp. 564–6.

1975. 'Preface' to *Bedae Venerabilis Opera*, Pars I, Opera Didascalica, CCSL 123A. Turnhout: Brepols, pp. v–xvi.

1976. 'Bede's Place in Medieval Schools' in Bonner (ed.), *Famulus Christi*, pp. 261–85.

1994. *Bede, the Schools and the Computus*. Aldershot: Ashgate.

Jones, G. R. J. 1995. 'Some Donations to Bishop Wilfrid in Northern England.' *Northern History*, 31: 22–38.

Kaczynski, B. M. 2001. 'Bede's Commentaries on Luke and Mark and the Formation of a Patristic Canon' in S. Echard and G. R. Wieland (eds.), *Anglo-Latin and Its Heritage: Essays in Honour of A. G. Rigg on His 64th Birthday*. Turnhout: Brepols, pp. 17–26.

Katzenellenbogen, A. 1959. *The Sculptural Programs of Chartres Cathedral: Christ, Mary, Ecclesia*. Baltimore, MD: Johns Hopkins University Press.

Kelly, J. F. 1993. 'Bede's Exegesis of Luke's Infancy Narrative.' *Mediaevalia*, 15: 59–70.

Kendall, C. B. 1984. 'Dry Bones in a Cathedral: The Story of the Theft of Bede's Relics and the Translation of Cuthbert into the Cathedral of Durham in 1104.' *Mediaevalia*, 10: 1–26.

1991. 'Introduction' to *Bede: Libri II De arte metrica et De schematibus et tropis: The Art of Poetry and Rhetoric*, pp. 15–33.

2006. 'The Responsibility of *Auctoritas*: Method and Meaning in Bede's Commentary on Genesis' in DeGregorio (ed.), *Innovation and Tradition*, pp. 101–19.

2008. 'Introduction' to *Bede: On Genesis*, pp. 1–61.

Kennedy, E. D. 1989. 'Chronicles and Other Historical Writing' in A. E. Hartung (ed.), *A Manual of the Writings in Middle English 1050–1500*. 11 vols. New Haven: Connecticut Academy of Arts and Sciences, vol. VIII, pp. 2,611–17.

Ker, N. R. 1957. *Catalogue of Manuscripts Containing Anglo-Saxon*. Oxford University Press.

Kershaw, P. 2008. 'English History and Irish Readers in the Frankish World' in P. Fouracre and D. Ganz (eds.), *Frankland: The Franks and the World of Early Medieval Europe*. Manchester University Press, pp. 126–51.

Keynes, S. and M. Lapidge. 1983. 'Introduction' to *Alfred the Great: Asser's 'Life of King Alfred' and Other Contemporary Sources*. London: Penguin Books.

King, J. 1982. *English Reformation Literature: The Tudor Origins of the Protestant Tradition*. Princeton University Press.

Kirby, D. P. 1983. 'Bede, Eddius Stephanus and the Life of Wilfrid.' *English Historical Review*, 98: 101–14.

1992. *Bede's 'Historia Ecclesiastica Gentis Anglorum': Its Contemporary Setting*. Jarrow Lecture. Jarrow: Jarrow Parish Council. Reprinted in Lapidge (ed.), *Bede and His World*, vol. II, pp. 903–26.

1995. 'The Genesis of a Cult: Cuthbert of Farne and Ecclesiastical Politics in Northumbria in the Late Seventh and Early Eighth Centuries.' *Journal of Ecclesiastical History*, 46: 383–97.

Laistner, M. L. W. 1933. 'Bede as a Classical and a Patristic Scholar.' *Transactions of the Royal Historical Society*, 16: 69–93.

1935. 'The Library of the Venerable Bede' in Thompson (ed.), *Bede: His Life, Times, and Writings*, pp. 237–66.

1957. 'Was Bede the Author of a Penitential?' in *The Intellectual Heritage of the Early Middle Ages*, ed. Chester G. Starr. Ithaca, NY: Cornell University Press, pp. 165–77.

and H. H. King. 1943. *A Hand-list of Bede Manuscripts*. Ithaca, NY: Cornell University Press.

Landes, R. 1988. 'Lest the Millennium be Fulfilled: Apocalyptic Expectations and the Pattern of Western Chronography 100–800 CE' in W. Verbeke, C. Verhelst and A. Welkenhuysen (eds.), *The Use and Abuse of Eschatology in the Middle Ages*. Leuven University Press, pp. 137–209.

Lapidge, M. 1986. 'The Anglo-Latin Background' in S. B. Greenfield and D. G. Calder (eds.), *A New Critical History of Old English Literature*. New York University Press, pp. 5–37.

   1988. 'Bede's Metrical Vita S. Cuthberti' in Bonner *et al.* (eds.), *St Cuthbert, His Cult and His Community*, pp. 77–93.

   (ed.) 1994. *Bede and His World: The Jarrow Lectures 1958–93*. 2 vols. Aldershot: Variorum.

   (ed.) 1995. *Archbishop Theodore: Commemorative Studies on his Life and Influence*. Cambridge University Press.

   1996. 'Aediluulf and the School of York' in *Anglo-Latin Literature, 600–899*. London: The Hambledon Press, pp. 381–98.

   2000. 'The Archetype of Beowulf.' *Anglo-Saxon England*, 29: 5–41.

   2006. *The Anglo-Saxon Library*. Oxford University Press.

   2008. 'The Career of Aldhelm.' *Anglo-Saxon England*, 36: 15–69.

   (ed.) and P. Chiesa (trans.). 2008–9. *Beda: Storia degli Inglesi (Historia ecclesiastica gentis Anglorum)*. 2 vols. Milan: Fondazione Lorenzo Valla/Mondadori.

   and M. Herren (trans.). 1979. *Aldhelm: The Prose Works*. Cambridge: D. S. Brewer.

Lebecq, S., M. Perrin and O. Szerwiniack (eds.). 2005. *Bède le Vénérable entre tradition et postérité*. Lille: CEGES.

Leclercq, J. 1961. *The Love of Learning and the Desire for God*, trans. C. Misrahi. New York: Fordham University Press.

Lehmann, P. 1918. *Mittelalterliche Bibliothekskataloge Deutschlands und der Schweiz, I: Die Bistümer Konstanz und Chur*. Munich: C. H. Beck'sche Verlagsbuchhandlung/Oskar Beck.

Leinbaugh, T. H. 1982. 'Ælfric's *Sermo de Sacrificio in Die Pascae*: Anglican Polemic in the Sixteenth and Seventeenth Centuries' in Berkhout and Gatch (eds.), *Anglo-Saxon Scholarship*, pp. 51–68.

Lendinara, P. 1991. 'The World of Anglo-Saxon Learning' in Godden and Lapidge (eds.), *The Cambridge Companion to Old English Literature*, pp. 264–81.

Levison, W. 1935. 'Bede as Historian' in A. H. Thompson (ed.), *Bede: His Life, Times, and Writings*, pp. 111–51.

   1946. *England and the Continent in the Eighth Century*. Oxford: Clarendon Press.

Levy, F. J. 1967. *Tudor Historical Thought*. University of Toronto Press.

Love, R. C. Forthcoming. 'The Library of the Venerable Bede' in R. Gameson (ed.), *The History of the Book in Britain I*. Cambridge University Press.

Lowe, E. A. 1934–72. *Codices Latini Antiquiores*. 11 vols and suppl. Oxford: Clarendon Press.

   1958. 'An Autograph of the Venerable Bede.' *Revue bénédictine*, 68: 199–202.

   1960. *English Uncial*. Oxford: Clarendon Press.

McClure, J. 1983. 'Bede's Old Testament Kings' in Wormald *et al.* (eds.), *Ideal and Reality*, pp. 76–98.

   1984. 'Bede and the Life of Ceolfrid.' *Peritia*, 3: 71–84.

McCluskey, S. 1998. *Astronomies and Cultures in Early Medieval Europe*. Cambridge University Press.

McCready, W. D. 1994. *Miracles and the Venerable Bede*. Toronto: Pontifical Institute of Mediaeval Studies.

　1995a. 'Bede and the Isidorian Legacy.' *Mediaeval Studies*, 57: 41–74.

　1995b. 'Bede, Isidore and the *Epistola Cuthberti*.' *Traditio*, 50: 75–94.

McKinnell, J. 1998. *The Sequence of the Sacrament at Durham*. Durham: North East England History Institute.

McKisack, M. 1971. *Medieval History in the Tudor Age*. Oxford University Press.

McKitterick, R. 2002. 'Kulturelle Verbindungen zwischen England und den fränkischen Reichen in der Zeit der Karolinger: Kontexte und Implikationen' in Joachim Ehlers (ed.), *Deutschland und der Westen Europas im Mittelalter*. Vorträge und Forschungen 56. Stuttgart: Jan Thorbecke Verlag, pp. 121–48.

McNally, R. E. 1973. *Introduction to Commentarius in epistolas catholicas Scotti anonymi and Tractatus Hilarii in septem epistolas canonicas*. CCSL 108B; Scriptores Hiberniae Minores 1. Turnhout: Brepols.

McNeill, J. T. and H. M. Gamer (eds. and trans.). 1990. *Medieval Handbooks of Penance*. New York: Columbia University Press.

Maddicott, J. R. 1997. 'Plague in Seventh-Century England.' *Past and Present*, 156: 7–54.

　2000. 'Two Frontier States: Northumbria and Wessex, c. 650–750' in J. R. Maddicott and D. M. Palliser (eds.), *The Medieval State: Essays Presented to James Campbell*. London and Rio Grande: Hambledon, pp. 25–46.

Markus, R. 1997. *Gregory the Great and his World*. Cambridge University Press.

Marner, D. 2000. *St Cuthbert: His Life and Cult in Medieval Durham*. London: British Library.

Marsden, R. 1995. *The Text of the Old Testament in Anglo-Saxon England*. Cambridge University Press.

Martin, L. T. 1989. 'The Two Worlds in Bede's Homilies: The Biblical Event and the Listeners' Experience' in T. Amos, E. Green and B. Mayne Kienzle (eds.), *De Ore Domini: Preacher and Word in the Middle Ages*. Kalamazoo, MI: The Medieval Institute, pp. 27–40.

　2006. 'Bede's Originality in his Use of the Book of Wisdom in his Homilies on the Gospels' in DeGregorio (ed.), *Innovation and Tradition*, pp. 189–202.

Mayr-Harting, H. 1976. *The Venerable Bede, the Rule of St Benedict, and Social Class*. Jarrow Lecture. Jarrow: Jarrow Parish Council. Reprinted in Lapidge, *Bede and His World*, vol. 1, pp. 404–34.

　1991. *The Coming of Christianity to Anglo-Saxon England*. 3rd edn. University Park: Pennsylvania State University Press.

Meyvaert, P. 1971. 'Bede's Text of the Libellus Responsionum of Gregory the Great to Augustine of Canterbury' in Clemoes and Hughes (eds.), *England Before the Conquest*, pp. 15–33.

　1976. 'Bede the Scholar' in Bonner (ed.), *Famulus Christi*, pp. 40–69.

　1979. 'Bede and the Church Paintings at Wearmouth-Jarrow.' *Anglo-Saxon England*, 8: 63–77.

　1996. 'Bede, Cassiodorus, and the Codex Amiatinus.' *Speculum*, 71: 827–83.

　1999. '"In the Footsteps of the Fathers": The Date of Bede's *Thirty Questions on the Book of Kings* to Nothelm' in W. Klingshirn and M. Vessey (eds.), *The Limits of*

Ancient Christianity: Essays on Late Antique Thought and Culture in Honor of R. A. Markus. Ann Arbor: University of Michigan Press, pp. 267–86.

2002. 'Medieval Notions of Publication: The "Unpublished" *Opus Caroli regis contra synodum* and the Council of Frankfort (794).' *Journal of Medieval Latin*, 12: 78–89.

2005. 'The Date of Bede's *In Ezram* and His Image of Ezra in the Codex Amiatinus.' *Speculum*, 80: 1,087–133.

Migne, J.-P. (ed.). 1862. *Patrologiae Cursus Completus*, Series latina 90. Petit-Montrouge: J.-P. Migne.

Miller, T. (ed. and trans.). 1890–8; reprinted 1959–63. *The Old English Version of Bede's Ecclesiastical History of the English People.* 4 vols. Oxford University Press.

Moisl, H. 1983. 'The Bernician Royal Dynasty and the Irish in the Seventh Century.' *Peritia*, 2: 99–124.

Moreton, J. 1998. 'Doubts about the Calendar: Bede and the Eclipse of 664.' *Isis*, 89: 50–65.

Morris, R. 1983. *The Church in British Archaeology.* London: Council for British Archaeology.

2004. *Journeys from Jarrow.* Jarrow Lecture. Jarrow: Jarrow Parish Council.

Murphy, M. 1967. 'Abraham Wheloc's Edition of Bede's History in Old English.' *Studia Neophilologica*, 39: 46–59.

Murray, A. 2007. 'Bede and the Unchosen Race' in H. Pryce and J. Watts (eds.), *Power and Identity in the Middle Ages: Essays in Memory of Rees Davies.* Oxford University Press.

Naylor, J. 2007. 'The Circulation of Early-Medieval European Coinage: A Case Study from Yorkshire.' *Medieval Archaeology*, 51: 41–61.

Nordhagen, P. J. 1977. *The Codex Amiatinus and the Byzantine Element in the Northumbrian Renaissance.* Jarrow Lecture. Jarrow: Jarrow Parish Council Reprinted in Lapidge (ed.), *Bede and his World*, vol. 1, pp. 435–62.

Ó Cróinín, D. 1983. 'The Irish Provenance of Bede's *Computus*.' *Peritia*, 2: 238–42.

1984. 'Rath Melsigi, Willibrord and the Earliest Echternach Manuscripts.' *Peritia*, 3: 17–42.

2003. *Early Irish History and Chronology.* Dublin: Four Courts Press.

Ohashi, M. 2005. 'Theory and History: An Interpretation of the Paschal Controversy in Bede's *Historia Ecclesiastica*' in Lebecq *et al.* (eds.), *Bède le Vénérable*, pp. 177–85.

O'Keefe, J. and R. Reno. 2005. *Sanctified Vision: An Introduction to Early Christian Interpretation of the Bible.* Baltimore: Johns Hopkins University Press.

O'Loughlin, T. 2007. *Adomnán and the Holy Places: The Perceptions of an Insular Monk on the Location of the Biblical Drama.* London: T. & T. Clark.

Olsen, G. 1982. 'Bede as Historian: The Evidence from His Observations on the Life of the First Christian Community at Jerusalem.' *Journal of Ecclesiastical History*, 33: 519–30.

Orchard, A. 2003. 'Latin and the Vernacular Languages: The Creation of a Bilingual Textual Culture' in T. Charles-Edwards (ed.), *After Rome.* Oxford University Press, pp. 191–219.

O'Reilly, J. 2001. 'The Library of Scripture: Views from the Vivarium and Wearmouth-Jarrow' in P. Binski and W. G. Noel (eds.), *New Offerings, Ancient*

Treasures: Essays in Medieval Art for George Henderson. Stroud: Alan Sutton, pp. 3–39.

2005. 'Idols and Islands at the Ends of the Earth: Exegesis and Conversion in Bede's *Historia Ecclesiastica*' in Lebecq *et al.* (eds.), *Bède le Vénérable*, pp. 119–45.

Orschel, V. 2001. 'Mag nEó na Sacsan: an English colony in Ireland in the seventh and eighth centuries.' *Peritia*, 15: 81–107.

Parker, M. S. 1985. 'An Anglo-Saxon Monastery in the Lower Don Valley.' *Northern History*, 21: 19–32.

Parkes, M. B. 1982. *The Scriptorium of Wearmouth-Jarrow*. Jarrow Lecture. Jarrow: Jarrow Parish Council. Reprinted in Lapidge (ed.), *Bede and his World*, vol. II, pp. 555–86, and in M. B. Parkes, *Scribes, Scripts and Readers: Studies in the Communication, Presentation, and Dissemination of Medieval Texts*. London and Rio Grande, OH: Hambledon Press.

Parsons, D. 1987. *Books and Buildings: Architectural Description Before and After Bede*. Jarrow Lecture. Jarrow: Jarrow Parish Council. Reprinted in Lapidge (ed.), *Bede and his World*, vol. II, pp. 729–74.

Partner, N. F. *Serious Entertainments: The Writing of History in Twelfth-Century England*. University of Chicago Press, 1977.

Picard, J.-M. 2004. 'Bede and Irish Scholarship: Scientific Treatises and Grammars.' *Ériu*, 54: 139–47.

2005. 'Bède et ses sources irlandaises' in Lebecq *et al.* (eds.), *Bède le Vénérable*, pp. 43–61.

Plummer, C. 1896. 'Bede's Life and Works' in *Venerabilis Baedae opera historica*. 2 vols. Oxford: Clarendon Press; reprinted as 1 vol., 1946, pp. ix–lxxix.

Rabin, A. 2005. 'Historical Re-Collections: Rewriting the World Chronicle in Bede's De temporum ratione.' *Viator*, 36: 23–39.

Raine, J. 1828. *St Cuthbert, with an Account of the State in which his Remains were Found upon the Opening of his Tomb in Durham Cathedral, in the Year 1827*. Durham and London: Geoffrey Andrews and J. B. Nicholls.

Ray, R. 1976. 'Bede, the Exegete, as Historian' in Bonner (ed.), *Famulus Christi*, pp. 125–40.

1980. 'Bede's *Vera Lex Historiae*.' *Speculum*, 55: 1–21.

1982. 'What Do We Know about Bede's Biblical Commentaries?' *Recherches de théologie ancienne et médiévale*, 49: 1–20.

1985. 'Augustine's *De Consensu Evangelistarum* and the Historical Education of the Venerable Bede.' *Studia Patristica*, 16: 557–63.

1987. 'Bede and Cicero.' *Anglo-Saxon England*, 16: 1–15.

2006. 'Who Did Bede Think He Was?' in DeGregorio (ed.), *Innovation and Tradition*, pp. 11–35.

Reinhardt, T., M. Lapidge and J. N. Adams (eds.). 2005. *Aspects of the Language of Latin Prose*. Oxford University Press.

Riché, P. 1976. *Education and Culture in the Barbarian West: Sixth through Eighth Centuries*, trans. J. Contreni. Columbia: University of South Carolina Press.

Robinson, B. 1994. 'The Venerable Bede as Exegete.' *The Downside Review*, 112: 201–26.

Rollason, D. 1989. *Saints and Relics in Anglo-Saxon England*. Oxford: Blackwell.

(ed.) 2000. *Symeon of Durham: Libellus de exordio atque procursu istius hoc est Dunhelmensis ecclesie*. Oxford Medieval Texts. Oxford: Clarendon Press.

2001. 'Bede and Germany.' *Jarrow Lecture*. Jarrow: Jarrow Parish Council.

2003. *Northumbria, 500–1100: Creation and Destruction of a Kingdom*. Cambridge University Press.

Russo, D. G. 1998. *Town Origins and Development in Early England c. 400–950 AD*. Westport, CT and London: Greenwood Press.

Salmon, P. 1962. *The Breviary Through the Centuries*. Collegeville, MN: The Liturgical Press.

Scheil, A. 2004. *The Footsteps of Israel: Understanding Jews in Anglo-Saxon England*. Ann Arbor: University of Michigan Press.

Scott, J. 1981. *The Early History of Glastonbury Abbey: An Edition, Translation and Study of William of Malmesbury's De Antiquitate Glastonie Ecclesie*. Woodbridge, Suffolk: The Boydell Press.

Scragg, D. 2000. 'Introduction' in Scragg and Weinberg (eds.), *Literary Appropriations of the Anglo-Saxons*, pp. 1–21.

and C. Weinberg (eds.). 2000. *Literary Appropriations of the Anglo-Saxons from the Thirteenth to the Twentieth Century*. Cambridge University Press.

Scully, D. 1997. 'Introduction' to *Bede: On Tobit and On the Canticle of Habakkuk*, pp. 17–37.

Shanzer, D. 2007. 'Bede's Style: A Neglected Historiographical Model for the Style of the *Historia Ecclesiastica*?' in C. D. Wright, F. M. Biggs and T. N. Hall (eds.), *Source of Wisdom: Old English and Early Medieval Latin Studies in Honour of Thomas D. Hill*. University of Toronto Press, pp. 329–52.

Sharpe, R. 2005. 'The Varieties of Bede's Prose' in Reinhardt *et al.* (eds.), *Aspects of the Language of Latin Prose*, pp. 339–55.

Sims-Williams, P. 1990. *Religion and Literature in Western England, 600–800*. Cambridge University Press.

Smetana, C. 1978. 'Paul the Deacon's Patristic Anthology' in P. Szarmach and B. Huppé (eds.), *The Old English Homily and its Backgrounds*. Albany: State University of New York Press, pp. 75–97.

Smyth, M. 1996. *Understanding the Universe in Seventh-Century Ireland*. Studies in Celtic History 15. Woodbridge: Boydell.

Snape, M. G. 1980. 'Documentary Evidence for the Building of Durham Cathedral and its Monastic Buildings' in Draper and Coldstream, (eds.), *Medieval Art and Architecture*, pp. 20–36.

Stancliffe, C. 1989. 'Cuthbert and the Polarity between Pastor and Solitary' in Bonner *et al.* (eds.), *St Cuthbert, His Cult and His Community*, pp. 21–44.

1995. 'Oswald, "Most Holy and Most Victorious King of the Northumbrians"' in Stancliffe and Cambridge (eds.), *Oswald*, pp. 33–83.

1999. 'The British Church and the Mission of Augustine' in R. Gameson (ed.), *St Augustine and the Conversion of England*. Stroud: Sutton Publishing, pp. 107–51. Reprinted in Stancliffe, *'Celt' and 'Roman'*.

2003. *Bede, Wilfrid, and the Irish*. Jarrow Lecture. Jarrow: Jarrow Parish Council. Reprinted in Stancliffe, *'Celt' and 'Roman'*.

2007. *Bede and the Britons*. Whithorn Lecture 2005. Whithorn: Friends of the Whithorn Trust. Reprinted in Stancliffe, *'Celt' and 'Roman'*.

Forthcoming. *'Celt' and 'Roman': An Evolving Controversy and its Impact on Identity and Historiography from Columbanus to Bede*. Turnhout: Brepols.

and E. Cambridge (eds.). 1995. *Oswald: Northumbrian King to European Saint*. Stamford: Paul Watkins.

Stansbury, M. 1999a. 'Early Medieval Biblical Commentaries: Their Readers and Writers.' *Frühmittelalerliche Studien*, 33: 49–82.

1999b. 'Source-Marks in Bede's Biblical Commentaries' in Hawkes and Mills (eds.), *Northumbria's Golden Age*, pp. 383–9.

Stevens, W. 1985. *Bede's Scientific Achievement*. Jarrow Lecture. Jarrow: Jarrow Parish Council. Reprinted in Lapidge (ed.), *Bede and His World*, vol. II, pp. 645–88.

1995. *Cycles of Time and Scientific Learning in Medieval Europe*. Aldershot: Variorum.

Sutcliffe. E. F. 1935. 'The Venerable Bede's Knowledge of Hebrew.' *Biblica*, 16: 300–6.

Tatlock, J. S. P. 1933. 'Geoffrey and King Arthur in "Normannicus Draci".' *Modern Philology*, 31: 113–25.

Taylor, H. M. and Joan Taylor. 1965–78. *Anglo-Saxon Architecture*, 3 vols. Cambridge University Press.

Thacker, A. 1981. 'Some Terms for Noblemen in Anglo-Saxon England, c. 650–900.' *Anglo-Saxon Studies in Archaeology and History*, 2: 201–36.

1983. 'Bede's Ideal of Reform' in Wormald *et al.* (eds.), *Ideal and Reality*, pp. 130–53.

1989. 'Lindisfarne and the Origins of the Cult of St Cuthbert' in Bonner *et al.* (eds.), *St Cuthbert, His Cult and His Community*, pp. 103–22.

1992. 'Monks, Preaching and Pastoral Care in Early Anglo-Saxon England' in Blair and Sharpe (eds.), *Pastoral Care Before the Parish*, pp. 137–70.

1995. 'Membra Disjecta: The Division of the Body and the Diffusion of the Cult' in Stancliffe and Cambridge (eds.), *Oswald*, pp. 97–127.

1996. 'Bede and the Irish' in Houwen and MacDonald (eds.), *Beda Venerabilis*, pp. 31–59.

2006. 'Bede and the Ordering of Understanding' in DeGregorio (ed.), *Innovation and Tradition*, pp. 37–63.

2008. 'Bede, the Britons, and the Book of Samuel' in Baxter *et al.* (eds.), *Early Medieval Studies*, pp. 129–47.

and R. Sharpe (eds.). 2002. *Local Saints and Local Churches in the Early Medieval West*. Oxford University Press.

Thomas, I. G. 1974. 'The Cult of Saints' Relics in Medieval England.' Unpublished PhD thesis, University of London.

Thompson, A. H. (ed.). 1935. *Bede: His Life, Times, and Writings: Essays in Commemoration of the Twelfth Centenary of his Death*. Oxford: Clarendon Press; reissued New York: Russell & Russell, 1966.

Treharne, R. F. 1967. *The Glastonbury Legends*. London: Cresset.

Van der Walt, A. G. P. 1986. 'Reflections of the Benedictine Rule in Bede's Homiliary.' *Journal of Ecclesiastical History*, 37: 367–76.

Wallace-Hadrill, A. 1986. 'Introduction' to *The Later Roman Empire*, ed. and trans. Walter Hamilton. Harmondsworth: Penguin Books.

Wallace-Hadrill, J. M. 1971. *Early Germanic Kingship in England and on the Continent*. Oxford University Press.

Wallis, F. 1999. 'Introduction' to *Bede: The Reckoning of Time*. Translated Texts for Historians 29. Liverpool University Press.

2005a. 'Bede' in S. Livesey, T. Glick and F. Wallis (eds.), *Medieval Science, Technology and Medicine: An Encyclopedia*. London: Routledge, pp. 139–41.

2005b. '"Number Mystique" in Early Medieval Computus Texts' in T. Koetsier and L. Bergmans (eds.), *Mathematics and the Divine: A Historical Study*. Amsterdam: Elsevier, pp. 181–99.

2006. '*Si Naturam Quaeras*: Reframing Bede's "Science"' in DeGregorio (ed.), *Innovation and Tradition*, pp. 61–94.

2007. 'Caedmon's Created World and the Monastic Encyclopedia' in A. Frantzen and J. Hines (eds.), *Caedmon's Hymn and Material Culture in the World of Bede*. Morgantown: West Virginia University Press, pp. 80–111.

Ward, B. 1990. *The Venerable Bede*. Outstanding Christian Thinkers Series. London: Continuum; republished in Cistercian Studies Series 169. Kalamazoo, MI: Cistercian Publications, 1998.

1991. 'Preface' to *Bede the Venerable: Homilies on the Gospels*.

1993. '"In medium duorum animalium": Bede and Jerome on the Canticle of Habakkuk.' *Studia Patristica*, 25: 189–93.

Watson, N. 1995. 'Censorship and Cultural Change in Late-Medieval England: Vernacular Theology, the Oxford Translation Debate, and Arundel's Constitutions of 1409.' *Speculum*, 70: 822–64.

Webster, L. and J. M. Backhouse. 1991. *The Making of England: Anglo-Saxon Art and Culture AD 600–900*. Toronto University Press.

Whitelock, D. 1960. *After Bede*. Jarrow Lecture. Jarrow: Jarrow Parish Council. Reprinted in Lapidge (ed.), *Bede and His World*, vol. 1, pp. 35–50.

1962. 'The Old English Bede.' Sir Israel Gollancz Memorial Lecture. *Proceedings of the British Academy*, 48: 57–90. Reprinted in E. G. Stanley (ed.), *British Academy Papers on ASE*. Oxford University Press, 1990, pp. 227–61.

1974. 'The List of Chapter-Headings in the Old English Bede' in R. Burlin and E. Irving, Jr (eds.), *Old English Studies in Honour of John C. Pope*. University of Toronto Press, pp. 263–84.

1976. 'Bede and His Teachers and Friends' in Bonner (ed.), *Famulus Christi*, pp. 19–39.

1979. *English Historical Documents I, c.500–1042*. 2nd edn. London and New York: Eyre Methuen and Oxford University Press.

Wood, I. 1987. 'Anglo-Saxon Otley: An Archiepiscopal Estate and its Crosses in a Northumbrian Context.' *Northern History*, 23: 20–38.

1995. *The Most Holy Abbot Ceolfrid*. Jarrow Lecture. Jarrow: Jarrow Parish Council.

2006. 'Bede's Jarrow' in C. A. Lees and G. R. Overing (eds.), *A Place to Believe in: Locating Medieval Landscapes*. University Park: Pennsylvania State University Press, pp. 67–84.

2008a. 'The Origins of Jarrow: The Monastery, the Slake and Ecgfrith's Minster.' *Bede's World Studies*, 1: 1–40.

2008b. 'Monasteries and the Geography of Power in the Age of Bede.' *Northern History*, 45: 11–25.

Woolf, A. 2006. *Anglo-Saxon and Viking Britain*. London: Franklin Watts.

Wormald, P. 1976. 'Bede and Benedict Biscop' in Bonner (ed.), *Famulus Christi*, pp. 141–69. Reprinted in Wormald, *The Times of Bede*, pp. 3–29.

1978. 'Bede, "Beowulf" and the Conversion of the Anglo-Saxon Aristocracy' in R. T. Farrell (ed.), *Bede and Anglo-Saxon England*. Oxford: BAR, pp. 32–95. Reprinted in Wormald, *The Times of Bede*, pp. 30–105.

1983. 'Bede, the Bretwaldas and the Origins of the Gens Anglorum' in P. Wormald *et al.* (eds.), *Ideal and Reality*, pp. 99–129. Reprinted in Wormald, *The Times of Bede*, pp. 106–34.

1991. 'Anglo-Saxon Society and Its Literature' in Godden and Lapidge (eds.), *The Cambridge Companion to Old English Literature*, pp. 1–22.

1992. 'The Venerable Bede and the "Church of the English"' in G. Rowell (ed.), *The English Tradition and the Genius of Anglicanism: Studies in Commemoration of the Second Centenary of John Keble*. Wantage: Ikon Productions, pp. 13–32.

1999. *Legal Culture in the Early Medieval West*. London and Rio Grande: Hambledon Press.

2006. *The Times of Bede: Studies in Early English Christian Society and Its Historian*, ed. S. Baxter. Oxford: Blackwell.

and D. Bullough and R. Collins (eds.). 1983. *Ideal and Reality in Frankish and Anglo-Saxon Society: Studies Presented to J. M. Wallace-Hadrill*. Oxford: Basil Blackwell.

Wright, N. 1981. 'Bede and Vergil.' *Romanobarbarica*, **6**: 361–79.

2005 'The Metrical Art(s) of Bede' in K. O'Brien O'Keeffe and A. Orchard (eds.), *Latin Learning and English Lore: Studies in Anglo-Saxon Literature for Michael Lapidge*. 2 vols. University of Toronto Press, vol. I, pp. 150–70.

Wright, R. 2000. 'Political and Ethnic Identity: A Case Study in Anglo-Saxon Practice', in W. Frazer and A. Tyrrel (eds.), *Social Identity in Early Medieval Britain*. London: Leicester University Press.

2002. *A Sociophilological Study of Late Latin*. Utrecht Studies in Medieval Literacy 10. Turnhout: Brepols.

Young, F. 2003. 'Alexandrian and Antiochene Exegesis' in A. Hauser and D. Watson (eds.), *A History of Biblical Interpretation, Volume 1: The Ancient Period*. Grand Rapids, MI: Eerdmans, pp. 334–54.

INDEX

Cambridge Companions to ...

AUTHORS

Edward Albee edited by Stephen J. Bottoms

Margaret Atwood edited by Coral Ann Howells

W. H. Auden edited by Stan Smith

Jane Austen edited by Edward Copeland and Juliet McMaster

Beckett edited by John Pilling

Bede edited by Scott DeGregorio

Aphra Behn edited by Derek Hughes and Janet Todd

Walter Benjamin edited by David S. Ferris

William Blake edited by Morris Eaves

Brecht edited by Peter Thomson and Glendyr Sacks (second edition)

The Brontës edited by Heather Glen

Frances Burney edited by Peter Sabor

Byron edited by Drummond Bone

Albert Camus edited by Edward J. Hughes

Willa Cather edited by Marilee Lindemann

Cervantes edited by Anthony J. Cascardi

Chaucer edited by Piero Boitani and Jill Mann (second edition)

Chekhov edited by Vera Gottlieb and Paul Allain

Kate Chopin edited by Janet Beer

Caryl Churchill edited by Elaine Aston and Elin Diamond

Coleridge edited by Lucy Newlyn

Wilkie Collins edited by Jenny Bourne Taylor

Joseph Conrad edited by J. H. Stape

Dante edited by Rachel Jacoff (second edition)

Daniel Defoe edited by John Richetti

Don DeLillo edited by John N. Duvall

Charles Dickens edited by John O. Jordan

Emily Dickinson edited by Wendy Martin

John Donne edited by Achsah Guibbory

Dostoevskii edited by W. J. Leatherbarrow

Theodore Dreiser edited by Leonard Cassuto and Claire Virginia Eby

John Dryden edited by Steven N. Zwicker

W. E. B. Du Bois edited by Shamoon Zamir

George Eliot edited by George Levine

T. S. Eliot edited by A. David Moody

Ralph Ellison edited by Ross Posnock

Ralph Waldo Emerson edited by Joel Porte and Saundra Morris

William Faulkner edited by Philip M. Weinstein

Henry Fielding edited by Claude Rawson

F. Scott Fitzgerald edited by Ruth Prigozy

Flaubert edited by Timothy Unwin

E. M. Forster edited by David Bradshaw

Benjamin Franklin edited by Carla Mulford

Brian Friel edited by Anthony Roche

Robert Frost edited by Robert Faggen

Elizabeth Gaskell edited by Jill L. Matus

Goethe edited by Lesley Sharpe

Günter Grass edited by Stuart Taberner

Thomas Hardy edited by Dale Kramer

David Hare edited by Richard Boon

Nathaniel Hawthorne edited by Richard Millington

Seamus Heaney edited by Bernard O'Donoghue

Ernest Hemingway edited by Scott Donaldson

Homer edited by Robert Fowler

Horace edited by Stephen Harrison

Ibsen edited by James McFarlane

Henry James edited by Jonathan Freedman

Samuel Johnson edited by Greg Clingham

Ben Jonson edited by Richard Harp and Stanley Stewart

James Joyce edited by Derek Attridge (second edition)

Kafka edited by Julian Preece

Keats edited by Susan J. Wolfson

Lacan edited by Jean-Michel Rabaté

D. H. Lawrence edited by Anne Fernihough

Primo Levi edited by Robert Gordon

Lucretius edited by Stuart Gillespie and Philip Hardie

David Mamet edited by Christopher Bigsby

Thomas Mann edited by Ritchie Robertson

Christopher Marlowe edited by Patrick Cheney

Herman Melville edited by Robert S. Levine

Arthur Miller edited by Christopher Bigsby (second edition)

Milton edited by Dennis Danielson (second edition)

Molière edited by David Bradby and Andrew Calder

Toni Morrison edited by Justine Tally

TOPICS